心无界 路同行

中国建材集团100位海外员工成长记

JOIN HANDS AND MOVE FORWARD WITH LOFTY PURSUITS

GROWTH STORIES OF 100 OVERSEAS EMPLOYEES OF CNBM

中国建材集团党委宣传部 编著

新 华 出 版 社

图书在版编目（CIP）数据

心无界　路同行：中国建材集团100位海外员工成长记 / 中国建材集团党委宣传部编著. -- 北京：新华出版社, 2023.8
ISBN 978-7-5166-6935-8
Ⅰ. ①心…　Ⅱ. ①中…　Ⅲ. ①建筑企业集团－先进工作者－先进事迹－中国　Ⅳ. ①K826.16
中国国家版本馆CIP数据核字（2023）第148067号

心无界　路同行：中国建材集团100位海外员工成长记

编　　著： 中国建材集团党委宣传部

责任编辑： 于　梦　周富祥
责任校对： 刘保利　　**封面设计：** 刘宝龙

出版发行： 新华出版社
地　　址： 北京石景山区京原路8号　　**邮　　编：** 100040
网　　址： http://www.xinhuapub.com
经　　销： 新华书店、新华出版社天猫旗舰店、京东旗舰店及各大网店
购书热线： 010－63077122　　**中国新闻书店购书热线：** 010－63072012

照　　排： 六合方圆
印　　刷： 三河市君旺印务有限公司

成品尺寸： 185mm × 260mm　1/16
印　　张： 26.5　　**字　　数：** 600千字
版　　次： 2023年8月第一版　　**印　　次：** 2023年8月第一次印刷

书　　号： ISBN　978-7-5166-6935-8
定　　价： 98.00元

版权专有，侵权必究。如有质量问题，请与出版社联系调换：010-63077124

序

人类因梦想而伟大，事业因赓续而辉煌。今年是共建“一带一路”倡议提出 10 周年。10 年来，“一带一路”倡议顺应时代潮流，秉持共商共建共享原则，弘扬开放包容、互学互鉴精神，以高标准、可持续、惠民生为目标，开启了中国高水平对外开放的新篇章，成为当今世界规模最大的国际合作平台和最受欢迎的国际公共产品之一。10 年来，中国建材集团（英文简称：CNBM）坚定不移走国际化道路，不断创新“走出去”模式，始终秉持“为当地发展作贡献、与当地企业合作、为当地人民服务”的合作共赢“三原则”，高水平建设了近 500 个水泥和玻璃工程，连续 15 年保持全球建材工程市场占有率第一，为“一带一路”沿线国家和地区提供高质量建材和工程技术服务，为构建人类命运共同体贡献了建材力量。

国有边疆，心无界限。“材料创造美好世界”是中国建材集团的企业使命，也是每一位中国建材人的目标使命。中国建材集团遍布全球的 2 万多名海外员工，他们肤色不同、民族不同、文化不同，但为了共同的目标理想，团聚到中国建材大家庭。他们干一行爱一行，钻一行精一行，在建设“一带一路”上团结协作奋斗，在砥砺奋进中书写精彩答卷，在企业发展中实现共同成长，在一个个小项目、小岗位上合力做出大工程、大事业，用一点一滴的默默奉献生动谱写“美美与共”美好蓝图。

道阻且长，携手同行。今年，中国建材集团正式提出，力争用10年左右的时间，在海外“再造一个中国建材”。任何宏大的目标和美好的愿景，只有把力量、智慧和辛碌落实在行动上，才有可能达成。要实现这个10年目标，没有快捷键，唯有团结更多志同道合的海外建材人，汇聚力量、并肩前行。本书收录中国建材集团100位海外员工的故事，就是其中的代表，他们在“一带一路”建设中播撒梦想的种子，付出辛勤的耕耘，收获喜悦的果实，书写了丰富多彩、生动鲜活的感人故事。相信未来会有更多“一带一路”建设者加入我们，为共建人类美好家园而团结奋斗。

行大道，人为本，利天下。中国建材人要志存高远，放眼全球，以世界一流为标杆，以恒心守望初心，用平凡铸就不凡，在共建“一带一路”的新征程中弘扬丝路精神，谱写丝路新华章，让“材料创造美好世界”的旋律传唱悠远。

中国建材集团有限公司党委书记、董事长

2023年8月

Foreword

Humans are great because of dreams. We have made amazing accomplishments by constantly building on our legacy. This year marks the 10th anniversary of the Belt and Road Initiative. Over the past decade, the Belt and Road Initiative has opened a new chapter of China's high-level opening up to the outside world by responding to the trend of the times, upholding the principles of extensive consultation, joint contribution, and shared benefits, promoting openness, inclusiveness, mutual learning, and mutual benefit, and pursuing the goals of high-standard development, sustainability, and improvement in people's livelihoods. It has become one of the largest international cooperation platforms and the most welcomed international public goods today. Over the past decade, China National Building Materials Group (CNBM) has unswervingly taken the path of internationalization, continuously innovating its "going global" model. By upholding the "three principles" of win-win cooperation -- "contributing to local development, collaborating with local enterprises, and serving local people," it has completed nearly 500 high-quality cement and glass projects. CNBM has held the world's largest share in the engineering market for the construction materials industry for 15 consecutive years. It has provided countries and regions along the Belt and Road with high-quality building materials and technologies, contributing its expertise to building a community with a shared future for humankind.

Countries have borders, but hearts have no boundaries. "Better Materials, Better World" is the corporate mission of CNBM as well as the shared mission of every CNBMer. The CNBM family has over 20,000 overseas employees across the globe coming from different ethnicities, nationalities, and cultures but sharing the same goals and ideals. Diligent at their work and meticulous in their specialties, they collaborate and strive together in the construction of the Belt and Road. By forging ahead with remarkable results, they grow together with CNBM. They have jointly accomplished significant projects and undertakings by satisfactorily performing their tasks and duties, and their dedication and contributions have helped to create a blueprint for a beautiful community of shared destiny.

The path ahead is arduous and lengthy, but we walk incessantly together. This year, CNBM formally proposed developing overseas operations equivalent to the current size of CNBM in about ten years. Big goals and inspiring visions are only achieved through focused effort, wisdom, and hard work. There is no easy way to achieve this 10-year goal. We must work with like-minded people in the overseas construction materials sector, pool our resources and talent, and march forward together. The stories of 100 overseas CNBM employees collected in this book are just a few examples of the many people who have worked hard and achieved great things along the Belt and Road. Their stories are a testament to their inspiring accomplishments. I believe more builders of the Belt and Road will join us in the future, working together to build a shared, beautiful home for humanity.

Let's walk the noble path, center on the needs of people, and pursue benefits for the world. We must have high aspirations and a global vision and take the world's leading enterprises as benchmarks. Stay true to the original aspiration and achieve the extraordinary in ordinary roles. We shall carry forward the Silk Road Spirit in the new phase of Belt and Road cooperation, writing new chapters of the Silk Road. Let the mission "Better Materials Better World" resonate far and wide.

Chairman of China National Building Material Group Co., Ltd.

August 2023

CONTENTS

大路同行篇

Joint Efforts of Chinese and Foreign Employees

丝路成材篇

Growth Stories of Young Employees

探路追梦篇

The Road to Realizing Dreams

一路坚守篇

Forging Ahead with Unwavering Perseverance

丝路连山海，合作谱新篇。

志同道合的海外建材人，在砥砺奋进中书写精彩答卷，在企业发展中实现共同成长。

他们，携手同行，守望相助，共建“一带一路”，展示中国力量。

The Belt and Road Initiative connects mountains and seas and opens up a new chapter of cooperation.

CNBM's overseas employees, with a shared vision, are forging ahead to achieve success and pursue common growth in the development of the enterprise.

They team up and support each other under the Belt and Road Initiative and demonstrate the strength of China.

大路同行篇

JOINT EFFORTS OF CHINESE AND FOREIGN EMPLOYEES

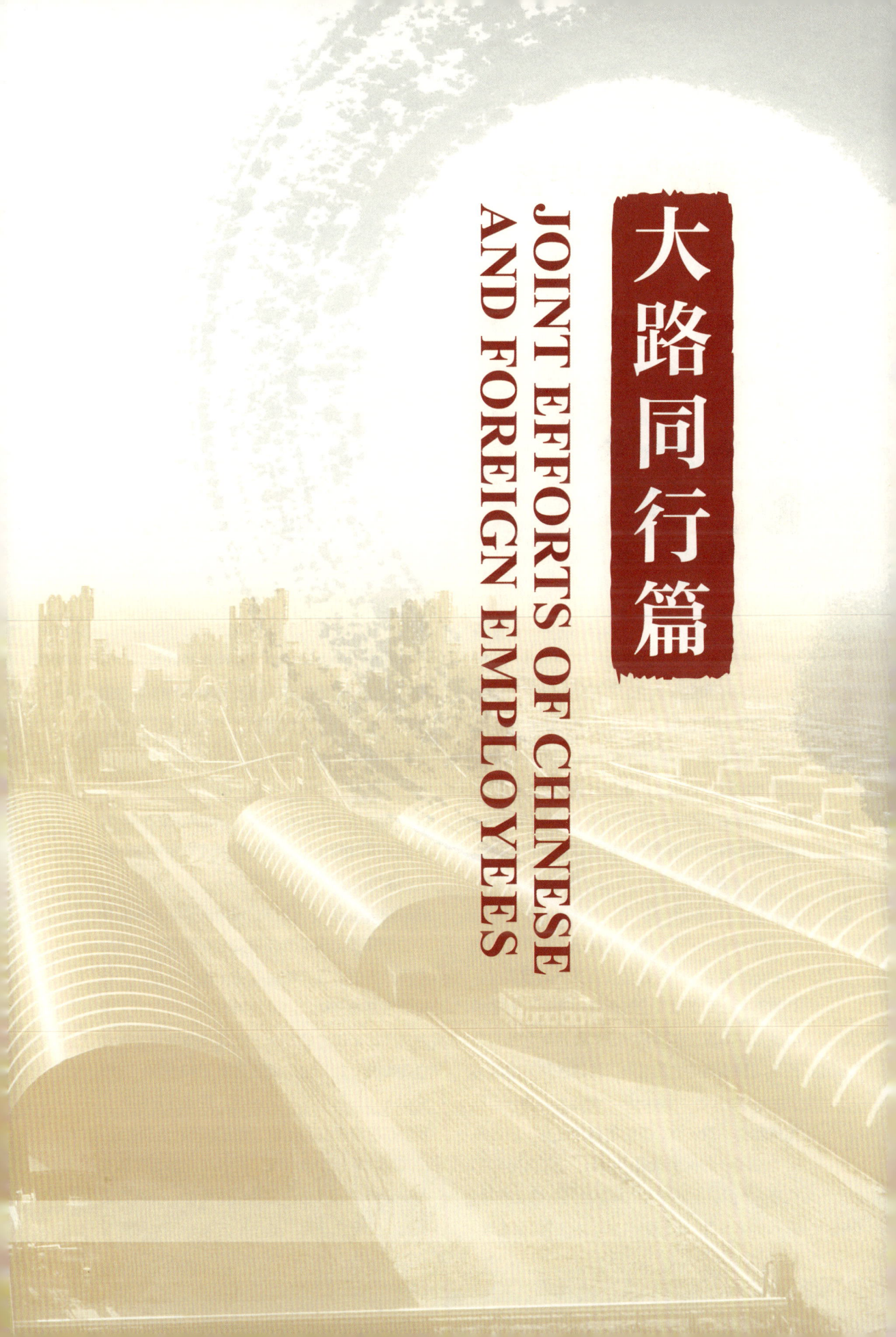

“零事故”守护者

麦坦提·摩根

2022 年加入中国建材

现任中国建材赞比亚工业园健康、安全、安保、环境和质量经理

我叫麦坦提·摩根，今年 39 岁，出生在赞比亚铜带省的恩多拉，毕业于非洲赞比亚大学中非函授学院。2022 年 3 月，我加入了中国建材赞比亚工业园，担任健康、安全、安保、环境和质量经理（以下简称安环经理）。此前，我在行业内也积累了丰富的健康、安全、安保和环境管理等方面的工作经验，同时也十分注重对赞比亚本地法律法规和国际规则的学习，尽可能全面系统地做好工业园的安全管理工作。

作为安环经理，我严于律己，按照公司的安全环保要求，结合公司安全生产实际状况，认真开展公司各项安全环保管理工作。为了更好地做好本职工作，我平日很重视对业务知识的学习和业务能力的提高，通过各种方式学习安全环保知识，锻炼自己工作能力，提升自己业务水平，对于上级下达的各项任务，总会尽全力在第一时间完成任务目标。2023 年年初以来，为促进企业安全生产形势持续稳定好转，深入贯彻落实“安全第一，预防为主，综合治理”的方针政策，我们围绕工艺装备、基础设施、作业环境、防控手段等方面存在的隐患，以及责任落实、遵章守纪、现场管理等方面存在的薄弱环节，重点督导完成了各类安全、环境隐患的排查和整改工作。

在日常管理中，大家常说我“铁面无私”，因为我深知“安全无小事”，要自己恪尽职守，更要人人做到履职尽责才能保证“零事故”目标的实现。我平时很少待在办公室，每月大部分时间都会深入一线作业现场，及时发现和解决生产环节上出现的各类安全环保问题，为业务不熟悉的员工详细讲解安全操作规程，一针见血地指出问题、消除隐患。我相信这样才能为生产经营工作的顺利开展创造有利条件，助力提高公司的安全环保管理水平和质量。按照公司安排，每年的 6 月份是“安全生产月”，我会积极带领部门同事，围绕当年的活动主题，在车间内悬挂安全横幅，在各车间醒目位置张贴安全标语，营造良好的宣传氛围。我还认真制定“安全生产月”的活动方案并下发给各车

间，在车间内组织开展多种多样的安环宣讲、演练、培训活动，全面提升大家的安全环保意识。

“既往不恋，纵情向前。”未来我将持续提升自身业务能力，认真学习更多的专业知识，不断充实自己，从而更好地为公司的安全工作服务。同时，我会加强与各部门的沟通、协调和合作，发动大家齐抓共管，多在现场组织召开安全生产分析会，查找原因，解决问题。针对一线作业现场存在的问题，制定一些切实可行的安全措施，尽量帮助一线管理人员做好现场安全管理工作。我希望可以通过这些努力在全公司内带动形成“人人讲安全、人人会应急”的氛围，大家共同推动公司的安全工作再上一个台阶，为中国建材的海外发展保驾护航。（中国建材赞比亚工业园）

个人体会 未来我将持续提升自身业务能力，认真学习更多的专业知识，不断充实自己，从而更好地为公司的安全工作服务。我希望可以通过这些努力在全公司内带动形成“人人讲安全、人人会应急”的氛围，大家共同推动公司的安全工作再上一个台阶，为中国建材的海外发展保驾护航。

The "Zero Accident" Guardian

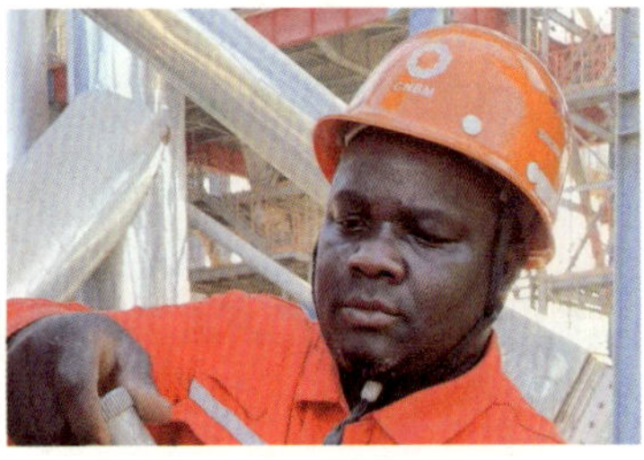

Mwitanti Morgan

Joined CNBM in 2022

HSSEQ Manager of CNBM Zambia Industrial Park

My name is Mwitanti Morgan. I am 39 years old. I was born in Ndola, Copperbelt Province, Zambia. I graduated from the University of Africa, and obtained my Master's degree in Basic Business Administration of Health and Safety Management from Acaciai University in the UK through distance education. In March 2022, I joined CNBM Zambia Industrial Park as its Health, Safety, Security, Environment and Quality (HSSEQ) Manager. Before that, I accumulated rich work experience in health, safety, security and environmental management in the industry, and also paid great attention to the study of local laws and regulations and international rules, so as to contribute to the safety management of the industrial park as comprehensively and systematically as possible.

As an HSSEQ manager, I am strict with myself, and conscientiously carry out the company's safety and environmental protection management in accordance with the company's safety and environmental protection requirements, combined with the actual situation of the company's safety production. In order to do a better job, I attach great importance to the study of business knowledge and the improvement of business ability, learn the knowledge of safety and environmental protection by various means, exercise my work ability and improve my business level, and always try my best to complete the assigned tasks as soon as possible. Since the beginning of this year, in order to promote the continuous and stable improvement of the production safety situation of the industrial park, and thoroughly implement the policy of "safety first, prevention-focused, comprehensive management", we have focused on the hidden dangers in process equipment, infrastructure, operating environment, prevention and control means, as well as the weak links in responsibility implementation, compliance and discipline, and on-site management. We've supervised inspections and rectification work for various safety and environmental hazards.

In daily management, my colleagues thought I am a strict and impartial person, because I know that "safety is no small matter." Every individual should fulfill his or her responsibilities, and collectively we should perform our duties to achieve the goal of "zero accidents". I rarely stay in the office, and spend most of my time at the front-lines to timely detect and solve various safety and environmental protection problems in the production process, explain the safety operation procedures in detail for employees who are unfamiliar with the business, and point out problems and eliminate hidden dangers. I believe that only in this way can we create favorable conditions for smooth production and operation, and help improve the company's safety and environmental protection management level and quality. According to the company's arrangement, every June is the "Safety Production Month". I will actively lead my department colleagues to hang safety-themed slogans and banners in the park, to create a good publicity atmosphere. We also carefully formulate the activity plan of the Safety Production Month and send it to all workshops, organize and carry out a variety of environmental safety awareness lectures, drills and training activities in the workshops to comprehensively enhance everyone's safety and environmental awareness.

"Leave the past behind, and indulge in moving forward." In the future, I will continue to enhance my business ability and earnestly learn more professional knowledge to enrich myself, so as to better serve the company's safety work. At the same time, we will strengthen the communication, coordination and collaboration with various departments, mobilize everyone to work together, organize and hold on-site safety production analysis meetings, identify the causes and solve the problems. We will develop some practical safety measures to support frontline management personnel in executing efficient on-site safety management. I hope that through these efforts, we can foster an atmosphere within the company where "safety is emphasized by all, and everyone understands emergency preparedness."and we can jointly promote the safety work of the company to a higher level and safeguard the overseas development of China National Building Material Group.

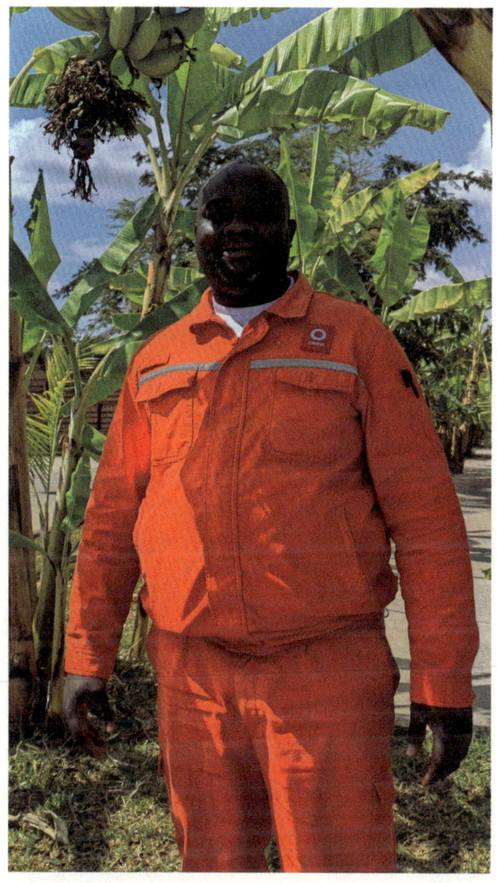

Personal Insights In the future, I will continue to enhance my business ability and earnestly learn more professional knowledge to enrich myself, so as to better serve the company's safety work. I hope that through these efforts, we can foster an atmosphere within the company where "safety is emphasized by all, and everyone understands emergency preparedness."and we can jointly promote the safety work of the company to a higher level and safeguard the overseas development of CNBM.

在自我成长中推动“一带一路”发展

怀斯 · 希布鲁

2018 年加入中国建材

现任中国建材赞比亚工业园水泥磨工段长

我的名字叫怀斯 · 希布鲁，今年 44 岁，出生在赞比亚南部一个叫 Choma 的小镇，我的职业是机械技术员。我于 2018 年 7 月加入中国建材赞比亚工业园。刚入职时，我只是一名普通的巡检工，主要负责对现场设备的巡查和维护。在日常的工作中，我凭借自己在职业学校期间所学的机械知识，再加上日常的工作实践，我的工作能力得到了很大的提升，现在的我担任水泥磨工段的工段长。

新的职位意味着更大的责任。刚担任工段长时，对于水泥磨系统工艺原理和设备的运行原理我了解得不是很透彻，于是我每天会拿上自制的小记录本，不停地记录着自己不懂不会的问题。我在水泥库底，观察水泥物料是如何输送的，观察这些设备是如何先后启动运行的。中方同事给了我一份工艺流程图后，我对照设备一一确认、标注物料的输送走势，抱着刨根问底的态度，一步一个脚印地走到今天。在多岗位轮岗期间，我未出现过工作失误，并且多次排查出设备隐患，并及时反馈给相关管理人员，避免了多起重大安全事故的发生。

机器设备是重要的生产工具，对于完成生产任务具有极其重要的作用，因此我会定期检查各台设备的运行时间以及电机运转情况等，在确保安全的前提下，及时消除设备的跑、冒、滴、漏，并要求自己的班组员工要爱惜设备，按照每台设备的安全操作规程正确使用设备，精心维护设备，保持设备的完好率和正常运行。另外，我还会利用班前、班后会的时间，定期开展员工培训，使他们弄懂设备结构，熟知设备检查的作用及方法、设备的维护保养及设备操作规程。在工作中，我会号召大家使用好设备，保养好设备，稳定设备功能，确保设备正常运行，以满足生产需要。

理论知识永远是指导生产的最有力标准。一个人只有不断学习，才能跟上时代的步伐。作为生产一线的员工，在保证生产的同时，我和班组其他员工会利用闲暇时间，一起讨论工作中的难点，我们会一起向中国“师父”请教，

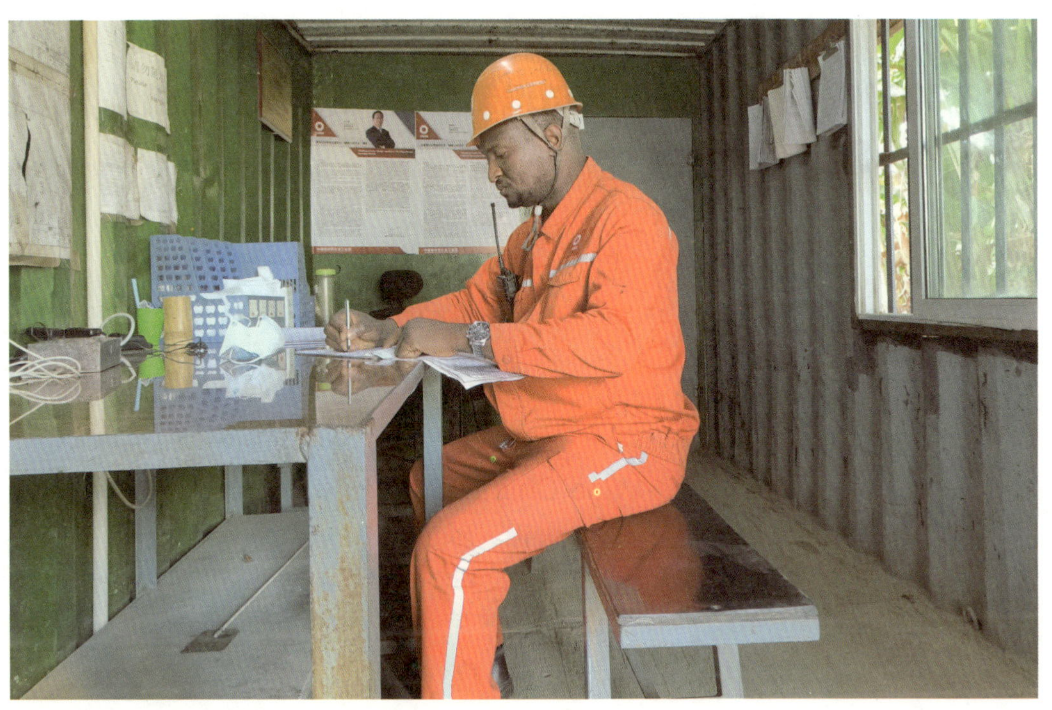

他们总会倾囊相授，每次我们都受益匪浅。只有将生产知识量化分解，使学习内容与生产实际灵活地结合在一起，才能更好地提高大家的工作质量，中国“师父”有针对性地讲解，既可以解决我们实际工作中的困难，又提高了大家的操作水平和综合素质，促使我们不断掌握新知识、新技能。

在带领班组人员搞好生产的同时，我们更注重“以人为本”的生产理念，狠抓落实安全生产管理责任制。为切实推动班组安全管理工作的进步，我们在车间建立了安全绩效考核，通过考核，明确班组职责，提高班组安全管理的主动性，划分区域，明确责任范围。另外，我还根据车间的实际情况，对生产中的安全隐患采取专项治理活动，我主要通过现场指导、会议等方式来开展工作，推进车间安全文化建设。通过会议、学习、标语、宣讲等方式，在车间形成安全生产文化氛围，提高员工安全意识，这样一来，全车间各班组齐抓共管的局面快速形成。

时光飞逝，转眼间，我已来到这里快 5 年了。中国建材赞比亚工业园就像一个大家庭，见证了我的每一步成长，让我从一个小小的巡检工，一路成长为可以独当一面的工段长。这期间，有我自己的努力，但更多的则是领导的栽培与同事的帮助。在以后的工作中，我要不断增强自己的业务知识，努力提升自身的管理水平，扎实开展日常工作，为班组员工做好榜样，从而为推动“一带一路”建设发展贡献更多的力量。（中国建材赞比亚工业园）

我已来到这里快5年了，中国建材赞比亚工业园就像一个大家庭，见证了我的每一步成长。在以后的工作中，我要不断增强自己的业务知识，努力提升自身的管理水平，扎实开展日常工作，为班组员工做好榜样，从而为推动“一带一路”建设发展贡献更多的力量。

To Promote the Development of the Belt and Road through Self-growth

Wise Chibulu

Joined CNBM in 2018

Chief of Cement Grinding Mill Section of CNBM Zambia Industrial Park

My name is Wise Chibulu. I am 44 years old. I was born in Choma, a small town in southern Zambia. I joined CNBM Zambia Industrial Park in July 2018. When I first joined, I was just an ordinary inspection worker, mainly responsible for inspection and maintenance of on-site equipment. In daily work, I have greatly improved my working ability thanks to the mechanical knowledge I learned in vocational school and from daily work practice. Now I am working as the foreman of the cement grinding section.

The new position means greater responsibilities. When I first became the monitor, I did not understand the process principles of the cement grinding system and the operation principles of the equipment thoroughly, so I would take a self-made small notebook every day and keep recording what I did not understand. At the bottom of the cement warehouse, I observed how the cement materials were transported and how these equipment were started and operated successively. After my Chinese colleagues gave me a process flow chart, I compared it with the equipment and annotated the material transportation route, and with an inquiring attitude, I have made progress step by step until today. During the position rotation period, I did not make any work mistakes, and repeatedly detected the potential safety hazards of equipment and promptly gave feedback to the relevant management personnel, preventing the occurrence of major equipment safety accidents.

Machinery and equipment are important production tools, which play an extremely important role in completing production tasks. Therefore, I will regularly check the running time of each set of equipment and the operation of the motor, etc. While ensuring safety, I will eliminate the flaws and errors in the operation of the equipment in time, and ask my team to cherish the equipment, using the equipment correctly according to the safe operation procedures, carefully maintaining the equipment to ensure its good condition and normal operation. In addition, I will also use the time before and after work to carry out regular training, so that they can understand the structure of the equipment, the role and methods of equipment inspection, as well as the maintenance and the operation procedures of equipment. In the work, we should use and maintain the equipment properly so that it can function stably and run normally to serve the production needs.

Theoretical knowledge is always the most powerful standard to guide production, a person can only keep up with the pace of the times by constant

learning. As an employee at the production site, while ensuring production, my collegues and I will use our spare time to discuss the difficulties in work, and we will consult the Chinese masters together. They always teach us everything, and we benefit a lot every time. Only by applying the production knowledge and integrating it with the production practice can we better improve the quality of our work. Our Chinese masters' targeted explanations can not only solve the difficulties in our work, but also improve our operational level and comprehensive performance, and promote us to constantly master new knowledge and new skills.

While leading the team to do a good job in production, we pay more attention to the "people-oriented" production concept and pay close attention to the implementation of the safety production management responsibility system. In order to effectively promote the progress of the safety management in our team, we have established a safety performance assessment system in the workshop. Through the assessment, we can clarify the responsibilities of the team members, enhance their initiative in safety management, and establish clear accountability by dividing the tasks and specifying responsibility boundaries. In addition, I have taken targeted measures to address safety hazards in production, based on the actual conditions in the workshop. I provide on-site guidance and conduct meetings as part of my work approach to promote the construction of safety culture in the workshop. Through meetings, training sessions, safety slogans, presentations, we have successfully cultivated a culture of safety in the workshop and improved the safety awareness of employees. In this way, an atmosphere has been quickly built up where all teams in the workshop work together to ensure safety and effectively manage potential risks.

Time flies, in a blink of an eye, I have been here for nearly five years, CNBM Zambia Industrial Park is like a big family, witnessing my every step of growth from a grassroots inspection worker all the way to a team leader. I attributed my growth during this period to my own efforts and, more importantly to the support of my leaders and the help from my colleagues. In the future, I will continue to enhance my professional knowledge, strive to improve my management capability, continue to work hard, and set a good example for my team, so as to contribute more strength to promoting the construction and development of the "Belt and Road".

Personal Insights I have been here for nearly five years, CNBM Zambia Industrial Park is like a big family, witnessing my every step of growth.In the future, I will continue to enhance my professional knowledge, strive to improve my management capability, continue to work hard, and set a good example for my team, so as to contribute more strength to promoting the construction and development of the "Belt and Road".

戈壁上开出的“管理之花”

陈鸿

2000 年加入中国建材

现任中国巨石二三分厂拉丝工段副主任

“Mr.Chen，我晋升成功了！”看到来自巨石埃及这条隔着六个小时时差的好消息，巨石二三分厂拉丝车间副主任陈鸿不禁露出了欣慰的笑容。回忆起在茫茫沙漠的那三年，现在留下的都是沙漠般金色的难忘回忆。

“他们埃及员工大多数都留着差不多的络腮胡，肤色也都一样，黑黑的，我那时候对他根本没有印象。”回忆当初，陈鸿的嘴角不禁流露微笑。2017 年 7 月，时任三分厂拉丝班组长的陈鸿被派往埃及，然而作为班组长去的他却被赋予了车间主任一般大的权利，因为他此行的唯一目的就是让“陈鸿班组管理方法”在埃及落地生根，改变埃及公司班组管理状况。

来到埃及公司的第 2 天，为了初步了解埃及拉丝车间的情况，时任埃及拉丝车间主任的刘祖发带着陈鸿深入车间，那是陈鸿第一次见到格里布。作为苏伊士当地人，格里布算得上当地的中产阶级，有自己的房子，还能接受相对较好的教育（获得大学学历），自巨石埃及公司成立之初，他就加入了该公司，他算得上公司“元老级”的员工。有学历、有技术的他在众多一线员工当中脱颖而出，成为一名老班组长。

一个下午，刚刚开完班组长会议的陈鸿回到了办公室，来不及坐下喝口水，一个声音叫住了他：“Mr.Chen，你看看，这是我们班组内部的先进工作者。”听到这句话，已经通过竞聘上岗成为埃及拉丝车间副主任的陈鸿不禁有些诧异。格里布说着将手机递给了陈鸿，图片上是格里布负责班组的内部光荣榜。陈鸿问道：“怎么想到在自己的班组里开展评比啊？我并没有要求这个！”“我觉得这个方法很有效，所以，为了提高我自己班组的工作，我也学着开展了一下！”格里布答道。

在陈鸿去到埃及公司之初，发现班组旷工现象严重，离职率居高不下，严重影响公司正常生产。授人以鱼不如授人以渔，对班组长的培养，陈鸿手把手地教，分析上一次各项生产数据，找到问题所在，然后再针对性地解决，在管理上实行“传帮带”。

在被派驻埃及的第 2 年，掌握了班组情况的陈鸿开始在拉丝车间开展光荣榜文化建设，激励员工工作激情。自推行光荣榜文化建设以来，一直是 6 个班组之间的评比，而格里布学以致用，率先在自己的班组开展了内部评比。这一举动也让陈鸿看到了格里布身上的高度执行力和创新意识。2018 年，陈鸿任命格里布为埃及拉丝车间的综合管理员。

由一名班组长到一名综合管理员，格里布从一线员工晋升到基层领导岗位。对他来说，陈鸿亦师亦友，那些他手把手教的管理方法让自己一生受用。2022 年，他又通过竞聘上岗成为巨石埃及公司公用部组长，和当班组长时相比，工资增长近 15%。

如今，陈鸿已经回到了桐乡，苏伊士的沙漠戈壁只能通过一张张照片来回忆。每到斋月期间，他还总能收到来自红海之滨的祝福。“陈鸿班组管理方法”到底有没有在埃及落地生根，长成参天大树？这一声声的感谢和祝福应该是最好的回答。（巨石埃及公司）

在埃及的经历让我收获满满，心中十分欣喜。对待埃及同事，我将中国最先进的玻纤生产技术和管理方法倾囊相授，让他们获得技术和实现成长。我也将持续提升自己的技术和管理水平，用优秀的管理经验推动公司高质量发展。

The Management Flower Blooming in the Desert

Chen Hong

Joined CNBM in 2000

Deputy Director of the Wire-drawing Section at Jushi Group Plant No. 2 & Plant No. 3

"Mr. Chen, I have been promoted." Upon seeing the good news from Jushi Egypt with a six hour time difference, Chen Hong, the deputy director of the wire-drawing workshop at the Second and Third Plant in Jushi, can't help but smile with relief. Recalling the three years in the vast desert, Chen is overwhelmed by those unforgettable memories.

"Most of Egyptian employees had similar whiskers and dark skin, and I had no impression of him at that time."Chen Hong recalled with a smile on his lips.

In July 2017, Chen Hong, who was then the leader of wire-drawing team at the Third Plant, was sent to Egypt. As a team leader, he was given the authority of a workshop director, as his only purpose in this trip was to make the "Chen Hong's Team Management Method" take root in Egypt and change the team management situation of Jushi Egypt.

On the second day of his arrival at Jushi Egypt, Chen Hong was guided by Liu Zufa, then the wire-drawing workshop's director for a tour of the workshop to get a grasp of the general situation there. It was then that Chen Hong first met Grib.

As a native of Suez, Grib comes from a local middle class family. He has his own house, and has also received relatively good education to obtain a bachalor's degree. He joined Jushi Egypt soon after it was set up, and can be regarded as a "senior" employee. With good education and skills, he naturally stood out among many frontline employees at the grassroots level and became an experienced team leader.

One afternoon, Chen Hong, who had just finished a team leader meeting, returned to the office. He was about to sit down for some water when he heard someone calling him.

"Mr. Chen, look, here is a list of the exemplary individuals in our team."

Upon hearing it, Chen Hong, who had already become the deputy director of the wire-drawing workshop, was quite surprised. Grib handed his phone to Chen Hong as he spoke, showing Chen a Honor List of his team.

"What inspired you to conduct evaluations in your own team? I didn't ask for this." Chen Hong asked.

"I think this method is very effective. So in order to improve the work of my own team, I also learned

from you and try out the evaluation method." Grib answered.

Chen Hong faced a lot of challenges when he first arrived in Egypt. The absentee and turnover rates remained high among teams, which had a negative impact on the company's normal production. "It's better to teach a person how to fish than to give him a fish." To cultivate team leaders, Chen Hong adopted a person-to-person approach, analyzing various previous production data, identifying the problems, and then addressing them in a targeted manner, acting as a mentor in management.

In his second year in Jushi Egypt, Chen Hong, who had a good grasp of the situation of the teams, began to cultivate the Honor List culture in the workshop, inspiring employees' work enthusiasm. The implementation of the Honor List involved competitions among six teams, but Grib took the lead in conducting similar evaluations within his own team by applying what he had learned. This move made Chen Hong find Grib's strong execution power and innovative mindset. In 2018, Chen Hong promoted Grib to become the comprehensive administrator of the wire-drawing workshop.

From a team leader to a comprehensive administrator, Grib successfully stood out from the frontline staff. For him, Chen Hong is both a teacher and a friend, and the management methods Chen taught him have benefited him all the way. In 2022, he became the leader of the public department of Jushi Egypt through competitive recruitment, with a salary increase of nearly 15% compared to when he was a team leader.

Now, Chen Hong has returned to Tongxiang, and the desert in Suez can only be recalled through photos. During Ramadan, he always receives blessings from the shore of the Red Sea. Has the "Chen Hong's Team Management Method" taken root in Egypt and grown into a towering tree? These messages of gratitude and blessings should be the best answer.

Personal Insights My experience in Egypt has rewarded me a lot and filled me with joy. I will impart the most advanced fiberglass production technology and management methods in China to Egyptian employees, to help them grow in pursuit of happiness. I will also continue to improve my technical and management skills, and promote the high-quality development of the company with my excellent management experience.

在企业发展中实现共同成长

阮俊羽

2020 年 12 月加入中国建材

现任中材膜材料越南有限公司综合部主管

2018 年 3 月 6 日，随着“协同出海，合作共赢”中国建材集团越南膜材料生产基地项目建设推进大会上具有象征意义的推杆仪式完成，中材膜材料越南有限公司的建设正式进入快车道。随着项目建设日益成熟，公司的各项经营管理工作逐渐走上正轨，许多怀揣着对事业和未来憧憬的越南青年进入公司，阮俊羽就是其中一员。从此，他的人生轨迹与一家中国公司紧紧联系在了一起。

2021 年初，越南本地疫情暴发，整个社会面临食物、药品、消杀物资、疫苗等严重短缺的局面，越南政府也进行了最严格的管控措施。为了将疫情对经营的影响降到最低，公司按照地方政府要求开始执行“三就地”政策，即在工厂“就地生产，就地用餐，就地住宿”。在企业运转最困难的时刻，阮俊羽主动站了出来，积极参与应急预案的制定、贯彻和执行。在实施封闭管理期间，阮俊羽冒着被病毒感染的风险，主动担当作为，外出采购生产经营和员工隔离生活所需物资，短时间内完成原辅材料、设备配件、生活物资和防疫药品等物资的采购工作；他还多渠道联系当地医院，请医院的医护人员定期来公司为全体员工做核酸检测，满足了隔离员工的基本生活需求，保证了生产经营的正常运转。

通过疫情的考验，不仅公司上下对阮俊羽勇于担当、积极作为的工作态度赞赏有加，他本人也在考验中获得成长，业务能力不断提升，所承担的岗位职责也愈加重要。在安全管控方面，由于越南南部地区常年处于高温状态，气候干燥，极易起火，当地政府对消防工作要求也十分严格，阮俊羽多次邀请同奈省公安、消防到公司对员工进行安全知识培训和消防演练，督促员工始终绷紧安全这根弦，公司日常安全管理工作扎实推进。在人力资源管理方面，受疫情的影响，在封闭管理环境下的部分越籍员工无法忍受物资匮乏、饮食单一、休闲娱乐缺失的状态，离职率剧增，企业用工缺口巨大。为了满足生产经营需要，同时确保防疫不放松，阮俊羽积极寻找招工渠道、寻求好友推荐，多

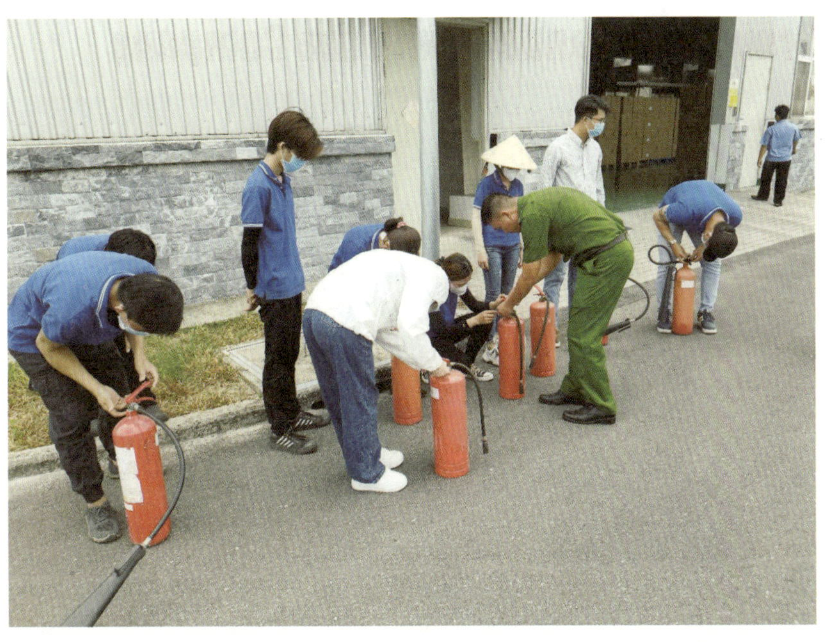

措并举保证了生产经营的用工需求。在行政管理方面，阮俊羽负责对接越南本土行政部门（如工业园区、公安局、消防局），在取得环评和房产证书的过程中，面对资料准备困难、取证经验不足等情况，阮俊羽通过多种渠道在两个月中多次奔波于省会与公司所在地之间，早出晚归，加班加点，从无怨言，在较短的时间内取得两证。在基础建设方面，阮俊羽带领团队完善了整个厂区视频监控系统建设，购置防恐设施，完成了生活楼前的人行道路加宽改造，增添了部分健身设施，扩建了垃圾房和车棚，根据厂区的实际情况对主要区域进行绿化工程建设，在美化公司环境的同时提升了公司形象。

不仅如此，他还和中国员工经常在一起研究如何改进优化工作流程，不断提升整体服务品质。中国员工和管理团队不怕困难、不怕疲惫，连续工作的精神感动了他，他说，越南本地有句谚语：“微风聚在一起，就有台风的力量”，他要向中国员工学习这种团结一致、攻坚克难的精神。

作为一名越南籍员工，阮俊羽无论是在疫情防控中还是在日常工作中都能够勇敢闯、加油干，勇扛使命担当，在砥砺奋进中书写精彩答卷，在企业发展中实现个人成长，在公司越籍员工中起到了榜样作用，也是“中越一家亲”的践行者。疫情过后，他与越南同学聚会，他津津乐道地和大家分享在中国企业工作的收获：“在这里，我能够和公司不断成长，通过每天不断学习，我感觉很充实、怀有希望。”

（中材膜材料越南有限公司）

个人体会 2022 年，我获得南京玻纤院“文明职工标兵”和微纤维公司“一线模范”的称号，这不仅是我个人的荣誉，更是全体越籍员工的骄傲。公司正在加快越南本土化骨干员工的培养，我将以自己的实际行动去影响更多的本土员工，为完成各项工作贡献自己的力量。

Growing in Tandem with the Company

Ruan Junyu

Joined CNBM in 2020
Manager of General Affairs Department of SINOMA Membrane Material Vietnam Co., Ltd.

On March 6, 2018, with a symbolic launch ceremony at the conference for advancing the construction of the CNBM Vietnam Membrane Materials Production Base Project held under the theme of "jointly going overseas with win-win cooperation", the construction of SINOMA Membrane Material Vietnam Co., Ltd. officially entered the fast track. With the advancement of the project construction, the management of the company gradually got on the right track. Many Vietnamese young people joined the company with a vision for their career and future, and Ruan Junyu was one of them. From then on, his life path was closely connected with a Chinese company.

In early 2021, COVID-19 epidemic broke out in Vietnam, and the whole society faced a serious shortage of food, medicine, disinfection supplies and vaccines, and the Vietnam government took the strictest control measures. In order to minimize the impact of the epidemic on operations, the company began implementing a "3 on-sites" policy in accordance with the requirements of the local government, which means "on-site production, on-site dining and on-site accommodation" at the factory. In the most difficult time of enterprise operation, Ruan Junyu took the initiative to stand out and actively participate in the development, implementation and execution of the emergency plan. During the implementation of the closed management, Ruan Junyu took the initiative to go out to purchase materials needed for production and management and the quarantine of employees, regardless of the risk of being infected by the virus. He completed the procurement of raw and auxiliary materials, equipment and accessories, daily supplies and anti-epidemic drugs in a short time, and contacted local hospitals through multiple channels to conduct nucleic acid testing for all employees. What he did met the basic living needs of the quarantined employees and ensured the normal operation of production and management.

Through the test of the epidemic, not only the company appreciated Ruan Junyu's courageous and active work attitude, but also he himself grew up during the test, and his business ability continued to improve, and the responsibilities of his position became more and more important.

In terms of safety control, the southern region of Vietnam is prone to fire incidents due to the consistently high temperatures and dry climate there. As a result, the government has implemented strict regulations regarding fire safety. Ruan Junyu has proactively arranged safety training sessions and fire drills conducted by the public security and fire departments of Dong Nai Province, urging employees to stay vigilant about fire safety. This has ensured the effective implementation of the company's daily safety management protocols. In terms of human resource management, some of the Vietnamese employees confined by the epidemic could not tolerate a shortage of supplies, monotonous diets, and lack of entertainment options, resulting in a significant rise in employee turnover and a substantial employment gap. To address these issues and maintain production and operational requirements without compromising on epidemic prevention measures, Ruan Junyu has taken proactive steps, including actively seeking recruitment channels and recommendations from acquaintances, to fulfill the labor demands for production and operations.In terms of administration, Ruan Junyu was responsible for liaising with local administrative departments in Vietnam, including the Industrial Park, Public Security Bureau, and Fire Bureau. In the process of obtaining environmental assessment and real estate certificates, Ruan had difficulties in preparing materials and getting other things done smoothly due to the lack of experience. Ruan then spent two months commuting between the provincial capital and the company many times through various channels, but he chose not to complain despite constantly working overtime.He managed to obtain the two certificates in a relatively short period of time. In terms of infrastructure, Ruan improved the construction of video surveillance system in the whole factory, purchased anti-terrorist facilities, widened the sidewalk in front of the living building, added some fitness facilities, expanded the garbage room and carport, and carried out greening works in the main area according to the actual situation of the factory, beautifying the company's environment while enhancing the company's image.

Besides, he also worked together with Chinese staff and studied how to improve and optimize the working process and continuously improve the service level. During the epidemic, he observed the unwavering determination and dedication displayed by the Chinese staff and management team, and was deeply touched by their relentless spirit.He said that there is a local proverb in Vietnam that when the breeze gathers together, it has the power of a typhoon, and he wants to learn from the Chinese team the spirit of unity in overcoming difficulties.

As a Vietnamese employee, Ruan Junyu is brave in epidemic prevention and control as well as in daily work. With the spirit of fighting and the courage to shoulder the mission, he has demonstrated the spirit of striving, and achieved common growth in the development of the enterprise. He has played a role model among the Vietnamese employees of the company, and he is also the practitioner of "China and Vietnam are one family".When he gathered with his Vietnamese classmates after the outbreak, he was all too happy to share what he had learned from working for a Chinese company. "Here, I am able to grow with the company, and I feel fulfilled and hopeful every day through the constant learning I do every day."

Personal Insights I was awarded the title of "Model Pioneer Employee" of Nanjing Glass Fiber Research and Design Institute in 2022 and the title of "Model Frontline Worker" of Microfiber Company in 2022. This is not only my personal honor, but also the pride of all the Vietnamese employees. The company is accelerating the training of local Vietnamese backbone staff.I will motivate and support more local staff with actions and commit myself to accomplishing various tasks.

非洲小伙 Augustine 成长记

奥尼亚卡·奥诺拉·奥古斯丁

2017 年加入中国建材

现任中材宁锐尼日利亚子公司驳船码头高级管理经理

我是奥古斯丁，今年 36 岁，来自尼日利亚最东部的阿南布拉州，毕业于 Nnamdi Azikiwe 大学机械工程专业，现任中材宁锐尼日利亚子公司驳船码头高级管理经理。

作为一个土生土长的非洲小伙，在加入 SINOMA Cargo 之前，我一直在当地企业从事维修方面的基层工作，微薄的收入和频繁的工作变动给我的生活带来很多不稳定性。一次偶然的机会，我看见 SINOMA Cargo 的招聘信息，抱着试试看的心态我投递了简历。很幸运，我自此开始了与 SINOMA Cargo 的故事。

2017 年 6 月 5 日，是我作为车队管理部维修主管入职 SINOMA Cargo 的第一天，通过 SINOMA Cargo 工作制度和流程的培训，我对中国人以及他们的工作方式有了深入的了解，他们时刻保持着良好的工作状态、高效的执行力，注重承诺、细节和时间管理，这些品质对我后续工作习惯的养成产生了潜移默化的影响。

作为当地的外企，我们的客户大多数是中国人，为了提高与客户的沟通效率，在领导的激励下，我开始利用闲余时间学习中文。经过半年的锻炼，我的中文水平得到了一定提升，我的中国客户对我的服务赞不绝口。我的努力也受到了公司的认可，在年终颁奖会上我受到了表彰，获得 2017 年度公司优秀员工称号。

在 2017 年的时候，我们的车队仅有 20 辆卡车，仅仅经过一年多时间的经营，卡车总数就达到 42 辆。在此期间，我主要负责供应商开发以及车辆维修管理工作。在这个过程中，身边的中国同事们毫不吝啬地分享他们的工作经验，并对我的管理能力提出更高的要求。在 SINOMA Cargo 的培养下，我的管理能力不断提升，我还通过业余时间学习并获得了 HSE 1 级、2 级、3 级证书，物流供应链证书以及项目管理证书，成为更加专业的工作者。

2019 年是我职业生涯中的重要转折点。随着公司的发展壮大，SINOMA Cargo 车队卡车总数已增加至 63 辆。同年 10 月，在距离拉各斯州 APAPA 码头 70 公里处，我们的

内河自有码头 SINOMA Port 正式运营。

鉴于突出的工作表现及管理能力，我被提拔为驳船码头发展事业部经理。车队运营规模的扩大以及驳船码头的运营为 SINOMA Cargo 带来新的挑战和机遇。在公司发展创新过程中，我与中国管理者们并肩作战，克服种种困难，在这个过程中我也接触和学习到了中国团队高效的管理方式。

2020 年初，新冠肺炎疫情蔓延全球，对于一家拥有 200 多名当地员工的国际物流公司而言，码头运营和车辆运输等各项工作面临巨大挑战。我主动请缨在疫情期间负责当地员工的防疫安全管理，在中方管理团队的远程指导下，我结合现场实际情况，组织安全员队伍积极落实疫情防控工作，定期开展疫情防控知识专题培训，对当地员工进行积极引导，严格执行疫情防控要求，尤其是在尼日利亚疫情肆虐时期，我们的团队工作成效显著。

今年是我在 SINOMA Cargo 的第 6 个年头，从起初的生活飘忽不定到现在的成家立业，我在这里实现了自己的价值，同时也见证了 SINOMA Cargo 的快速发展。

中国有句古话："滴水之恩当涌泉相报"，我很感激公司给予我的工作机会和锻炼平台，在今后的工作中我一定再接再厉，竭尽所能做得更好，与 SINOMA Cargo 共同成长！〔中材国际（南京）〕

这是我第一次入职中国企业，在这里我感受到了大家庭般的温暖，中国人的"授之以渔"让我逐渐实现了自己的价值。在今后的工作中，我一定竭尽所能，与公司共同成长。

From Struggle to Success: Inspiring Story of Augustine

Onyeaka Onuorah Augustine

Joined CNBM in 2017

SINOMA Port Admin Manger of SINOMA Cargo International Nigeria Ltd.

I'm Augustine and I'm 36 years old. I come from Anambra State in the easternmost part of Nigeria and graduated from Nnamdi Azikiwe University with a major in Mechanical Engineering. I'm currently the SINOMA Port Admin Manger of SINOMA Cargo International Nigeria Ltd.

I was born and raised in Africa. Prior to joining SINOMA Cargo, I worked as a grassroots maintenance worker at a local enterprise. Meager income and frequent job changes brought a lot of instability to my life. By chance, I saw the recruitment information of SINOMA Cargo and submitted my resume with a try-and-see attitude. Fortunately, this marked the beginning of my journey in SINOMA Cargo.

I joined SINOMA on June 5, 2017 as the Maintenance Supervisor of the Fleet Management Department. After receiving training on SINOMA Cargo's work systems and procedures, I had an in-depth understanding of the Chinese people and their work methods. They always maintain a positive working state with efficient execution, and they focus on commitment, details and time management. These qualities have had a subtle influence on the subsequent cultivation of my work habit.

As a local foreign enterprise, we have mostly Chinese clients. In order to improve the efficiency of communication with our clients, I began to use my spare time to learn Chinese with encouragement from my leaders. After six months of practice, my Chinese improved to a certain level, and my Chinese clients were full of praise for the services provided by me. My efforts were also recognized by the company. I was commended and awarded the title of "Outstanding Employee of the Company 2017" at the year-end award ceremony.

In 2017, our fleet only had twenty trucks. And after just over a year of operation, the total number of trucks in our fleet reached 42. During this period, I was mainly responsible for supplier development and vehicle maintenance management. During this process, my Chinese colleagues generously shared their work experience and put forward higher requirements for my management abilities. Under the cultivation of SINOMA, my management abilities had been continuously improved. By studying in my spare time, I obtained HSE Level 1, Level 2 and Level 3 certificates as well as logistics supply chain certificate and project management certificate, and became a more professional worker.

The year 2019 was an important turning point in my

career. With the development and growth of the company, the total number of trucks in the fleet of SINOMA Cargo increased to 63. In October 2019, 70 kilometers away from the APAPA Terminal in Lagos State, our own inland river terminal SINOMA Port was officially put into operation.

In consideration of my outstanding work performance and management abilities, I was promoted to the position of Manager of the Barge Terminal Development Division. The expansion of the fleet's operating scale and the operation of the barge terminal had brought new challenges and opportunities to SINOMA Cargo. As the company developed and innovated, I worked alongside Chinese managers to overcome all kinds of difficulties. During the process, I was also exposed to and learnt about the efficient management methods of the Chinese team.

In the beginning of 2020, the COVID-19 pandemic swept the world. For an international logistics company with more than 200 local employees, the pandemic had posed great challenges to terminal operation and vehicle transportation. I volunteered to take charge of COVID-19 prevention and safety management of local employees during the pandemic. Under the remote guidance of the management team from China, I organized a team of safety officers to actively implement COVID-19 prevention and control measures in consideration of the actual situation on site, periodically carrying out special training on COVID-19 prevention and control knowledge, providing positive guidance for local employees, and strictly enforcing COVID-19 prevention and control requirements. Our team achieved great results especially at the height of the pandemic in Nigeria.

This year is my sixth year in SINOMA Cargo. From living an unstable life to getting married and starting a career, I've realized my value here and I've also witnessed the rapid development of SINOMA Cargo.

As an old Chinese saying goes, "The grace of dripping water should be reciprocated by a gushing spring." I'm quite grateful to the company for offering me a job and a platform to cultivate myself. In my future work, I'll redouble my effort to continue to do my job well and grow together with SINOMA Cargo.

Personal Insights This is my first time to work in a Chinese company, where I feel the warmth of a big family. The Chinese people's concept of "teaching a man to fish" has gradually made me realize my own value. In the future, I will do my best to grow together with SINOMA Cargo.

绽放非洲的巾帼风采

庄园
2019 年加入中国建材
现任中材宁锐尼日利亚子公司运营管理部经理

“婚后第 9 天，我老公再次返尼工作，那天天气很冷，地上的雪很是刺眼，在送他去车站回来的路上我便暗自下定决心：跟随他的脚步……”2019 年，英语专业的庄园应聘中材宁锐，她应聘的岗位为尼日利亚子公司综合管理。当我们问其原因，她的回答是：“他可以，我也可以！”

在海外工作，背井离乡，环境艰苦，远离亲友的陪伴，没有光鲜的穿着打扮和优越的生活环境，她能坚持吗……这样的疑惑很快就被消除！3 年来，作为子公司唯一一名女员工，她抗住了外部环境和工作内容改变带来的重重压力，带着一腔热忱挥洒汗水投身到公司海外属地化的建设中，与尼日利亚的当地人同办公、共奋斗，从单纯熟悉外贸的“小庄”一步步成长为子公司综合管理方面独当一面的“庄主任”。

刚到尼日利亚便迎来了子公司六月安全生产月活动，因为没有任何安全管理方面经验，子公司领导便安排庄园前往 Dangote 炼油厂项目部进行安全生产管理经验学习。那是她在尼日利亚的第一次远行，也是在那时候她感受到了尼日利亚的路况有多糟糕，雨季来势有多凶猛。从项目部返回公司后，在领导的指导和同事们的帮助下，她顺利开展了子公司安全生产月的活动。此次安全生产月活动也让她深刻意识到安全的重要性，为今后的管理工作打下了坚实基础。

2019 年 7 月，中材宁锐尼日利亚子公司受邀参加拉各斯大学毕业典礼暨中资企业校园招聘会，庄园作为企业代表上台为优秀毕业生颁奖。此次活动正式拉开子公司与拉各斯大学孔子学院的合作帷幕。此后，在庄园的积极推动下，子公司每年为该校应届生提供大量实习岗位，促进解决学生就业问题。对于应聘上岗的属地员工，庄园积极探索培养方式，通过“传帮带”的形式，将来自拉各斯大学毕业的近 40 名大学生培养为公司属地化骨干员工，为学生们提供了可持续发展的平台和机会。

2020 年初，尼日利亚新冠疫情暴发。因尼日利亚医疗技术落后，防疫物资短缺，作为后勤保障部门，庄园的主要精力都集中在口罩、消毒液和米面油等生活物资的采购上面。第一次面对这样突发的情况，她深知自己工作的重要性，结合境外公司实际情况，积极与上级单位对接，制定防疫紧急预案，安排防疫应急演练，定期安排抗体检测，更新物资报表，对生活区楼层定期进行消杀。在她的努力下，中材宁锐尼日利亚子公司创造了零感染、零疑似的奇迹。

非洲的社会环境对职场女性来说很有挑战性，特别是疫情期间，各种意外状况发生频率更高。在一次外出办事返程途中，庄园乘坐的车辆途经 APAPA 高架遭遇堵车，此时高架旁的大型储油罐正在发生爆燃，随时都有可能爆炸。那是她感到最无助的一次，好在最终平安无事。虽然经历了这样的意外，但时至今日她仍选择坚守。

“她胆子很小，有时候见到小虫子都会怕得躲起来”，但就是这样一位“胆小”的女性，面对当地员工、办公室和宿舍物业的一些无理要求，她总是摆事实，讲道理，据理力争，坚持原则和底线；面对政府部门的苛刻检查，她又能变换沟通技巧，灵活且友好地解决问题。她，用自己柔而刚的一面撑起了子公司管理工作的“半边天”。

成长的脚步匆匆，作为中材宁锐首次派驻海外的女性员工，庄园用柔弱又坚毅的双肩扛起责任与使命，脚踏实地，用辛勤汗水浇灌海外管理事业的苗圃。她的故事让我们看到了巾帼坚守的力量，也让我们坚信，巾帼的力量可以在企业不断发展的浪潮中汇聚成企业前进的大江大河，成为推动其海外建设的强大力量。〔中材国际（南京）〕

我选择去更多的地方，看不同的风景，结交不同的人，并在其中不断探寻自我的可能性。愿与大家一同不断开拓国际市场，为推动公司海外建设贡献巾帼力量。

She Power: Zhuang Yuan and Her Endeavours in Africa

Zhuang Yuan

Joined CNBM in 2019
Manager of Operations Management Department of SINOMA Cargo International Nigeria Ltd.

"On the ninth day after our wedding, my husband departed for Nigeria, resolute and determined, despite the biting cold and unforgiving snow-covered terrain. As I bid him farewell at the station, a firm resolve took hold: I would follow in his footsteps". In 2019, as an English major graduate, Zhuang Yuan took a bold step and applied for a position at SINOMA Cargo. With determination, she applied for the role of General Administration at the Nigeria subsidiary. When we inquired about her motivation, her response was resolute: "If he can do it, so can I!"

Working overseas far away from her hometown, living in a difficult environment without the company of friends and relatives, and having no glamorous dressing or luxurious living conditions, can she overcome these challenges and persevere? Such a doubt was quickly dispelled. Over the course of three years, as the sole female employee of the subsidiary, she faced and overcame the pressures arising from the external environment and the evolving nature of her work. With a passionate dedication, she invested her sweat and efforts into fostering the company's localization efforts overseas. Alongside the local people in Nigeria, she embarked on a journey of shared struggles, gradually transforming from a relatively experienced individual in foreign trade to a well-rounded director, assuming full leadership responsibilities for the subsidiary's comprehensive management.

Upon her arrival in Nigeria, she was greeted by the subsidiary's June production safety month activities. Despite her lack of prior experience in safety management, the subsidiary's leadership made arrangements for her to visit the Dangote refinery project estate to learn from their expertise in production safety management. During her first travel in Nigeria, she had a firsthand experience of the challenging road conditions and the intensity of the rainy season, which made her realize the severity of the situation. Upon her return to the company from the project department, she effectively organized a series of activities for the subsidiary's production safety month, drawing guidance from her leaders and receiving valuable assistance from her colleagues. The safety production activities provided her with a profound understanding of the significance of safety and established a strong groundwork for her future management endeavors.

In July 2019, the Nigerian subsidiary of SINOMA Cargo received an invitation to attend the University of Lagos graduation ceremony and the Chinese enterprises' campus recruitment event. As a representative of the company, she took the stage to present awards to exceptional graduates. This event marked the beginning of a fruitful collaboration between the subsidiary and the Confucius Institute at the University of Lagos. Since then, with the enthusiastic support of the Zhuang Yuan, the subsidiary has been offering numerous internship opportunities to graduating students from the university, contributing to easing the employment challenges faced by young graduates. With a strong commitment to the development of local employees, Zhuang Yuan diligently explores innovative training approaches, passing on her experience to them. As a result, about 40 graduates from the University of Lagos have been trained to become the company's localized backbone workforce.This initiative provides a platform and continuous growth opportunities for the graduates.

At the onset of 2020, Nigeria faced an outbreak of the Covid-19. Due to the limited medical resources and scarcity of epidemic prevention supplies in Nigeria, the logistics support department, led by Zhuang Yuan, focused its efforts on procuring essential supplies such as masks, disinfectants, as well as basic necessities like rice, flour, and oil. Confronting an unprecedented situation, Zhuang Yuan recognized the significance of her role. Considering the specific circumstances of the company, she proactively coordinated with higher authorities, devised emergency plans for epidemic prevention, organized drills, implemented regular antibody testing, and ensured timely updates on material inventory and disinfection procedures in the living quarters. Through her dedicated efforts, SINOMA Cargo's Nigerian subsidiary achieved the remarkable feat of "zero infection and zero suspected case".

The working conditions for women in Africa can be particularly challenging, especially given the even more unpredictable circumstances during the epidemic. At one time, she encountered a distressing situation on the APAPA elevated road on her way back to the office—an immense oil storage tank adjacent to the road suddenly erupted

in flames, posing an imminent risk of explosion. That was one of the most unsettling moments she had ever experienced, making her feel utterly powerless. However, she managed to emerge unhurt, feeling relieved and grateful for her safety. Having experienced such a harrowing accident that rattled her, she bravely chooses to stay.

"She is a timid girl. A small bug will get her.",But when confronted with unreasonable requests from local staff, and the office and dormitory property management personnel, she always presents factual evidence and logical reasoning, firmly upholding principles and defending her bottom line. Moreover, when faced with rigorous inspections by government departments, she adeptly adapts her communication skills, demonstrating flexibility and a friendly demeanor to effectively resolve problems. With her blend of gentleness and strength, she has played a vital role in supporting the management of the subsidiary.

As the first female employee from SINOMA Cargo to be sent overseas, she shouldered the responsibility and mission with unwavering determination, channeling her dedication and perseverance into the fruitful results of overseas management. Her story shows the resilience of women and strengthens our firm belief that women have the power to make a big difference in the fast growth and development of enterprises, and their strength can be pooled to serve as a strong driving force for the enterprises' overseas construction.

Personal Insights I choose to work in more places, see different scenery, meet different people, and constantly explore the possibilities of myself. I hope to work with people to continuously tap the international market and contribute to pushing forward the company's development overseas as a female.

“凡人微光”照亮前进征程

王丽惠

2019 年 1 月加入中国建材

现任中国建材印度尼西亚 CITEC 工程公司行政部部长

2019 年初，CITEC 印度尼西亚工程公司从加里曼丹省坤甸招聘了一名人力资源经理，她的中文名字叫王丽惠（英文名：Wiwin Chandra）。

没有惊天动地的事迹，没有激动人心的语言，只有匆匆的步履和默默的付出。虽然她只是一名普通员工，在普通的岗位上从事平凡的工作，但她让每一个身边人都能感受到她春天般的温暖，她就是天津院印尼公司行政部办公室负责人王丽惠。她以踏实细致的工作作风和认真负责的工作态度，在平凡的岗位上默默地奉献自己的青春，树立了一个新时代优秀青年工作者的形象。

凡是了解王丽惠的人都知道，她在工作中不仅认真负责，而且注重细节。不论是办公用品管理、伙食费用账务核算，还是公司固定电话和移动电话的缴费工作，她都处理得一丝不苟、毫厘不差。

在普通人眼中，办公室行政工作或许就是每天准时上班、按点下班，但王丽惠做行政工作有所不同。就拿餐厅账务核算工作来说，其中项目之多、核算之烦琐，只要稍有疏忽就可能出现差错。这类工作一环扣一环，急不得，乱不得，这就要求员工必须思维敏捷、逻辑清晰、有条不紊。有时候，王丽惠白天忙于各种事务性工作，没有时间处理当天的账目，只能晚上把工作带回家，加班至深夜才能完成，但她毫无怨言，坦然面对工作中的困难和挑战，并且不允许自己出现任何差错。正因为她对工作认真负责，所以收获了同事们的信任和赞誉。

王丽惠在工作上积极主动，执行力强，凡事都坚决服从公司安排，始终以坚持到“最后一分钟”的心态去工作。2020 年，凭借良好的工作态度和敬业精神，王丽惠被评为天津水泥院优秀外籍员工。

王丽惠除了完成自己的本职工作之外，还能够积极主动参与其他工作。由于行政工作的特殊性，各项任务具有突发性，很多工作在部门内部没有明确的职责划分。但每次遇到突发情况，即使到了下班时间，只要把工作交给王丽惠，她都会加班加点、按时完成，而且没有丝毫怨言。

在团队合作中，加强沟通是激发团队活力的主要途径。在工作中，王丽惠经常和同事互相交流、相互学习、彼此关心。她经常借用“木桶原理”激励团队：只有加强沟通，才能发挥最短板的最大效应。不久前，行政部入职了两名新员工，王丽惠主动承担起对两名新人的“传帮带”工作，在完成自己工作的同时帮助他们快速步入工作正轨。

王丽惠还带头厉行节约、践行低碳理念。她办公桌上的台灯用了快 10 年了；水笔笔芯的墨用完了，她不领新笔，而是更换一支笔芯；用 A4 纸，力争双面打印……一件件小事体现着她勤俭节约、以公司为家的优秀品格。

王丽惠在平凡的工作岗位上埋头苦干、兢兢业业、任劳任怨，做出了不平凡的业绩，闪烁着凡人的微光。未来，她将继续尽职尽责、勤勉奋进，为公司的高质量发展贡献出自己的一份力量。（中材国际所属天津水泥院）

个人体会 不畏艰难、追求卓越。我始终保持积极态度，全身心、无私地投入到真心热爱的工作中。我以进取、过硬的专业能力为公司贡献力量，以真诚、友善的服务宗旨为身边的同事带来温暖。

A Dedicated and Heartwarming Worker

Wiwin Chandra

Joined CNBM in 2019
Head of the Administrative Department of PT CITEC Engineering Indonesia

At the beginning of 2019, PT CITEC Indonesia Engineering recruited Wiwin Chandra from Pontianak, Kalimantan Province as the human resources manager.

There was no earthshaking story. She was just an ordinary employee of PT CITEC. Wiwin Chandra,as the head of the administrative department office, works in an ordinary administrative position and engages in ordinary office work but can always make everyone feel the warmth. She silently devotes her youth to ordinary positions with her inherent down-to-earth and meticulous work style, serious and responsible work attitude, and good professional ethics, establishing the image of an excellent young employee.

Anyone who knows Wiwin Chandra knows that she is not only very serious and responsible in her work, but also strives for perfection in details. In her work, whether it's office supplies management, food expense accounting, payment of company fixed and mobile phones, or even daily work chores, she always maintains a rigorous work attitude.

In the eyes of ordinary people, the job of the office is to go to work on time every day and finish work on time. But for Wiwin Chandra, the idea is completely different. Taking the accounting of restaurant accounts and the payment of company fixed and mobile phones as an example. If there is a slight difference in the details, given the complexity of accounting task, the results may be fallacious. This type of work is closely linked, urgent and chaotic. Therefore, the job requires agile thinking, rigorous logic, meticulous attitude. Sometimes, during the day, she is busy with various temporary tasks or customer reception, so at night, she brings the work accounts home. She often works overtime until midnight to complete them, but she has no complaints and bravely faces every difficulty and pressure in her work, not allowing herself to make any mistakes. Her excellent work performance not only reduced the workload of the next work step, but also received praise from colleagues. From her, we have learned that the key to achieving success lies in having a firm belief and a persistent pursuit of dreams in one's heart, in order to achieve a happy and confident life.

Wiwin Chandra is proactive and has strong execution ability. She firmly obeys the arrangements of superiors and strictly implements everything. She always works with a "last minute" mentality, always doing her daily work well, and is able to take the initiative to work and report. With a good work attitude and effectiveness, Wiwin Chandra was awarded the title of "Outstanding Foreign Employee of Tianjin Institute" in 2020.

In addition to completing her own duties, Wiwin Chandra is also able to actively take on other works. Due to the unique nature of administrative work, tasks often come suddenly, without clearcut responsibilities among employees within the department. However, no matter when the tasks come, as long as the work is handed over to Wiwin Chandra, she is always willing to work overtime and take the initiative to complete it on time without any complaints. Wiwin Chandra is doing ordinary work in an ordinary job position, but her diligent and willing spirit of dedication makes her shine.

In team collaboration, strengthening communication with each other is the main way to stimulate strength of the team. Wiwin Chandra often says that she learned from the principle of wooden barrels that only by strengthening communication can the barrels have the biggest volume. Therefore, in her work, she not only works hard on her own, but also handles things very well with her colleagues. In addition to learning from each other at work, she also often communicates with colleagues to understand their thoughts, and comes up with ideas and solutions for each other. She has always had a harmonious relationship with her colleagues, gained everyone's trust, and actively participated in various activities organized by the company. Recently, two new employees were hired in the administrative department. Wiwin Chandra took the initiative to assist the newcomers and provided them with assistance while completing their own work, enabling them to quickly get their work on track.

Wiwin Chandra also attaches great importance to

saving resources. She always cherishes every asset of the company with a sense of ownership. The desk lamp on her desk has been used for almost ten years and has never been replaced with a new one. The pen has run out of ink, and instead of claiming a new pen, a new refill has been replaced. She always prints on both sides of A4 papers, and so on. These small things reflect her noble character of loving the company and considering the company as her home.

Wiwin Chandra from the administrative department has always been diligent and hardworking in ordinary work positions, and has made extraordinary achievements. In her future, she will continue to contribute to the company's high quality development with her enthusiasm, diligence, and serious work style.

Personal Insights Fearless of challenges and pursuing excellence, I always maintain a positive attitude and wholeheartedly dedicate myself to the work I sincerely love. With proactive and strong professional capabilities, I contribute to the company, and with a sincere and friendly service principle, I bring warmth to my colleagues around me.

“YES MAN”德基·普拉约嘉

德基·普拉约嘉

2016 年 4 月加入中国建材

现任中国建材印度尼西亚 CITEC 工程公司采购部采购助理

德基·普拉约嘉是中材国际所属天津水泥院印度尼西亚工程公司的一名员工。德基来自一个叫作万隆的小城市，没有相关的工作经验，但无论你交给他什么任务，即使他并不了解这项任务该如何做，他也总是会说：“Yes”。乍看起来，他并不像一名优秀的员工。起初，公司只将一些简单的任务交给他。然而，随着时间的推移，他逐渐积累了工作经验，并开始承担更大的责任。无论面对何种困难，他始终保持积极的态度，勇于创新、敢于挑战，他越来越熟练地完成工作并不断取得进步，逐渐成为团队中不可或缺的一名成员。

德基的职业道路起始于总务部门，他承担的是税务工作。最初，他对这份工作并不十分熟悉，但凭着对工作的认真和执著，他逐渐成为税务工作的“百事通”，他总是通过电子邮件、电话、短信与总公司、现场多方协调沟通。在过去的 5 年里，他多次帮助财务部门圆满完成地方税务服务报告。无论事情有多复杂，他总能自觉承担起责任，以出色的专业技能和坚定的决心推动工作顺利进行。他出色的表现得到了领导的高度认可，并被安排到采购部去迎接更大的挑战、承担更重要的责任。

在印尼 CITEC 项目执行期间，德基一直担任采购工作，他始终坚守原则，确保每一件商品的采购和发货都井然有序，在强化采购程序和控制方面作出了巨大努力，实现了降低成本的目标。面对紧急、复杂的情况，他也能灵活运用自己的才智和经验处理棘手问题。德基的专业能力和领导才能使他在项目团队中脱颖而出，赢得了同事们的钦佩和尊重。

此外，德基还是一位人际交往小能手。他在现场与当地人紧密合作，凭借优秀的沟通技巧，推进各项工作顺利实施。面对语言、文化等方面的挑战，德基以他超强的人际交往能力和敏锐的洞察力赢得当地人的信任，促进跨部门、跨国界的合作，帮助团队解决各种问题。由于一贯出色的表现，他被评为了天津水泥院 2022 年度优秀外籍员工，也逐渐成为整个公司最受欢迎的人。

面对新冠肺炎疫情，德基起到了“领头人”的作用，严格遵守公司制定的疫情防控措施，并积极向当地员工讲解疫情的风险以及公司采取疫情防控措施的必要性，带领当地员工共同维护公司形象，有效保障了公司全体员工的生活稳定和人身安全。

在工作逐渐恢复正常后，德基凭借他的语言优势和真诚务实、勤奋担当的工作作风，在客户和项目部之间发挥着重要的桥梁作用。他作为“YES MAN”，全身心投入到完成业务运营、运输车辆调度、采购等各项任务中。他的努力和奉献让他成为团队中的核心人物，他的故事激励着我们追求卓越，并以积极进取的态度迎接新的挑战。

德基已经在公司工作了 7 年，成为采购部门不可或缺的重要成员。他说：“在一家中国企业的工作经历不仅使我不断成长，也改变了我的命运，我真诚希望中材国际所属天津水泥院未来能在印尼取得更大的发展。”（中材国际所属天津水泥院）

个人体会

无论面对何种困难，我始终保持积极态度，勇于创新、敢于挑战。我希望用自己的成长故事来感染每一个脚踏实地、努力拼搏的人，我真诚希望公司未来能在印尼取得更大的发展。

The"YES MAN"

Decky Prayoga

Joined CNBM in 2016

Assistant to Procurement Department in PT CITEC Engineering Indonesia

Decky Prayoga is an employee of PT CITEC Engineering Indonesia of Tianjin Cement Industry Design & Research Institute Co., Ltd. (TCDRI) , a subsidary of SINOMA International. Hailing from a small town called Bandung, Decky joined the company without any relevant work experience. However, no matter what task was assigned to him, even if he didn't know how to do it, he always responded with a resounding "Yes." At first glance, he might not appear to be an outstanding employee. Initially, the company only entrusted him with small tasks. However, as time went on, he gradually accumulated work experience and began to assume greater responsibilities.

In the face of any difficulty, he consistently maintains a positive attitude, willingly embraces innovation, and dares to take on challenges. He becomes more proficient in completing his work and steadily makes progress, gradually becoming an indispensable member of the team.

Decky's career journey began in the general affairs department, where he took on tax-related tasks. Initially, he wasn't very familiar with this line of work. However, as time passed, he gradually became a "jack of all trades" when it came to tax matters. He consistently coordinated and communicated with the headquarters and onsite team through emails, phone calls, and text messages, assisting the finance department in completing local tax service reports over the past five years. No matter how complex the situation, he always took responsibility, driving the smooth progress of work with excellent professional skills and unwavering determination. His outstanding performance received high recognition from his superiors, leading to his assignment to the procurement department to embrace greater challenges and take on more significant responsibilities.

During the implementation of the CITEC project in Indonesia, Decky served in the procurement role. He steadfastly adhered to core principles, ensuring that every purchase and delivery of goods proceeded in an orderly manner. He invested significant effort in strengthening procurement procedures and controls, achieving the goal of cost reduction. Even in urgent and complex circumstances, he demonstrated flexibility in applying his intellect and experience to handle challenging issues. Decky's professional competence and leadership qualities set him apart within the project team, earning him the admiration and respect of his colleagues.

Furthermore, Decky is skilled in interpersonal communication. He closely collaborates with local individuals on site, using his exceptional communication skills to facilitate the smooth implementation of various tasks. Despite language and cultural challenges, Decky's extraordinary interpersonal abilities and keen insight enable him to earn the trust of local individuals, promoting cooperation across departments and national boundaries, and helping the team solve various problems. Due to his consistently outstanding performance, he was recognized as the TCDRI's Outstanding Foreign Employee for the year 2022, gradually becoming one of the most popular individuals within the entire company.

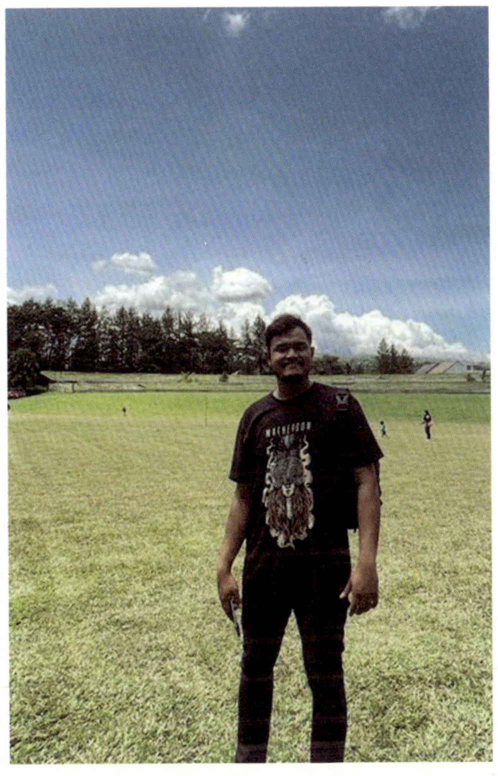

At the beginning of the COVID-19 pandemic, Decky led local employees to firmly adhere to the epidemic prevention and control measures formulated by the company. He carefully explained the risks of COVID-19 to local employees and the necessity for the company to take epidemic prevention and control measures. He led local employees to jointly maintain the company's image, effectively ensuring the life and personal safety of all CITEC employees.

After normal operation resumed, the client and project department relied on his language advantages, as well as his sincere, pragmatic, diligent, and responsible work style. Taking a "Yes Man" work attitude, he has effectively undertaken business inventory, transportation vehicle scheduling, and procurement work, ensuring that transportation vehicles accurately arrive at their destination.

Decky has been working in the CITEC department of TCDRI for 7 years and has become an indispensable and important member of the procurement department. During this period, Decky also grew rapidly and gradually became the backbone of the procurement department. He said that his work experience in a Chinese company not only enabled him to continuously grow and develop, but also changed his fate. He shares a common destiny with the Chinese company and its employees, and hopes that CITEC, TCDRI, and SINOMA International can achieve greater development in Indonesia in the future.

Personal Insights Despite facing various challenges, I always maintain a positive attitude, demonstrating a willingness to innovate and embrace challenges. I hope that my story of personal growth can inspire each one of you who are hardworking and determined. I sincerely hope that the company will achieve even greater development in Indonesia in the future.

实干追梦的海外员工蒙塔兹

蒙塔兹·穆斯塔法·阿布·法赫拉·马卡维

2016 年 10 月加入中国建材

现任成都建材院埃及 EL Dabaa Corridor 38 万吨粮食储库项目现场土建施工经理

近年来，中材国际海外业务不断拓展，随着国际化、属地化、本土化的不断推进，越来越多的外籍人员加入中材国际这个大家庭中。蒙塔兹·穆斯塔法就是中材国际成都建材院在深耕埃及市场、持续加强属地化经营过程中表现突出的员工之一。

2016 年，26 岁的埃及人蒙塔兹怀揣着为家乡建设作贡献的梦想来到了中材国际成都建材院，作为土建技术员加入埃及 GOE BENI SUEF 6X6000TPD 熟料水泥生产线总承包项目的建设大军。他主要负责全场道路的施工管理，每天面对数十个分包商和几十个工作电话，他需要及时协调各方转运设备材料，清理被占用场地，理顺土建、排水管网等相关专业施工工序，组织大量道路施工机具和材料有序进场施工作业，按照项目计划加班加点及时提供规定区域通畅的厂区通道，他常常笑称："自己手机的电池不耐用。"也正是这些响个不停的工程电话、不断出现的突发情况和棘手问题锻炼了他的统筹协调能力，让他做事更加严谨踏实，同时，他的蜕变让所有人都记住了这个年轻精干的小个子。

2019 年，蒙塔兹被评为成都建材院优秀外籍员工，获得前往中国参观、学习培训和接受表彰的机会。来到中国，他走进成都建材院总部，走进国内在建项目现场，近距离了解公司的发展历程，感知公司的企业文化，感受国内项目管理的科学化和规范化，学习国内项目管理的先进理念和方法。此次培训让他对公司的发展历史、现状及未来规划有了更加清晰的了解和认识，对属地化经营和总承包项目管理有了更加深入系统的理解和掌握。在成都总部培训结束后，蒙塔兹与其他 6 位优秀外籍员工前往云南滇西宾川总承包项目部，进行了为期 3 天的项目现场体验式学习，通过室内教学、施工现场实地参观、问题答疑等形式，全方位、多角度地学习国内水泥生产线先进的施工技术和项目管理经验。

2019 年 1 月，蒙塔兹作为成都建材院承建的埃及苏伊士运河 EL-FERDAN 大桥总承包项目的土建主管，第一批到达项目现场。从项目临

建到土建施工的全过程，每一步都烙印着蒙塔兹深深的足迹。由于大桥项目东靠西奈半岛，当时，当地社会安全局势紧张，整个项目处于军事作战部队管理戒严区域，项目参与人员、机械设备和材料进出都面临非常严格的审核与检查，稍有疏忽就会耽误项目进度。但这些困难并没有难倒蒙塔兹，他凭借出色的沟通能力，提前策划，积极协调业主与军方的关系，精心组织，周密安排，保证了项目人员、设备及材料按计划运送到场，为项目的顺利开展打下坚实基础。

不同的国家有着不同的风俗与文化，在埃及传统文化中，穆斯林的斋月是重要而特殊的。对于在埃及承建项目的单位来说，如何保障项目的顺利推进也是不小的考验。每到斋月期间，许多当地工程师都会休假戒斋，导致项目人员短缺，部分工作暂时停工，可是像桩基等需要连续作业的工作一旦停滞将会对桥体工程的进度和质量产生极大的影响。作为主管工程师的蒙塔兹主动扛起责任，一根水下桩基从开孔到浇筑完成需要 18 个小时连续作业，任何一个环节他都坚守把关，他在近 40 摄氏度的高温下连续工作 18 个小时，滴水未沾，这需要极大的耐力，但蒙塔兹却一直坚守，毫无怨言。许多人问他，为什么能坚守，他满腔热血地回答道：“在勤奋和坚持的同时，我心中有着一份热爱。”有着 45 年工作经验的业主监理也直夸他是“Iron Man”（钢铁侠）。

蒙塔兹在中国接受表彰、发表感言时曾这样说：“我能加入中材国际成都建材院是幸运的，能为家乡建设作贡献是光荣的，能与 SINOMA 中国同事们共进退、共成长、互学习是难得而自豪的。”目前，公司在海外总承包项目及分（子）公司均有外籍员工，他们参与项目建设、生产经营、业务管理，也创造着共同的辉煌。蒙塔兹只是公司优秀外籍员工的一个缩影，他们都在各自的岗位上发光发热，我们的大家庭也因为有了这群优秀的外籍员工而更加精彩！（中材国际所属成都建材院）

在成都建材院工作的 7 年里，我不仅实现了个人职业梦想，还为我的国家的经济发展作出了贡献，这对我而言意义非凡。我将在成都建材院继续努力工作，实现更大的价值。

Motaz, "Iron Man" with Passion

Moataz Mostafa Abou fakhra Makkawy

Joined CNBM in October 2016
Site Manager of Civil Construction for El Dabaa Corridor 380,000 Tons Grain Silo Project undertaken by CDI in Egypt

Over the years, SINOMA has been constantly expanding its overseas operations. With the continuous development of international, localized and indigenized operations, more and more foreign employees have joined the big family of SINOMA. Motaz Mustafa is a prominent member of Chengdu Design & Research Institute of Building Materials Industry Co., Ltd. (CDI), a subsidiary of SINOMA, as it dives deep into the Egyptian market and continues to enhance localized operations.

In 2016, Motaz, a 26-year-old Egyptian, joined CDI with the dream of contributing to the construction of his hometown. As a civil engineering technician, he joined the construction team of the GOE BENI SUEF 6X6000TPD clinker cement production line general contracting project in Egypt. He was mainly responsible for the construction management of all the roads at the construction site. Faced with dozens of subcontractors and answering dozens of work-related phone calls every day, he timely coordinated various parties to transport relevant equipment and materials to clean up the occupied area, straightened out professional construction processes of civil engineering, water supply and drainage pipelines, etc., organized a large number of road construction machineries and materials to enter the construction site in an orderly manner, and worked overtime to provide smooth access to the designated area in a timely manner according to the project plan. He often joked that "my phone's battery is not durable". It's precisely these incessant engineering-related phone calls, constantly emerging emergencies and thorny issues that have honed his overall planning and coordination skills, making him more rigorous and down-to-earth in his work. Meanwhile, as he gradually realizes his personal transformation, everyone has remembered this capable young lad.

In 2019, Motaz was recognized as an outstanding foreign employee of CDI, and was given the opportunity to visit, study, train and receive commendation in China. After arriving in China, he visited the headquarters of CDI and the construction sites of projects under construction in China, so as to understand the company's development history close up, experience the company's corporate culture, witness the scientific and standardized project management in China, and learn about the advanced concepts and methods of project management in China. This training enabled him to have an even clearer understanding and awareness of the company's development history, current situation and future plans, allowing him to have an even more in-depth and systematic understanding and mastery of localized operations and general contracting project management. After the training at the headquarters in Chengdu, Motaz and six other outstanding foreign employees headed to the Binchuan General Contracting Project Department in West Yunnan for a 3-day on-site experiential learning, learning about the advanced construction technologies and project management of cement production lines in China by comprehensive and multi-dimensional forms such as indoor teaching, construction site visits, and Q&A sessions.

In January 2019, Motaz served as the civil engineering supervisor for Egypt's Suez Canal EL-FERDAN Bridge General Contracting Project undertaken by CDI, arriving at the project site among the first batch of personnel. Throughout the entire process from temporary facility construction to civil engineering construction, Motaz's footprints were everywhere. As the bridge project was adjacent to the Sinai Peninsula in the east, the tense social security situation meant that the entire project was within the restricted area controlled by the military's combat units. The entry and exit of all of the project's personnel, mechanical equipment and materials had to undergo extremely strict examination and inspection. Any slight negligence would delay project progress. But this did not hinder Motaz. With excellent communication skills, he made plans in advance, actively coordinated the relationship between the project owner and the military, carefully organized and meticulously arranged relevant matters, and ensured that the project's personnel, equipment and materials were delivered to the project site on schedule, so as to lay a solid foundation for the smooth progress of the project.

Different countries have different customs and cultures. In traditional Egyptian culture, the Muslim month of Ramadan is quite important and special, but this has posed quite a challenge for entities undertaking projects in Egypt. During the month of Ramadan, many local engineers will take their leave and fast. The project will face staff shortages and some construction work will come to a halt. But for tasks like pile foundation that require continuous operation, a work stoppage will have a significant impact on the progress and quality of bridge engineering. As the supervising engineer, Motaz took the initiative to shoulder the responsibility. It took 18 hours of continuous operation from drilling to the completion of concrete pouring for an underwater pile foundation, and he would be on site throughout the process. It required great endurance to work continuously for 18 hours without drinking a single drop of water in temperature reaching approximately 40 degrees Celsius. But Motaz remained steadfast in his position without any complaint. Many people asked him why he could endure such hardship, and he would always answer with enthusiasm, "Apart from diligence and persistence, there is a passion in my heart". Even the project owner's supervisor who has 45 years of working experience would praise him and call him the "Iron Man".

Many willing minds will achieve great success, and many talents will contribute to great achievements. SINOMA's recognition and value of outstanding foreign employees has further enhanced the company's magnet for international talents, stimulating the foreign employees' sense of belonging and laying a solid talent foundation for the Group to build a world-class enterprise with global competitiveness.

Personal Insights During my seven years working in Chengdu Design & Research Institute of Building Materials Industry Co. Ltd., I have not only realized my personal career dream, but also contributed to the economic development of my country, which means a lot to me. I will continue to work hard in Chengdu Design & Research Institute of Building Materials Industry Co. Ltd. to realize my greater professional value.

我与 SINOMA 共成长

班米 · 奥沃乔里
2009 年加入中国建材
现任中材建设尼日利亚有限公司拉各斯仓库经理

我叫班米 · 奥沃乔里，中国同事们亲切地叫我“班米”。我于 2009 年 8 月 20 日加入 SINOMA，成为中材建设尼日利亚拉法基 EWEKORO 项目部的一名当地员工。受学历所限，我只能从事项目部简单的一些力工工作，但是时任该项目部的项目经理李明对我的基础工作给予了肯定，很感谢公司能给我提供一份在家门口工作的机会，让我能够维持家庭日常的开销。

2013 年，随着拉法基项目的结束，中材建设尼日利亚 SOKOTO 项目又给了我一次继续为 SINOMA 贡献力量的机会。9 月份，时任 SOKOTO 项目部项目经理助理的戴辉来整理拉法基项目后期的一些项目物资，目的是运输这些物资到 SOKOTO 项目部继续使用。这次接触使我有机会认识和了解了他，也为我能够继续在中材建设尼日利亚公司工作奠定了基础。经过现场考察，我们发现调拨物资种类很多，而且需要把这些物资登记、整理、归类到不同的集装箱，从而完成发运工作。由于人员、机具缺少，我们一致认为，此项工作预计在一周左右完成。为了更好地完成此项工作，我组织了其余三名同事加入，大家一起开始了这项细致且烦琐的工作。4 天时间，4 个人，从早晨 7 点到晚上 9 点，我们顺利完成了此项工作，也得到了领导的肯定，于是，我的工作关系立即调入了 SOKOTO 项目部，开启了又一个崭新的篇章。

SOKOTO 项目地处尼日利亚西北部沙漠地带，自然环境恶劣。我远离妻子和孩子，项目部考虑到我个人生活习惯，为我提供了免费的住宿，并为我提供了新的工作岗位——材料管理员兼安全管理员。我的工作稳定下来，在此期间我的第二个和第三个孩子相继出生，我的生活也逐步得到了改善。记得刚调入 SOKOTO 项目部的时候，一件事情坚定了我继续为中材建设工作的信念。随着项目的推进，越来越多的中国新同事来到了项目部，他们对我的工作不是很了解。记得那天，我拿着材料领用登记表追着一名中国员工要签字，由于语言差异，他以为我故意找事，我们争吵了起来，还闹到了领导那里。因为我是一名材料管理员，要对自己的工作负责，领用材料是必须要记录在案的，此项工作得到了项目部领导的充分肯定与支持，最后，那名中国员工也理解了我的工作，补了签字，并对我工作的认真细致表示肯定。此后，“死抠门”成为中国员工对我的昵称，感谢他们对我工作的理解和肯定。

还有一项工作是我从项目开始到项目竣工独自一人完成的，由于项目的特殊性，现场施工和生活用电均来自发电机发电。为了确保项目部正常供电，几年来我风雨无阻，每天拿着一个小本本，一个油桶一个油桶地记录油位，确保如实记录每天柴油用量，并及时反馈项目部采购部订购柴油量，项目部自始至终从未断过油、断过电。也正是由于我出色的工作表现，我被评为中材建设 SOKOTO 项目部优秀员工。

其间，还发生了一件让我铭记一辈子、感谢中材建设一辈子的事。2016 年 9 月 7 日上午，我接到了家里的电话，我的爱人 MRS. OWOJORI ANU 得了重病，医院下了病危通知。当时家里还有 3 个孩子无人照顾，SOKOTO 到拉各斯有着 1100 多公里的距离，以尼日利亚的道路情况，如果坐汽车回家至少需要 1 天 1 夜。时任项目经理田宝得知此消息后，立即为我订了

一张直飞拉各斯的机票，确保我能在第一时间赶回家见妻子最后一面。

我与 SINOMA 之间的故事一直在继续，我与 SINOMA 也一直在共同成长。随着这些年中材建设尼日利亚有限公司业务的扩大，我也成为尼日利亚有限公司拉各斯的仓库经理，目前负责公司彩石瓦产品和硅酸钙板产品的仓储和销售工作。加入公司已经 13 年，我一直为我是中材建设的一名员工而感到骄傲和自豪。中材建设是一个包容的公司，无论中国员工还是本土化员工，全部一视同仁。只要有责任心，有为公司奉献的精神，无论学历高低、能力高低，最终都能找到适合自己的岗位。我就是那个 13 年来，从简单的基础工作做起，做到仓库经理的“死抠门”。今后我会继续保持我的工作态度，坚持做好本职工作，让我与 SINOMA 在尼日利亚这片土地上共成长。（中材国际所属中材建设）

个人体会

我已经在公司工作 13 年了，这 13 年来我从一名普通属地化员工成长为一名有责任心的仓库经理，我能够在离家最近的地方安心工作和照顾家庭，我要感谢中材建设对我的培养和关怀。我会尽我最大的努力好好工作，在我的国家将两国友谊继承和发扬下去。

Grow with SINOMA

Bunmi Owojori

Joined CNBM in 2009

Lagos Warehouse Manager of SINOMA Nigeria Co., Ltd.

My name is BUNMI OWOJORI, and my Chinese colleagues always call me "Bunmi" amiably. On August 20, 2009, I joined SINOMA as a local employee of the EWEKORO project department of SINOMA Nigeria for the Lafarge Group. Although I could only do some simple manual work caused by my limited education background, the project manager, Mr. Li Ming, praised my basic work. I do appreciate that he could give me a chance to work near home, so that I could afford the daily expenses of my family.

In 2013, after the Lafarge project, the SOKOTO project of SINOMA Nigeria gave me another opportunity to contribute to SINOMA. In September, Dai Hui, then project manager assistant of the SOKOTO project department, came to Lafarge to sort out some unused project materials to transport them to the SOKOTO project department for further use. It was my first time to know him, which paved the way for me to devote myself to SINOMA Nigeria continuously. After site inspection, we found that many kinds of materials to be transferred should be registered, sorted out and categorized into different containers for shipping. Due to the lack of personnel and equipment, we all agreed that the work would take about a week. To complete this work better, I arranged the other three colleagues to finish this meticulous and tedious work. We worked from 7:00 a.m. to 9:00 p.m. for four days and completed the work successfully. Our efforts were recognized by the leaders. Therefore, I was transferred to the SOKOTO project department immediately, starting a new chapter in my work.

The SOKOTO project is located in the desert area of northwest Nigeria, characterized by a harsh natural environment. Working there meant I had to live far away from my wife and child. Considering my living habits, the project provided me with free accommodation and assigned me a new position as the material manager and security manager. With a stable job, I experienced the joy of welcoming my second and third children during this period, and my life quality was gradually improved. I will always remember an incident when I was just transferred to the SOKOTO project department, which strengthened my determination to continue working for CBMI. As the project progressed, more and more new Chinese colleagues joined the project department, and they did not know much about my work. One day, I approached a Chinese employee to sign a material consumption registration form. Due to the language barrier, he thought I was bothering him deliberately, so he quarreled with me angrily and reported it to the leader. As a material manager, I should be responsible for my own work, and ensure accurate record-keeping of material consumption. After learning what happened, the leader of the project department praised and supported my work. Eventually, the Chinese employee came to understand my role and willingly added his signature, acknowledging my meticulousness. Since then, "cheapskate" has gradually become a commendatory term and a nickname for me among Chinese employees, and I'm really grateful for their understanding and affirmation of my work.

There was a piece of work that I did on my own from the project commencement to completion. Because of my excellent performance, I was awarded as an outstanding employee of the SOKOTO project department of SINOMA. Due to the unique nature of the project, the electricity for on-site construction and domestic use were all generated by generators. To ensure the stable power supply of the project department, in the past few years, regardless of the elements, I recorded the oil level of each oil tank every day on a small notebook, so as to ensure the record of daily diesel consumption and timely inform the purchasing department of the project to order diesel. It is my excellent performance that partly ensures the stable supply of diesel and electricity for the project department from beginning to end.

During this period, there was also another incident that I'll remember forever and left me grateful to CBMI for a lifetime. On the morning of September 7, 2016, I received a phone call from home saying that my wife, Mrs. OWOJORI ANU, was seriously ill and the hospital had issued a notice of critical condition. My three children were left unattended at home, and as Sokoto is more than 1,100 kilometers away from Lagos, given Nigeria's road conditions, it would take at least one day and one night to get home by bus. Upon hearing the news, Tian Bao, the then project manager, immediately booked me a direct flight ticket to Lagos to make sure that I would get home as soon as possible to see my wife one last time.

I have been growing with SINOMA, and our story will never end. With the expansion of SINOMA Nigeria's business over the years, I have become the warehouse manager of SINOMA Nigeria's Lagos project, and I'm currently responsible for the warehousing and sales of the company's color stone tile products and calcium silicate board products. I have been proud to be a member of CMBI for 13 years. CMBI is an inclusive company, where all Chinese and local employees are treated equally. With a sense of responsibility and dedication to the company, employees will eventually find a suitable position, regardless of their educational background and ability. In my case, I have progressed from a grassroots worker to a warehouse manager in thirteen years. In the future, I will maintain my working attitude and complete my own work strictly, so that SINOMA and I can grow together in Nigeria.

Personal Insights I have been working in the SINOMA Nigeria for 13 years. Over the past 13 years, I have grown from an ordinary local employee to a warehouse manager, and managed to work close to home so that I can take care of my family. I would like to express my gratitude to SINOMA for its investment and support in my development. I will continue to try my best at work and contribute to the ever-lasting friendship between our two countries.

优秀市场经理的成长记

莎拉波夫·凯瑞·瓦莱里耶维奇

2012 年加入中国建材
现任中材建设俄罗斯公司副总经理

莎拉波夫·凯瑞·瓦莱里耶维奇于 2012 年加入中材国际所属中材建设有限公司，工作至今，他先后在拉豪 FER 项目、长城汽车总包俄罗斯汽车厂项目工作，现在是中材建设俄罗斯公司副总经理。他工作努力、踏实能干，曾获得“长城汽车总包项目杰出贡献奖”“优秀外籍员工”等荣誉称号。

莎拉波夫大学学的是硅酸盐工艺，虽然在中材建设的工作与其所学专业对口，但正式工作后他才发现，理论和实际有很大差距。在 FER 项目工作的经历让他从一个只有理论知识的新生成长为一名真正的工程师。

进入俄罗斯市场后，由于技术、标准、规范的不同，全引进生产线从技术、设备、调试到生产都需要经过俄罗斯特有的 GOST 认证体系认证。因此，入职后的他便与中国同事一起，深度参与了项目的认证体系工作。

为了熟悉中国技术和中国设备，莎拉波夫告别新婚燕尔的妻子，申请入住现场临建房。3 年多的时间里，他在项目上与中国同事同吃同住，互帮互助，不仅对中国技术有了更深刻的了解，提升了工作能力，还收获了来自中国同行的友谊。

在大家的共同努力下，FER 项目 1.9 万吨、5.8 万立方米的货物按时发运、顺利清关。作为进驻俄罗斯当地水泥工程 EPC 领域的第一家外国企业，创造了在俄大型项目物流、清关的奇迹。与计划工期相比，该项目提前两个月取得运营许可，业主对 SINOMA 不可思议的速度竖起了大拇指，表示赞叹。

FER 项目结束后，莎拉波夫来到由中材建设有限公司承建的中国长城汽车公司在俄罗斯汽车厂的项目担任总工程师。这个项目与水泥工程行业完全不同，不仅涉及的施工方面多、整体工期短，并且所有设计均采用俄罗斯技术规范，施工则是以本土化为主，项目操作难度特别大。在这里，莎拉波夫主要负责项目管理工作、现场技术指导，与俄籍业主团队、监理、设计单位等协调工作。他白天跑现场，负责施工管理，晚上修改合同，变身商务经理，

为项目解决了一个又一个难题。由于施工时间跨越冬季，他时常会在零下 30 多摄氏度的极端天气以及暴雪袭击的情况下工作，他始终率领团队攻坚克难，保证项目顺利履约，体现了 SINOMA 勇者无畏的奋斗精神。

2019 年，长城项目工厂在中俄两国元首的见证下启动生产。莎拉波夫说：“看到第一辆汽车从工厂开出时，我深深地为自己奋斗的项目感到激动和自豪。”由于表现出色，莎拉波夫在那一年获得“长城汽车总包项目杰出贡献奖”，还被公司评为“年度十大优秀外籍员工”。他被公司邀请来到中国，进一步了解公司，了解中国的发展，了解中国的文化。这次中国之行给他带来人生中最难忘的一次经历，他说：“我为自己能成为这里的一分子而感到骄傲，我深深地热爱中国，热爱培养我的公司”。

2018 年开始，根据公司工作部署，莎拉波夫开始担任俄罗斯公司市场部经理，负责俄罗斯市场的开拓。为了让中材国际属地化经营顺利开展，他策划了品牌宣传方案，走访各大水泥业主，积极参加各类商务会议。除了传统水泥项目外，俄罗斯公司在多元项目、水泥工程 + 方面也取得了一些成绩，与新加坡丰益国际、海尔集团、拉豪集团均签订了项目合同。

2020 年，疫情使俄罗斯本就低迷的工程市场雪上加霜。莎拉波夫在做好自身防护的同时，坚持开展工作，带领市场部的同事积极跟踪项目，中标 9 个项目，签约 21 个备件合同，圆满完成年度目标任务。

在 SINOMA 大家庭 11 年的时间里，他已经能用英文自如交流，中文也学得不错，还不时和自己的朋友们炫上几句。

他时常和别人说，他的人生中做出的最重要、最正确的选择有两个：一是与妻子结婚，二是加入中材建设。在这里，没有感觉到中外员工的差别，只有家的温暖和亲情。在中材建设，大家在工作中、生活中的相互帮助和鼓励让所有人都有家的感觉。

他说：“中材建设是我的家，谁不会为自己的家庭谋求更好的明天呢。”（中材国际所属中材建设）

个人体会 11 年来与公司的相伴，我和我的中国同事都成了好朋友。很庆幸 11 年前的选择，让我能在世界 500 强的企业中学习和工作，很感谢公司的信任，让我成为俄罗斯公司副总经理，我将与同事们一起，尽最大的努力让公司在俄罗斯更好地发展壮大，做一名中俄友好的积极践行者。

Growth Story of an Excellent Marketing Manager

Sharapov Kirill Valeryevich

Joined CNBM in 2012

Deputy General Manager of SINOMA Rus Co., Ltd.

Kirill Sharapov joined CBMI Construction Co., Ltd. affiliated with SINOMA International in 2012. He has worked on LafargeHolcim FER Project and Great Wall Motor's Russia Automobile Plant Project as the General Contractor. Currently, he serves as a deputy general manager of the SINOMA RUS CO.,LTD, the subsidiary of CBMI Construction Co. Ltd. Due to his arduous efforts and down-to-earth work attitude, he has won honorary titles such as "Great Wall Motor EPC Project Outstanding Contribution Award" and "Excellent Foreign Employee".

Sharapov studied Silicate Production Technology at University. His major matches well with his work in CBMI. But he quickly found a big gap between theory and practice after taking on the work. The experience in the FER project has transformed him from a freshman with only theoretical knowledge into a qualified engineer.

After entering the Russian market, due to the discrepancy in technology, standards and specifications, he realized that all-exported production lines are required to be certified by Russia's unique GOST certification system, covering such aspects as technology, equipment, commissioning and production. Thus, he actively participated in the project certification work together with his colleagues in China after induction.

To familiarize himself with China's technology and equipment, Sharapov parted from his newlywed wife and applied to stay in on-site temporary housing. Over more than three years, he has lived and worked with Chinese colleagues on the project and helped each other. Finally, he has improved his work abilities and gained a deeper understanding of China's technology and forged friendship with his Chinese counterparts.

With joint efforts, 19,000 tons and 58,000 cubic meters of goods in the FER project were delivered on time and the customs clearance was completed successfully. As the first foreign enterprise to enter the EPC field of local cement projects, it has created a miracle in logistics and customs clearance for large-scale projects in Russia. The project obtained operating permission 2 months faster than projects of its like, leaving the client amazed at SINOMA's incredible speed and efficiency.

Upon the completion of the FER project, Sharapov came to Great Wall Motor undertaken by CBMI and served as a chief engineer in Russia Automobile Plant

Project. Totally different from the cement engineering industry, the project, with a shorter construction period, involved numerous construction aspects. Furthermore, the project adopted Russia's technical specifications for all the designs, resulting in mainly localized construction and tremendous difficulties. In the project, Sharapov was mainly responsible for project management, on-site technical guidance and coordination with the Russian client's team, supervisors and designers. He managed construction on site during the daytime, and solved problems one by one at night, acting like a business manager. As the construction period spanned winter, he often worked in extreme weather with a temperature of minus 30°C and facing snowstorms. He always led his team to overcome difficulties and ensure the smooth completion of the project, reflecting the endeavoring spirit of SINOMA.

The GWM project plant started production under the witness of the heads of state of China and Russia in 2019. Sharapov said that he was extremely excited and proud of the project he had worked so hard for when seeing the first car roll out of the factory. Due to his outstanding performance, Sharapov won the "Great Wall Motor EPC Project Outstanding Contribution Award" and was also recognized as one of the "Top Ten Annual Excellent Foreign Employees" that year by the company. The company invited him to China to learn more about the company, China's development and culture. The trip to China brought him the most impressive experience of his life. He said, "I am so proud to be a part of the company. I love China so much and I also love my company."

Starting from 2018, Sharapov, according to the arrangement of the company, served as the Marketing Department Manager of the Russia Branch, responsible for expanding the market there. To guarantee a smooth localized operation of SINOMA International, he developed the brand promotion schemes, visited major cement owners and actively participating in various business conferences. In addition to traditional cement projects, Russia Branch scored plenty of achievements in diversified projects and cement engineering +, signing projects with Wilmar International (Singapore), Haier Group and LafargeHolcim Group.

The pandemic worsened Russia's already sluggish engineering market in 2020. While taking strict protective measures himself, Sharapov persisted in conducting his work and led colleagues to actively track the projects, winning 9 bids, signing 21 spare parts contracts and completing the annual objectives and tasks.

Over the 11 years in SINOMA, he has become frequent in English and learned Chinese quite well, occasionally showing off a few words to his friends.

He often said that two most important and correct choices in his life were to marry his wife and join CBMI. He does not feel any gap between Chinese and foreign employees here, only familial warmth and affection. In CBMI, everyone helps and encourages each other in work and life. It is just like a warm family.

He says, "CBMI is my home. Who would not strive for a better future for their family?"

Personal Insights I am extremely happy that 11 years ago I chose to study and work in a Fortune 500 company, and I am grateful for the trust of our company, which made me a Deputy General Manager of the Russia Branch. Together with my colleagues I will do my best to ensure the company's better development in Russia and make continuous efforts for the development of friendly relations between China and Russia.

在工作中积淀　在淬炼中成长

拉斐尔·乌默孔
2022 年加入中国建材
现任中材建设尼日利亚有限公司产品销售部客户经理

今年 30 岁的尼日利亚帅气小伙拉斐尔·乌默孔于 2022 年 3 月加入中材建设尼日利亚有限公司，现担任产品销售部门的客户经理。自加入公司以来，拉斐尔全身心投入工作，成为中材建设尼日利亚有限公司最优秀的销售业务员之一，是 FABCOM 工厂家喻户晓的“明星”人物。

拉斐尔出生于 1993 年 11 月 1 日，2020 年毕业于尼日利亚阿克瓦伊本州立大学，所学专业是政治学。他此前做过许多工作，例如行政专员、书记员等。微薄的收入和日益加剧的生活压力迫使他不得不辞去那些工作。为了给自己一个更好的发展空间，以及给家人创造一个更好的生活环境，他试图寻找和进入一个前景更加广阔的领域。一次偶然的机遇，他加入了中材建设尼日利亚有限公司这个大家庭。为了实现自己的梦想，他从进入工厂的那一刻起就开始不停地学习和实践。正是这种积极主动的精神，让他用最短的时间融入团队并完成角色转换。他充分利用尼日利亚文化背景知识和本地员工身份的双重优势，从一名普通工厂员工晋升至销售部的客户经理，成为一颗冉冉升起的新星。

初入中材建设尼日利亚有限公司，拉斐尔不屈不挠的精神和不断学习的热情给大家留下了深刻印象。他开始跟随中方师傅学习生产、销售等理论知识，为了方便与中方师傅的交流，他主动学习汉语。理论学习期间，遇到不明白的技术原理、专业术语，他反复请教中方员工，直到学懂弄通。从最初对生产设备、原材料和彩石瓦产品的陌生，到能够独立领导产品装运、生产和销售，强烈的责任感促使他不断提高自身的技术水平和实践能力，他抓住一切机会学习专业知识，不但自己学，还与其他成员探讨交流。拉斐尔说：“学习是进步的阶梯，自己要学的东西还有很多。”现在，他依然保持着随身携带记事本的习惯，把工作中遇到的问题随时记下来，回去慢慢“补功课”。为了做好屋面产品市场调研和销售工作，他的足迹踏遍了阿布贾的各个区域。为了按时保质完成销售

任务，他工作勤奋，经常加班加点，与不同的经销商、房地产开发商和工程师等洽谈业务。经过不断努力，他在销售业绩上取得了骄人的成绩。他在工作中也有着自己的愿望和理想。拉斐尔曾说：“我最大的愿望就是在我的工作岗位上认认真真地做好自己的工作。作为一名销售客户经理，就是要保证每一样屋面产品都符合质量要求，并且保证将它们准确无误地送到客户手中，努力做到100%让顾客满意。这些产品和设备就像是我的孩子，我必须清楚它们每一个的情况，我要让它们健健康康地成长。”

自加入中材建设尼日利亚有限公司以来，拉斐尔的付出和努力为他赢得了诸多人的称赞和肯定。他也从最初工厂里的一名普通销售人员成长为产品销售部的客户经理。新的职位是对他前期成绩的充分肯定，也让他有机会更深入地参与到业务中去。如今他已然成为销售部不可或缺的重要成员。他表示，中材建设尼日利亚有限公司是一个充满机遇的地方，在这里，他学习了很多新的知识，认识了很多新的朋友，获得了比较可观的收入。他在这个团队度过了许多美好时光，每一分、每一秒对他来说都很重要。他突破空间的局限和文化的差异，和中国同事像家人一样相聚在一起，组成一个团队，拼搏一份事业，共同创造着属于建材人更美好的未来。这个岗位，不仅证明了他具有专业能力，还激励着他成为更好的自己。他为中材建设在尼日利亚和世界各地的工程建设所取得的成绩感到骄傲，也为能够成为中材建设的一员感到荣幸。在未来，他会继续努力工作，与公司携手同行让尼日利亚人民住上更舒适的房间，享受更美好的生活。（中材国际所属中材建设）

个人体会 我热爱中材建设，更热爱我的工作。我能成为一名优秀的客户经理离不开公司和领导的支持。未来，我会再接再厉，勇创佳绩，不辜负公司提供的如此优秀的平台，为公司和我自己的梦想继续奋斗。

Improve Abilities in Work and Excel Through Challenges

Rafael Umerkong

Joined CNBM in 2022
Account Manager of Product Sales Department of SINOMA Nigeria Co., Ltd.

Raphael, a 30 year-old handsome and talented young man from Nigeria, joined SINOMA-FABCOM in March 2022 as a customer manager in the product sales department. Since his arrival, Raphael has demonstrated unwavering dedication to his work, quickly establishing himself as one of the best sales executives at FABCOM, and a "star" of the company.

Born on November 1, 1993, Raphael graduated from Akwa Ibom State University in 2020 with a degree in political science. His early career included positions as a Commissioner of Administration and a clerk, but faced with limited income and growing life pressures, he made the difficult decision to resign from these jobs. Motivated to create a better future for himself and his family, Raphael sought opportunities in a more promising field. By chance, he became part of a FABCOM's family in Nigeria. Determined to pursue his dreams, Raphael embarked on a journey of continuous learning and practical experience from the moment he joined the company. His proactive attitude enabled him to quickly integrate into the team and adapt well to his new role. As a local employee who understand well about Nigerian culture, he swiftly moved up from an ordinary factory worker to a customer manager in the sales department.

Raphael's unwavering determination and passion for continuous learning impressed everyone when he first joined FABCOM. He eagerly immersed himself in learning theoretical knowledge in production and sales from Chinese teachers. Recognizing the importance of effective communication, he took the initiative to learn Chinese to facilitate better interaction with his teachers. During his theoretical studies, he sought guidance from Chinese staff, relentlessly striving to comprehend technical principles and professional terminology. From initially being unfamiliar with production equipment, raw materials, and colored stone tile products, Raphael's strong sense of responsibility drove him to continuously enhance his technical expertise and practical skills. He seized every opportunity to expand his knowledge, not only for himself but also to foster exchange with fellow colleagues. "Learning is a ladder of progress," Raphael emphasized. "There is always more to learn." He maintains the habit of carrying a notebook, diligently recording encountered challenges and referring back to them for continual improvement. To conduct thorough market research and promote roofing products, Raphael embarked on journeys to various regions of Abuja. To ensure timely and high-quality completion of sales targets, he diligently worked overtime and negotiated business deals with diverse distributors, real estate developers, and engineers. Through persistent efforts, he achieved remarkable results in sales. Furthermore, he holds deep aspirations and ideals in his work, saying "My greatest desire is to approach my job with utmost dedication. As a sales account manager, I ensure that every roofing product meets stringent quality standards and is promptly delivered to customers, striving for 100% customer satisfaction. These products and equipment are like my children, and I need to take good care of them and ensure their healthy growth."

Raphael's dedication and accomplishments since joining FABCOM have earned him widespread praise and recognition. He has risen from being an ordinary salesman in the factory to becoming a customer manager in the product sales department. This promotion reflects the high recognition for his past achievements and provides him with the opportunity to delve deeper into his responsibilities. Today, he is an indispensable and valued member of the Sales Department, fully recognized for his contributions. Raphael views FABCOM as a place of immense opportunities. He has acquired a wealth of new knowledge, forged meaningful friendships, and earned a substantial income. Every moment spent in this team holds significant value to him. He has overcome spatial and cultural barriers in the company, and together with his Chinese colleagues, they have formed a tight-knit team, akin to a family. Their collective efforts aim to create a brighter future for FABCOM. His current position not only validates his professional abilities, but also serves as a source of personal inspiration. Raphael takes great pride in the progress of the company's construction projects in Nigeria and worldwide, and he feels honored to contribute to these endeavors. Moving forward, he is committed to continuing his hard work, collaborating with the company to improve living conditions and create better opportunities for Nigerians.

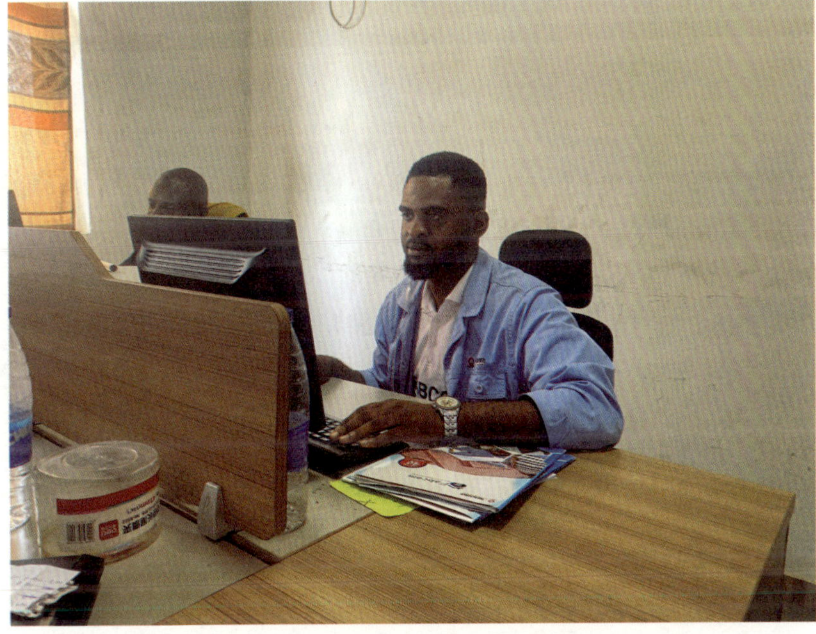

Personal Insights I love CBMI and my work. I can not become an excellent customer manager without the support of the company, I will continue to work hard and strive for new achievements, live up to the excellent platform provided by the company, and work for company's future development and my personal dreams.

一名外籍员工的别样奉献

欧碧阿格里·克里蒙蒂娜·亨肖

2015 年加入中国建材

现任中材建设尼日利亚有限公司人力资源经理

快言快语的欧碧阿格里·克里蒙蒂娜·亨肖是中材建设尼日利亚有限公司人力资源经理。热爱学习的她本科毕业于天津大学中文系，后又负笈南开大学国际关系学院，两年后，如愿以偿地拿到了硕士学位。2015 年她加入中材国际，抱着“心存感恩”的态度，全身心投入工作，按照她的说法：“快速赢得了大家的赞赏和拥戴，有赖于忘我的奉献。”

“作为公司人力资源经理，带动培养当地员工的工作意识和热情一直是我的首要任务，这对尼日利亚公司的发展也至关重要。我认为，从本土化角度而言，我们可以通过寻找和培养更多的本地年轻人才来加入我们的团队，对他们进行专业培训，同时加强公司战略引导，使他们逐步认同和接受公司的发展战略。”谈起自己的工作，欧碧条分缕析，有板有眼。

8 年来，她一以贯之地踏实工作，把所负责的人力资源档案、劳动合同、人力资源信息统计、招聘面试等工作做得井井有条。“只有把井挖得更深才能喝到更甜的水”，这句尼日利亚谚语让她深有体会，为此，她在工作中积极落实部门和岗位职责，主动帮助各部门完善人力资源工作，及时提供各种信息、政策和可行性建议，为部门工作效能的提高作出积极的贡献。与此同时，她还利用作为本地人的优势，为公司各部门提供服务，为经营团队做好助手，特别是在对外关系沟通方面，她紧紧围绕与公司业务相关的警察局、移民局、劳动局开展公关工作，工作效率得到极大提升。

在公共关系开拓与维护的过程中，欧碧一方面热忱服务，另一方面也向尼日利亚当地人传达 SINOMA 的文化和价值理念，通过 instagram、linkedin 和 facebook 等媒介推销公司产品给当地人，向尼日利亚人民传播 SINOMA 品牌。“但凡碰到问题，只要欧碧在，基本上没有她不能沟通和解决的。”她的同事说，作为一名外籍人士，如此努力和敬业，她赢得了大家应有的尊重。

“奥贡河不是一条河，它有许多姐妹。”欧碧深谙其道，她知道团队力量的巨大，她也明白团队精神的神奇，她在工作上严格服从上级领导安排，并与其他部门之间协调一致，为提高公司整体效益竭尽全力。就像奥贡河要奔向大西洋一样，对于认定的目标，欧碧和她的团队永不言放弃。“我很感恩上帝给我这样的机会和朋友，”她说，“他们让我明白很多中国的箴理，也让我在这样的环境中学到未知和协作。” 欧碧落落大方地回答笔者的问题。

在日常工作和生活中，她深切感受到了中国文化及和谐融洽的公司氛围。“中国同事积极乐观、勤劳踏实的工作精神时时激励着我，在他们的影响下，我很快适应了公司的步伐，并在这里获得了良好的职业发展机会。感谢公司给予我的平台，在这里，我找到了属于自己的人生。在中文氛围的影响下，我的孩子们也会用中文进行一些简单的沟通，甚至邻居也会偶尔用中文与我寒暄，中华文化已融入我的生活。”欧碧操着流利的汉语娓娓道来。

西方有句谚说：“在一个屋檐下容易握手。”由于欧碧有着良好的中国留学背景，她在一定程度上更能理解中国人的工作态度和思考方式，也帮助了更多人了解中国文化。出于对中国文化的热爱，她每周两次教授当地员工中国语言和文化，此举有助于增进文化沟通，使外籍员工更好地了解他们的中国同事，并为大家创造一个提升知识和能力的平台，这对企业员工间的有效沟通至关重要。

当大家对她的工作和行为表示赞赏时，她总是谦虚地笑着说：“能够为这样卓越的企业服务是值得骄傲的事情，我这样做也是一名员工应尽的义务，对大家进一步认识企业和熟悉企业或许是有帮助的。”

谈及未来的工作，欧碧自信满满地说：“SINOMA 是国际水泥领军企业，尼日利亚公司在尼日利亚有着深厚的根基，我将不断提升自己的综合实力，让更多更优秀的尼日利亚当地人才加入公司，我将为公司的屋面系统产品做好宣传推广，为公司的属地发展添砖加瓦，为公司高质量发展贡献智慧。”（中材国际所属中材建设）

个人体会 8年来，我对公司的热爱与日俱增。中材建设是国际水泥领军企业，尼日利亚公司在尼日利亚有着深厚的根基。我热爱我的工作，我将与其他属地员工一道为我们的企业做好宣传推广，为公司的属地发展添砖加瓦。

A Devoted HR Manager

Obiageri Clementina Henshaw

Joined CNBM in 2015

The HR Manager of SINOMA Nigeria Co., Ltd.

Obiageri C. Henshaw, a candid HR manager at CBMI Nigeria, is an inquisitive person. She graduated from the Chinese Department of Tianjin University and later studied at the School of International Relations at Nankai University. Two years later, she successfully obtained her master's degree. She joined SINOMA International in 2015 and devoted herself to work with "a grateful heart". According to her, she "quickly received appreciation and support from people around her, thanks to her selfless dedication."

"As the HR manager of the company, my top priority has always been to foster the local employees' will to work and inspire passion in them, which is also crucial for the development of the company in Nigeria. From the perspective of localization, I think we can find and train more local young talents to join our team. By offering them professional training and highlighting the company's strategic guidance, they can gradually understand and accept the company's development strategy." When talking about her job, Obi shows her expertise and gives a lot of details.

For eight years, she has been working diligently, managing her tasks in an orderly manner, such as processing HR files, labor contracts, HR information statistics, and job interviews, etc. "The deeper the well, the sweeter the water." The Nigerian proverb has inspired her to proactively fulfill the duties of her position, assume the responsibility of helping other departments improve their HR work, and provide timely information, policies, and feasible suggestions and make a positive contribution to the work efficiency of the departments. Meanwhile, she also uses her advantage as a local to provide services for different departments of the company and serves as a helpful assistant to the management team, especially in handling external communications and liaising with the police departments, immigration offices, and departments of labor that handle corporate affairs. Her endeavor has facilitated related work.

During the development and maintenance of public relations, Obiageri C. Henshaw not only provides service with enthusiasm, but also conveys SINOMA's culture and values to the local people in Nigeria. She promotes the company's products to the locals through Instagram, Linkedin, and Facebook, building SINOMA brand awareness among Nigerian people. "Whenever there is a problem, there is basically nothing Obiageri C. Henshaw can't communicate and solve as long as she is present," her colleagues said, "As a foreign employee, her hard work and professionalism have earned her the respect she deserves."

"The Ogun River is not alone. She has many sister rivers." Obiageri C. Henshaw knows the power and magic of teamwork. She strictly complies with the arrangements of her superiors at work and coordinates with other departments to improve the overall efficiency of the company. Just as the Ogun River runs uninterruptedly towards the Atlantic Ocean, Obiageri C. Henshaw and her team never give up on their goals. "I am very thankful to God for giving me this opportunity and the friends," she said, "they have made me understand a lot of Chinese wisdom and allowed me to learn about the unknown and collaboration in an environment like this." Obiageri C. Henshaw answered the author's questions in a frank and confident manner.

In her everyday work and life, she has felt the profoundness of Chinese culture and the harmonious atmosphere of the company. "I've been always inspired by my Chinese colleagues' positive attitude and their diligent and down-to-earth work ethic. Under their influence, I quickly adjusted to the company's pace and have achieved great career development here. I am grateful that the company has given me this platform where I found my own life. Surrounded by Chinese language, my children can also speak some Chinese. And even my neighbors would occasionally greet me in Chinese. Chinese culture has become a part of my life," said Obiageri C. Henshaw in fluent Chinese.

As a western proverb says, "It's easier for peole living under the same roof to shake hands." Due to the strong Chinese educational background, Obiageri C. Henshaw can understand the work attitudes and thinking styles of Chinese people. She helps others understand Chinese culture and learns to be dedicated in her work. Out of her love for Chinese culture, she teaches Chinese language and culture to local staff twice a week, which is helpful for cultural communication and allows employees to have a better understanding of their Chinese colleagues. This can also create a platform for knowledge and skill improvement, which is a crucial element for effective communication.

When people praise her work and what she's done, she always responds with a humble smile and says, "It is my honor to serve such an outstanding company. And as an employee, it is my duty to do so. My effort may help people know the company better."

Talking about future work, Obiageri C. Henshaw has unshakeable confidence. "SINOMA is an international leading cement company. CBMI Nigeria has deep roots in Nigeria. I will continuously improve my comprehensive abilities and encourage more excellent local Nigerian employees to join the company. I will also promote the company's roof system products and contribute to the company's local development. I'll continue to contribute my efforts and wisdom to the company's high-quality development."

Personal Insights I have been with the company for eight years, and my love for the company has grown day by day. CBMI is an international leader in the cement industry. CBMI Nigeria has been developing on a strong footing locally. I love my work. Going forward, I will continue to work with other local employees to promote our company and contribute to the company's localized development.

拼搏进取的海外逐梦人

刘渠东

2006 年加入中国建材

现任区域总监兼中东公司总经理兼沙特 ACC 项目总经理

刘渠东，中国中材海外科技发展有限公司区域总监、中东公司总经理、沙特 ACC 项目总经理。曾多次获得公司“先进工作者”称号和海外赤子奖；2013 年度被评为集团劳动模范；2022 年度被评为中材国际劳动模范。

自 2006 年接受公司外派后，到目前为止，刘渠东持续 17 年坚守海外现场，从阿联酋 UCC 项目到阿曼 OCC 项目，再到整个中东公司，从刚刚毕业的毛头小伙子，逐步变成身经百战的海外分公司负责人，其中有艰辛，有痛苦，亦有喜悦和收获。这期间，在经历了结婚无蜜月、初为人父却不能伴妻儿左右的遗憾后，他依然坚定信念、无怨无悔，从他的身上，我们看到了一位海外赤子的拳拳之心。

近几年，中东地区经济受国际油价持续下行和新冠疫情的影响，众多在建项目停滞。刘渠东带领中东公司市场拓展团队始终贯彻落实公司属地化经营战略，坚持疫情防控和安全生产，市场拓展“两手抓，两不误”，攻坚克难、积极进取。截至目前，中东公司会同国

内部门顺利签约 ISC 5000TPD 熟料水泥生产线 EPC 总承包项目、CEC 5000TPD 熟料水泥生产线 EPC 总承包项目、斯里兰卡 2×50TPH 移动模块化水泥粉磨站项目、菲律宾德拉特立尼达 10MW 风电项目、伊拉克磨

机供货合同、沙特 SCC 窑筒体改造及备件合同、沙特 ACC 粉磨站收尾项目等。

刘渠东不仅业务精悍，工作能力、组织能力也非常强，特别是与业主及项目当地人的沟通和协调能力在业界口碑极佳。疫情期间，作为中东片区 3 个项目团队的疫情防控总负责人，他第一时间成立应急工作组，制定应急管理计划，执行严格的疫情防控措施和预案。此外，他带领现场团队不仅抓市场、紧生产，还心系国内，克服重重困难，采购输送防疫物资，展现了“海外人”团结、守望、互助的大爱情怀。这期间，所有中外员工实现了零感染、零疑似、零确诊的“三零目标”；中东片区的各项目均实现了零事故、零事件、零罚款的“三零安全管理”。

海外一线工作形势复杂多变，刘渠东深谙团队凝聚力的重要性，他犹如一缕红色纽带，将团队成员紧紧地凝系在一起。他以认真、负责、努力的工作态度团结每一位员工，了解和掌握每位员工在市场拓展、项目执行过程中和日常生活中的需求，传授项目管理与执行的经验和知识。

刘渠东坚持以工作需要为出发点，以极富热忱的工作态度和甘于吃苦、勇于争先的市场开拓精神，以及时刻把公司利益放在第一位的敬业精神为公司同事树立起良好的工作榜样。这就是刘渠东，一个综合素质高、业务能力强的基层干部；一个面对困难永不退缩、敢于挑战、永不言败的区域负责人。他积极进取、只争朝夕，在公司海外项目的商务执行和市场开拓中，勇挑重担、锐意进取、开拓创新，为将公司打造成国际一流企业而贡献力量。（中材国际所属中材海外）

个人体会 我热爱海外工程 EPC 总承包项目的执行、市场拓展和境外分（子）公司经营管理等方面的工作，我愿意用近二十年的海外工作经验，带领海外团队，攻坚克难，为中东运营中心的建设和发展、为集团国际化征程贡献力量。

A Dream-chaser Who Strives for Progress

Liu Qudong

Joined CNBM in 2006
Regional Director,
General Manager of SINOMA Middle East,
General Project Manager of Saudi ACC Project

Mr. Liu Qudong, an accomplished leader in SINOMA Overseas Development Company Limited, holds multiple esteemed positions including Regional Director, General Manager of Middle East Company and General Manager of Saudi ACC Project. Recognized for his outstanding contributions, he has received awards such as "Excellent Worker," and "Overseas Compatriot". Furthermore, he was honored as a Model Worker of the Group in 2013 and received the esteemed accolade of SINOMA International Model Worker in 2022.

Since his assignment abroad by the company in 2006, Liu Qudong has been unwaveringly stationed on the front lines of overseas operations for 17 years. Beginning as a young and ambitious project lead in the UAE UCC project, he progressed to the Oman OCC project and eventually assumed leadership of the entire Middle East division. Throughout his journey, he encountered challenges and hardships, but also tasted the sweetness of success and personal growth. Despite the sorrow of missing out on his honeymoon and the birth of his first child, he remained resolute in his principles, embracing his choices without any hint of regret. He epitomizes the company's global presence and exemplifies the unwavering commitment of a dedicated overseas employee.

In the face of challenging circumstances, including the impact of declining international oil prices and the COVID-19 pandemic, Liu Qudong, leading the market development team of the Middle East Company, has successfully implemented the company's localization management strategy. With a steadfast commitment to epidemic prevention and control, safety in production, and market development, they have overcome obstacles and remained proactive in their approach. As a result of their efforts, Middle East Company, in collaboration with domestic departments, has achieved significant milestones. They have secured the EPC contracts for ISC 5000TPD clinker cement production line and CEC 5000TPD clinker cement production line. Additionally, they have successfully undertaken the 2*50TPH mobile modular cement grinding plant project in Sri Lanka, the 10MW wind power project in Deira Trinidad, Philippines, the mill supply contract in Iraq, the SCC contract in Saudi Arabia for kiln shell renovation, as well as the spare parts contract in Saudi Arabia. Furthermore, they have accomplished the ACC grinding plant finishing project in Saudi Arabia, among other notable achievements.

Liu Qudong's outstanding business skills are complemented by his exceptional work ethic and organizational abilities. Notably, his communication and coordination skills with project owners and local stakeholders have earned him a stellar reputation in the industry. During the challenging period of the epidemic, Liu Qudong served as the General Manager of Epidemic Prevention and Control for the three project teams in the Middle East region. Swiftly responding to the situation, he established an emergency work group and developed comprehensive management plans to ensure stricter epidemic prevention and control measures were in place. Additionally, he led the onsite team in not only maintaining market stability and production efficiency but also demonstrated a deep commitment to the welfare of the local community. Overcoming logistical challenges, he facilitated the procurement and delivery of essential epidemic prevention supplies, demonstrating the unity, vigilance, and mutual assistance that characterize the spirit of "overseas Chinese." Under Liu Qudong's leadership, all Chinese and foreign employees achieved remarkable results, with "three zeroes" being accomplished - zero infections, zero suspected cases, and zero confirmed cases. Furthermore, all projects in the Middle East region achieved "three zeroes safety management" with zero accidents, zero incidents, and zero fines.

In the intricate and ever-changing landscape of overseas front-line work, Liu Qudong deeply understands the significance of team cohesion. He acts as the red ribbon that binds team members together, fostering a strong sense of camaraderie. With a sincere, responsible, and diligent approach, he forges deep connections with every employee, attentively understanding and addressing their needs throughout the process of market development, project execution, and daily life.

Sharing his wealth of experience and knowledge in project management and execution.

Liu Qudong remains steadfast in prioritizing the needs of the work, exemplifying an incredibly enthusiastic work ethic and a willingness to endure hardships for the sake of achieving success in market development. His unwavering dedication to putting the company's interests above all else serves as a shining example and inspirational leadership for his colleagues. Liu embodies the qualities of an exemplary grassroots leader, showcasing strong loyalty and integrity, outstanding comprehensive abilities, and exceptional business acumen. As a regional leader, he never backs down in the face of challenges, fearlessly embraces adversity, and perseveres relentlessly. With an enterprising spirit, he constantly strives for a better future. In the execution of the company's overseas projects and the pursuit of market development, he shoulders the weighty responsibilities, forging ahead with unwavering determination, pioneering new paths, and fostering innovation. His wholehearted dedication serves as a testament to his commitment in contributing significantly to the company's aspirations of becoming an internationally renowned enterprise.

Personal Insights I have a great passion for executing overseas EPC turnkey projects, marketing expansion, and the management of overseas subsidiaries. With nearly twenty years of experience, I am dedicated to fulfilling my duties in the development of the operation center in the Middle East Region. I will lead the overseas team to promote business, overcome all challenges and contribute to the internationalization of CNBM group.

时不我待　只争朝夕

程金

2005年加入中国建材

现任苏州中材总经理助理、中材国际埃塞子公司总经理

在埃塞俄比亚11年，对于程金来说，是一生难忘的记忆，作为中材国际埃塞俄比亚子公司总经理的他，不仅要关心项目的施工进度，而且要全权负责埃塞子公司的运营。他带领团队，越过无数次坎坷不平，跨过无数个艰难险阻，最终业有所成。这其中的酸甜苦辣只有程金自己能深刻体会。他用平静内敛的气质、雷厉风行的作风，无怨无悔地谱写着中国建材人的最美篇章。

曾经，埃塞俄比亚国内形势动荡、骚乱事件经常发生。2016年，埃塞俄比亚处于国家紧急状态，武装冲突频繁发生。有一次，埃塞俄比亚Dangote水泥厂项目受到冲击，厂区外围道路几近被阻断，通信全部中断，项目人员面临生命安全威胁。程金当时临危不乱，穿越危险区，前往100公里外的中国大使馆寻求安保支援，最终得到大使馆的大力支持。

2020年，新冠肺炎疫情暴发。身在异国他乡，程金积极组织防疫小组，安排部署防疫工作，亲自组织项目部和隔离点开展防疫培训，讲解防疫知识，叮嘱大家要合理饮食，注意休息，加强锻炼，同时，对大家进行心理疏导，程金成了大家的主心骨。众志成城的力量，最终抵挡住了疫情的入侵，当时，整个子公司无一人感染。

2016年以后，埃塞俄比亚政局波动，外汇异常短缺，很多行业对外国人不再开放。为了提高子公司在当地的生存能力，完成集团在非洲的战略布局，程金开始在周边国家开展经营活动，索马里、南苏丹、厄立特里亚等地区都留下了他的足迹。多元工程项目开始初期，无机具、无人员，他和少量管理人员带着一百多名当地员工自力更生、真抓实干，连续奋战、不眠不休是常事。

在疫情持续下的2021年，程金作为中材国际埃塞俄比亚子公司总经理，带领团队，迎难而上，主动出击，取得一个又一个新的突破：签订Hawassa纺织工业园项目总承包合同、Lemi建材产业园项目启动。这两个项目不仅提升了子公司在当地的声誉，也助推了埃塞俄比亚的经济发展，造福了当地人民，增进了中埃人民的深厚友谊。

这些年来，中材国际埃塞俄比亚子公司在程金的领导下积极履行社会责任，在用工上推行属地化管理，长期雇用当地员工 107 人，其中本科 11 人、海外留学硕士 2 人。子公司还注重对当地员工的培训，中国工人传授给他们知识和技能，接受培训的当地员工对 SINOMA 的认同度和自豪感大大增加。随着持续的合作，越来越多的员工还进入管理岗位。与此同时，程金还倡议组织有当地员工参加的各种文体和健身活动，大大增加了当地员工的归属感。2021 年，子公司举行以“抗击疫情 强身健体 回归自然”为主题的爬山活动，当地员工 Wodesen 获得了冠军。登临山顶，他开心地说：“感谢 SINOMA 这个大家庭给我创造了一次锻炼身体、磨炼意志的机会。”

在做大做强企业的同时，程金没有忘记帮助当地有困难的人。他多次向上级公司申请物资，捐献给当地的学校、医院等；组织人员定期为学校维修桌椅板凳；多次给当地居民运送干净的饮用水；遇到当地发生交通事故时，项目部有时会调用重型机械吊车帮助处理现场；项目部的医疗团队也经常为当地重病患者诊疗。“我们身上都贴着‘中国’标签，要树立中国人的良好形象，要为祖国增光添彩。”程金经常跟大伙儿这样说。

40 岁的程金，将自己的青春尽情挥洒在海外的土地上。现场工作纷繁复杂，加班加点早已经成为他的生活常态，他对家人的关心自然很少。面对妻子和孩子，他总是满怀愧疚。由于疫情，程金在埃塞一待就是两年多，妻子一个人在国内拉扯两个孩子，照顾着上上下下一大家子，任劳任怨，无怨无悔。这些年来，她用理解、信任、支持和奉献为程金撑起家庭这一片天，让程金安心工作，没有后顾之忧。

作为一个平凡的建设者，程金在海外度过了十多个春节。他错过了太多陪伴家人的重要时光，却唯独没有错过每个新项目的合同签订，没有错过每个项目的竣工投产，更没有错过每个现场的精彩瞬间。他用行动扛起责任，用汗水诠释担当，用实干践行着“时不我待，只争朝夕”的誓言。他将与自己的团队振奋精神，再鼓干劲，向着更高更远的目标奋进。（中材国际所属苏州中材）

个人体会 我知道，我肩负着公司给予的重任，承载着家人的全力支持和殷殷期待。我必将用行动扛起责任，用汗水诠释担当，用实干践行“时不我待，只争朝夕”的誓言。我将与自己的团队振奋精神，再鼓干劲，全力拓展公司海外业务，向着更高更远的目标奋进。

"Time and tide wait for no man, we should make the best of every minute!"

Cheng Jin

Joined CNBM in 2005

Assistant General Manager of SINOMA(Suzhou) and General Manager of SINOMA International Engineering Co. Ltd. (Ethiopia Branch)

The eleven years in Ethiopia is unforgettable for Cheng Jin. As the general manager of the Ethiopia subsidiary of SINOMA International, he should not only focus on the construction progress of projects, but also take full charge of the subsidiary's operations. As the team leader, he overcame countless ups and downs, and finally achieved great success. Only he can deeply understand the joys and sorrows in this process. Calm and resolute, he is one of the most excellent CNBM workers.

Ethiopia is a volatile country with frequent riots. In 2016, Ethiopia was under a state of emergency, and armed riots occurred monthly. Once, the Dangote Cement Plant project in Ethiopia was attacked, the roads outside the plant were nearly all blocked, and communications were completely interrupted, which was a major security threat for all project personnel. However, under the premise of ensuring his own safety, Cheng Jin crossed the danger zone calmly and went to the Chinese Embassy 100 kilometers away to seek security assistance, and finally got strong support from the embassy.

In 2020, the COVID-19 epidemic broke out. In a foreign country, Cheng Jin organized an epidemic prevention team actively, deployed epidemic prevention, personally arranged the project department and the quarantine units to carry out epidemic prevention training, and popularized the knowledge of epidemic prevention, repeatedly advising his colleagues to eat, rest and exercise properly. He also provided psychological counseling, thus becoming the backbone of his colleagues. With concerted efforts, they finally fended off the epidemic, with no one in the subsidiary infected.

After 2016, Ethiopia experienced political turbulences and an unusual shortage of foreign exchange, and many industries were exclusive to domestic enterprises. To improve the viability of the subsidiary in Ethiopia and complete the Group's strategic goals in Africa, Cheng Jin began to explore business potentials in neighboring countries such as Somalia, South Sudan, and Eritrea. At the beginning of the diversified projects, with a shortage of equipment and personnel, he and a small number of managers with more than 100 local employees had to work hard on their own tirelessly.

In 2021, when the epidemic was rampant, Cheng Jin, as the general manager of the Ethiopia subsidiary, led the team to meet the challenges and took the initiative to achieve successive breakthroughs: signing the EPC contract of

Hawassa Textile Industrial Park Project and launching the project of LEMI Building Materials Industrial Park. These two projects have not only enhanced the local reputation of the subsidiary, but also boosted the economic development of Ethiopia, benefiting the Ethiopian people and deepened the profound friendship between the two peoples.

Over the years, under the leadership of Cheng Jin, the subsidiary in Ethiopia has actively fulfilled its social responsibility and implemented localized management in employment, with 107 long-term local workers, including 11 with a bachelor's degree and 2 with a master's degree. Meanwhile, the subsidiary has paid attention to the training of local employees. Chinese workers pass on knowledge and skills to them, and the local employees who received training have greatly increased their recognition and pride in SINOMA. With continued cooperation, more and more employees are transferred to management positions. Kebede, a field engineer in the production and operation project, said, "I do enjoy working in SINOMA, for I not only learn a lot of skills and valuable experience, but also earn a good salary to provide for my family." At the same time, Cheng Jin has proposed to organize various recreational, sports and fitness activities involving local employees, which has greatly increased the sense of belonging of local employees. In 2021, the subsidiary held a mountain climbing activity with the theme of "exercising to fight the epidemic and returning to nature", and Wodesen, a local employee, won the champion. "Thanks to the SINOMA family for giving me a chance to exercise both my body and toughen my mind." The winner said happily at the top of the mountain.

While developing his business, Cheng Jin helped local people in trouble. He has repeatedly applied to the superior company to donate materials to local schools, hospitals, etc. He organized staff to repair desks and chairs for schools regularly and provided clean drinking water to the local population. In case of local traffic accidents, the project department offered heavy machinery cranes to help clear the site. The medical team of the project department often treats local patients with serious illnesses. "We Chinese people should behave well and build a good image and reputation for our motherland." Cheng Jin often said.

Cheng Jin, 40, has spent his youth overseas. He faced complex work on-site and often worked extra hours, leaving little time for his family. He remains regretful for his wife and family. Due to the epidemic, Cheng Jin had to stay in Ethiopia for more than two years, so his wife had to take care of their children and parents alone in China. Over the years, she has managed the family well with trust, support, understanding and dedication, so that Cheng Jin can focus on his work.

As an ordinary constructor who has worked overseas for 17 years, Cheng Jin has spent more than 10 Spring Festivals overseas. Although he has lost so much important time with his family, he has never missed the signing of every new project contract, the completion and operation of every project, as well as every wonderful moment on site. With the oath of "racing against time, for time waits for no man", he has taken responsibility with practical actions and worked hard tirelessly, advancing bravely with great ambitions for better goals together with his team.

Personal Insights I am shouldering heavy responsibilities of the company, and carrying the full support and expectation of my family. "Time and tide wait for no man, we should make the best of every minute!" I will fulfill my responsibilities with concrete actions and all-out efforts, and lead my team to fully devote ourselves to expanding the overseas market and striving for the higher targets.

优秀的“安全卫士”

亨德拉

2013 年加入中国建材
现任中材国际印尼子公司项目安全员

亨德拉是印尼 Bayah 项目所在地的本地人，专业为安全管理，于 2013 年 7 月大学毕业后加入中材国际印尼 Bayah 一期项目部，参与了 Bayah 一期、Bayah 电厂和 Bayah 二期项目的建设工作。

亨德拉工作勤勤恳恳，任劳任怨，通过大学所学到的安全专业理论知识和在工作现场学到的实践经验，在日常工作中及时检查作业环境，消除安全隐患，为项目部和相关分包方提供专业的安全方案，在项目施工中严格执行公司安全规章制度和地方相关法律法规。虽然家里距项目现场仅 25 公里，但是为了现场安全和防疫工作，疫情期间他主动坚守在项目部，没有回家，为项目“零事故”安全管理目标的实现作出了自己贡献。

亨德拉除了安全管理工作外，还负责协调公司和地方政府的关系，办理相关政府审批文件，比如，施工之前跟当地劳工部申请办理余热发电锅炉图纸审批，施工结束后申请办理特种设备使用证书等，他要确保项目建设和运行符合地方政府法律法规；在人员签证方面他要和当地移民局、劳工部、警察局等相关部门保持密切联系；他还要配合相关部门的定期检查工作，及时办理相关手续，确保现场所有中国人员符合当地移民局和劳工部的规定。

同时，亨德拉对家乡的公益事业也很热心，积极为项目部和当地社区牵线搭桥，组织了多次捐赠活动，比如，地震后为当地驻军捐赠帐篷等救灾物资，为当地敬老院捐赠生活物资，为当地学校捐赠文具、课本等学习用品，这些公益捐赠活动使公司在当地社区赢得了口碑，获得了当地政府和民众的大力支持。

亨德拉不仅工作努力，还好学上进。在这几年工作期间，他参加了多项当地大学和政府部门举办的培训，并考取了多个资质证书。在平常工作中，亨德拉和项目部同事建立了融洽的朋友关系。他说：“中国同事都是我的朋友和老师，我跟他们不仅学会了很多中文表达，而且学到了很多项目管理方面的知识和技能，我非常感谢 SINOMA 及中国同事给我的工作

机会和帮助，SINOMA Bagus（非常棒）！”

属地化是公司海外发展的一个重点方向。近年来公司在印尼积极推进人员属地化发展，充分发挥属地化人员的语言优势和技术优势，把培养优秀属地化人才作为公司海外发展的一个重要措施。项目部聘用了很多当地技术和管理人才，亨德拉就是其中的一个代表，他以优异的工作成绩和踏实肯干的工作作风得到项目部领导和同事的一致肯定和好评。（中材国际所属苏州中材）

个人体会

能够成为SINOMA的一员是我的荣幸，SINOMA是一个温暖的大家庭，我喜欢和SINOMA的同事一起工作。在SINOMA工作的10年间，我学到了很多，从项目安全管理到中文语言能力，从神奇的中国文化到美味的中式菜肴，中国的各个方面都吸引着我，希望有机会能到中国去看看。

Excellent Safety Guard

Hendrayana

Joined CNBM in 2013

Project Safety Officer of PT. SINOMA Engineering Indonesia

Hendra, a native of the Bayah project site in Indonesia and a graduate with a bachelor's degree in safety management, joined SINOMA International's Bayah Phase I project department in Indonesia in July 2013. He actively contributed to the construction endeavors of Bayah Phase I, Bayah Power Plant, and Bayah Phase II projects.

Drawing upon his theoretical knowledge of safety acquired during his college education and practical experience in the field, Hendra diligently conducts thorough inspections of the working environment. He proactively identifies and rectifies potential safety hazards, offering expert safety solutions to the project department and subcontractors involved. With unwavering commitment, Hendra ensures the strict adherence to the company's safety regulations and complies with local laws and regulations throughout the project's construction phase. Despite residing a mere 25 kilometers from the project site, Hendra chose not to return home during the epidemic to prioritize on-site safety and epidemic prevention measures. His selfless dedication played a vital role in contributing to the project's overarching goal of achieving "zero accidents" through meticulous safety management.

Apart from his responsibilities in safety management, Hendra also takes charge of liaising with the local government to obtain necessary government approval documents. This includes submitting waste heat boiler drawings to the Ministry of Labor for approval prior to construction and acquiring a special equipment use permit after completion. These meticulous efforts ensure that the project adheres to the laws and regulations set by the local government throughout the construction and operation phases. Regarding personnel visas, Hendra establishes and maintains strong relationships with the Immigration Bureau, Ministry of Labor, Police Department, and other relevant departments. He collaborates with regular inspections conducted by these departments and promptly handles all necessary procedures. This ensures that all Chinese personnel working at the site comply with the regulations set by the local Immigration Bureau and Ministry of Labor.

Simultaneously, Hendra demonstrates great enthusiasm for public welfare initiatives in his hometown. He actively connects the project department with the local community, organizing numerous charitable events. Examples include donating tents and other essential supplies to the local garrison after an earthquake, providing living essentials to local nursing homes, and contributing stationery, textbooks, and other educational materials to nearby schools. These acts of philanthropy have not only enhanced the project department's reputation within the local community but also garnered the support of both the local government and residents.

Hendra is not only diligent in his work but also highly committed to continuous learning. In the past few years, he actively engaged in various training programs organized by local universities and government entities, acquiring multiple certifications. Hendra also gets along quite well with his colleagues in the project department. He said with gratitude, "My Chinese colleagues have become not only my friends but also my mentors. Through their guidance and support, I have not only acquired proficiency in spoken Chinese, but also gained invaluable project management knowledge and skills. I am immensely thankful to SINOMA and my Chinese colleagues for granting me this opportunity to work and for their unwavering assistance. SINOMA Bagus (SINOMA is truly remarkable!)"

In recent years, the company has been actively advancing the localization of personnel in Indonesia, capitalizing on the language and technical expertise of local employees. The training and development of exceptional local talent have become key strategies for the company's overseas expansion. Hendra stands as an exemplary figure, highly regarded and praised by project leaders and fellow employees alike for his outstanding work ethic, dedication to learning, and remarkable job performance.

Personal Insights It's my great honor to be a member of SINOMA. SINOMA is a warm family, and I like working together with SINOMA colleagues. During 10 years working with SINOMA colleagues, I have learnt a lot, from project safety management to Chinese language, from wonderful Chinese culture to delicious Chinese food. I am interested in everything about China. I hope to visit China in the near future.

塔哈的工作

塔哈·阿里夫·阿卜杜勒卡里姆

2007 年加入中国建材

现任中材工贸（伊拉克）有限公司外事管理员

2007 年，苏州中材第一次走进伊拉克，作为总承包方承接了伊拉克苏莱曼尼亚 SCP 日产 5000 水泥熟料生产线项目，正式开启了在伊拉克的开拓耕耘，也翻开了公司国际市场拓展的新篇章。作为中国建材集团旗下致力于水泥工程板块的骨干企业，十多年来，苏州中材在伊拉克市场一路高歌猛进，践行了“一带一路”倡议，并成功扎根伊拉克，深耕伊拉克，创造了辉煌的成绩，树立了水泥工程领域的品牌，塑造了中国企业良好的国际形象。

然而，成就是来之不易的，跟所有的励志故事一样，苏州中材在伊拉克的起步也充满艰辛，尤其是当初刚刚抵达苏莱曼尼亚时，在一个陌生的、百废待兴的国家里，项目的开展举步维艰，我们今天故事的主角——塔哈，正是在那时加入苏州中材的团队，作为公司的当地员工，他既是这个故事中的主角，又是公司整个发展历程的见证人。

2007 年 4 月的一天，不到 30 岁的塔哈第一次来到苏州中材位于苏莱曼尼亚市的临时办事处，这个满脸胡茬的人跟他年龄不那么相称，不过因为他在来之前曾在中铁的项目上干过 1 年多，还会说一些中文，所以很快就融入公司的团队，这个渴望用双手以实际行动来建设库尔德的伊拉克人，正式成为苏州中材的一名员工。

这个时候，伊拉克战争还没有结束，大量美军驻扎在伊拉克，苏莱曼尼亚位于伊拉克北部库尔德地区，相对比较安全，政治也相对稳定，但是，针对美军和伊拉克政府机构的袭击仍然时有发生。当地的中资企业非常少，塔哈不但做了司机的工作，做一些翻译工作，还要负责一些安全防护的工作，以保证大家的安全。当地有什么风吹草动，塔哈会主动联系大家，确保大家无虞。

自 SCP 项目的临建设施完成，项目现场就要开始准备后续的机具、材料和设备，由于苏莱曼尼亚深处内陆，项目现场离合同约定的位于土耳其的中转港口梅尔新有 1200 公里陆路，其中伊拉克境内有约 400 公里。经过长

年的战乱，这段道路通畅情况、沿途的桥梁承重情况、空中障碍情况等尚无确切信息，需要安排人员实地考察，塔哈又理所当然地承担起“带路党”的重任。为安全起见，他携带了一把枪在随行车上，临时当上了考察组的安保员。经过三天两夜的高强度工作，考察组对边境至项目现场的每一座桥梁、每一处高压线距离、每一个检查站都做了详细的测量和记录，为后续物流运输的顺利开展提供了第一手的翔实数据。

2010 年 6 月，伊拉克 SCP 生产运营项目成立，塔哈顺理成章地成为项目部的一员。项目初期，人员紧张，物资匮乏。塔哈一人身兼数职，任劳任怨。他既是项目部的司机，各种工程车辆如数家珍，又负责物资、备件的采购，因为会说英文，他还兼职现场的翻译，在项目部与当地政府打交道的过程中，塔哈利用他的影响力和人脉，始终是打头阵的人。

2020 年 2 月份以来，新冠肺炎疫情突如其来，整个伊拉克变得人心惶惶。为了接送人员离厂返厂，塔哈经常需要连夜往返机场，甚至还需深入伊朗边境。因为疫情，项目部工作人员尽量减少外出以及和外界沟通，很多业务就必须要塔哈出面与外界进行沟通，每次他总是高效地完成，从来没有怨言。他总是用简单的一句话来解释：“这是我的工作”。

不论环境如何变化，始终在平凡的岗位上坚守，终将成就不平凡。2018 年，塔哈毫无意外地被公司评选为海外优秀员工，并于 2019 年受邀前往公司总部参观学习。在塔哈心里，这应该是公司对他最大的认可。

15 年的时间，苏州中材在伊拉克耕耘出了新的天地，作为苏州中材的一名员工，塔哈的生活也变得更加美好。（中材国际所属苏州中材）

个人体会 我非常喜欢中国，在 SINOMA 工作很愉快，也喜欢跟中国朋友在一起工作。在 15 年的工作时间里，我和中国朋友一起经历了很多快乐的事情，共同克服工作中的困难，现在我已经能独立做一些管理当地员工、本地采购、机具租赁和维护等工作，希望 SINOMA 在伊拉克再创佳绩！

"This is my job"

Taha Arif Abdalkarim

Joined CNBM in 2007
Foreign Affairs Administrator of SINOMA Industry & Trade (Iraq) Co., Ltd.

In 2007, Suzhou SINOMA ventured into Iraq for the first time, taking on the SCP 5000t/d cement clinker production line project in Sulaymaniyah. This marked a significant milestone in the company's history, as it not only embarked on a pioneering journey in Iraq but also initiated a new phase of international market expansion. As a key player in the cement engineering sector under CNBM Group, we have made remarkable strides in the Iraqi market over the past decade, actively contributing to the implementation of the Belt and Road Initiative and expanding our global presence. Through our unwavering commitment, we have firmly established ourselves in Iraq, deepening our roots, achieving remarkable milestones, and setting a distinguished reputation in the field of cement engineering. Chinese enterprises have been rejuvenated and their image refreshed through our outstanding accomplishments in Iraq.

Nevertheless, the road to success was far from smooth. Suzhou SINOMA's foray into Iraq was riddled with formidable challenges, particularly upon its arrival in Sulaymaniyah. Operating in an unfamiliar country struggling to get back on its feet posed a significant hurdle for the project's implementation. Taha joined the Suzhou SINOMA team during that period. As a dedicated employee of the company, Taha played a pivotal role in shaping this remarkable story and bore witness to the entire developmental journey of company.

In April 2007, Taha, then in his 20s, stepped into Suzhou SINOMA's temporary office in Sulaymaniyah. Taha's previous experience working on a China Railway project for over a year, along with his knowledge of the Chinese language, allowed him to swiftly assimilate into the company's team. With a deep-rooted desire to contribute his efforts to the betterment of the Kurdish region, this passionate Iraqi officially joined the ranks of Suzhou SINOMA as an employee.

During that period, the Iraq War in 2003 was still fresh in people's memories, and a significant presence of American troops remained in the country. Sulaymaniyah, situated in the politically stable and relatively secure northern Kurdish region, experienced sporadic incidents of attacks targeting American forces and government establishments. Given the scarcity of Chinese companies operating in the area, Taha took on the role of a driver while also fulfilling translation duties. He played a crucial role in ensuring the safety of everyone by primarily focusing on security protection work. Whenever there was a local incident or movement, Taha took it upon himself to proactively reach out to everyone, ensuring their safety and keeping them updated on the latest developments.

After the completion of the temporary construction facilities for the SCP project, the project site embarked on preparations for the arrival of machinery, materials, and equipment. However, due to its remote location deep within Sulaymaniyah, the project site was situated 1,200 kilometers away from the contracted transit port of Mersin in Turkey. Approximately 400 kilometers of this distance lay within Iraq. After years of conflict, detailed information regarding road conditions, bridge load-bearing capacity, and potential aerial obstacles remained elusive. A field inspection was necessary to gather accurate data, and Taha naturally assumed the crucial role of leading the way. In consideration of safety, Taha carried a firearm in the accompanying vehicle, temporarily taking on the responsibility of a security guard for the inspection team. Over the course of three days and two nights, the team conducted exhaustive work, meticulously measuring and documenting vital details such as road conditions, bridge integrity, and potential obstacles along the route. This firsthand information proved instrumental in ensuring smooth logistics and transportation for the project.

In June 2010, with the establishment of the Iraq SCP production and operation project, Taha naturally became a member of the project team. During the initial phase, the project faced challenges such as staff and material shortages. Taha took on various responsibilities. He served as the driver of the project department, with vast knowledge of various engineering vehicles. He was responsible for material procurement and the sourcing of essential spare parts. Moreover, Taha's proficiency in English allowed him to fulfill the role of an on-site translator, bridging the language barrier between the team and local stakeholders.

In February 2020, the sudden outbreak of the COVID-19 epidemic sent shockwaves across Iraq, instilling fear and uncertainty throughout the country. Taha often drove at night to transport people between the factory and the airport, and sometimes could drive as far as the Iranian border. Due to the epidemic, the project department minimized interactions and contacts with the outside world. Taha willingly took on the responsibility of communications with outsiders on behalf of the team, efficiently handling various business matters without ever expressing any complaints.

Regardless of the changing environment, one can achieve miracles by steadfastly sticking to everyday. In 2018, Taha was honored as an Exceptional Overseas Employee and received a well-deserved invitation to visit the company's headquarters for a study program in 2019. To Taha, this recognition from the company meant more to him than anything else.

Over the course of 15 years, Suzhou SINOMA has created a new realm in Iraq, and Taha's life, as an integral part of Suzhou SINOMA, has blossomed with dreams and aspirations, reflecting the positive transformation brought about by his association with the company.

Personal Insights I love China, and I am very happy to work in SINOMA with my Chinese friends in SINOMA. In the past 15 years, a lot of nice memory I have had with my Chinese friends, and we have overcome a lot of problems and difficulties together. I can now do some work such as management of local employees, local procurement, machinery and tool sourcing and maintenance, I hope SINOMA will make more success in the future.

运输车队的排头兵

奥利弗·布瓦利亚

2020 加入中国建材

现任中材国际赞比亚分公司运输车队助理

奥利弗·布瓦利亚是中材国际赞比亚分公司赞比亚籍员工，1972 年出生于分公司所在城市 Edola，1995 年专科毕业之后参加工作，具有丰富的社会工作经验，包括生产管理、车辆保险及车队运营工作。2022 年，公司开始组建自营车队，他经社会招聘加入车队，当前职位为运输物流部助理，主要负责车队的日常运营、司机的日常管理以及车队涉外沟通和应急处理等工作。

中材国际赞比亚分公司经过多年的发展，广泛发展了水泥、煤炭、建材等跨境贸易，伴随着业务量的增加，运输车队的短缺成为制约分公司贸易发展的最重要因素。为了公司的进一步发展，赞比亚分公司开始购买车辆筹建自营车队，但分公司并没有车队运营管理相应的人才储备，经过一段时间的社会招聘，具备多年车辆保险和运输公司管理经验的奥利弗·布瓦利亚脱颖而出。

自营车队成立伊始，奥利弗·布瓦利亚从司机招聘着手，包括文件办理、车辆整备、人员培训，并逐一建立健全车队运营及管理制度。起初，由于司机对运输路线和津巴布韦、刚果通关文件等不熟悉，车队运营一度极其缓慢，运输周期甚至不到其他运输公司的 70%。在中方管理人员的带领下，奥利弗·布瓦利亚和车队管理办公室的同事一起逐一跟踪车辆信息，发现问题，逐一分解，制定办事流程，从每个步骤抠时间，挤进度，向同行取经。经过两个月的优化，车队运输效率得到了巨大提升，并结合自有清关保税的便利，目前的车队运输效率超越了大部分同行。

伴随着精益化的管理和公司投资的逐步增加，目前分公司的自有车队逐渐壮大，现已增加至 60 台车，至最终客户的月运力约 5000 吨，不仅为公司贡献了可观的利润，也使车队成为赞比亚分公司以及贸易物流板块发展的压舱石。日常运营中，车辆运输途中的紧急维修、文件及通关问题等也是无法避免的，奥利弗·布瓦利亚利用公司提供的平台，积极联系拓展内外资源。近则亲自按需带维修人员或者清关代理前往处理，较远或者跨境时则发动事发地人脉资源紧急处理各种车辆问题，保障了车队的安全、高效运行。

除了车队管理外，奥利弗·布瓦利亚也兼顾部分车队油库管理工作，每次出库入库时他都一丝不苟，认真检查铅封和文件明细，发现铅封损坏和数据不一时则一丝不苟，立即汇报和处理，避免公司出现损失。

自营车队目前是中材国际赞比亚分公司推行属地化管理的排头兵，除一名中方主管外，日常管理工作主要由车队助理负责，奥利弗·布瓦利亚不论是在理解公司运行管理，与中方管理人员沟通协调，还是管理赞比亚籍员工，都能积极应对、妥善处理并认真做好执行工作。

伴随着自营车队规模的逐渐扩大，工作的逐渐深入，奥利弗·布瓦利亚对 SINOMA 的企业归属感也越来越强。中材国际赞比亚分公司正是有了这样一批专业、实干、擅长沟通管理的当地骨干，才一步一步成为中国建材集团和中材国际在海外的排头兵。（中材国际所属苏州中材）

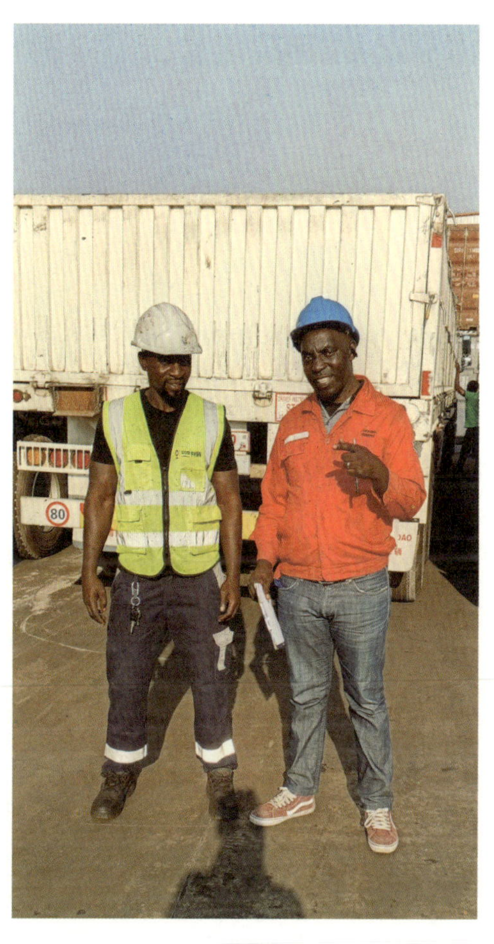

个人体会 我来到运输物流部近一年了，中材国际工作是一种很棒的体验，让我实现了人生目标，为此，我心存感激。我非常荣幸见证了运输物流部以及自身的成长，也非常期待公司未来的发展和更好的自己。

In the Vanguard of the Fleet

Oliver Bwalya

Joined CNBM in 2020

Transportation Team Assistant of SINOMA International Engineering Co. Ltd. (Zambia Branch)

Oliver Bwalya is a local employee of the Zambian branch of SINOMA. He was born in Edola, the city where the branch is located, in 1972. He graduated from a vocational college in 1995 and has a rich background in social work, including production management, vehicle insurance, and fleet operation. In 2022, the company began to establish a self operated fleet and he was recruited and recommended to join SINOMA. Currently, he serves as an assistant to the self operated fleet, mainly responsible for the daily operation of the fleet, daily management of drivers, internal and external coordination, as well as foreign communication and emergency response of the fleet.

After years of development, SINOMA Zambia Branch has extensively developed cross-border trade in cement, coal, building materials, and other industries. With the increase in business volume, the shortage of transportation fleets has become the most important factor restricting the branch's trade development. After approval, the Zambian branch started purchasing vehicles to establish a self-operated fleet, but the branch does not have the corresponding talent reserve for fleet operation and management.

After a period of social recruitment and recommendation, Oliver Bwalya's years of experience in vehicle insurance and transportation company management made him stand out.

Since the establishment of the self-operated fleet, Oliver Bwalya has been recruiting drivers, including document processing, vehicle preparation, personnel training, and gradually establishing and improving fleet operation and management systems.

When the self-operated fleet was first established, it faced many challenges, such as inexperienced drivers, unfamiliar transportation routes, and complex customs clearance procedures. The fleet's transportation efficiency was very low compared to other transportation companies. Oliver Bwalya worked closely with the Chinese management staff to track and troubleshoot vehicle information, develop and improve fleet operation and management systems, optimize each step of the transportation process, learn from peers, and leverage the advantages of self-owned customs clearance and bonded. After two months of hard work, the fleet's transportation efficiency improved significantly and even surpassed most of its competitors. With lean management and increased investment from the company, the self-operated fleet expanded to 60 vehicles with a monthly transportation capacity of about 5000 tons to the final customer. The fleet has become a key contributor to the company's profits and a pillar for the development of the Zambian branch and trade logistics sector.

In daily operations, emergency repairs, document and customs clearance issues during vehicle transportation are also unavoidable. Oliver Bwalya utilizes the platform provided by the company to actively explore internal and external resources. If things happen nearby, he personally brings maintenance personnel or customs clearance agents as needed to handle the situation. When such needs occurred far away or across borders, he mobilizes resources from the affected area to urgently handle various vehicle issues, ensuring the safety and efficient operation of the fleet.

In addition to fleet management, Oliver Bwalya also takes into account the management of some fleet oil depots. He is meticulous in every delivery and warehousing, carefully checks the lead seals and document details. If he finds that the lead seal damage and data inconsistency, he immediately reports and handles them to avoid the company's losses.

The self operated fleet is currently at the forefront of implementing localized management in the Zambian branch. Except for a Chinese supervisor, daily management work is mainly carried out by the fleet assistant. Oliver Bwalya is able to actively respond, properly handle and conscientiously carry out execution work, whether in understanding the company's operational management, communicating and coordinating with Chinese management personnel, or managing Zambian employees.

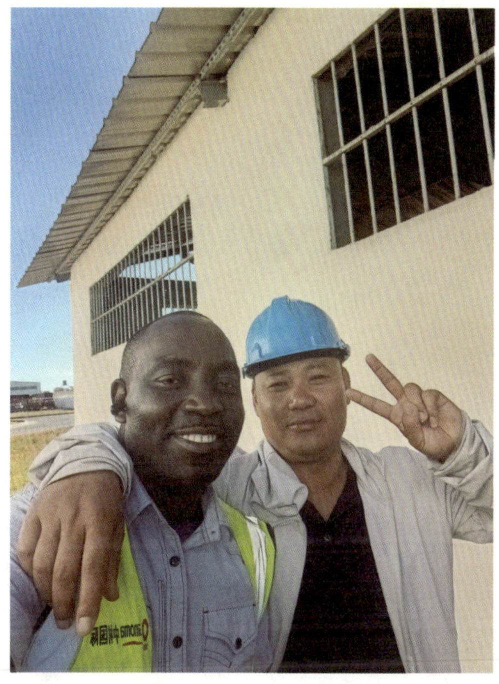

With the gradual expansion of the self operated fleet and the deepening of work, Oliver Bwalya and SINOMA have also established a deep friendship and a strong sense of corporate belonging. Zambia Branch also has such a group of professional and practical local backbone who is good at communications management, and is now gradually becoming the bridgehead, ballast and pacesetter of the whole China Building Materials Group and SINOMA International's overseas businesses.

Personal Insights I've worked for the transport and logistics department for almost a year. It's been a great experience for me and helped me achieved my goals in my life, for which I am very grateful. With a sound management in place, I've been really happy to see the development of the transport and logistics department as well as myself. Looking ahead, I am really excited to see what the company will grow into and what I can achieve.

踔厉奋发　勇毅前行

梅拉库·特威特姆·德加菲

2021 年加入中国建材

现任苏州中材埃塞莱米万吨线项目电气工程师

苏州中材埃塞莱米日产万吨水泥线项目是SINOMA 与西部国际控股有限公司 20 年合作与友谊的重要见证。20 年前，苏州中材与西部国际控股有限公司相遇、相识、相知，20 年后的今天，我们在埃塞非洲之星再次相逢，共同延续 20 年的友情，我们携手共进，共赢未来，在埃塞俄比亚市场一路高歌猛进，践行“一带一路”倡议，并成功扎根埃塞俄比亚，深耕埃塞俄比亚，创造辉煌的成绩，SINOMA 树立了水泥工程领域的品牌、刷新了中国企业的形象。

然而，成就是来之不易的。起步时，在项目开展初期，在物资匮乏的莱米镇，中方人员对这个地方是完全陌生的，项目开展举步维艰，生活设施条件差，没水没电，就在此时，梅拉库加入公司，一步步协助项目部解决了通电通水等问题。

他时常废寝忘食，走遍大街小巷寻找临建所需的电气用材，独自安装临建线路。工作间隙时，同事们问梅拉库：“是什么让你这么拼？”他用蹩脚的汉语说：“中非友谊万岁，我喜欢中国，更喜欢 SINOMA 的企业文化。”

自 2022 年 12 月 25 日起，窑尾框架开始浇筑垫层，全厂区内的临时用电全面按照临时用电专项方案开始布置，他协助中方人员布线、接线、安装配电柜等各项工作，有时为了现场进度，他会独自前往施工现场，完成接线、调试等各项工作，坚守着苏州中材“特别能吃苦、特别能奉献、特别能攻关、特别能战斗”的企业精神。

项目正常有序推进以后，由于临建工作的结束，临时用电布置接近尾声，他本人向项目安环科申请利用业余时间学习安全管理知识。项目部的同事问他：“你是一个电气工程师，为什么想学安全管理？”他回答说：“因为SINOMA 是一家国际化大公司，我想学习国际化大公司的各项工作内容，安全无小事，我就从安全管理开始学习。”他从自身做起，践行“安全为天，质量第一”的理念。身为电气工程师的他兼职安全员，给项目部的安全管理

工作作出了巨大的贡献，比如，项目部在安装监控系统时，他会从安全管理的角度，结合属地环境、人文环境等方面，给监控点的布置提供至关重要的建议，保障了监控系统的安全。

在日常工作中，虽然他是一名电气工程师，但也会在工作之余钻研安全管理，挂在他嘴边的一句话："管安全就是做善事，我要多做善事。"他的言行深深触动着大家。梅拉库是电气工程师里面最好的安全管理人员，更是安全管理人员里最懂施工用电的人。他从专业角度，多次给属地员工进行安全用电知识的宣讲，培训出一批批合格的属地电工，为埃塞莱米万吨线项目的顺利开展，作出了很大的贡献。

不论环境如何变化，他始终在平凡的岗位坚守，踔厉奋发、勇毅前行。（中材国际所属苏州中材）

个人体会 我非常喜欢 SINOMA，更敬佩 SINOMA 员工的职业精神和技术能力；我学到了很多技术上的知识，更学到了吃苦耐劳的奉献精神。我喜欢 SINOMA"特别能吃苦、特别能奉献、特别能攻关、特别能战斗的'狼'文化"。希望 SINOMA 在埃塞俄比亚再创佳绩。

Work Hard, Move Forward with Courage

Melaku Tewetm Dgafie

Joined CNBM in 2021

Electrical Engineer of SINOMA (Suzhou)'s Ethiopian Lemi 10000t/d Cement Clinker Production Project

Ethiopia's Lemi 10,000t/d line project is an important manifestation of the 20-year cooperation and friendship between SINOMA (Suzhou) and West International Holding Limited. 20 years ago, SINOMA (Suzhou) and West International Holding Limited met and got to know each other. Today, 20 years later, we meet again in Ethiopia, the Star of Africa, and we will continue our long-lasting friendship. We will go forward hand in hand, work together for a win-win future. We have made remarkable progress in the Ethiopian market, actively participating in the Belt and Road Initiative and the "Going out" strategy. We have successfully established ourselves in Ethiopia, deeply invested in its development, and achieved outstanding results. SINOMA (Suzhou) has become a renowned brand in the field of cement engineering, enhancing the reputation of Chinese enterprises.

However, achievements are hard-won. Like all inspirational stories, the project also faces all kinds of difficulties and challenges at the beginning. When Melaku first arrived at the project, he found himself in a new and unfamiliar place, where the project development was tough, the living conditions were poor, and there was no water and electricity. It was precisely because of his joining that the project department was able to solve the problem of electricity and water gradually.

In the early stage of the project, the town of Lemi lacked materials, and Chinese personnel were completely unfamiliar with this place. Melaku often ate one meal a day and worked tirelessly to find electrical materials needed for temporary buildings in the streets and alleys, and installed temporary construction lines alone. During work breaks, we asked Melaku what made him work so devotedly, and he said in poor Chinese: Long live the China-Africa friendship, I like China, and I like the enterprise spirit of SINOMA even more. Starting from December 25, 2022, the kiln tail frame began to pour the cushion, and the temporary power consumption in the entire factory area began to be arranged according to a special temporary power usage plan. He assisted Chinese personnel in wiring, connecting and installing power distribution cabinets etc. Sometimes electricity was urgently needed for the progress of the site. Due to external environmental problems, Chinese personnel could not arrive at the site at night, and he would go to the construction site alone to complete wiring, debugging, etc. He completed all tasks diligently and stuck to the "wolf culture" of SINOMA (Suzhou), which features hard work, dedication, problem-sovling skills and fighting spirit.

After the project began to be run in an orderly

manner, Melaku applied to the project safety and environmental section to learn safety management knowledge in his spare time. The project department asked him, "Since you are an electrical engineer, why do you want to learn safety management?" He answered, "Because SINOMA is a large international company, I want to learn various aspects of management kills of a large international company. Safety is not a small matter, so I started with safety management." He led the local employees to practice the concept of "safety is paramount, quality first". As an electrical engineer, he worked as a part-time safety officer. He made great contributions to the safety management of the project department. For example, when the project department began to install the monitoring system, he, from the perspective of safety management, taking into account the conditions such as the local environment and culture, provided crucial suggestions for the layout of monitoring points, which helped reduce theft incidents at the project site. He also learned superb Chinese skills during the whole installation process.

As he delicates his spare time to learning safety management, he always says,"To manage safety is to do a good deed, and I want to do more good deeds." His word deeply touched us. Melaku is the best safety manager among electrical engineers, and the one who knows the most about electricity usage during the construction among the safety managers. Based on his professional knowledge, he has given many lectures on the safe use of electricity to the local employees, trained a group of local electricians, and made great contribution to the development of the project.

No matter how the circumstances change, he always sticks to the ordinary position, and will eventually make extraordinary achievements by working hard, and going forward bravely.

Personal Insights I like SINOMA very much, and I admire the professionalism and technical ability of employees in SINOMA even more. During the period of working for the project, I learned a lot of technical things, and learned the spirit of hard work and dedication. I esteem SINOMA's superb technology, and admire SINOMA's "wolf culture" that is features hard work, dedication, problem-sovling skills and fighting spirit. I sincerely hope that SINOMA will achieve more success in Ethiopia.

让产品富有更高价值

托比亚斯·施吕特

2006 年加入中国建材
现任 HAZEMAG 产品经理

“我非常高兴能成为 HAZEMAG 团队的一员，并竭诚为它的成长贡献智慧。”36 岁的工业工程师托比亚斯·施吕特高兴地说，“这是我的新起点，也是我的努力所获。”

2022 年 1 月，托比亚斯·施吕特的职位从销售经理变为产品经理。“这不同于我过去担任的职位，在这个职位上，我将和 HAZEMAG 集团的所有部门和公司之间建立一种新的、成功的沟通文化。”在履新之际，托比亚斯·施吕特如此界定工作的价值。

作为产品经理，不能独断专行，相反，需要把来自不同部门的员工如销售、研发、运营、服务和控制等聚集在一起。“在 HAZEMAG 集团内部，跨国界的横向团队致力于跨越部门和国家之间的障碍，进行高效地沟通和交流，以达成最优解决方案。” 托比亚斯·施吕特表示。

有志者，事竟成。经过团队的努力，技术研发部门和产品管理部门之间的沟通有了明显的改善，并提高到了一个前所未有的水平。“我们一起能够创造出新颖和现代的产品。” 托比亚斯·施吕特说。在一个由高度积极的员工、同事和朋友组成的团队中，他将利用新的团队精神，更有力地推广 HAZEMAG 这个知名的品牌，“我将加强 HAZEMAG 品牌的影响力，以标准化和模块化的产品组合促进企业增长。”为此，托比亚斯·施吕特所在的全球测试和研究中心密切参与产品标准化开发工作。目前，托比亚斯·施吕特团队已部署通过 CRM 软件为所有的标准化产品自动创建实施方案，保证企业对客户的要求能快速做出反应。

新产品信息的标准化包括新的和统一的图片语言以及所有产品的相同外观和感觉，使托比亚斯·施吕特的团队能够以最佳方式推销 HAZEMAG 的设备。从现在开始，HAZEMAG 在世界各地的所有员工都可以获得统一的、标准化的产品信息。这些新信息能够以统一和专业的方式向客户和商业伙伴展示，保证了公司能够以统一、便捷的方式展示所有产品系列的不同产品细节。“这种成功的

新的标准化产品信息也将被 HAZEMAG 集团的其他公司所采用，”托比亚斯 · 施吕特激动地说，“主动收集改进意见和随后积极推动实施，使公司内部的处理工作得到了改善和提高。在整个 HAZEMAG 集团内发展持续改进方法是公司成功转型的关键，也是我的主要动力之一。”

整个一年中，托比亚斯 · 施吕特参与了大量改善整体业务发展和业绩的工作，并取得了巨大成功。“我与我们的营销部门一起，为公司的产品制定了社会媒体战略，这将保证公司的产品得到最好的推广。同时，成功与否可以通过公司社交媒体平台上迅速增加的订阅数量以及公司的主页提供的增益的客户流量和咨询量来衡量。这清楚地表明，这种方法可以成功推广到集团内的所有公司。我所做的一切都以公司的盈利增长为重点，并加强公司组织内优秀人员之间的沟通。”托比亚斯 · 施吕特肯定地说。

谈到今后的工作，托比亚斯 · 施吕特表示，将在 HAZEMAG 集团和下属的所有公司进一步推广使用这种新颖的工作方式和实践经验。“无疑，这将使 HAZEMAG 集团的业务水平更上一层楼。”他说。（中材国际所属 HAZEMAG）

个人体会

我从 2006 年开始以实习生的身份在 HAZEMAG 工作。工作至今，历经多个岗位，因此能够学习和获得丰富的知识和经验。自 2021 年以来，我转任产品经理。我很自豪能成为这样一个以高技术标准生产和制造产品的集团的一员。

Making Products More Valuable

Tobias Schlueter

Joined CNBM in 2006
Product Manager of HAZEMAG

"I'm very happy to become a member of HAZEMAG and I will devote my wisdom to its growth wholeheartedly," said Tobias Schlueter, a 36-year-old industrial engineer, "This is my new starting point and a reward for my hard work."

In January 2022, Tobias Schlueter was transferred from sales manager to product manager. "This is a position different from my previous one. In this position, I will implement a new, successful communication culture with all departments and companies of the HAZEMAG Group." Tobias Schlueter defined the basic duties and values of the job as he was about to take on his new role.

As a product manager, he can't judge for himself. Instead, he needs to bring together people from different departments, such as sales, R&D, operations, services and control. "I lead a virtual team in the HAZEMAG Group to enable more purposeful communication among departments to ensure the best solutions of our company." Tobias Schlueter said.

Where there is a will, there is a way. Thanks to team efforts, the communication between the technology R&D department and the product management department has been obviously improved to an unprecedented level. "Together, we can create innovative and modern products." With a team of highly motivated employees, colleagues and friends, Tobias Schlueter will take advantage of the new team spirit to promote the well-known brand of HAZEMAG more vigorously. "I will strengthen the brand of HAZEMAG and create business growth with a standardized and modular product portfolio." To this end, the Global Testing and Research Center where Tobias Schlueter works is closely involved in development of product standardization. At present, Tobias Schlueter's team has implemented proposals automatically created from CRM software for all standardized products, which ensures a faster response to customers' requirements.

The standardization of new product information, including new and unified pictures and language, and the same look and feel of all products, enables Tobias Schlueter to market HAZEMAG's machines in the best possible way. From now on, all HAZEMAG's employees around the world will have access to unified and standardized product information. This new information can be presented to customers and business partners in a unified and professional way, which ensures that the company can more easily present different details of all product lines in a consistent form. "This successful

new standardized product information will also be adopted by other companies of the HAZEMAG Group," Tobias Schlueter said excitedly. "Proactively collecting suggestions for improvement and subsequently actively promoting implementation led to improved and enhanced processing within the company. Developing an approach to continuous improvement across the HAZEMAG Group is the key to the successful transformation of the company and one of my main motivations."

HAZEMAG's initiative to identify and define best practice processes and workflows was very prominent throughout the year. Tobias Schlueter was heavily involved in improving overall business development and performance and achieved great success. "Together with our marketing department, I developed a social media strategy for promoting the company's products. Its success can be measured by the increased number of followers of the company's account on social media platform and increased customer traffic and inquiries on the company's homepage. This approach can be easily adopted by all companies within the Group. "Everything I do is focused on the profit growth of the company and strengthening the communication and working relationship between outstanding employees in the company." Tobias Schlueter said.

Looking ahead, Tobias Schlueter said such new processes, efficient workflows and best practices will be further promoted in the HAZEMAG Group and all of its affiliated companies. "Undoubtedly, this will bring the HAZEMAG Group's business to a higher level."

Personal Insights I have been working at HAZEMAG since 2006, when I started as a intern. I have already worked on various positions in the company and have thus acquired rich knowledge and experience. Since 2021, I have been responsible for product management in the company. I am proud to be part of such a successful Group that manufactures and sells products with the highest technical standards.

托瑞与中建投巴新公司 22 年的“守望相助”

托瑞·托尔德·米里亚
2001 年加入中国建材
现任中建投巴新公司商务经理

2001 年 3 月 19 日，一个阳光明媚的清晨，一位年轻的小伙儿面带着朝阳般灿烂的笑容踏入了中建投巴新公司。这是 22 岁的托瑞，或许当时的他没有想过，自己此后的人生会与这家公司紧紧联系在一起。

“在上学时我就了解到中国人民是勤劳而热情的，进入中国企业工作对我来说将是一种全新的经历，最终我抓住了这个机会。”不过，由于文化差异，刚进入中国企业工作的托瑞在思维方式、语言交流等方面遇到了不少困难，但在中国同事的帮助下，这些难题迎刃而解，托瑞也和中国同事结下了深厚的友谊。他说：“最初我觉得在中资企业困难重重，担心自己不能胜任工作，是我的中国同事和朋友不断鼓励我，让我有动力坚持到了今天。”

在加入中建投巴新公司后的时间里，托瑞表现出了超乎常人的热情、勤奋和努力，并且从未停止过进步。基于他优秀的工作能力和对公司的贡献，中建投巴新公司决定支持他继续完成学业。2018 年，托瑞顺利从巴布亚新几内亚大学毕业，他说：“难以想象工作之后我竟然还有机会完成学业，巴新公司真是一个包容的、能让员工实现价值的平台。”

从分店的应收账款专员、应收主管、店长助理到总部人事经理，再到如今的商务经理；从工作到完成学业，再到成家立业，这 22 年来，托瑞不断转换角色，实现了一次又一次蜕变，巴新公司也从最初的 3 家分店发展到如今的 12 家，整体规模不断扩大，可以说，他与巴新公司共同见证了彼此的成长。

现在，作为公司商务经理的托瑞积极承担岗位职责，他花费了大量的时间和精力研究当地商业法规和程序，确保相关合同等材料完善无误，确保公司相关申请符合政府规范要求。在公司管理层的支持和指导下，托瑞参与了巴新公司多个地区重要项目的筹备建设，不论是莱城的马莱塔店、莫港的润柏店、西高地省的哈根店，还是如今即将开业的北部省波蓬德塔店和东高地省戈罗卡店，都留下过他奋斗的身影。他为每个项目的用地审批提供关键支持，高效办理分店营业执照、消防认证等相关手续，极大助力了公司的市场开拓，助推了海外建材超市的发展。

托瑞觉得自己是幸运的，他说："我很荣幸能够参与公司成长发展过程中的这些重要项目，从项目中我不断地获取经验，不断学习、进步。我也很高兴能够为巴新公司贡献自己的一份力量，如果当初我没有来到巴新公司工作，也许就会碌碌无为。"

"这是我人生的第一份工作，我想也会是最后一份。"这是托瑞对公司最真挚的情感表达。他和巴新公司二十多年的"守望相助"也被他的亲人、朋友看在眼里，记在心里，他们认为像巴新公司这样的中资企业是非常好的就业选择。如今，在"一带一路"倡议下，中国与巴布亚新几内亚两国合作前景广阔，多层次、宽领域的合作也推动了当地经济发展和社会进步，为当地民众提供了大量的就业岗位。托瑞相信，将会有越来越多的当地民众选择加入中资企业，他为此感到非常自豪。（中建投巴新公司）

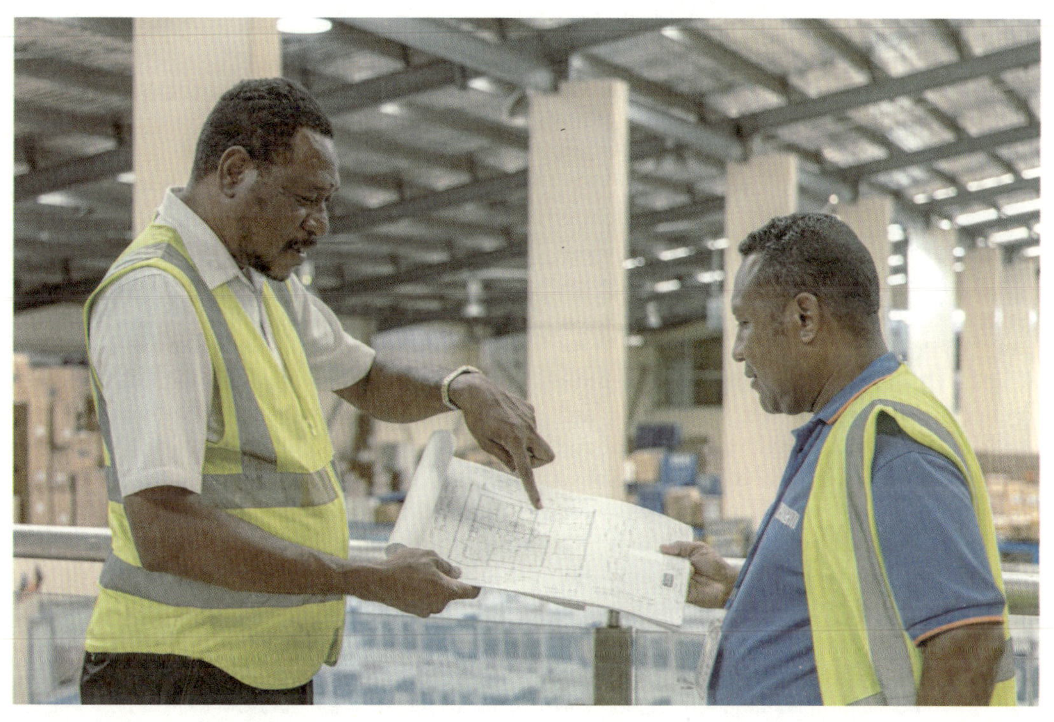

个人体会

我于2001年加入中建投巴新公司，已经在公司工作了22年，现在担任商务经理。回顾过去的工作和生活，我切实感受到成为世界500强企业的一名员工的幸运，为有一群善良、踏实、能干的同事感到骄傲，为能在这里充分展现自我感到自豪。

22 Years of Solidarity with BNBM PNG LTD

Torre Tord Miria

Joined CNBM in 2001
Business Manager of BNBM PNG Ltd.

On March 19, 2001, a bright and sunny morning, a young man with a radiant smile stepped into BNBM PNG LTD. Torre, then a 22-year-old, was unaware of the profound connection his life would forge with this company in the years to come.

"When I was in school, I learned that the Chinese people are hardworking and passionate. For me, the opportunity to work in a Chinese company represented a whole new experience, and I eventually seized that chance. However, due to cultural differences, I encountered several challenges in terms of mindset and language communication when I first joined the Chinese company. Fortunately, with the help of my Chinese colleagues, these difficulties were overcome, and I formed deep friendships with them," said Torre, "Initially, I felt overwhelmed by the challenges in a Chinese company and worried about my competence. It was my Chinese colleagues and friends who constantly encouraged me and gave me the motivation to persist until today.'"

After joining BNBM PNG Ltd., Torre displayed an extraordinary level of enthusiasm, diligence, and hard work, never ceasing to strive for improvement. Recognizing his outstanding work capabilities and contributions to the company, Company decided to support him in continuing his education. In 2018, Torre successfully graduated from the University of Papua New Guinea. He said, "It's hard to imagine that I had the opportunity to complete my studies while working. BNBM is truly an inclusive platform that allows employees to realize their value."

In the span of 22 years, Torre went through various role transitions, starting as an Accounts Receivable Officer at the branch level, then progressing to become the Accounts Receivable Supervisor, Assistant Store Manager, HR Manager at the headquarters, and finally reaching the position of Business Manager. Alongside his professional growth, Torre also accomplished personal milestones such as completing his education and starting a family. During these 22 years, BNBM PNG Ltd. has also experienced significant development, expanding from its initial three branches to twelve branches today, with continuous growth in overall scale. It can be said that Torre and BNBM have witnessed each other's growth throughout this journey.

As the Business Manager of the company, Torre actively fulfills his job responsibilities. He invests a significant amount of time and effort into studying local business regulations and procedures to ensure the accuracy and completeness of relevant

contracts and materials. He also ensures that the company's applications comply with government regulations. With the support and guidance of the company's management team, Torre has been involved in the preparation and construction of several important projects in various regions.

Whether it was the Malaita Branch in Lae City, the Rainbow Branch in Moresby, the Hagen Branch in Western Highlands Province, or the upcoming openings of the Popondetta Branch in Northern Province and Goroka Branch in Eastern Highlands Province, Torre has left his mark through his hard work. He provides critical support for land approvals in each project, efficiently handles procedures such as branch business licenses and fire safety certificates, greatly assisting the company's market expansion and promoting the development of overseas building materials branch stores.

Torre considers himself fortunate and says, "I am honored to be involved in these significant projects that contribute to the growth and development of the company. Through these projects, I continuously gain experience, learn, and progress. I am also delighted to contribute my efforts to BNBM in Papua New Guinea. If I hadn't joined the company, perhaps I would have led an unremarkable life."

"This is my first and likely my last career." This is Torre's sincere expression of his emotions towards the company. His dedication and loyalty towards BNBM PNG LTD for the past 22 years have been recognized and cherished by his family and friends. They believe that Chinese companies, like BNBM PNG LTD, are excellent employment choices. Today, with the prospects of China-PNG cooperation under the Belt and Road Initiative, multi-level and wide-ranging collaborations have propelled the economic development and social progress of PNG. This has provided numerous job opportunities for the local population. Torre believes that more and more people will choose to join Chinese companies, and he takes great pride in this trend.

Personal Insights I joined BNBM PNG Ltd. in 2001 and have been working with the company for 22 years. Currently, I hold the position of Business Manager. Looking back on my work and life, I truly feel fortunate to be an employee of a Fortune 500 company. I take pride in working alongside a group of kind, diligent, and capable colleagues, and I am proud to have the opportunity to give my abilities full play here.

做中巴新文化融合的助力者

艾莉森·帕特森

2012年加入中国建材

现任中建投巴新公司人事经理

“艾莉森工作能力突出，而且非常有上进心。”

这位让同事们赞不绝口的艾莉森，是中建投巴新公司的人事经理，主要负责公司人员招聘、选拔和培训等工作，她熟悉当地的劳动法、就业法等法律法规，具备丰富的从业经验。加入公司11年来，她不仅能专业高效地处理员工的各类问题，维护员工权益和公司声誉，还从企业对人力资源管理的需求出发，为管理层建言献策，提升公司的属地化管理水平，助推公司的市场开拓和生产经营。

艾莉森深入了解公司的战略目标和发展需求，她意识到人才储备的重要作用，并积极协助中建投巴新公司管理层实施人才储备计划，例如实施管培生计划，招聘大学毕业生并提供专业培训和轮岗机会。每年毕业季，艾莉森都会带领团队进驻校园开展招聘工作，她以专业的眼光和独到的选人方式，为公司甄选了一个又一个的优秀人才。通过此计划入职公司总部的菲奥娜，在实习期间就展现出很强的学习能力，新员工通常需要两个月才能熟悉上手的工作，她一个月就可以完成。转正后，她更是以突出的工作表现连续两年获得办公室年度优秀员工。

作为人事经理，艾莉森非常重视员工关系建设，她与员工保持开放和透明的沟通，倾听员工的意见和需求，解决员工关注的问题。她为本地员工提升福利待遇积极建言，增强员工的工作满意度和忠诚度。她还在公司实行绩效管理的过程中，与员工一起设定明确的目标，并提供及时的反馈和指导，帮助他们不断改进和成长。她说：“我的工作是确保员工的工作表现能够与公司的目标和标准相匹配。当我看到我招聘和培养的员工实现他们的职业和个人目标时，我感到快乐和满足，也正是这样的时刻让我感到有用不完的动力继续为公司服务。”

艾莉森了解中国与巴布亚新几内亚两国的文化差异，她鼓励中外员工互相分享自己的文化背景和习俗等，并积极协助公司组织文化融合活动，例如，她在两国的传统节日组织员工

分享各自国家传统节日的起源、传统习俗，并安排趣味活动，帮助员工体验不同文化，增进彼此了解，尊重彼此的文化差异。她不仅是跨文化融合的助力者，还是实践者。4 年前，她把小儿子西蒙斯送往中国学习，如今西蒙斯已顺利毕业并进入巴布亚新几内亚银行工作。他表示，自己非常幸运能够了解中国文化、中国人民和中国美食，他将把自己在中国学到的知识和收获分享给更多的青年，希望他们能够更了解中国、爱上中国。

得益于自己在中资企业的工作和孩子在中国留学的经历，艾莉森对中国有着特殊的感情。今年是“一带一路”倡议提出 10 周年，在谈及中国与巴布亚新几内亚两国合作的愿景时，艾莉森的眼中流露出一种别样的期待，她说：“中国与巴布亚新几内亚在经济、文化、社会层面都具有广阔的合作前景。中国为巴布亚新几内亚发展给予的支持使我们有能力也有责任为自己的国家带来繁荣。‘一带一路’倡议宏远而伟大，我希望中国与巴布亚新几内亚两国在合作的路上越走越好。”（中建投巴新公司）

个人体会

我为能加入中建投巴新公司和成为中国建材集团这个全球化大家庭的一员而感到自豪，这让我有机会了解中国与巴布亚新几内亚两国的不同文化。我将积极履行岗位职责，努力助力两国文化融合，为公司发展贡献一份力量，与公司携手共进，共创未来。

Facilitator of China-Papua New Guinea Cultural Integration

Allison Patterson

Joined CNBM in 2012
HR Manager of BNBM PNG Ltd.

"Allison demonstrates outstanding work abilities and possesses a strong drive for self-improvement."

Allison, a highly praised employee, serves as the Human Resources Manager at BNBM PNG Ltd. In her role, she is primarily responsible for personnel recruitment, selection, and training within the company. With a deep understanding of labor laws, employment regulations, and practices in Papua New Guinea, she brought a wealth of professional experience to her position.

Throughout her 11 years with the company, Allison has not only efficiently handled various employee-related matters but also safeguarded the rights of employees and upheld the company's reputation. Additionally, she actively contributes to the development of the company by providing valuable insights and recommendations to the management team, aiming to enhance the localization of human resources management and drive market expansion and operational efficiency for company.

Deeply understanding the company's strategic goals and development needs, Allison recognizes the importance of building a talent pipeline and actively assists the management in implementing talent reserve plans. For instance, she spearheads the implementation of a management trainee program, recruiting university graduates and providing them with professional training and job rotation opportunities. Every graduation season, Allison leads her team to campus for recruitment activities. With her professional eye and unique selection methods, she has identified numerous outstanding talents for the company.

One notable success story is Fiona, who joined the company's headquarters through this program. During her internship, Fiona demonstrated exceptional learning abilities, completing tasks that typically take new employees two months to grasp in just one month. After her official employment, Fiona continued to excel in her work and was recognized as the Office's Outstanding Employee for two consecutive years.

As a Human Resources Manager, Allison places great importance on building employee relations. She maintains open and transparent communication with employees, actively listens to their opinions and needs, and addresses their concerns. She actively advocates for improved benefits and welfare for local employees, aiming to enhance their job satisfaction and loyalty. In the company's performance management process,

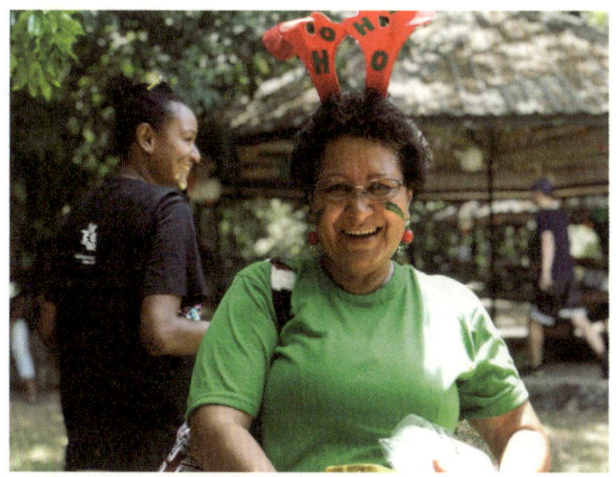

she collaborates with employees to set clear goals and provides timely feedback and guidance to help them improve and grow.

She states, "My job is to ensure that employees' performance aligns with the company's goals and standards. It brings me joy and fulfillment to see the employees I have recruited and nurtured achieving their career and personal goals. These moments serve as an endless source of motivation for me to continue serving the company."

Allison has a deep understanding of the cultural differences between China and Papua New Guinea. She encourages both Chinese and foreign employees to share their cultural backgrounds, customs, and traditions with each other. She actively assists the company in organizing cultural integration activities, such as employee sharing sessions on the origins and traditional customs of festivals celebrated in both countries. She also arranges fun activities to help employees experience different cultures, fostering mutual understanding and respect for cultural differences.

Not only is she a catalyst for cross-cultural integration, but she is also a practitioner herself. Four years ago, she sent her younger son, Simmons, to China to pursue his education. After graduation, Simmons joined a bank in Papua New Guinea. He expresses immense gratitude for the opportunity to learn about Chinese culture, the people, and the beloved Chinese cuisine. He intends to share the knowledge and experiences he gained in China with more young people in Papua New Guinea, hoping that they will develop a deeper understanding of and love for China.

Thanks to her experience working in Chinese companies and her child's study in China, Allison has developed a special affection for China. This year marks the tenth anniversary of the Belt and Road Initiative. When discussing her vision for cooperation between China and Papua New Guinea, Allison's eyes are filled with anticipation. She says, "The cooperation between China and Papua New Guinea holds vast prospects in terms of economy, culture, and society. The support that China has provided for Papua New Guinea's development has given us the ability and responsibility to bring prosperity to our own country. The Belt and Road Initiative is far-reaching and magnificent, and I hope that China and Papua New Guinea will continue to progress along this path of cooperation."

Personal Insights I am proud to be part of BNBM PNG LTD and to become a member of the global family of CNBM GROUP. This opportunity allows me to gain insights into the cultural differences of China and Papua New Guinea, and further recognize the role of culture in cross-border human resources management. And I will contribute my efforts to the developement of the company and work hand in hand with my colleagues to create a bright future.

当好新时代海外财务人的排头兵

张月德

2017 年加入中国建材

现任中建材投资赞比亚有限公司财务经理

2017 年，毕业于深圳大学会计系的张月德，满腔热情地加入中建投巴新公司财务部门，经过系统培训，快速成长。人手紧张时，他同时负责巴新首都、莱城等 4 家大体量建材店的财务工作。在巴新的经历，既磨炼出他吃苦耐劳的品格，也让他总结出一套高效的工作经验。

2019 年，在中建材投资赞比亚有限公司（以下简称赞比亚公司）运营之初，张月德按照上级工作安排被调往赞比亚。他快速融入新环境，提出了一系列接地气、好操作、有效果的工作方法，助推赞比亚公司管理水平的提升。

运营初期的赞比亚公司，门店销售、财务系统暂未实现对接，数据无法实现实时更新，张月德通过重新设计 SAP 系统报表，使当日数据可准确传送至公司总部，加强总部对分店的财务管控；得益于与业财数据的对接，在应收账款管理上他也更加得心应手，赞比亚公司应收账款周转率提升 59%。另一方面，他结合公司运营模式和财务管控要求，对业务及财务流程进行重新梳理和优化，使得公司内控水平大幅提高。同时，张月德主导推行线上办公流程，在保证提升办公效率的情况下，也为新冠疫情期间最大限度减少人员接触作出积极贡献。

经过系统升级和流程改进，赞比亚公司财务核算水平明显提高，月结工作效率提升 2.5 个工作日，审批操作效率提升了 50%。运营及管理效率的提升为公司高质量发展夯实基础。

在日常工作中，张月德深入学习赞比亚劳工法、地产政策、运营商行业资料等相关文件，同时积极与当地相关机构进行探讨，挖掘公司降本潜力，推动精细化管理水平。他提出对百余名外籍员工的劳务合同由短期合同转为长

期合同，配合定期考评制度，解决因短期合同造成的补偿款问题，有效降低10%的当地人工成本；他多次与赞比亚公司业主磋商协调，掌握谈判主动权，为公司成功压减27%的租金费用；他还通过优选服务运营商，在保证服务水准的前提下进行二次筛选，促使通信服务费用降低60%。

为提高当地财务人员工作的积极性，张月德选择以“引导机制+竞争机制+人文关怀”的组合原则来带领团队。为员工明确其未来职业发展方向，提供互动式培训，确保在特定模块人人会操作、人人在培训中受益，提升员工忠诚度和自豪感。为更好地融入当地员工队伍，他一直重视对员工的关怀，在一名员工妻子手术期间，他主动前往医院探望；在新员工表现不佳时，他经常引导其学习并且监督跟进、给予鼓励。目前，财务部已组建一支能独立完成财务核算的属地化团队。

“心中有阳光，脚下有力量”，作为新时代青年，张月德始终将外派机会看作一次珍贵的锤炼，在这个能扩展国际视野的平台上吸取能量，丰富学识，勇挑重担，不断解决问题、破解难题，为公司海外业务发展添砖加瓦。（中建材投资赞比亚有限公司）

个人体会 刚毕业能够加入中建材投资赞比亚有限公司，我感到十分幸运，公司海外平台完善的培训体系让我受益匪浅。从负责基础财务核算到财务管理，我与公司共同成长，希望为公司海外业务高质量发展作出更多贡献。

Competent Finance Manager in the New Era

Zhang Yuede

Joined CNBM in 2017
Finance Manager Of CNBM investment Zambia Ltd.

In 2017, Zhang Yuede, who graduated from Shenzhen University with a degree in accounting, joined the finance department of BNBM. He worked with enthusiasm and improved quickly after systematic training. When the department was extremely understaffed, he was responsible for the accounting of a total of four large building material stores in the PNG capital and Lae at the same time. It is because of the experience in PNG that he has honed his hard-working character and developed an efficient work approach.

In 2019 when CNBM Investment Zambia just started operation, Zhang Yuede was transferred to work in Zambia. He quickly integrated into the new environment and proposed a series of pratical and effective work methods, which helped to improve the management level of the company.

In the early stage of operation of the Zambia company, the sales and financial systems of stores were not yet connected, and the data could not be integrated in real time, Zhang Yuede redesigned the SAP system reports so that the data of the day could be accurately transmitted to the headquarters of the company to strengthen the financial monitoring of the stores; Thanks to the interface of business finance data, accounts receivable management is also more convenient, and the accounts receivable turnover rate of the Zambian company has increased by 59%. On the other hand, he combined the company's operation model and financial management requirements, reorganized and optimized the business and financial processes, significantly improving the company's level of internal management. At the same time, Zhang Yuede led the implementation of online work processes to ensure improved work efficiency while also making a positive contribution to minimizing human contact during the epidemic.

After system upgrade and process improvement, the financial accounting level of the Zambia company has been significantly improved, the efficiency of month-end closing has been improved by 2.5 working days, and the efficiency of approval operation has been increased by 50%. Improvements in operational and management efficiency provide a solid foundation for the company's high-quality development.

In his daily work, Zhang Yuede studied Zambian labor law, real estate policy, operator industry information and other related documents, while actively discussing with relevant local institutions to explore the company's cost reduction potential and

promote refined management to the next level. He proposed to change the labor contracts of more than 100 foreign employees from short-term contracts to long-term contracts, and with the help of the regular appraisal system, solved the problem of compensation payments caused by short-term contracts, effectively reducing local labor costs by 10%; He repeatedly negotiated and coordinated with the landlords of the company to get the upper hand in negotiation, successfully reducing rental costs by 27% for the company; By selecting service operators through secondary screening without compromsing on guaranteed service standards, he got a 60% reduction in the cost of communications services.

In order to improve the motivation of local finance staff, Zhang Yuede chose to lead the team with a combination of "guidance mechanism + competition mechanism + humanistic care". He provides interactive training to ensure that everyone knows how to operate the specific modules and benefits from the training to enhance employee loyalty and pride. In order to better integrate into the local workforce, he has always attached importance to the care of employees. When an employee's wife underwent a surgery, he went to the hospital to extend his care; when new employees performed poorly, he regularly offers them guidance, push and encouragement. At present, the Finance Department has set up a team consists of local employees that can complete financial accounting independently.

"With sunshine in your heart, there is power under your feet."As a young man in the new era, Zhang Yuede always regards every opportunity of working abroad as a precious training. He gains capabilities and enriches knowledge on the international platform that can expand vision, takes up heavy responsibilities, constantly solves problems and cracks difficulties, and contributes to the company's overseas business development.

Personal Insights I feel very fortunate to join CNBM Investment Co., Ltd. immediately after graduation, and I have benefited from the perfect training system of the company's overseas platform. From the position of basic financial accounting to financial management, I grow with the company and hope to make more contributions to the high-quality development of the company's overseas business.

为碲化镉太阳能电池插上腾飞的翅膀

贝蒂娜·施帕斯博士

2010 年加入中国建材

现任中国建材工程子公司 CTF Solar 研发部副主任

贝蒂娜·施帕斯博士杰出的科学生涯始于德国达姆施塔特。她在黑森州风景如画的本斯海姆小镇长大，对科学产生了浓厚的兴趣，这促使她进入了材料科学领域。她的学术之旅始于达姆施塔特大学，在那里，她在Jaegermann 教授的指导下学习半导体方面的专业知识。

贝蒂娜·施帕斯博士对材料科学的深刻理解使她在 Jaegermann 教授的“表面科学”研究小组中完成了关于碲化镉薄膜太阳能电池的毕业论文。随后，她在教授的指导下继续她的研究，攻读博士学位，专注于碲化镉薄膜太阳能电池的界面和背接触特性。

博士毕业后，贝蒂娜·施帕斯博士移居德国德累斯顿，将她的材料科学专业知识应用于半导体行业。她的主要职责是改进和调整用于生产存储芯片的等离子蚀刻工艺。

她对太阳能技术的兴趣使她回到了太阳能行业，在那里，她从事硅太阳能电池的表征工作。她在这一领域的重大贡献使她将焦点转移回碲化镉薄膜太阳能电池，该技术因其高转换效率和大规模生产潜力而受到关注。2010 年，贝蒂娜·施帕斯博士加入当时的中国建材工程子公司 CTF Solar，在那里，她利用自己对材料和半导体技术的理解来推动碲化镉薄膜太阳能电池技术的进步。

在 CTF Solar，她发挥了重要作用，利用自己的知识和经验，推动了碲化镉薄膜太阳能电池技术的进步。在此期间，她与德国弗劳恩霍夫研究所（FEP）建立了密切的合作。

她还在 CTF Solar 成立了一个研究和开发部门。这个部门最初由 3—4 名科学家组成，为今天的 20 人的研发部门奠定了基础。CTF Solar 指定并开发了几个试验性工具，以实现提高太阳能电池效率的工艺开发。

首先，心脏工具 CSS 镀膜被投入使用。公司成立了一个化学部门，并测试了最新的化学工艺。贝蒂娜·施帕斯博士主要负责溅射工艺和计量工具。

当时，贝蒂娜·施帕斯博士还推动了金属

无铜背面接触的发展。第一批效率超过 13% 的无铜太阳能电池被开发出来。位于德国凯尔克海姆的前实验室的一些工具被转移到德累斯顿并投入使用。

2011 年，中国建材集团旗下的中国建材工程收购了 CTF Solar。研发部门不断壮大，因此搬到了德累斯顿北部的一个更大的实验室。该实验室占地面积为 300m^2。贝蒂娜 · 施帕斯博士与同事们一起组织了实验室的搬迁，并建立了一个完全改进的实验室。

贝蒂娜 · 施帕斯博士在 2012—2015 年的几个项目中作出了重要贡献，并将碲化镉薄膜太阳能电池的转化效率提高到 15% 以上。实验室工艺被转化为生产工具的规范。作为一名科学家和工艺工程师，贝蒂娜 · 施帕斯博士支持溅射、激光和退火机器以及计量工具的规范，这需要她与供应商密切互动，以及在多个地点验收程序。

2016 年，贝蒂娜 · 施帕斯博士和同事们的研发和调查成果被转化到 CTF Solar 在中国的第一条生产线上。鉴于她的专业知识，贝蒂娜 · 施帕斯博士于 2017 年被提升为 CTF Solar 研发部门的副总监。她领导了一个由 20 名员工组成的团队，制定了公司的研究议程，并营造了一个创新的环境。她的领导能力和科学敏锐性对推动公司的成功和进一步提高公司的声誉起到了重要作用。2016—2022 年，贝蒂娜 · 施帕斯博士领导了两个受资助项目，每个项目为期 3 年，资金为 150 万欧元。2020 年，CTF Solar 再次搬迁至新址，占地面积达

1000m^2。

自 2016 年以来，在 CTF Solar 的研发部门，碲化镉薄膜太阳能电池的效率从 17.8% 提高到 20.85%，10 × 10cm^2 组件的效率从 14.4% 提高到 18.3%。

贝蒂娜 · 施帕斯博士于 2023 年 4 月访问邯郸生产线后，她十分支持采用碲化锌工艺。在 CTF Solar 团队的技术支持下，碲化镉薄膜太阳能组件的效率达到了 17%。贝蒂娜 · 施帕斯博士高度赞扬了邯郸碲化镉团队的辛勤工作。此次合作的成功给了贝蒂娜 · 施帕斯博士与邯郸碲化镉团队一起克服未来所有挑战的自信。她相信，在大家的共同努力下，薄膜太阳能市场的前景将更加广阔。（中国建材工程子公司 CTF Solar）

个人体会 在中国建材集团旗下从事太阳能行业工作，特别是在 CTF Solar 工作，对我有许多积极的影响，这是一个令人振奋和有成就感的职业选择。总的来说，在 CTF Solar 工作不仅令人满意，而且还可以通过提供清洁能源的解决方案为世界带来切实的改变。

Contributing to the Development of Cadmium Telluride Solar Cells

Dr. Bettina Späth

Joined CNBM in 2010

Vice Director of the R&D Department at CTF Solar

Dr. Bettina Späth's distinguished career in science began in Darmstadt, Germany. Growing up in the picturesque town of Bensheim in Hessia, she developed a keen interest in science, which propelled her into the field of material science. Her academic journey started at Darmstadt University, where she honed her expertise in semiconductors, guided by Professor Jaegermann.

Dr. Späth's impressive understanding of material science led to her completing her diploma thesis on CdTe thin film solar cells within Professor Jaegermann's "surface science" research group. She then continued her research under the professor's mentorship, pursuing a PhD focused on the interface and back contact properties of CdTe solar cells.

Post-PhD, Dr. Späth moved to Dresden, Germany, to apply her material science expertise in the semiconductor industry. Her primary responsibility was to improve and adapt plasma etching processes for the production of memory chips.

Her interest in solar technology drew her back to the solar industry, where she worked on silicon solar cell characterization. Her significant contributions in this field led to her shifting focus back to CdTe (Cadmium Telluride) solar cells, a technology gaining attention for its high conversion efficiency and potential for mass production. In 2010, Dr. Späth joined Roth&Rau/CTF Solar, where she leveraged her understanding of materials and semiconductor technology to drive advancements in CdTe solar cell technologies.

At CTF Solar, she took on a significant role, utilizing her knowledge and experience to drive advancements in CdTe solar cell technologies. During this time, she established a close cooperation with the German Fraunhofer Institute FEP.

She set up a research and development department in CTF Solar. This department, initially consisting of 3-4 scientists, laid the foundation for today's 20-person research and development department. Initially located at Fraunhofer FEP/Dresden, Germany, the entire front-end process chain was developed. CTF Solar specified and developed several pilot tools to enable the development on processes to increase the solar cell efficiency.

First, the heart tool CSS coating was put into operation. A chemical department was established and the latest chemical processes were tested.

Dr Bettina Späth was mainly responsible for the sputtering processes and metrology tools.

At that time, Dr Bettina Späth was able to drive forward the development of the metallic copper-free back contact. The first copper-free solar cells with an efficiency of >13% were developed. Several tools from the former laboratory in Kelkheim, Germany were transferred to Dresden and put into operation.

In 2011, CTIEC, part of the Chinese CNBM Group, acquired CTF Solar. The research and development department was growing and therefor moved to a bigger laboratory in the north of Dresden. The laboratory covered an area of 300 m^2. Together with her colleagues, Dr. Bettina Späth organized the transfer of the tools to the new location. New tools were specified and purchased and a complete upgraded laboratory was established.

Dr. Bettina Späth contributed in several founded projects in 2012-2015 and with this help, the CdTe conversion efficiency was rised to >15%. The laboratory processes were transferred into specifications of production tools. As a scientist and process engineer, Dr. Bettina Späth supported the specification of the sputtering, lasering and annealing machines as well the metrology tools. This included a close interaction with suppliers as well as several acceptance procedures at several location.

The results of the developments and investigations of Dr. Bettina Späth and her colleagues were transferred onto the first production line of CTF Solar in China in 2016. In recognition of her expertise, Dr. Späth was promoted to the role of Vice Director in the R&D department of CTF Solar in 2017. She led a team of 20 employees, shaping the company's

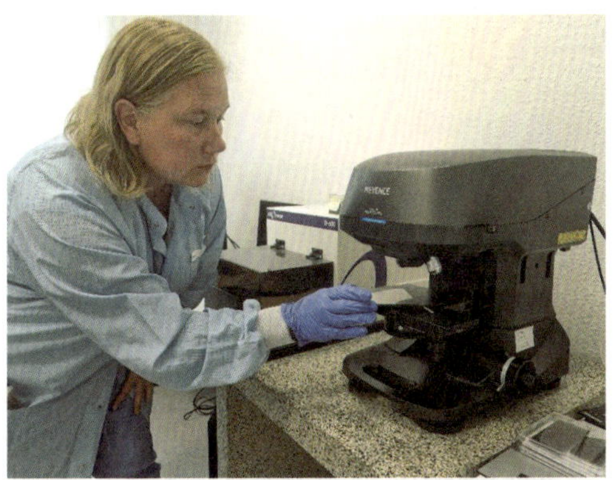

research agenda and fostering an innovative environment. Her leadership skills and scientific acumen were instrumental in driving the company's success and furthering its reputation. From 2016-2022 Dr. Bettina led two funded projects, each with a duration of 3 years and a funding of € 1.5 million. In 2020 CTF Solar moved again to a new location, covering an area of 1000 m^2.

Since 2016, the efficiency of CdTe solar cells has been improved from 17.8% to the remarkable value of 20.85% and that of 10*10 cm^2 modules from 14.4% to 18.3% in the R&D department of CTF Solar.

After Dr. Späth visited the Handan production line in April, she fully supported introducing the ZnTe process. With the technical support from CTF Solar team, the efficiency of CdTe thin film solar module reached 17%. Dr. Späth highly commended the hard work of HDN team. With the success of this cooperation, she has full confidence that we together can meet all challenges in the future. She believes that the prospect of CdTe solar cells market will be broader through everyone's efforts.

Personal Insights Working in the solar industry, specifically at CTF Solar, a subsidiary of the CNBN Group, offers numerous positive facets. In essence, working at CTF Solar not only offers professional fulfillment but also the chance to make a substantial difference to the world by offering clean energy solutions.

一腔热血赴重洋　硬汉亦有柔情时

薛承文

2016 年加入中国建材

现任上海凯盛节能工程技术有限公司工程管理部员工

“爸爸……”听着国内视频中传来的 1 岁零个月的女儿咿咿呀呀的学语声，远在千里之外的薛承文满含柔情地应和着。

这一幕发生在中国建材集团上海凯盛节能工程技术有限公司在土耳其 BASTAS 项目的工地上。由于时差的关系，薛承文正在利用中午饭后的时间和远在国内的幼女视频连线互动，这个家在山东的汉子此刻流露出的柔情让人动容。由于工作的关系，他舍下尚在襁褓中的女儿，踏上了国外项目管理的征程。

时间退回到 3 个月前，接到公司通知后，当他办理签证准备前往土耳其的时候，他深感压力重重，在和妻子、父母的沟通中，满是担忧和顾虑，奶奶和父母年事已高、孩子年幼、房子装修在即等问题都要抛给妻子一个人去承担，他始终难以启齿，当不得不说的时候，他的妻子已经感觉到了他的为难，主动提出让他不要想太多，趁着年轻去奋斗，家里的事情交给她处理。就这样，薛承文在匆忙中舍下家里的事情，风尘仆仆地奔赴土耳其 BASTAS 项目工地。

“Stop，stop……”薛承文大声对工长喊着，原来 SP 锅炉在安装中一名土耳其当地公司的工长把管片的吊装方向搞反了，这样会导致后面工序无法施工。工长很不理解地赶紧让吊装停了下来，他知道，薛工让停下来一定是有重要的问题，当他们拿着图纸和薛工对照时才明白过来，明白了原因后，大家纷纷给薛工竖起了大拇指，这位工长说：“是我们疏忽了，没有分清楚左视图和右视图的关系，谢谢薛工及时提醒，否则我们返工得浪费好几天的时间。”薛工谦虚地说：“这是我们两国图纸表达习惯不同造成的，只要我们以后多沟通交流，就可以避免。”工长主动和薛工握手，表示感谢。

这一幕发生在项目安装施工的高峰期，薛工来项目工地不到一个多月，很快就和所有人员打成一片，融入项目的工作氛围中。薛工成熟的技术、丰富的施工经验及满含激情的工作态度深深感染着项目团队的每一个成员。

“薛工，薛工……走，去吃饭了”，都很晚了，薛工一下班就躺下没有起来，到现在饭都没有去吃。薛工的这种异常情绪是很少见的。当第二天早上同事找他的时候，他满脸悲戚地沉声说：“昨天接到家里的信息，我的奶奶去世了。今天上午先转点钱过去，上午就能处理好，晚点过去上班，工地还有几件事需要去处理。”薛工自小在奶奶身边长大，对奶奶有着深厚的感情，他心底的悲伤是可以想到的，男儿有泪不轻弹，只是未到伤心时。此刻，拍拍肩膀胜过千言万语。这一幕发生在薛工刚来项目工地的半个月。

在繁忙的工作之余，团队成员经常一起交流，他积极提倡的一个观点：虽然中土文化、习惯截然不同，但是实事求是地看待问题、面对问题，大家才能形成客观的共识，否则各有角度，看法各有不同，那将导致无休止的争论，解决问题的效率将大打折扣，而且双方容易形成对立情绪，陷入恶性循环中。朴实的语言将解决问题的本质讲得通透，也很容易让人理解接纳。

薛工是一个平易近人的人，一个土耳其管理人员对他的评价让人记忆犹新：他忧郁的眼神中略带儒雅而又不失激情。

薛工就是这样一个好“战友”，虽然他还很年轻，然而他对妻儿满怀柔情，对长辈充满深情，对工作一腔激情！这样三份情贯穿在他的生活和工作中，他让同他一起工作过的同事们钦佩不已！时代需要英雄，但是时代更需要千千万万像薛工这样的平凡的人，在各自的岗位上书写时代的光荣与梦想。（上海凯盛节能工程技术有限公司）

个人体会 自入职上海凯盛节能工程技术有限公司以来，栉风沐雨，同舟共济，我与所有员工一样，见证了公司的蓬勃发展、蒸蒸日上，也在这个大家庭里不断成长。搭着“一带一路”的春风，乘坐在上海凯盛这艘行驶在丝绸之路的大船上，为土耳其 BASTAS 项目尽自己一份绵薄之力。

Tenderness of an Iron Man

Xue Chengwen

Joined CNBM in 2016

Employee of the Engineering Management Department at Shanghai Triumph Energy Conservation Engineering Co., Ltd.

"Papa...Papa..." Xue Chengwen's one-year-and-eight-month-old daughter babbled from home thousands of miles via a video call, and Xue Chengwen answered her tenderly.

This scene took place at the construction site of the Bastas project in Turkey, a key stop along the Belt and Road for the Shanghai Triumph Energy Conservation Engineering Co.,Ltd. Due to the time difference, Xue Chengwen was video chatting with his infant daughter back in China during his lunch break. Xue had to leave her behind when he went abroad to work on the Turkish project.

Three months ago, Xue Chengwen's company told him to get ready for his visa to Turkey. He felt a lot of pressure. He worried about his infant daughter, his elderly grandparents, and his home renovation. He didn't want to burden his wife, who had to handle everything alone. But when he finally shared his concerns, she supported him. She told him to focus on his career and not to worry too much. She said she could manage the home affairs. So Xue Chengwen left his family behind and went to the Bastas project site in Turkey.

"Stop, stop..." Chengwen Xue Chengwen shouted to the foreman. The foreman at the local Turkish company had incorrectly hoisted the pipe sections during the installation of the SP boiler. This mistake would cause problems in the later construction stages. The foreman, puzzled, immediately stopped the hoisting. He knew that if Xue asked them to halt, there must be a significant issue. After referring to the blueprints with Xue, they understood the problem and gave Xue a thumbs-up. The foreman said they had mixed up the left and right views and thanked Xue for his timely correction, which would save them several days of rework. Xue responded that this was just due to different drawing habits between the two countries, and it could be avoided with more communication in the future.

This incident occurred during the peak of project installation. Despite having arrived at the project site less than a month ago, Xue quickly integrated with the team and adapted to the project's working atmosphere. His mature technical skills, rich construction experience, and passionate work attitude deeply impressed every Chinese and Turkish manager and construction worker on the project.

"Xue, Xue... Let's go, it's time for dinner." One evening, Xue fell asleep right after work without eating dinner. He looked unsually sad. The next

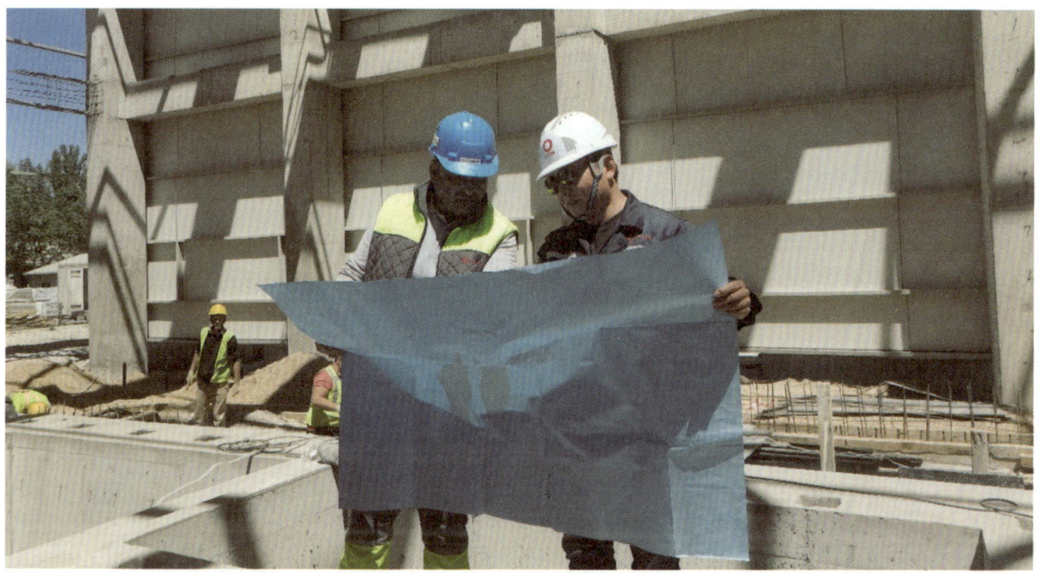

morning, he said with a sorrowful expression that his grandmother had passed away. His colleagues expressed condolences and asked him to take a few days off to deal with family matters. However, Xue refused, saying he would transfer some money home in the morning and come back to work later that day as there were a few tasks on site that he needed to do. Having grown up by his grandmother's side, Xue deep-seated grief.

Xue often said that even though Chinese and Turkish cultural customs are starkly different, but we could still cooperate effectively by adopting a realistic and objective attitude when facing issues. He said we had to avoid arguments and conflicts that would waste time and energy. He spoke clearly and confidently, and everyone respected him for that.

Xue Chengwen is approachable and popular. One Turkish manager remembers him vividly, describing his thoughtful gaze as subtly refined yet filled with passion.

Xue is an excellent "comrade-in-arms". Although young, he has deep love for his wife and child, profound respect for his elders, and unbridled enthusiasm for his work. Such a character has been fully displayed through his life and work, inspiring admiration from his colleagues. Our era needs heroes, and it relies on countless individuals like Xue Chengwen as its sturdy foundation.

Personal Insights Since joining Shanghai Triumph Energy Conservation Engineering Co.,Ltd., I've sailed through challenges alongside all other employees. I have witnessed company's vigorous development and rise, while also keep growing and emulating within this big family. Thanks to the Belt and Road Initiative, I've boarded the vessel of Shanghai Triumph as it keeps sailing on the Silk Road, contributing my best efforts to the BASTAS project in Turkey.

行劳神不倦，奋斗趁年华。

志存高远的海外建材人，扎根一线拓市场，团结协作创佳绩。

他们，挥洒青春，奋发向上，助力互联互通，贡献中国智慧。

Strive hard with a fighting spirit in the prime years.

CNBM's ambitious overseas employees firmly establish themselves on the frontline to explore new markets, collaborating to achieve remarkable results.

They dedicate their youth and take an active role in enhancing connectivity and contributing Chinese wisdom to the world.

丝路成材篇

GROWTH STORIES OF YOUNG EMPLOYEES

让每一分耕耘都有收获

亨利·卡瓦利卡
2018 年加入中国建材
现任职于中国建材赞比亚工业园财务部

我是资产财务部的亨利·卡瓦利卡，出生于赞比亚恩多拉，今年 30 岁，毕业于卢萨卡国家公共行政学院。2018 年我来到中国建材赞比亚工业园，已经在这里工作了四年多。我是一个性格开朗、喜欢结交朋友的人。自进入本公司工作以来，我努力通过“理论知识 + 应用实践”双驱动快速实现自我提升，并在我的中方同事们的帮助和鼓励下，高效地推动了各项工作的有序开展。

中国有句老话：“不积跬步，无以至千里。”我作为一名会计，肩负着细致且烦琐的工作，这要求我有足够的细心和耐心，将所见所学应用于实践。刚入职时，我压力很大，于是我先给自己制定了一个“小目标”：要在短时间内迅速掌握业务知识，丰富理论储备，实现独立上岗。面对新工作、新业务，我明白一个道理：只有自己积极主动、虚心好学，方能以勤补拙。于是我在学好专业知识的基础上，利用业余时间阅读了大量的书籍，拓展了视野。

从最初入职时小毛病不断，到现在成长为一名业务熟练的基础核算会计，我一方面“苦练内功”，另一方面向与我朝夕相处的领导、同事学习。在平时的工作中，遇到不清楚的问题我会向中方主管会计请教，他的专业指导使我少走了很多弯路，受益匪浅。不仅如此，我还积极参加公司组织的各类社会实践活动和各种文体活动，通过参与这些活动增进了我与中国同事之间的了解，加深了彼此的友谊。工作中我们是携手奋进的伙伴，生活中我们是亲密无间的“铁哥们儿”。

疫情期间，我积极响应公司的疫情防控管理措施，每天接班后主动承担起办公区的防疫消杀工作，对办公室内的键盘、鼠标、办公桌以及地面进行消毒液的喷洒或酒精擦拭，在班组的防疫工作中贡献了自己的一份力量。当我的赞籍同事家中有事请假、岗位临时空缺时，我都会主动代班。“团结一心、互帮互助”是我在这个大家庭中的深刻体会，我坚持将这一理念付诸实践。

目前公司收入款项业务较多，开支单据异常频繁。在审核每笔单据报销或支付时，我都会认认真真地审核报账手续是否齐全、报销原始单据是否合法有效、大小写金额是否正确，只有完全符合公司管理规定的单据，我才予以支付。因此，我实现了全年支付业务“零差错”，准确率为 100%。未来，我会尽心履行好一名会计的岗位职责。

“问渠哪得清如许，为有源头活水来”，活水在哪里？在领导无微不致的指导与关怀里，在同事们勤劳协作、无私奉献里，在个人无怨无悔的艰辛劳动里。在广阔的建材平台上，因为财务工作，我发挥了自我价值、磨炼了我的意志、让我收获到了快乐。但我清楚，我距离“优秀的财务人员”的目标还有一定的差距，不过，我坚信，“一份耕耘，一份收获”，只要秉承“敬业、勤奋、求精、务实”财务工作精神，肩负“材料创造美好世界”的使命，以满腔热忱投入工作，明天我将收获更多！（中国建材赞比亚工业园）

个人体会 在广阔的建材领域，在财务工作中，我实现了自我价值。这份工作磨炼了我的意志，让我收获到了快乐。秉承“敬业、勤奋、求精、务实”的财务工作精神，肩负“材料创造美好世界”的使命，以满腔热忱投入工作，明天我将收获更多！

Dedicated CNBMer in Zambia: Effort Pays off

Henry Kawalika

Joined CNBM in 2018

Asset Finance Department of CNBM Zambia Industrial Park

My name is Henry Kawalika from the Asset Finance Department of CNBM Zambia Industrial Park. I was born in Ndola, Zambia. I am 30 years old and graduated from Lusaka National Institute of Public Administration. I came to CNBM in 2018 and have been working here for more than 4 years. I am a cheerful person who likes to make friends. Since I started working at this company, I have tried to achieve rapid self-improvement through the dual drive of "theoretical knowledge & application practice". With the help and encouragement of my Chinese colleagues, I have effectively promoted the orderly implementation of various works.

An ancient Chinese saying goes, " A long journey can be covered only by taking one step at a time". As an accountant, I shoulder meticulous and tedious work, which requires sufficient carefulness and patience from me to apply what I have learned into practice. When I first joined the company, I was under great pressure. So I set "small goals" for myself – to learn the business knowledge in the short time and enrich the theoretical reserves to work independently. Faced with new work and business, I understand that only by being proactive, humble, and studious can I make up for my shortcomings through diligence. Therefore, on the basis of learning professional knowledge well, I read abundant books to broadened my horizons.

I often made mistakes when I first came, but now I have grown into a skilled basic accounting accountant. On the one hand, it benefits from self-training, on the other hand, I also learn from my leaders and colleagues with whom I get along day and night. During daily work, I often ask the Chinese accountant in charge for advice when I had some confuses. His professional guidance has saved me a lot of detours and benefited a lot. Besides, I have also participated in various social practice activities and sports and cultural activities organized by company, which enhanced the understanding and friendship between me and my Chinese colleagues. In work, we are team partners forging ahead hand in hand, and in life, we are close buddies side by side.

During the pandemic, I actively responded to our company's epidemic prevention and control

management measures, and undertook the epidemic prevention work in our office. I sprayed disinfectant and wiped alcohol on the public keyboard, mouse, desk and floor, making my own contribution to the epidemic prevention work of the team. When there is a temporary vacancy of our colleagues, I will take the initiative to cover for them. “Solidarity and mutual help” is my profound experience in this big family, and I'd like to put it into practice.

At present, our company has a lot of income and frequent expense bills. When reviewing the reimbursement or payment of each document, I will carefully check whether the procedures are complete, whether the original documents are legal and valid and whether the case amount is correct. Only when the document fully complies with the regulations, can I pay. Therefore, I have achieved "zero errors" in the payment business throughout the year, with an accuracy rate of 100%, and fulfilled my duties as an accountant with all my heart.

"Ask where the canal is so clear, because there is flowing water from the source", where is the flowing water? Under the meticulous guidance and care of the leaders, in the hard work of colleagues, in the selfless dedication, in the hard work of individuals without complaints or regrets. Because of the financial work, I have demonstrated my self-worth; because of this job, I have tempered my will, and every time I complete the work well, I will feel a sliver of happiness, because happy work makes me feel happy. Although I have made certain achievements in the financial work position, there is still a certain gap from the goal of excellent financial personnel. However, I firmly believe that "hard work pays off", as long as I enthusiastically adhere to the financial work spirit of "dedication, diligence, refinement, and pragmatism", I will definitely do better in financial work tomorrow.

Personal Insights On the stage of CNBM Zambia, I exert my self-worth, temper my will, let me harvest happiness due to my work. As long as adhering to the "dedication, diligence, excellence, pragmatic" spirit of financial work, shoulder the "material to create a better world" mission, with enthusiasm into the work, tomorrow I will gain more!

光速成长的管理新手

易卜拉欣·森戈·穆罕穆德

2022年加入中国建材
现任北新建材工业（坦桑尼亚）有限公司石膏板坦桑厂车间主任助理

一口流利的中文、满脸灿烂的笑容，文质彬彬的易卜拉欣毕业于多多马大学孔子学院汉语专业，在坦桑尼亚属于妥妥的高学历人才。

2022年，懂汉语的易卜拉欣加入了北新建材所属坦桑北新。短短一年间，他从一位石膏板行业的“小白”，光速成长，蜕变为一名基层管理人员，现担任石膏板坦桑厂车间主任助理。

易卜拉欣光速成长的背后，不仅仅是因为他拥有聪明才智。

入职北新后，面对石膏板生产这个全新的领域，易卜拉欣无惧挑战，积极主动学习石膏板产品知识和岗位操作技能。在公司安排下，他在石膏板生产线不同的岗位进行轮岗学习。

每个岗位，他都是满怀热情、全心投入。他谦虚好学，利用自己的语言优势，如饥似渴地向中方技术专家学习。

每天，他都带着问题来上班，积极向老员工请教解惑，然后自己再思考、实践。工作中，他时刻留心观察设备运行状态，特别是异常情况以及设置不同技术参数时对产品质量的影响，及时做好记录。经过不断地摸索和学习，易卜拉欣进步神速，很快便基本掌握了石膏板生产基本工艺流程及各岗位操作技能。

对于坦桑北新这样的海外企业来讲，促进中外员工的融合至关重要，而翻译起着重要的作用。

易卜拉欣利用自己的语言优势，工作中积极协助中方管理人员把生产、经营、管理的理念准确地传达给每一位坦桑员工，也把坦桑员工的想法、创意、建议及时反馈给公司的管理人员，促进了坦桑北新管理层与坦桑员工之间良好的沟通和公司的融合发展。

他协助坦桑北新落实“一带两训”员工管理模式，把中文翻译成当地语言，让坦桑籍员工能更好地理解岗位职责、产品工艺技术要求等，更好地掌握产品质量控制知识、岗位操作规程等，不断提升专业技能和岗位技能水平，从而使公司培养出更多的坦桑籍技术骨干。

在翻译的过程中，他不厌其烦、耐心给同

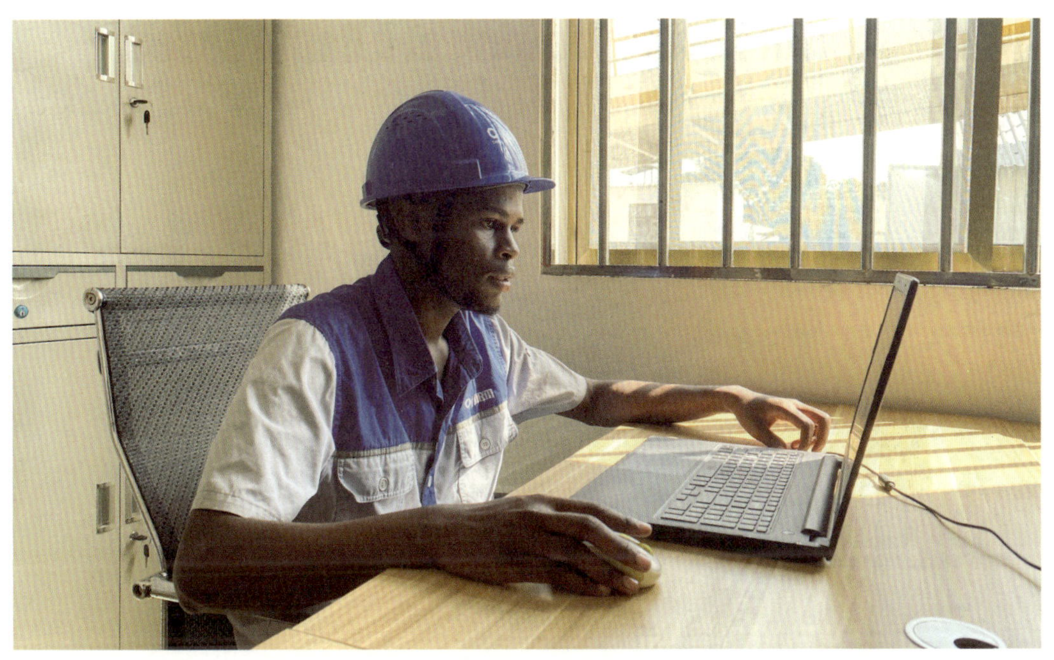

事一遍遍讲解，直至他们理解。而他自己也在一次次翻译过程中，不断吸取养分，进一步加深对坦桑北新和工作的认知，学到了更多中方员工的工作技能，实现了自我成长。

光速成长的易卜拉欣很快便承担起部分管理和培训工作。他积极学习公司的各项规章制度，并翻译成斯瓦西里语后对当地员工进行培训和宣贯，协助公司将制度要求更好地在广大当地员工中落实落地。

他还承担起公司的安全管理工作，积极贯彻落实公司“三不伤害”——不伤害自己、不伤害他人、不被他人伤害原则，时刻提醒和监督当地员工按照安全操作规程开展工作，以确保所有生产活动都是在安全、规范的前提下进行，提升了员工们的安全意识。

“我在坦桑北新工作得很开心，也感谢公司给我提供了这么好的机会。公司非常尊重我们本地员工的信仰和习惯，考虑到我们的饮食习惯，把午餐时间定为中午 1 点到 2 点；在‘8 · 28 文化节’期间举行我们最喜爱的足球比赛……这些都让我感受到公司满满的关怀。今后，我也会更加努力工作，用工作成绩来回报公司的信任。”易卜拉欣感动地说。

易卜拉欣年仅 24 岁，好学又努力，这位管理新手正在快速成长为一名既懂技术又善管理的复合型人才，为坦桑北新属地化经营和人才培养提供了成功的样板和宝贵的经验。〔北新建材工业（坦桑尼亚）有限公司〕

个人体会 当我刚来坦桑北新工作时，没有太多操作自动化设备的经验，但现在我已经学会了如何操作设备，而且还能给其他同事进行培训。感谢坦桑北新让我有机会为我的国家坦桑尼亚工业化发展贡献自己的微薄力量，今后我将继续提升我的技能和知识，以便能够在公司内承担更多责任。

A Management Novice Growing at a Rapid Speed

Ibrahim Sengo Mohamed

Joined CNBM in 2022

The Assistant to the Workshop Director of the gypsum board plant of BNBM Building Materials Industry (Tanzania) Limited

Ibrahim Sengo Mohamed, who is fluent in Chinese and gentle, and smiles brightly, graduated from the Confucius Institute at the University of Dodoma, majoring in Chinese. In Tanzania, Ibrahim is undoubtedly a well-educated talent.

In 2022, Ibrahim, who can speak Chinese, joined BNBM Tanzania affiliated to BNBM. In just one year, he grew up at a rapid speed from a "green hand" in the gypsum board manufacturing to a grass-roots manager, and now he is the assistant to the workshop director of the gypsum board Tanzania plant.

Ibrahim's growth at a rapid speed is not just because he is clever or gifted.

After joining BNBM, facing the brand-new field of gypsum board production, Ibrahim actively learned the product knowledge and operation skills of gypsum board without fear of challenges. Under the arrangement of the company, he studied in rotation in different posts on the gypsum board production line. In every post, he is full of enthusiasm and dedication. He is modest and eager to learn. Through taking advantage of language, he eagerly learns from Chinese technical experts.

Every day, he comes to work with questions, actively asks senior staff for answers, and then thinks and practices by himself. During his work, he always pays attention to the running status of equipment, especially the abnormal situation and the influence of setting different technical parameters on product quality, and makes records in time. After continuous exploration and study, Ibrahim made rapid progress, and soon basically mastered the basic technological process of gypsum board production and the operation skills of each post.

For an overseas enterprise like BNBM Tanzania, it is very important to promote the integration of Chinese and foreign employees, and translation plays an important role.

Th rough taking advantage of language, Ibrahim actively assisted Chinese managers in accurately conveying the concepts of production, operation and management to every Tanzanian employee, and timely fed back the ideas, creativity and suggestions of Tanzanian employees to the managers of the company, which promoted good communication between the management of BNBM Tanzania and Tanzanian employees and the integrative development of the company.

He assisted BNBM Tanzania in implementing the new employee management mode of "Guidance and Training", and translates Chinese into the local language, so that Tanzanian employees could better understand job responsibilities and product process technical requirements, better master product quality control knowledge and operation procedures, as well as constantly improve their professional skills and post skills, thus enabling the company to cultivate more Tanzanian technical backbones.

In the process of translation, he patiently explained to his colleagues over and over again until they understood. In which, he also constantly absorbed knowledge, further deepened his understanding of BNBM Tanzania and work, learned more work skills from Chinese employees, and achieved self-growth.

Ibrahim, who grew up at a rapid speed, soon undertook some management and training work. He actively studied the company's rules and regulations, translated them into Kiswahili, trained local employees, and assisted the company in better implementing the system requirements among local employees.

He also undertakes the safety management of the company, actively implements the principle of "three no injuries", which is not hurting himself, not hurting others or being hurt by others. Besides, he always reminds and supervises local employees to work in accordance with safety operation procedures, so as to ensure that all production activities are carried out on the premise of safety and standardization, enhancing employees' safety awareness.

"I have a great time working in BNBM Tanzania and I would like to express my gratitude to the company for providing me with such a good opportunity. The company has great respect for the beliefs and habits of our local employees. Considering our eating habits, the company sets lunch time from 13:00 to 14:00, and holds our favorite football match during the Company Cultural Festivals on August 28, which make me feel the full care of the company. In the future, I will work harder and repay the trust of the company with my achievements. "Ibrahim said with emotion.

Ibrahim is only 24 years old, studious and hard-working. This management novice is rapidly growing into a compound talent who understands technology and is good at management, providing a successful model and valuable experience for the new localized management and talent training in BNBM Tanzania.

Personal Insights When I first started my new job in BNBM Tanzania, I didn't have much experience in operating automation equipment, but now I have learned how to operate the equipment and can train other colleagues. Thanks to BNBM Tanzania for giving me the opportunity to contribute to the industrialization of my country Tanzania. I will continue to upgrade my skills and knowledge in the future so that I can take on more responsibilities in the company.

真诚以待的暖男

阿兹江·霍希莫夫

2019 年加入中国建材

现任北新建材中亚外资有限公司行政兼翻译

阿兹江·霍希莫夫个头不高，肌肉不少，大大的眼睛眨呀眨，仿佛会说话，他是一位名副其实的乌兹别克斯坦暖男。

他曾留学中国，是公司里少有的掌握几门语言的乌兹方员工，会说乌兹语、俄语和汉语。2019 年 8 月加入北新建材所属中亚北新后，他担任行政兼翻译工作。他爱岗敬业、尽职尽责，获得公司和同事的一致认可，经过 4 年的历练，如今已经成长为公司的骨干员工，对外事务方面的工作更是做得有声有色。

在项目建设前期，他积极与政府部门沟通协调，及时准确地传达双方的意见和建议。一次次谈判、一封封信函、一通通电话……在不知道忙碌了多少个日夜后，各种问题一一解决。他一次次的辛苦付出最终换来了项目建设的稳步推进。在解决问题的过程中，他不断积累，进一步了解了政府流程、银行事务、税务规定、签证制度等，并将自己学到的知识与其他同事分享。

2020 年年初新冠肺炎疫情暴发后，中亚北新回国的中方人员受疫情影响无法及时返回，即便辗转返回也需要长时间的隔离观察，人员短缺问题对项目建设工作产生很大的影响。

困难时刻，阿兹江站了出来。他冒着被感染的风险，加班加点，完成当地政府对 36.9 公顷项目地块要求的所有手续，顺利取得土地使用权证。他还督促工厂围墙的施工进度，及时拍照传回国内并定期汇报，让国内领导及时了解围墙施工进度。他还积极配合和协助中方员工顺利完成了各项工作任务，保障了项目按照进度有序推进。

2021 年 10 月，中亚北新土建正式开始施工。在此之前，阿兹江协助公司拿到项目环评结论和施工许可，完成消防和天然气图纸的审批。

在中亚北新员工间流传着一句话：有事就找阿兹江。可见阿兹江的好人缘。他不仅脾气温和，待人友善，乐于助人，而且办事妥帖周到，得到了大家一致认可。

他还很贴心，是个十足的暖男。疫情期间，在中方人员感染新冠后，他不惧感染、不怕麻烦，贴身照顾，每天带着笑容鼓励他们，帮助他们尽快康复，让大家深受感动。平时，他也会问候生病的同事，送小礼物给予安慰，还会时不时地从浩罕市里带来同事爱吃的点心，在同事的惊喜中，他大大的眼睛笑成了一条缝。

这就是阿兹江，他对公司的爱、对同事的爱是发自内心的，并不断感染着身边的同事。他的付出也换来了公司领导的信赖和同事们的尊敬。在他结婚时，公司的领导全员出席，直到现在他还经常拿出结婚录像给大家观看；他女儿出生的时候，全体员工又共聚一堂，用心为他庆祝，分享他的喜悦。

4 年的时光里，阿兹江见证了中亚北新从无到有的过程。他也与公司一起成长进步，变得更加自信、更加从容。

阿兹江只是中亚北新外籍员工的一个代表、一个缩影。越来越多的当地员工在各自的岗位上兢兢业业，努力掌握专业技能，做好本职工作的同时，开始学习汉语，了解中国文化。他们同中方员工一样，都是中亚北新不可或缺的宝贵财富。（北新建材中亚外资有限公司）

个人体会 真的很荣幸能加入北新建材这个大家庭。亲爱的领导和同事们，在我什么也不会的时候，有你们教我；在我迷茫彷徨的时候，有你们指路；在我受到委屈的时候，有你们宽慰；在我大喜的日子，有你们一起分享。认识你们，此生之幸！

Warm-Hearted Young Man of BNBM CENTRAL ASIA

Azizjon Hoshimov

Joined CNBM in 2019

The Administrator and Interpreter of BNBM Building Materials Central Asia

Azizjon Hoshimov is a young and warm-hearted man from Uzbekistan. Despite his modest height and well-built physique, his big eyes blink as if they can speak.

Having studied in China, Azizjon is one of the few employees in the Company who is proficient in multiple languages, including Uzbek, Russian, and Chinese. Since joining BNBM CENTRAL ASIA in August 2019, he has been working in administration and translation. He is dedicated and responsible, earning recognition from the Company and his colleagues. After four years of working, he has grown into a backbone employee of the Company, particularly excelling in his work in external affairs.

During the initial stages of project construction, he played an active part in communicating and coordinating with government departments, promptly and accurately conveying opinions and suggestions of both sides. Through numerous negotiations, letters, and phone calls, and after countless days and nights of hard work, all the issues were resolved smoothly. His hard work ultimately led to the steady progress of the project. In the process of solving problems, he accumulated knowledge and gained a deeper understanding of governmental procedures, banking affairs, tax regulations, and visa systems, and shared the knowledge he acquired with his colleagues.

In early 2020, when the COVID-19 pandemic broke out, Chinese personnel from BNBM CENTRAL ASIA who had returned to China were unable to come back promptly due to the pandemic. Even if they managed to return, they had to undergo long periods of quarantine, causing a personnel shortage, which had a significant impact on the project construction.

It was Azizjon who offered his hand during this challenging time. Despite the risk of being infected, Azizjon still worked overtime to complete all the procedures required the approval from the government of Fergana Region for the use of 36.9-hectare land plot, and obtained the land use right certificate successfully. While supervising the construction of the plant's perimeter wall, he would also take photos and send them back to China together with regular reports, allowing the domestic leadership to stay informed about the progress. He also actively cooperated with and assisted Chinese employees in completing various work tasks, ensuring that the project progressed in an orderly manner according to the schedule.

In October 2021, the civil construction of BNBM CENTRAL ASIA officially commenced. Prior to this, Azizjon assisted the company in obtaining the project's environmental impact assessment conclusion and construction permit, completing the approval of fire protection and natural gas drawings.

A saying circulates among BNBM CENTRAL ASIA employees: "If you need help, go find Azizjon," which shows how well-liked he is. With a gentle temperament, Azizjon treats people with kindness, and works in a meticulous and thoughtful manner, which earns him recognition from everyone.

He is considerate and is a truly warm-hearted man. During the pandemic, when Chinese personnel were infected with COVID-19, he took care of them fearlessly and selflessly, encouraging them with a smile every day and helping them recover as soon as possible, leaving a deep impression on his colleagues. He would also care about colleagues who were ill and give them small gifts for comfort. Apart from that, he would bring snacks from Kokand that his colleagues loved, and his big eyes would turn into slits as he smiled in response to their surprised and grateful thanks.

This is Azizjon. His care for the company and his colleagues comes from the bottom of his heart and is evident in his words and actions, constantly infecting those around him.

His dedication has earned him the trust of company leaders and the respect and affection of his colleagues. When he got married, all the company leaders attended his wedding, and even now he often brings out the wedding video for everyone to watch and relive the moment. When his daughter was born, all the employees gathered together to celebrate and share in his joy.

Over the course of four years, Azizjon has witnessed the transformation of BNBM CENTRAL ASIA from nothing to something. He has grown and progressed alongside the Company, becoming more confident and composed.

Azizjon is just one representative, one epitome, of the foreign employees at BNBM CENTRAL ASIA. More and more local employees are working diligently in their respective positions, striving to master professional skills and performing their duties while starting to learn Chinese and understand Chinese culture. Same as the Chinese personnel, they are an indispensable and valuable asset to BNBM CENTRAL ASIA.

Personal Insights I am truly honored to be part of the BNBM family. Dear leaders and colleagues, it's you who taught me when I knew nothing; it's you who guided me when I was lost and confused; it's you who comforted me when I felt wronged; and it's lucky to have you share my joy on my happiest days. It is the greatest fortune in my life to know all of you!

中国企业为我们带来了实惠和好处

阿罕默德·瑟利曼

2012 年加入中国建材

现任巨石埃及公司副总经理

技术输出，树立榜样，“授人以鱼，不如授人以渔”。

上午 8 时左右，阿罕默德·瑟利曼来到公司，安排好当天工作计划后，便与几位分管部门负责人召开晨会。布置完工作，他马不停蹄地前往生产计划、成品仓库办公室，了解排产计划和出货情况。

瑟利曼是中国巨石埃及玻璃纤维股份有限公司副总经理。2022 年年底，巨石埃及年产 12 万吨玻璃纤维生产线投入使用，使得巨石埃及玻璃纤维基地年设计总产能达到 32 万吨，目前是非洲大陆最大的玻璃纤维生产基地。由此，瑟利曼的工作更加忙碌，也有了更大成就感。

时间回到 11 年前，瑟利曼通过巨石埃及公司的 Facebook 招聘平台应聘加入公司。当时公司还在建设当中，为了给日后投产储备足够的技术和管理人员，新招聘的一批员工都会被送往中国巨石总部进行为期半年的学习培训，这对埃及刚毕业的大学生来说是一个再好不过的机会了。这源于巨石埃及通过各种方式招聘本地员工，包括在国外社交媒体平台上发布广告招聘大学生，之后，将他们送到中国总部培训，优化巨石埃及的员工培养体系。

瑟利曼同其他人一样想珍惜这个机会，但当时他的父亲身患重病，需要人照顾，他犹豫再三，在征得家人同意后，最终选择去中国培训。就在他培训临近结束的时候，他得知父亲去世的消息，于是他征得公司同意后立即返回埃及料理后事。

当时正赶上大批量的生产设备和办公用品从国内发过来，很多集装箱因来不及卸货而滞留在公司，如不及时清理集装箱，多放一天公司就要多支付一天的费用。瑟利曼只用了一周的时间将家里的事情处理完就回到公司上班，他积极组织人员清理集装箱，每天都干到筋疲力尽，最终，在他的带领下，所有集装箱被及时清理，为公司节省了一大笔滞箱费。当问到他为什么这么拼命时，他只说：“为了抓住巨石这个机会，父亲在生病的时候我没能照顾他，

但在巨石中国总部培训时，我被巨石的规模震撼到了，我要抓住这个机会，利用好这个平台，努力提升自己的能力，让家里人过上好日子，让父亲放心！”

公司投运后，瑟利曼从一名络纱工艺员做起，伴随着巨石埃及公司一路成长，2014 年，他从一名工艺员晋升为车间主任，生产现场成为他提升和磨炼自己的平台，他认真钻研车间管理，很快就找到了既符合生产要求又符合当地实际的管理方法。在他的带领下，车间从现场到生产都有了很大的改观和进步，他也成为公司不可或缺的埃方管理人才。因其出色的工作表现，他连续 3 年获得公司先进工作者称号，并于 2017 年顺利晋升成为埃及公司第一位分管生产的埃方高管。

他继续积极创新管理方法，加强质量控制，使车间各项生产指标都顺利达标，在他的梳理下，车间的管理变得顺畅和通达，他将埃及本土文化和巨石文化融为一体，成为埃及公司本土化推进过程中的一面旗帜，为埃及当地员工树立了榜样。

在人才培养方面，巨石搭建了学习和晋升的平台。在这里，每个员工都能像瑟利曼一样，通过努力工作实现自身的价值。每年优秀的业务骨干还可以去中国巨石总部学习交流，把先进的技术和管理理念带回埃及，造福建设自己的家乡。近几年，埃方高管和埃方中层本土化比例提升较快，目前，7 人高管队伍中已有 2 名埃方高管，并对埃方高管提出培养后备高管人选的考核指标，使得本土化推进工作在埃及中层队伍中形成自我造血功能。

11 年时间，在巨石埃及，他从青涩走向老练；从络纱工艺员成长为副总经理，哪里需要他就出现在哪里，带领着团队为巨石发展、为埃及发展贡献自己的力量。（巨石埃及公司）

个人体会 现在我已经在公司工作 11 年了，这 11 年，我从对企业生产管理一窍不通的大学生成为有技术有经验的中资企业的高管，这一切是我一开始不敢想象的。我要感谢巨石对我的培养，在这里我感觉和中国同事都是一家人，我愿意为公司的“十四五”规划再添砖加瓦。

Chinese Enterprises Bring Real Benefits to Us

Ahamed Soliman

Joined CNBM in 2012
The Deputy General Manager of Jushi Egypt

Give a man a fish and he will eat for a day. Teach a man to fish and he will eat for the rest of his life.

Around 8 a.m., Ahmed Soliman arrived at the company and made the working schedule for the day before holding morning meetings with several department directors in charge. After assigning work, he went to the production planning and finished product warehouse office immediately to see the production scheduling and shipment situation.

Soliman is the Deputy General Manager of Jushi Egypt. At the end of 2022, Jushi Egypt put into use a glass fiber production line with an annual output of 120,000 tons, making the annual designed total production capacity of Jushi Egypt glass fiber base reach 320,000 tons. Currently, it is the largest glass fiber production base in Africa. As a result, Soliman's work became busier and he felt a greater sense of achievement.

Back 11 years ago, Soliman applied to join the company through the Facebook recruitment platform of Jushi Egypt . At that time, the company was still under construction. In order to reserve sufficient technical and managerial personnel for future production, the new recruit were sent to the headquarter in China for a six-month study and training. This was a great opportunity for newly graduated Egyptian college students. At the same time, it optimized the company's employee training system.

Soliman, like everyone else, wanted to cherish this opportunity. But at that time, his father was seriously ill and needed someone to take care of him. He hesitated, and after obtaining the consent of his family, he ultimately chose to go to China for training. Near the end of his training, he learned of the news of his father's death, so he immediately returned to Egypt with the company's permission to take care of his affairs.

At that time, a large number of production equipment and office supplies were being shipped from China, and many containers were stuck in the company. If the containers can't be loaded in a timely manner, the company will pay an additional fee per day. Soliman only took one week to complete his family affairs and returned to work. He actively organized personnel to clean the containers and worked until exhausted every day. In the end, under his leadership, all containers were loaded in time, saving the company a large amount of demurrage fees. When asked why he worked so hard, he only said, "In order to seize the opportunity of Jushi, I couldn't take care of my father when he was sick. However, during the training at Jushi's headquarter in China, I was shocked by the scale of the company. I want to seize this opportunity, make good use of this platform, and strive to improve my abilities, so that my family can live a good life and my father can rest in peace."

After the company was put into operation, Soliman started as a winding craftsman and grew with Jushi Egypt. After improving and refining himself, he was promoted from a craftsman to a workshop director in 2014. He diligently studied workshop management and quickly found management methods that met production requirements and local realities. Under his leadership, the workshop has made significant changes and progress in both on-site and production, and he has also become an indispensable Egyptian management talent for Jushi Egypt. Because of his excellent work performance, he was awarded the title of Exemplary Individual for three consecutive years, and in 2017, he was successfully promoted to become the first Egyptian executive in charge of production in Egypt.

He continued to actively innovate management methods, strengthen quality control, and make all production indicators of the workshop reach the standard smoothly. And the workshop management became smooth and accessible. He integrated Egypt's local culture and the company's culture, promoting localization of Jushi Egypt and setting an example for local employees.

In terms of skill cultivation, Jushi has built a platform for learning and promotion. Every employee can achieve their own value through hard work, just like Soliman. Every year, outstanding business backbones can also go to the headquarters of Jushi in China to learn and exchange advanced technology and management concepts, bringing them back to Egypt to benefit the construction of their hometown. In recent years, the localization ratio of Egyptian executives and Egyptian middle-level cadres executives has increased rapidly. Currently, there are two Egyptian executives in the 7-person executive team, and evaluation indicators for cultivating reserve executive candidates have been proposed for Egyptian executives, promoting localization and forming a self-hematopoietic function in the Egyptian middle-level cadres' team.

During the past 11 years in Jushi Egypt, Soliman went from green to experienced,growing from a winding craftsman to a deputy general manager. He appears wherever in need, leading the team to contribute to the development of the company and the Egypt.

Personal Insights I have been working in the company for 11 years now. In these 11 years, I have grown from a college student with no knowledge to a senior executive in a Chinese enterprise with technology and experience, which I couldn't imagine at the beginning. I would like to thank Jushi for nurturing me. Here, I feel like I am part of the big family, and I am willing to contribute to the company's 14th Five-Year Plan.

女中层干部的幸福生活

迪娜·默罕默德·哈桑·哈桑

2013 年加入中国建材

现任巨石埃及公司计调物流部副经理

巾帼不让须眉——这句话不分国别，在巨石埃及公司，就有这样一位代表。

她没有豪言壮语，只有默默耕耘，她用行动，用表率，用先进的力量，感召着自己身边的每一个人。娇小女子的内心藏着巨大的力量，她给自己立下军令状，开启一段不可思议的成长之旅。

迪娜来自埃及苏伊士一个小城市，2013 年加入巨石埃及公司，至今已近 10 年了。她目前是巨石埃及计调物流部的副经理，也是巨石埃及公司里唯一的女性中层管理者。能够登上管理岗位，她深感责任重大，她对工作的态度也让公司的同事由衷地感到佩服。

回顾近 10 年的经历，刚来公司时的迪娜还是一名职场新人，最开始的几年里，什么都不太懂，工作效率也很低。但是她十分勤奋，同事们每天从办公室下班后都还会看到她的身影，她对工作经常投入到忘我的程度，甚至吃饭都还在核对文件。有时候她还需要同事的提醒，才想起放下手里的文件。在巨石埃及公司工作的这些年里，让迪娜感触最深的是，许多埃及当地公司与员工家庭的互动较少，但在巨石埃及公司里，如果员工家庭有任何问题，公司总是会提供支持和帮助，使得她更加坚信自己的选择。

她在工作上仔细认真的态度使她在计调物流部取得了不小的成就，曾获得公司 2014 年及 2018 年度先进工作者荣誉称号，她的工作能力得到同事们的认可。

有一次，巨石埃及公司 301 生产线遇到有史以来最大的一次突发事件——停电，这一次停电因事发突然，大家根本来不及做出反应。迪娜深知停电对公司影响巨大——停电 1 分钟都会给公司带来巨大的损失，她心系公司，丝毫没有犹豫，当即组织部门同事奔向车间。她也第一时间核对产品质量，区分不合格产品，并迅速与销售沟通，重新安排生产。经过一整夜的奋战，在迪娜的带领下，大家把巨石埃及公司的亏损降到了最低。

经过这一次突发事件，巨石埃及公司的领

导及同事对她刮目相看。对于思想相对保守的埃及人来说，很多女性可选择的工作领域少之又少，更不用说是干出一番业绩了。而迪娜获得的成绩没有让她骄傲，她，还是那个认真的她，还是那个工作到忘我的她，还是那个平时温文儒雅、面对困难毅然冲锋陷阵的她。迪娜是巨石埃及公司当之无愧的女强人。

巨石给员工带来的不仅仅是工作上的满足感，更有生活上的幸福感。迪娜现在立足生产计划调度的本职工作，每天都到拉丝车间、络纱车间、检装车间进行生产安排和沟通，合理安排生产产品结构；同时她深入立体库，时刻了解最新的产品库存状况。

在生活上，公司还为她带来了一段美好的姻缘。迪娜说，她和丈夫在巨石相识、相知、相恋，他们在一起工作，一起规划生活和职业生涯。公司也为他们这对“上阵夫妻兵”提供了员工宿舍。她说，现在她和丈夫住在员工宿舍，宿舍的小区里还配备了篮球场、足球场，这完全满足了他们的业余生活所需，她觉得公司从员工的需求出发，为员工办实事，使她深深地感受到了家一般的温馨。（巨石埃及公司）

个人体会

我们生产的玻璃纤维产品95%以上通过苏伊士运河销往欧洲、美洲等地。巨石在国际玻璃纤维市场上的占有率超过20%，全球每3片风电叶片中就有1片使用了巨石的玻璃纤维。我心中无比自豪，期待巨石埃及的产品未来能走向更广阔的市场。

The Happy Life of Female Middle-level Cadres

Dina Mahmoud Hassan Hassan

Joined CNBM in 2013

The Deputy Manager of Scheduling and Logistics Department

Women are no inferior to men. This statement applies to all countries, and there is such a representative in the Jushi Egypt.

She has no bold words, but silently inspires everyone around her with action. There is great power hidden in the petite woman's heart. She set a goal for herself and made an incredible growth.

Dina comes from a small city in Suez, Egypt. In 2013, she joined the Jushi Egypt and has been with the company for nearly 10 years. She is currently the deputy manager of the planning, dispatching and logistics department, and the only female middle-level management in the company. On the management position, she feels deeply responsible, and her attitude towards work also makes colleagues sincerely admire.

Looking back at her experience in the past 10 years, Tina once was a newcomer in the workplace when she first joined the company. In the first few years, she didn't understand much and she did not completely had good command of the work. But she was very hardworking, and the other employees would always see her working every day after work from the office. She often immersed herself in her work and even checked documents for meals. Sometimes she needed a reminder before she remembered to put down the documents in her hand. During several years working at Jushi Egypt, what impressed Dina most was that many local companies in Egypt had less interaction with employee families. However, at Jushi Egypt, if there were any issues with employee families, the company would always provide support and assistance, which made her more confident in her choices.

Due to her careful and conscientious attitude in work, she had made great achievements in the department, and won the honorary title of Exemplary Individual in 2014 and 2018, which was recognized by colleagues.

On one occasion, the 301 production line encountered the largest emergency in history - a power outage, which occurred suddenly and there was no time to respond. Dina knew that power outage would have a great impact on the company, and every minute without power is a huge loss. She was concerned about the company and with no hesitation, she immediately organized her colleagues to rush to the workshop. She also checked the product quality as soon as possible, identified sub-quality products, and quickly

communicated with sales to rearrange production. After an all-night battle, under the leadership of Dina, the loss of the company was reduced to minimum. After this sudden incident, the leaders and colleagues of the company were great impressed by her. In Egypt, which is relatively conservative-minded, many women have few job options, not even making achievements. But all these did not make her proud,she was still the serious one, the selfless one who worked, and the gentle one who faced difficulties but dared to take the lead. She was a well-deserved female powerhouse in Jushi Egypt.

Jushi not only brings employees a sense of satisfaction at work, but also a sense of happiness in life. Currently, Dina mainly works on production planning and scheduling. Every day, she goes to the drawing workshop, winding workshop, and inspection and assembly workshop to arrange and communicate the production and product structure. She also checks the warehouse to keep abreast of the latest product stock status.

Jushi Egypt also brought Dina a beautiful love story. Dina said she and her husband met and fell in love at Jushi. They worked together, planned their lives and careers together, and established their own family. The company also provided employee dormitories for the couple. Dina said that she and her husband now live in the employee dormitories equipped with a basketball court and football field, which fully meet their leisure life. She feels that the company really concerns about the needs of employees, does practical things for them, and makes them deeply feel the warmth of home.

Personal Insights More than 95% of our glass fiber products are sold to Europe, America, and other places through the Suez Canal. Jushi has a market share of over 20% in the international glass fiber market, and one out of every three wind turbine blades worldwide uses Jushi's glass fiber. At present, I am extremely proud of this and looks forward to Jushi's products in Egypt moving towards a broader market for the future.

青春因奋斗而闪亮

刘忠宝

2005年7月加入中国建材

现任成都建材院巴基斯坦 Maple Leaf 项目机械工程师

他，在进入公司工作的15年时间里，完成了几十条生产线耐火材料的设计，参与了十多个总承包项目的现场施工管理；他的青春在大漠、在高原、他在每一个项目建设需要他的地方发着光。他，就是成都建材院工艺机械所高级工程师刘忠宝。

2005年秋天，刚参加工作两个月的刘忠宝被派往公司总承包建设的山东枣庄东源水泥项目，开始了他职业生涯的首秀。在那里，他主动学、踏实干，虚心向前辈请教，在解决问题中不断积累实战经验，为日后的成长打下了坚实的基础。之后，他陆续参与了安徽海螺、贵州金沙、云南保山、云南云维、哈萨克斯坦 HKCC 等项目的建设，通过多年项目一线工作的磨炼，他逐渐成长为独当一面的业务骨干。

2016年，公司签署了埃及 GOE Beni Suef 6×6000t/d 生产线总承包项目。项目意义重大、任务艰巨。作为公司出色的耐火材料及保温专业技术人员，刘忠宝责无旁贷地加入了建设大军，同时负责六条水泥生产线耐火材料的设计和施工，对他来讲是从来没有过的经历，压力大、责任重。那时的工作状态用他自己的话来形容就是“疯狂”。做图纸设计时，半夜两点走出公司办公大楼是家常便饭，挑灯夜战到四五点也习以为常。到达项目现场后，除了白天睁眼就是40多摄氏度的高温天气和漫天飞舞的黄沙，还有各种挑战：6条线、2家施工单位、10个小分包队伍、交叉作业多……作为在同一地点、同一时间、同步建设的世界最大规模水泥建设项目的亲历者，他时常感慨：“看到项目如期成功点火，看到项目顺利通过考核，得知项目获得中国建设工程‘鲁班奖’的消息时，觉得一切的辛苦和付出都是值得的。”

没有任何停歇，2018年，刘忠宝又投入到格鲁吉亚 Kaspi 项目的建设中。该项目业主为德国海德堡公司，项目的设计、施工和调试要完全执行欧洲标准。海德堡公司素来以要求严苛著称，在项目外保温设计这个环节上，他们对于标准的坚持没有任何商量余地。为了推动图纸审核和施工进度，刘忠宝主动请缨去啃这个“硬骨头”。他结合多年工作经验，和耐火材料专业的同事们一起起早贪黑，大量查阅专业书籍，连续加班一个月，终于绘制出符合现场实际情况和业主要求的外保温施工标准图和安装说明书。

项目建设需要的专业以外的知识——我学！业主要求的详细施工方案——我写！正是刘忠宝和伙伴们这种不畏艰难、刻苦钻研的精神，为项目建设取得成功和顺利完成以欧洲标准为检验前提的合同性能考核加码助力。该项目是中国总承包商第一次全面接受第三方德国公司独立严格考核的项目，谱写了公司与世界最大的水泥制品生产商之一——海德堡公司成功合作的新篇章。

2020 年，刘忠宝的脚步又踏上了青藏高原。6 月初，他接到了前往西藏祁连山项目担任项目耐火材料设计施工负责人的通知。该项目所在地西藏山南海拔高达 3700 米，大病初愈尚在恢复期的他知道高原地区氧含量低，会增加身体的负担，不利于康复。他犹豫过和担心过，项目部了解情况后也再三强调要他做好身体评估是否可以前往。但是项目进度不等人，项目建设需要他。在向医生询问相关注意事项后，他义无反顾地踏上了行程。初到项目部，身体处于恢复期，加上不适应高原气候，他发起了低烧，一连好几天都无法正常工作，只能靠吸氧和吃药坚持，待病情稍有好转，他立即

全身心地投入了工作。

长期工作生活在工程项目一线，他难免会感到单调与枯燥，但生活永远不会缺少发现美的眼睛。看着西藏湛蓝的天空、山谷中金色的麦浪、枝叶相连的绿柳白杨和一股正奔向远方的清流，喜欢赋词作诗的刘忠宝不觉间落笔成诗：

青谷幽涩秋依软，山似丘垄云如颠。
绿柳白杨擎天路，一碧斜照照千颜。
眉痕尚浅衣渐宽，生肖未减青丝满。
待到露华乘风去，玉在穹苍我在前。
…………

远看，站在百米高的塔架上的刘忠宝是渺小的，从旋风筒管道里爬出来的刘忠宝是“脏兮兮”的。然而，在公司发展的历程中，“刘忠宝们”的形象却是高大的、闪闪发光的！刘忠宝说：“我会一直在路上，在为公司发展贡献绵薄之力的路上。”（中材国际所属成都建材院）

在新的征程中，我将继续义无反顾、信诺忠义、勇毅前行，继续把我的足迹留在大漠和高原，继续在热爱的岗位上散发光和热，展现独属于奋斗者的青春风采，为公司高质量发展奉献智慧和汗水。

Youth Shines with Struggle

Liu Zhongbao

Joined CNBM in July 2005

The Mechanical Engineer of Maple Leaf Project undertaken by CDI in Pakistan

During the 15 years of working in the company, he completed the design of refractories for dozens of production lines and participated in the site construction management of more than ten projects. His youth is shining in the desert, in the plateau, and in every project that needs him. He is Liu Zhongbao, a senior engineer of Institute of Process Machinery, Chengdu Design Research Institute of Building Materials Industry Co., Ltd.

In the autumn of 2005, Liu Zhongbao, who had just worked for 2 months, was dispatched by the company to Dongyuan Cement Project in Zaozhuang, Shandong Province, and began his career debut. There, he worked hard, humbly learned from his predecessors and accumulated practical experience, laying a solid foundation for future work. Later, he successively participated in the construction of some projects, including Anhui Conch, Guizhou Jinsha, Yunnan Baoshan, Yunnan Yunwei, and Kazakhstan HKCC. After years of work in the frontline, he has gradually grown into a backbone of the company.

In 2016, the company signed the general contract project of Egypt GOE Beni Suef 6× 6,000 t/d production line, which has great significance. As an excellent professional technician in refractories and thermal insulation, Liu Zhongbao joined the construction army. At the same time, with great pressure and heavy responsibilities, he was responsible for the design and construction of six cement production lines of refractories. He described the working state at that time as "crazy". When making the drawing design, it was common to leave the office building at 2:00, even 4:00 or 5:00 o'clock in the morning. And the working condition was very serious: the temperature was as high as over 40°C and yellow sand flying all over the sky. After arriving at the project site, he had to face more challenges in woke: six lines, two construction organizations, 10 small subcontracting teams, and many cross-jobs... As a witness of the world's largest cement construction project, he often said, "Seeing the project being successfully commenced as scheduled, seeing the project has successfully passed the assessment, and knowing that the project won 'The Luban Prize' for construction projects in China, I felt that all the hard work and efforts are worthwhile."

Without any rest, in 2018, Liu Zhongbao was engaged in the construction of the Georgian Kaspi project. The owner of the project is Germany Heidelberg Company, and the design, construction and commissioning of the project are completely subject to European standards. Heidelberg has always been known for its strict requirements, and there was no room for discussion on the standards in the external thermal insulation design of the project. To promote drawing review and construction progress, Liu Zhongbao volunteered to take charge of the "hard work". Combined with years of work experience, he and his colleagues got up early to look up a lot of professional books. Working overtime for one month in a row, they finally drew standard drawings for external insulation construction and installation instructions meeting the requirements.

They learned the knowledge required by the project construction and wrote the detailed construction plan required by the owner. Their hard work contributed to the success of the project construction and the successful completion of the contract performance assessment based on European standards. This project is the first one in which China's general contractor fully accepted the independent and rigorous assessment of a third-party German company, which has written a new chapter in the successful cooperation between the company and Heidelberg, one of the largest cement product manufacturers in the world.

In 2020, Liu Zhongbao set foot on the Tibetan Plateau again. In early June, he was notified that he would be heading to Xizang Qilian Mountain project as the project refractory design and construction manager. The project is located in Shannan, Tibet, an altitude of up to 3700 meters. At that time, he was still recovering from a serious illness, he clearly knew that the low oxygen content in the plateau

area will increase the burden of the body and is not conducive to rehabilitation. He was hesitant and worried, the project department also repeatedly stressed that he should make a physical assessment whether he could go. However, the project schedule does not wait anymore, he is needed for the project construction! After asking the doctor about the relevant precautions, he embarked on the trip without hesitation. When he first arrived at the project department, since his body was in the recovery period, coupled with not adapting to the plateau climate, he started a low fever and could not work normally for several days. He could only rely on oxygen inhalation and medicine. When his condition improved slightly, he immediately threw himself into work.

Seeing from a distance, Liu Zhongbao, standing on a 100m-high tower, is small. Liu Zhongbao, who crawled out of the cyclone pipe, is "dirty". However, in the development course of the company, he is tall and shining. Liu Zhongbao said that he will always make contributions to the development of the company.

Personal Insights On the new journey, I will keep working hard and moving forward without hesitation and being faithful to my commitments. I will go on to leave my footprint in the desert and the plateau, devote my passion to the work I love so much, show the world the shining day of every fighter, and dedicate my wisdom and sweat to the high development of my company.

笃行致远　不负芳华

赵鑫

2007 年 7 月加入中国建材

现任成都建材院埃及 WNCC 替代燃料项目经理

人们常说：“青春需早为，岂能长少年。”在成都建材院埃及 EC 日产 6000 吨熟料水泥生产线项目（以下简称埃及 EC 项目）就有着这样一位在青春里不懈拼搏、在奋斗中拥抱梦想的人，他就是奋斗者赵鑫。在项目部同事的眼中，他既是一个在工程管理上遇事先觉果断、心思缜密、协调周全的“智将”，又是一个技术管理上专业扎实、思路开阔、技能出众的“能者”，更是一个在团队协作中，引领大家攻坚克难的“旗手”。

毕业至今，赵鑫已在中材国际成都建材院工作了 16 年。在这漫长而又充实的岁月里，他曾辗转广州惠州、阿联酋、加纳、多哥等多个项目，始终保持着谦虚好学、严谨认真的工作态度，收获了勇毅与顽强，悟透了责任与担当。如今，赵鑫依然秉持着踏实笃行的态度，为项目建设贡献着自己的光和热。

项目进度控制的关键是什么？用赵鑫的话来说：“关键工序主线明晰，土建机电各专业并行不悖，质量、进度、经济指标各得其所。”作为项目管理人员，要能提前思考、洞悉表里、精细规划、大胆实践、灵活务实，只有这样才能够成为项目蓝图的绘制者。

2018 年 4 月，埃及 EC 项目执行遇到了第一个抉择难点。土建施工阶段面临材料周转困难的问题，项目核心子项存在进度超期的风险。赵鑫结合项目实际情况，果断组织土建专业和安装专业讨论对策，并提出土建应将非关键子项的所有资源集中到生料磨、煤磨和水泥磨的大布袋车间。而这时几个要撤出生产资源的子项已经出地面，如再有 2 至 3 个月的时间就可以完工。“手心手背都是肉”，何处“保”、哪里“舍”成为关键抉择。

在难题面前，赵鑫凭借丰富的管理经验以及胆大心细的做事态度，精心组织、科学筹划，尽可能从外部调集资源的同时，暂停了现场原料配料站、水泥配料站两个子项的施工，拆除主体框架下的脚手架管并投入到生料磨和煤磨的大布袋车间的施工中。同时，为了不浪费两个配料站土建暂时放缓的窗口期，他及时调整安装工序，将施工困难的仓底安装提前执行，

使得原本要在 8 月份才能移交的核心子项，在 6 月陆续实现交工，核心子项的安装工作得以全面铺开。

项目部的同事们赞叹道：“先觉果断，心思缜密，协调周全，这就是我们的赵经理！”

项目上的同事们亲切地称呼赵鑫“胖哥”。“有困难？找胖哥，只要他在现场，这个事情就能解决”，这已经成了埃及 EC 项目遇到抢修问题时大家的口头禅。

埃及 EC 项目投产伊始，联合取料机遭遇链盘故障，虽然现场技术人员很快解决了引起故障的电气问题，但要让链盘回位，需要大量人力，而疫情当前，现场人员紧缺，这也为解决链盘回位问题增加了难度。此时，如果不能在 5 个小时内修复好设备重新向生料磨投料，刚刚启动的生产线就需要按下暂停键。

人手短缺，但力量不缺！越是紧急时刻越不能自乱阵脚。赵鑫通盘考虑后，利用现有人员，迅速做出安排。

在有条不紊地安排好各小组的工作后，赵鑫立即开始巡视各小组的工作情况，反复提醒安全注意事项，亲自查看维修过程中的技术细节和指标。仅用了 3 小时 55 分！项目团队拧成一股绳，奋力排除了故障。在确认系统安全后，他擦了擦早已满是汗珠的脸说：“让我们试运行一下，恢复生产就没问题了。”一句没有过多修饰的话，却在瞬间驱散了当时项目现场所有人心中的阴霾。

新时代我们要做起而行之的行动者，当攻坚克难的奋斗者。愿我们每个人都能够竭尽全力靠近，不遗余力超越，在奋斗的路上并肩前行。（中材国际所属成都建材院）

个人体会

“仰望奋斗魂，神州风采熠；你我皆奋起，中华早复兴。”我热爱成都建材院这个大家庭，加入这里后也不断提升自己，秉持着踏实笃行的态度，继续奋战在项目一线，彰显青春底色，贡献自己的光和热。

Living up to Prime Years While Acting Sincerely and Aiming High

Zhao Xin

Joined CNBM in July 2007

The Project Manager of WNCC Alternative Fuel Project undertaken by CDI in Egypt

As a poem of Tang Dynasty said, "Try hard as early as you can. Can you prolong your prime?" On the site of Egypt EC Nissan 6,000-ton cement clinker production line project, which was handled by Chengdu Design & Research Institute of Building Materials Industry Co., Ltd., ("Chengdu Building Materials"), there is a young man who untiringly struggles and bravely embraces dreams. He is Zhao Xin. In the eyes of his colleagues from Project Department, he is a "wise man", who is decisive, meticulous and thoughtful in engineering management, a "capable man", who is highly professional, open-minded and excellently skilled in technical management, and a "pathfinding man", who can lead one after another struggle against obstacles in teamwork.

Since he graduated from university, Zhao Xin has worked in Chengdu Building Materials for 16 years. In these years, he ever participated in quite a few projects, including the ones in Huizhou (Guangdong province), the United Arab Emirates, Ghana and Togo. The modest and knowledge-thirsty man, he reaped fortitude and tenacity and understood real meaning of responsibility. Now he still adheres to his down-to-earth and sincere attitude to work and continues to make his own contribution to the project construction.

What is the key to the control of project progress? Zhao Xin once said, "The key procedure must have a clear-cut line, the electromechanical disciplines of civil engineering are compatible, and quality, progress and economic indicators all reached the expected level." To draw a blueprint for each project, a project manager must be forward-looking, insightful, well-thought, bold in practice, and feasible and pragmatic.

In April 2018, Egypt EC project was faced with the first hard choice. Specifically, the construction of civil engineering project was troubled by unsmooth circulation of raw materials, and the core sub-projects had the risk of overdue construction. After the project's reality was taken into consideration, Zhao Xin immediately arranged civil engineering technicians and installation technicians to discuss about the countermeasures, and he proposed that all the resources of those non-key sub-projects should be channeled to the big-bag workshop of raw material mill, coal mill and cement mill. But several sub-projects from which production resources would be removed had been erected on the ground, their construction would be completed two to three months later and the installation work would be started. How to balance the "gain" with the "loss" is a critical choice.

Whenever encountering difficulties, Zhao Xin carefully organized and made scientific plans by leveraging extensive management experience and a bold yet cautious work style. While he tried to mobilize resources from external sources, he suspended the construction of two sub-projects including raw material batching station and cement batching station, dismantled the scaffold pipes from main framework, and used the pipes in the construction of the big-bag workshop of raw material mill and coal mill. During the window period created by the slowdown of civil engineering construction of two batching stations, he adjusted installation procedures timely and arranged the installation of warehouse bottom with difficult construction. As a result, the core sub-projects that should have been handed over in August were completed in June and its installation work could be rolled out on a full scale.

The colleagues from Project Department all praised him, "Zhao is a forward-looking, decisive, meticulous and considerate manager."

The colleagues in the project gave him a nickname "Brother Fat". "Have any problems? Go find Brother Fat. As long as he's on the site, it'll be surely settled." These words have become pet phrases of all who came across the repair headaches in Egypt EC project.

Soon after the project was put into operation, the combined reclaimer was troubled by chain fault. The on-site technicians solved the electric problem that caused this fault, but it took considerable manpower to get chains to their original position. As the pandemic continued, understaffing made this problem harder to deal with. If the equipment could not restart operation and materials could not be fed into raw material mill within five hours, the production line had to be suspended.

Understaffing was a problem, but there is always backup. At the critical moment, staying calm is more important. Having considered all factors concerned, Zhao Xin made arrangements for all on the site.

After he assigned the task to each group, he started at once to inspect each group's work, repeatedly reminded group members of safety precautions, and checked technical details and indicators in the process of maintenance. It only took 3 hours and 55 minutes. The project team worked together to troubleshoot the problem. After the system safety was confirmed, he wiped sweats off his face and said, "Let's have a try. If nothing is wrong, we'll be able to resume production." His words, though undecorated, dispelled haze in everyone's mind.

"Looking up at the soul of struggle, I find our country shining brilliantly. If we forge ahead with determination, the Chinese nation will see its rejuvenation soon." His inspiring words are the belief of every struggler and the direction that every struggler should strive for. In the new era, we must become action and hardship conquerors. Hope each of us can do our best to approach our goals and outperform ourselves. Let's march forward shoulder by shoulder on the road to success!

Personal Insights "Looking up at the soul of striving, I find our country shining brilliantly. If we forge ahead with determination, the Chinese nation will see its rejuvenation soon." I love the big family of CDI, where I may never cease to challenge myself and go beyond myself. I will stick to working perseveringly, keep fighting at the frontline of project construction, demonstrate the best aspect of my youth, and devote myself whole-heartedly to the bright future of CDI.

事无巨细的现场管家

廖伟

2006年加入中国建材

现任合肥院江西奉新时代锂电项目现场经理

“一带一路”倡议提出以来，无数的中国建材技术人员在异国他乡辛勤工作、挥洒汗水、贡献力量，在世界舞台上展示着中国成熟的水泥工艺和中国方案，展现出中国先进的管理理念及履约精神，合肥院的廖伟就是其中一员。

廖伟同志一直在工程总承包项目现场担任现场经理一职，参与了巴基斯坦ASKARI、芜湖南方、广东蕉岭、新疆青松建化、苏丹berber、越南缘何等众多项目的建设，参建的项目多次荣获建材行业工程总承包奖。廖伟对每次项目参建机会都非常珍惜，也备感压力，他竭尽全力，设定并严格执行项目各阶段的任务目标，把压力转换为动力，完成领导交代的任务，表现出现场经理的职责与担当。

2022年在巴基斯坦ASKARI项目上，他十分注重项目实施过程中的各项管理工作，把塑造和谐、阳光的工作环境放在极为重要的位置。他带领项目成员规范制度，以身作则，面对外界阻力，他不卑不亢，树立和维护合肥院的形象；积极主动与业主代表沟通，建立良好的沟通渠道及方式，组织协调现场2000多中巴施工人员，及时化解各种矛盾，众志成城，全力推进项目有序开展。

每天一早，廖伟都要在ASKARI项目现场工地转一圈，发现问题及时解决。“一年三百六十日，多是横戈马上行”，在项目上严排工期，注重效率，围绕各节点工期目标，克服种种困难，逐一跟进，逐步实现。对业主不卑不亢，对分包单位严格要求，带领团队在住宿区开辟了幸福农场，积极营造“家”的氛围，是现场的主心骨和定心神。国内春风和煦，ASKARI现场已经炎热难耐，从一片荒芜到形成规模，凝聚了项目部所有成员的心血，更离不开廖伟的辛勤付出与组织。

在项目施工过程中，只要关乎质量问题，他从不放过。身为现场经理，廖伟狠抓工程技术和工程质量，在设备安装时，廖伟严格把关，与设备工程师进行多次技术交流，强调质量是建设高品质工程的前提。

他始终把安全管理工作放到第一位，亲自

组织开展安全定期大检查，设备安装专项安全技术交底，把安全责任压实，真正把安全生产、生命至上的精神贯彻落实下去；针对“安全永远是零容忍”，把安全生产做到可控范围。

面对巴基斯坦的安全环境、恶劣的气候和当时的疫情形势，项目建设面临巨大挑战，他内心备感压力，但他依然身先士卒。作为项目的现场经理，他以一往无前的奋斗姿态与永不懈怠的精神状态，以身作则，带领项目部成员团结一心，众志成城，迎难而上，攻坚克难。

随着项目建设的推进，看着现场每天的变化，他就像看着自己家孩子每天在茁壮成长，廖伟干劲儿十足地说：“世上无难事，只要肯攀登。国内公司和国外现场同频共振，一起见证项目每天的进展。”

ASKARI 项目经过项目部团队长期的努力，最终提前到 2022 年 10 月 20 日点火，10 月 27 日一次性投料成功。当项目投料那一刻，项目团队所有人激动不已，业主巴基斯坦管理团队与项目团队为点火投料而拥抱在一起的时刻完美地诠释了中巴友谊。项目建成的喜悦还未散去，廖伟很快又整装待发，准备好迎接新的任务和挑战。（中材国际所属合肥院）

个人体会 工作不仅是获得报酬，也是实现人生价值的重要载体，我热爱工作，且始终充满激情。项目目标一旦设定，就不要去找任何借口。不吃工作的苦，就不会有成功的甜，相信自己，坚持不懈，胜利一定会到来。

A Micromanaging Steward on Project Site

Liao Wei

Joined CNBM in 2006

The Site Manager of Fengxin Era New Energy Co., Ltd.

Since the Belt and Road Initiative was put forward, numerous Chinese construction materials technicians have dedicated their efforts in foreign countries, perspiring and contributing their expertise. They have showcased China's well-established cement technology and provided Chinese solutions on the global platform, exemplifying China's advanced management principles and compliance ethos. Among these remarkable individuals is Liao Wei from the SINOMA International Hefei Cement Research & Design Institute Corporation Ltd.

Liao Wei has served as an on-site manager at EPC project sites, actively contributing to the construction of numerous projects, such as ASKARI in Pakistan, Wuhu South, Guangdong Jiaoling, Xinjiang Qingsongjianhua, Sudan Berber, and Vietnam Yuanhe. These projects have received multiple accolades, including the EPC Prize for the Building Materials Industry. Liao Wei values each project opportunity and embraces the associated challenges with a sense of responsibility. He diligently sets and rigorously follows project objectives at every stage, transforming pressure into motivation. He successfully completes assigned tasks, fulfilling the responsibilities and obligations of an on-site manager.

During the ASKARI project in Pakistan in 2022, Liao Wei demonstrated a strong commitment to project management, emphasizing on harmonious and positive working environment. Recognizing the importance of maintaining a favorable image for the Hefei Institute, he led the project team in implementing standardized systems and effectively addressing external challenges. Liao Wei proactively engaged with the owners' representatives, establishing effective communication. He skillfully organized and coordinated a workforce of over 2,000 Chinese and Pakistani construction workers, promptly resolving conflicts and ensuring smooth project progress. His dedication and efforts contributed to the orderly and successful execution of the project.

Every morning, Liao Wei diligently conducts site inspections at the ASKARI project site, proactively identifying and resolving any issues that arise. With a disciplined and efficient approach to construction projects, he diligently follows the strict schedule, overcomes challenges, and systematically achieves the goals for each construction phase. He upholds a respectful approach towards the property owners, ensuring their dignity is maintained, while also holding subcontractors to rigorous standards. As a leader, he spearheaded the establishment of a harmonious "Happy Farm" in the accommodation area, fostering a warm and welcoming atmosphere akin to a true "home." With his unwavering presence, he serves as the backbone on the site, guiding the team towards success. Liao Wei's dedication and organizational skills have played a pivotal role in transforming ASKARI from a barren land into a thriving and bustling project site.

Liao Wei's commitment to quality is unwavering throughout the project construction. As an on-site manager, he possesses a deep understanding of project technology and places great emphasis on ensuring high-quality standards. During equipment installation, Liao Wei conducts meticulous inspections and engages in frequent discussions with equipment engineers. He consistently emphasizes that maintaining exceptional quality is a fundamental requirement for the construction of top-notch projects.

Liao Wei prioritizes safety management above all else and takes personal initiative in conducting regular safety inspections. He ensures the implementation of special safety technologies and actively reinforces safety responsibilities. Liao Wei exemplifies the spirit of prioritizing production safety and valuing human lives. He maintains a "zero-tolerance approach towards safety violations" and consistently implements stringent safety measures to maintain a controlled and secure working environment.

In the face of Pakistan's security environment, harsh climate conditions, and the challenging epidemic situation, the project encountered tremendous obstacles, placing immense pressure on Liao Wei and his team. Despite being impacted by the pandemic, as the on-site manager, he remained relentless in his efforts and never wavered in his commitment. Leading by example, he fostered

unity among the project department members, encouraging them to face challenges head-on and overcome obstacles together.

As the project construction unfolds, Liao Wei witnesses the daily transformations feeling like observing one's own children thrive and flourish. Liao Wei embraces his role wholeheartedly, firmly believing that no challenge is insurmountable as long as one has the determination to overcome it. The synchronicity between domestic companies and foreign sites resonates harmoniously to witness the progress of the project every single day.

After countless moments of perseverance and dedication from the project team, the ASKARI project reached a significant milestone on October 20, 2022, as it was successfully ignited. The culmination of this achievement was celebrated with great enthusiasm on October 27, 2022, bringing forth immense excitement from the project team owner. The heartfelt embrace between the owner's Pakistan management team and the project team during the celebratory event perfectly exemplified the deep-rooted friendship between China and Pakistan. Although the elation of completing the project still lingers, Liao Wei is already gearing up to embrace new tasks and challenges that lie ahead.

Personal Insights Work is not only for payment, but also an important carrier to realize the value of life. I love work, and I am always full of passion. Once a project goal is set, don't make any excuses. Do not endure hardships in the work, there will be no sweetness of success. Believing in yourself and persisting, victory will sure come.

用平凡铸就不凡

邱怀磊
2018 年加入中国建材
现任中材建设尼日利亚有限公司销售经理

他是迎风的赶路人，做着看似普通而平凡的工作，却习惯骄阳与骤雨，挫折与困难；他是坚定的守望者，将不懈的努力藏在笑容背后，秉承初心，行稳致远；他是探索的先锋军，在岗位上书写不平凡的青春，步履不停，永攀高峰；他的脸上总是挂着自信的微笑，坚毅执着的内心永远怀揣着梦想，他用实际行动诠释着中材国际员工的担当、敬业和奉献精神，他就是中材建设尼日利亚有限公司销售经理邱怀磊。

邱怀磊本科毕业于哈尔滨商业大学电子商务专业，于 2018 年 10 月入职中材国际所属中材建设尼日利亚有限公司。初入职场，邱怀磊就进入产品销售部门进行学习。与此同时，邱怀磊对“建材人”的身份有着强烈的归属感和荣誉感。他主动关注公司宏观层面的海外业务规划，对公司的海外市场开拓策略和推进计划积极献言献策。4 年来，他以公司为家，全身心融入团队，在品牌推广、市场开发等工作中发挥了重要的作用，为推进中材建设国际化经营事业和公司属地化屋面系统产业发展作出了重要贡献。

2019—2022 年，他负责签约的大型代理商多达 14 家，并多次与大型厂商进行合作。与此同时，为了打响 FABCOM 品牌，他多次筹划并组织展会、宣讲会等宣传活动，线上利用 FACEBOOK、INS 等平台对公司屋面瓦产品进行宣传。通过他超强的工作能力与精益求精的工作态度，FABCOM 品牌在尼日利亚的市场份额得到了迅速提升。

与此同时，邱怀磊在工作中一直努力打造一支专业化的市场营销团队。他认为，一个优秀的营销团队是销售体系能否正常运行的关键因素。截至目前，邱怀磊已建立拥有销售经理 3 人、客户经理 5 人、外部市场员工 22 人的销售团队，且已拥有 3 家安装合作公司、4 家运输合作公司等外部合作团队，既为公司降低了成本和风险，又为客户提供了最优质的服务。

自 2020 年全球新冠疫情暴发后，公司屋面瓦产品销售等业务面临市场低迷、竞争加剧、人员紧缺、疫情防控任务重等诸多困难。面对困难，邱怀磊毅然选择放弃回国休假的机会，继续坚守工作岗位，让其他同事先回国。为了完成公司既定目标，邱怀磊有条不紊地制订销售计划、安排人员分工，带领销售队伍主动出击，不仅积极参与尼日利亚所举办的线上线下多个房屋展会活动，还一直不断地思考开拓市场的新方案，勇于求新求变，积极与客户和代理商保持沟通与联系，并且通过对营销数据和市场信息的分析，积极构建区域性营销网络。

在他的不懈努力下，2019—2022 年度，他率领销售团队销售金属彩石瓦共计 156 万平方米，销售金属彩钢瓦共计 14.8 万平方米。邱怀磊说："公司屋面系统是一个极具潜力的产业，每年都有极大规模的市场需求，我们也将不断提高市场占有率，从而为公司创造更多价值，满足公司战略规模布局的要求。"

骐骥一跃，不能十步；驽马十驾，功在不舍。邱怀磊始终兢兢业业、竭诚付出，用忠诚和责任践行使命担当，在看似平凡的工作中不断超越自我，用始终如一的工作热情默默耕耘，坚持用敬业和奉献诠释平凡人的不凡。这种精神也体现在每一个奋斗在海外一线建设者的身上，激励着全体中国建材人携手奋进，并肩前行，共赴未来！（中材国际所属中材建设）

个人体会　我热爱中材建设屋面系统产业，此产业承载了我与公司的共同梦想。我将时刻保持积极进取的心态和艰苦奋斗的精神，不畏艰难，不怕辛苦，为中材建设屋面系统产业的发展贡献我年轻的力量，书写自己的奋斗篇章。

Molding the Exceptional with Everyday Simplicity

Qiu Huailei

Joined CNBM in 2018

The Sales Manager of SINOMA NIGERIA COMPANY LTD

He embodies the spirit of a relentless adventurer, engaging in seemingly mundane and unremarkable tasks. However, he is no stranger to enduring the elements of success and setbacks, persisting through the sunshine and rain, frustration and obstacles. Behind his cheerful smile lies a steadfast observer, dedicated to his original purpose and steadily progressing towards distant horizons. As a trailblazer of exploration, he etches an extraordinary tale of youth upon his chosen path, ceaselessly journeying and forever ascending towards the summit. His countenance is perpetually adorned with confidence, his unwavering determination and resolute heart carry the weight of a cherished dream. He exemplifies the essence of commitment, devotion, and selflessness of SINOMA International employees. He is Qiu Huailei, sales manager of SINOMA NIGERIA COMPANY LTD.

After successfully completing his e-commerce studies at Harbin University of Commerce, Qiu Huailei embarked on a new chapter by joining SINOMA NIGERIA COMPANY LTD, a subsidiary of SINOMA International, in October 2018. Qiu Huailei took the initial steps of his professional journey by immersing himself in the product sales department. Simultaneously, Qiu Huailei deeply embraces and takes immense pride in his affiliation as one of the SINOMA International team fostering a profound sense of belonging and honor. With unwavering enthusiasm, he consistently keeps a close eye on the company's overseas business plan, actively engaging in the formulation of overseas market development strategy and promotional initiatives. Over the past four years, he has wholeheartedly embraced the company as his home, seamlessly integrating into the team. His significant contributions to brand promotion, market development, and other vital initiatives have played a pivotal role in the development of the company's international business and its territorialized roofing system industry.

From 2019 to 2022, he was responsible for signing up to 14 large agents and cooperated with large local manufacturers many times. Simultaneously, to propel the recognition of the FABCOM brand, he meticulously strategized and orchestrated numerous exhibitions, seminars, and promotional events. Harnessing the power of social media platforms such as Facebook and Instagram, he skillfully maximized the online presence of the company's roofing tile products. With his exceptional professional skills and unwavering work ethic, he has catalyzed a remarkable surge in the market share of the FABCOM brand within Nigeria.

Concurrently, Qiu Huailei has devoted relentless efforts to establish and cultivate a proficient marketing team. He firmly upholds the belief that an exceptional marketing team is the crucial linchpin for the smooth functioning of the sales system. To date, Qiu Huailei has successfully assembled a formidable sales team, comprising three adept sales managers, five skilled account managers, and a dedicated workforce of 22 external market employees. Additionally, he has forged strategic partnerships with three cooperative installation companies and four cooperative transportation companies, a symbiotic collaboration that not only mitigates costs and risks for the company but also ensures the delivery of unparalleled quality services to valued customers.

Since the outbreak of COVID-19 pandemic in 2020, the company has encountered a multitude of challenges, including a downturn in sales and heightened competition, compounded by staffing shortages and the demanding responsibilities of epidemic prevention and control. Confronting these challenges head-on, Qiu Huailei made a resolute decision to forgo the opportunity to return to his home country for vacation, instead choosing to remain steadfastly dedicated to his responsibilities, allowing his colleagues to prioritize their own returns. With the company's targets firmly in mind, Qiu Huailei diligently devised a comprehensive sales plan, meticulously assigning roles and responsibilities within the team. Leading by example, he proactively guided the sales team to take initiative, actively participating in both online and offline housing exhibition events held in Nigeria. Continuously seeking innovative solutions to penetrate the market, he fearlessly embraced change and consistently maintained open communication and connections with customers and agents. Leveraging marketing data and market intelligence, he tirelessly worked towards establishing a robust regional marketing network.

Through his unwavering dedication, he successfully steered the sales team to achieve remarkable results. In the period spanning 2019 to 2022, they accomplished the sale of an impressive 1.56 million square meters of stone-coated metal roofing tiles and 148,000 square meters of metal color steel tiles. Qiu Huailei said, "The roofing system industry has immense potential, witnessing substantial market demand year after year. We remain committed to expanding our market share further, generating enhanced value for the company, and aligning with the strategic goals of our expansive growth."

An untiring horse can endure ten journeys because he never gives up. Qiu Huailei embodies unwavering dedication and a wholehearted commitment to his responsibilities. With loyalty and a strong sense of responsibility, he embraces his mission wholeheartedly, consistently surpassing his own limits in seemingly ordinary tasks. Through silent dedication and unwavering enthusiasm, he exemplifies the extraordinary essence of ordinary individuals who remain steadfast in their devotion and commitment. This spirit runs through every SINOMA International representative who works tirelessly on the overseas frontline. It profoundly inspires all SINOMA International members to march forward hand in hand and unites for the common vision of the future.

Personal Insights I love roofing system industry, which carries the common dream of me and the company. I will always maintain a positive attitude and adhere to the spirit of struggle, and contribute my young strength to the development of SINOMA's roof system industry without fear of difficulties and hard work, and write my own struggle chapter.

属地化经营的坚守者

尚以国

1997 年加入中国建材

现任中材建设总监、俄罗斯公司总经理

25 年来，尚以国从中材建设的一名班组实习员到分公司经理，可谓筚路蓝缕。17 年的海外工作，他将汗水和青春留在了公司海外业务中，生动诠释了中材建设人担当、敬业、奉献的优秀品质，谱写了建材人的精彩人生。

2012 年，尚以国来到了公司在俄罗斯承建的日产 5000t 水泥生产线总承包项目。项目团队冒着严寒，在俄罗斯度过长达 4 个半月的冬季施工期，创造了俄罗斯 5000t 水泥 EPC 生产线最短时间投产的记录，受到业主拉法基集团的高度赞赏，为公司在俄罗斯市场树立了品牌，提高了知名度。项目结束后，在转战新工地之际，公司领导高瞻远瞩地制定了属地化经营策略，俄罗斯项目留下部分机具、人员和物资，就地成立属地化经营公司，尚以国被任命为俄罗斯公司总经理，从此开启了他带领俄罗斯公司团队积极践行“扎根属地、深耕经营”的公司战略的征程。

在国家“一带一路”倡议下，中国企业相继走出国门，俄罗斯公司利用中材国际品牌效应、属地化经营优势成功签约了俄罗斯长城汽车厂项目，这是中材国际彼时最大的多元类项目。面对陌生的行业、复杂的地质条件、短暂的施工周期，在公司的大力支持下，他带领俄罗斯公司的项目团队因地制宜，改变传统项目操作模式，以“本土化员工为主，中亚劳务为辅”的方式大胆创新，最终圆满完成项目建设工作。该项目最终取得了良好社会效益和经济效益，获得了业主的高度赞赏。随后他带领俄罗斯公司先后承接了海尔工业园、丰益国际食品厂、TH 牛奶厂等多元业务工程，按照公司化治理的中材建设俄罗斯公司当前已拥有完整的施工总承包、设计、消防资质，具备独立招投标能力和项目施工管理能力，成为中材建设境外 6 大区域中心之一。

2020 年 2 月疫情期间，俄罗斯项目正在施工高潮中，尚以国坚守在疫情防控的第一线，坚守在分公司的业务和项目的工程中，这一坚守就是 28 个月，即使在整个疫情期间中俄两国间的航线始终保持畅通的情况下，他也丝毫

没有动摇过坚守的决心，“我是中材建设俄罗斯公司项目部的负责人，也是疫情防控的第一责任人。在项目紧张施工中，我有义务和责任坚守一线，即使具备回国条件也应优先考虑一线职工的回国需求”。

每当谈论起家庭时，他的笑容掩不住对家人的愧疚，他说：“自从工作离开老家后，25 年来没能在家向父母尽孝，父亲重病和离开时也因我身在海外未能见他最后一面。结婚后与爱人一直分居两地，两个孩子出生都没有在她身边，也基本缺席了孩子的成长过程，作为儿子、丈夫、父亲，我深深地感到对不起他们。”2021 年 10 月，公司派代表专程到坚守海外的员工家里进行慰问，帮助解决实际困难，他深深地感受到了公司大家庭的温暖，他说：“这种大家庭的爱深深地温暖着我和我的家人，这是一种动力。我将继续努力工作，扎根属地经营，创造更好业绩，为公司高质量、可持续发展贡献力量。”

（中材国际所属中材建设）

个人体会 这应该是我这辈子唯一的职业了，虽然有愧对家人的遗憾，但我仍然热爱着它。26 年，伴随着公司一路走来，见证了公司扬帆深蓝、蓬勃发展的昨天，亦能清晰看见公司鹏程万里、不断壮大的明天，很荣幸在这千万人的奋斗身影中也有一个我，在这平凡的人生中体现出自我价值。

The Defender of Localized Operation

Shang Yiguo

Joined CNBM in 1997
The Director of CBMI and General Manager of SINOMA RUS CO.,LTD

Over the past 25 years, Shang Yiguo has endured great hardship in his promotion from a team intern to the subsidiary manager of SINOMA CBMI Construction Co., Ltd. During 17 years of overseas assignment, he has sweated and contributed his youth to the company's overseas business, which has vividly demonstrated the excellent quality of responsibility, devotion and dedication of employees of SINOMA and composed their wonderful lives.

In 2012, Shang Yiguo participated in the general contracting project of cement production line with a daily output of 5,000t undertaken by the company in Russia. After overcoming four and a half months of severe winter, the project team set a record for the shortest commissioning of the 5,000t cement EPC production line in Russia. It was highly appreciated by the owner Lafarge Group, which has established a brand and improved its popularity in the Russian market. After the project, upon moving to the new construction site, the company leaders were forward-looking and worked out the localized operation strategy. Some equipment, personnel and materials were left in Russia to form the localized operation company, and Shang Yiguo was assigned as the general manager of the Russia branch to lead the company team to actively practice the corporate strategy of "taking root in local place for in-depth operation".

Under the "Belt and Road" Initiative, Chinese enterprises went abroad one after another. Using the brand effect of SINOMA International and advantages of localized operation, the Russia branch successfully undertook the Russian Great Wall Motor Factory Project, which was the largest multi-type project undertaken by SINOMA at that time. Facing the unfamiliar industry, complex geological conditions, and short construction period, with the strong support from the company, Shang Yiguo led the Russia branch and the project team to change the traditional project operating mode in accordance with local conditions. He carried out bold innovation in the way of localization construction, supplemented by Central Asian labor, and finally successfully completed the project construction work. With sound social and economic benefit, the project was highly praised by the owner. Subsequently, he led the Russia branch to undertake projects of businesses of Haier Industrial Park, Wilmar International Food Factory, TH Milk Factory, and so on. The Russian branch currently has a complete total construction contracting, design, fire protection qualifications. It is now one of SINOMA's regional centers with independent bidding capabilities and project construction management capabilities.

During the outbreak in February 2020, the project construction in Russia was in full swing. Shang Yiguo remained not only at the frontline of epidemic prevention and control, but also in the business and project of the branch, which lasted for 28 months. The unblocked flight routes between China and Russia didn't affect his unwavering resolution to stick to his post during the epidemic. "I am the backbone of the Russia branch and the Project Department, and the person responsible for epidemic prevention and control here. I have the responsibility and obligation to remain at the frontline when the project is under construction in a tight time limit. When we are allowed to return to China, the priority should be given to other workers."

When talking about family, his smiles indicated the sense of guilt. He said, " I haven't been able to display filial piety towards my parents for 25 years after I left my hometown. When my father got ill and passed away, I couldn't come back to see him because I worked overseas. After marriage, my wife and I lived separately in two places. When she gave birth to two children, I wasn't with her. I was even absent in the growth of my children. As a son, husband and father, I was deeply sorry." In October 2021, the company paid special visits to the family members of workers remaining overseas to help solve practical problems. Shang Yiguo deeply felt the warmth of the company as a big family. He said, "The love from the company warmed me and my family profoundly, giving me impetus. I will keep in mind my original aspiration and mission, continue to work hard, take root in localized operation, create better achievements, and contribute to the high-quality and sustainable development of the company."

Personal Insights This should be the only career in my life, although I have guilt for my family, I still love my work. Following the company along the way for 26 years, I have witnessed the vigorous development of the company, and I can clearly see the positive growth of it in the future. I am honored to be one of the thousands of people who strive for excellence their work and embody their self-worth in ordinary life.

勇敢开拓的“大漠赤子”

魏强

2014 年加入中国建材

现任沙特 YAMAMA 项目部总经理兼叙利亚项目部总经理

2014 年，魏强入职中材国际所属中国中材海外科技发展有限公司，历任津巴布韦 100TPH 粉磨站项目经理、津巴布韦办事处总代表，现任叙利亚日产 6500 吨水泥生产线项目现场经理，现任沙特 YAMAMA 项目部总经理，多次荣获公司先进工作者荣誉称号及海外赤子奖。2019 年，在叙利亚政局尚未完全平稳之际，魏强响应公司号召，以强烈的责任感和使命感，不畏艰险，率队前往大漠戈壁，驻扎海外项目现场。

在最开始的时候，项目现场的洁净水源供应尚未稳定，有时需要用井水来维持日常生活；地处沙漠，夏天闷热干燥，蚊虫令人不堪其扰。在这种条件下，魏强带领团队一住就是一整年，在他眼里，这些都不算苦。

为了控制项目风险，他坚持以收定支，不投入大额资金购买固定资产。厂区较大，巡视一圈下来要 1 个多小时，他始终坚持走路去现场。疫情暴发后，面对叙利亚缺医少药的窘境，他制定防护方案和措施，守住了一方净土，坚定了员工信心，有力地推进了项目进展。

在工作中，魏强不断以创新的思维探索国际化项目管理组织架构。叙利亚项目是个分段分步招标的项目，处于战后重启的状态，魏强不断创新和探索工作方法，他与业主共同梳理项目组织操作中的各执行环节，查漏补缺，多次向业主提出最佳解决方案，帮助业主解决了很多疑难杂症，收获了业主信任，业主多次将新增的施工标的交给 SINOMA 完成。

魏强在工作期间大力推行属地化战略，除了在一些日常岗位上大量招募本地员工外，一些相对关键的岗位也对外籍专业人士开放，魏强对当地竞聘者进行面试和考核，深入了解他们的想法和履历。属地化战略的实施，既解决了当地人员就业问题，也大大降低了劳动成本，更为关键的是，这些本地员工的加盟让项目部在当地遇到的很多难题都顺利解决。

疫情期间，魏强始终在思考如何开拓市场，不放弃任何机会，积极参加叙利亚水泥线上研讨会。魏强说：“既然我们在这，就要让市场

知道我们的存在，客户知道有我们在就会与我们对接需求，这就是我们在这的价值。”

多年工作生涯中，魏强做过总承包项目执行，也做过属地化市场开拓，他能够把市场开拓和项目执行进行很好地融合。在叙利亚项目执行期间，他续签了现场非标设备制作合同、钢结构制作合同等。

UCG 项目执行期间，面对各种基础和供货的技术问题，他总能和团队一起分析，一起策划，最终给出合理的技术方案。

魏强连续多年奋战在境外现场一线，为公司赢得了效益和荣誉，但他对于自己的家庭却深感亏欠。2017 年，孩子出生后尚未满月，他就奔赴了境外工作。近年来，他感觉到年迈的父母身体状态不如从前，庆幸的是妻子一直支持他的工作，将家里老人孩子的照料全都包揽下来。为了项目工作的顺利开展，2020 年，他再次放弃回家过年，奔赴叙利亚项目现场，和父母一起过年、过节的愿望至今没能实现。

“要说不难过，那是不真实的，我连续 5 年没有在家过年了，父母年龄大了，两个孩子还小，我就是家里的顶梁柱。可是想一想在万里外的项目现场，还有一些兄弟奋战在一线，作为负责人，我又怎能安心在家过节呢？换作谁，都一样的。”魏强说。

在大漠深处，他和他的团队一起躬于勤、勉于专，付出智慧，流下汗水，深度实践公司属地化战略，总结了一套丰赡、有序的宝贵经验，为公司高质量发展打下了坚实的基础。

魏强是众多奋战在海外一线的建材人的一个缩影。在大漠之外，更多的建材人正在冲破艰险、跨越障碍，正是他们无私的奉献，正是他们“有一分热、便发一分光”的精神，凝聚在一起，照亮着公司的美好未来。（中材国际所属中材海外）

虽然做国际工程项目很辛苦，远离亲人，压力大，但做好项目执行已成为我的乐趣。我愿意用我 20 年的经验积累，为沙特项目无私奉献、精细管理，带领团队把沙特项目打造成项目标杆，为公司国际化和属地化发展贡献自己的力量。

A Sincere Person Who Is Bravely Exploring the Desert

Wei Qiang

Joined CNBM in 2014

The General Manager of Saudi YAMAMA Project Department and Syria Project Department

Wei Qiang joined SINOMA Overseas Development Co., Ltd., a subsidiary of SINOMA International, in 2014. He ever took offices such as the project manager of Zimbabwe 100TPH cement grinding station, general representative of Zimbabwe Office, the site manager of Zimbabwe cement production line project with daily output of 6,500 tons, and he is now the General Manager of YAMAMA Project in Saudi Arabia. He has been honored as the company's Advanced Worker and the Patriotic Chinese Working Abroad multiple times. In 2019, he responded to the company's call even before Syria' s political situation stabilized, and with a strong sense of responsibility and mission, he led a team of colleagues to the project site in the Gobi Desert.

The clean water at the project site did not have a stable supply at the outset. Sometimes, well water became essential if they wanted to have a normal life. Summer in the desert was sultry and dry and mosquitos were a torturing trouble. Under this circumstance, Wei Qiang stayed there for a whole year. These hardships were nothing in his eyes.

To keep the project risks under control, he upheld the principle that "expenditure is determined according to income" and he objected to the practice of purchasing fixed assets by utilizing large sums of capital. It usually took him more than one hour to complete a tour inspection within the huge plant, but he did not change his habit of walking to the site. After the COVID-19 pandemic broke out, he made prevention and control plan to keep the project site safe from the pandemic. That strengthened the confidence of the staff and effectively promoted the progress of the project.

Wei Qiang constantly explores the organizational framework of internationalized project management with innovative thinking. The project in Syria, which involves segmented and step-by-step bidding, is in the phase of post-war restart. Wei Qiang kept innovating and exploring feasible methods in work and examined all the links of the project organization and operation together with the owner. He proposed the best solutions for the owner several times to help tackle some thorny problems. He was trusted by the owner, so the owner decided to assign the new construction projects to SINOMA.

Wei Qiang unsparingly promotes localized strategy in work. He recruits lots of local employees, and even makes some key posts accessible to foreign professionals. Interviews and assessments help him learn much about locals' experience and thoughts. His localized strategy offers jobs for local people and reduces labor costs for the company. More importantly, these local employees are a key to many tough problems that Project Department meets locally.

Wei Qiang kept thinking about how to expand the market during the pandemic period. He tried to seize any possible opportunity and actively participated in Syria Cement's webinar. He said, "Since we're operating here, we must make our presence known to market. If clients are aware of our presence, they will come and find us. It is where our value lies."

In his years of work, he has ever handled the execution of turnkey project and the expansion of localized market. He could perfectly align market expansion with project execution. For instance, when he was responsible for the execution of Syria project, he renewed the contract for on-site non-standard equipment production and the contract for steel structure product. Now the contracts for construction, design and supply are also under negotiation.

In the execution of UCG project, he analyzed various basic technical problems and supply-related problems with his team, and planned and offered workable technical solutions at last.

As a frontline employee working abroad for years, Wei Qiang has earned benefits and honors for the company. However, he has owed so much to his own family. In 2017, he bade farewell to his newborn baby and went abroad to work. In recent years, his parents are not so healthy as in the past. Fortunately, his wife is a strong support for his work. She takes good care of his parents and young children. To ensure the project's success, he again

gave up the chance of spending the Spring Festival at home in 2020 and went to work at the site of Syria project. In fact, his wish of spending the Spring Festival with the family has not come true so far.

"It is impossible not to feel sorry. I have not spent the Spring Festival with my family for five years in a row. My parents are old and two children are still young. I am the backbone of my family. But whenever I think of the project and those brothers working hard there, how can I, as a team leader, spend the holiday at home? If others were in my shoes, they would do the same," Wei Qiang said.

He and his team contributed their sweat and wisdom in the vast desert. They apply the company's localized strategy in every aspect of their work and extract valuable experience, laying a solid basis for the company's high-quality development in the future.

Wei Qiang is the epitome of many frontline employees working for overseas projects of SINOMA International. Beyond the desert, there are more of SINOMA's employees who are overcoming hardships and surmounting barriers. It is their selfless dedication and concerted efforts that brighten up the company's future.

Personal Insights Although working overseas is hard, away from family and stressful, but I enjoy successfully completing the projects. I am willing to use my 20 years of experience to make solid dedication and fine management for the Saudi project. I will lead the team to make the Saudi project a benchmark, and make my own contribution to the internationalization and localization development of the company.

项目管理领域的坚守者

陈波

2008 年加入中国建材
现任中国建材印尼佳通项目经理

陈波，领导和同事眼中“善于解决棘手疑难问题”的现场经理，自己口中“普普通通的工程人”，妻子和女儿心中的“工作狂”。工作 15 年来，6 个春节在项目现场度过，每年平均在项目现场的时间为 330 天。

“这里有个设备参数出现异常，请电气工程师立即联系厂家查明原因，及时采取措施，确保设备稳定运行。”最近，陈波正在忙着印尼佳通日产 6000 吨总承包项目熟料线点火准备事宜，他的每天微信运动步数均超 2 万步。从早上 7 点到晚上 10 点甚至更晚，这是他每天的工作时间表；从原料处理车间到生料粉磨车间，再到熟料煅烧车间，这是他每天的路线图。虽然工作特别忙碌，但眼看着 4 年前的一片荒地变为如今生机勃勃的厂房，即将迎来检验工程成果的一刻，他的内心充满了喜悦。4 年前初到印尼的一幕幕又浮现在他的眼前。

2017 年初，公司安排陈波及另一名同事前往印尼中爪哇省格罗波干县开展项目前期调研工作。当时，印尼对于中材智科（原南京凯盛）而言是一个陌生的市场。当地人英语普及率不高，大部分人讲的是印尼语。怎么解决语言问题呢？陈波依靠的是手机翻译软件，他将问题提前准备好。当地交通设施不完善，100 多公里的路程常常需要花费七八个小时的时间。他通常利用地图软件，提前查好机构名称及地址，然后组合使用各种交通工具前往，每天在路上颠簸十来个小时对他来说太正常不过了。

就这样，经过长达半年的调研和准备，陈波与当地移民局、警察局、税务局等多个政府机构建立了良好的联系，与农村基层长老建立了深厚友谊，现场开工事宜也一一筹备完毕，为项目的平稳开工奠定了坚实的基础。

2021 年 6 月，Delta 病毒来袭，由于即将点火的需要，现场无法封闭施工，业主及外协人员进场增加了病毒传播风险，高峰期公司上百人处于隔离状态。在这段时间内，陈波又化身心理咨询师，每天对心理波动较大的人员

进行心理疏导，耐心讲解防疫政策及应急措施，积极协调国内医疗专家在线答疑解惑，并通过各种途径协调当地医疗机构为症状较重者提供必要的医疗救助。

“有担当、有主见，解决疑难问题的能力很强，每个任务都能不折不扣地完成。”佳通项目部项目经理吴晓给予陈波很高的评价。

陈波的妻子、时常被人误认为是单亲妈妈的伍江艳说起丈夫，没有抱怨，但语气中略带遗憾。她记得有次陈波刚休假没两天，女儿发烧到 40.2 摄氏度，此时项目部一个电话打来，他二话不说就奔赴现场。

在评价自己作为丈夫和父亲的角色时，陈波深感惭愧：“项目的里程碑节点我都在，但孩子成长的里程碑我都错过了，第一次走路，第一次说话，第一次上学……”

无论任务有多棘手，无论条件有多不利，无论是否有大部队支援，他都勇往直前，义无反顾，全力以赴，使命必达。这份豪迈和荣耀，理当属于中材智科（原南京凯盛）项目管理领域的坚守者——陈波。〔中材国际所属中材智科（原南京凯盛）〕

个人体会 从青春年少到不惑之年，我加入公司已有十五年，为公司多个总承包项目挥洒汗水与青春。为公司发展而努力，我感到很自豪。未来，我将继续把责任扛在肩上，立足岗位，提升技能，为公司作出更大的贡献。

Unyielding Persistence within the Realm of Project Management

Chen Bo

Joined CNBM in 2008

The Project Manager of China National Building Materials Group Indonesia Giti Project

Chen Bo, the site manager recognized by leaders and colleagues as a skilled problem solver, humbly describes himself as an "ordinary engineering person." Meanwhile, his dedication to work is affectionately acknowledged by his wife and daughter, who lovingly refer to him as a "workaholic." Over the past 15 years, he has celebrated six Spring Festivals at the project site. Remarkably, his average duration of stay at the project site amounts to 330 days per year.

"We have detected an irregularity in one of the equipment parameters. Please ask the electrical engineer to promptly contact the manufacturer to investigate the cause and implement necessary measures, ensuring the operation of the equipment." Lately, Chen Bo has been engrossed in the preparations for the clinker line ignition of the Indonesia Giti project with 6,000 tons per day. Remarkably, he consistently achieves over 20,000 steps on his daily WeChat exercise tracker. His daily schedule stretches from 7 am to 10 pm and often extends even further. From overseeing raw material processing to managing raw material grinding and clinker calcining, he navigates a comprehensive roadmap each day. However, Chen Bo's heart brims with joy as he witnesses the remarkable transformation of a barren wasteland, which stood four years ago, into a thriving plant. A vivid memory from his initial visit to Indonesia four years ago resurfaced in his mind.

In early 2017, Chen Bo and a colleague, was assigned to embark on a pre-project research mission in Grobogan County, located in Central Java Province, Indonesia. During that period, Indonesia was an uncharted market for SINOMA International Intelligent Technology Co.,Ltd (Nanjing Kisen). The level of English language proficiency among the local population was considerably low, with the majority conversing in Indonesian. How to solve this problem? Chen Bo used translation app to prepare for potential challenges in advance. He practiced simple questions in Indonesian while on the go, taking the time to hone his language skills. For more complex inquiries, he displayed the questions on his mobile phone or seeking the assistance of a local translator for support. The local transportation was notably inadequate, often resulting in arduous journeys of seven to eight hours for distances exceeding 100 kilometers. As part of his routine, he relied on map software to retrieve the names and addresses of various organizations. Using a combination of transportation methods, he would navigate his way to each destination, often spending approximately 10 hours on the road daily.

Through six months of dedicated research and meticulous preparation, Chen Bo successfully established effective communication channels with local immigration bureaus, police, tax bureaus and other relevant agencies. Additionally, he fostered connections with rural elders at the grassroots level, fostering a strong foundation in preparation for the project's commencement and laying the groundwork for a seamless project launch.

In June 2021, the site faced the outbreak of the Delta virus. As the ignition phase was imminent, closure of the construction site was not feasible. However, the entry of the project owner and outsourced workers posed a heightened risk of virus transmission. During the peak period, hundreds of individuals were placed under quarantine measures. During this unprecedented period, Chen Bo took on the additional role of a psychological counselor. Each day, he tirelessly moved from one person to another, offering psychological counseling and support to individuals experiencing significant psychological fluctuations. He patiently explained the epidemic prevention policies and emergency measures, while also coordinating with domestic medical experts to address inquiries online. Furthermore, through various channels, he facilitated cooperation with local medical institutions to ensure necessary medical assistance was provided to those with severe symptoms.

"Chen Bo exhibits a remarkable sense of responsibility and assertiveness, coupled with a formidable aptitude for resolving complex issues. He tackles every task with unwavering determination, ensuring their completion without any compromises." Wu Xiao, the project manager of the Giti project department speaks highly of Chen Bo's performance and contributions.

Wu Jiangyan, Chen Bo's wife, has frequently being mistaken for a single mother. But talking about her husband, Wu Jiangyan's voice carries a hint of wistfulness but no trace of complaint. She remembered that once her husband had been on vacation for two days, their daughter had a fever of 40.2 degrees. But when the project department called, he immediately rushed to the site without uttering a word.

Reflecting on his role as a husband and father, Chen Bo acknowledges his absence during significant moments of his children's growth, such as their first steps, first words, and first day of school.

Irrespective of the challenges that lie ahead, regardless of the adverse circumstances and the absence of substantial support, he will press on with unwavering determination, wholeheartedly devoted to the cause, ensuring that the mission is accomplished. This heroic and glorious, are embodied by Chen Bo, an unwavering figure in the realm of project management at SINOMA International Intelligent Technology Co.,Ltd (Nanjing Kisen), who stands tall and resolute.

Personal Insights From youth to the age of 40, I have joined the company for 15 years, and shed sweat and youth for many contracted projects of the company. I am very proud to work hard for the development of the company. In the future, I will continue to take responsibility on my shoulders, based on my position, improve my skills, and make greater contributions to the company.

深耕细作　开拓创新

杨厚建

2000 年加入中国建材

现任中材国际赞比亚分公司总经理

“我就是个电气工程师，哪算得上贸易专家。”2021 年杨厚建在走访客户过程中，面对某大型矿区负责人的称赞，如是说道。赞比亚分公司在苏州中材的领导下，坚持“做一个项目，交一方朋友，树企业口碑”的原则。在疫情期间，他带领团队克服物价波动、物流缓阻等不利因素，精心组织，积极开拓，逆势完成了公司制定的各项贸易指标，得到了客户及合作伙伴的一致好评。“大家齐心，其利断金，精耕细作，勇于创新。赞比亚分公司取得的成就，是大家一起努力的结果。”杨厚建谦逊地说。

杨厚建刚刚担任赞比亚分公司负责人时，赞比亚 Dangote EPC&M 项目正处于移交阶段。适逢公司提出“246+”海外发展思路，分公司亟须开辟新赛道，实现发展目标。经反复调研、周密筹划，在得到公司批准后，他决定以水泥销售为突破口，开展贸易业务。面对未知领域，依托 SINOMA 品牌和分公司在当地积攒的资源和人脉，他带领团队联系拜访各个行业的龙头企业，虚心请教，从无到有，带领着分公司逐步将贸易业务发展壮大。从分公司其他同事口中了解到，贸易业务开展前期，杨厚建给团队留下的最深印象就是“常走夜路”。为向客户提供更好的服务，杨厚建要参考施工管理模式，对贸易流程进行精细化管理，这就需要他亲临每一个采购供应点和客户卸货点，亲自确认路线、产品质量和各个供应、物流环节的操作，他往往一次出差就是几天，吃饭休息均在车上度过。

一次在刚果（金）调研期间，在不懂当地语言、沿途道路崎岖险峻且中途得不到任何补给的情况下，杨厚建陪同客户深入远离城市 300 公里的群山中对煤矿进行实地考察。到了夜晚，大雨滂沱，随行的当地司机面对坑洼不平的道路和一侧陡峭的山崖，吓得不敢继续前进。可这里荒无人烟，被困在野外后果不堪设想，杨厚建挺身而出，凭借过硬的车技和良好的心理素质，一路坎坷总算将车驶离逾 30 公里的险要地段，直到行驶至一座殖民时期遗留的简陋教堂，大家才如释重负。在没水没电的

教堂安顿下来后，大家拿出干粮还没吃完，他早已和衣倒地，酣然入睡。

2020 年 3 月，面对疫情，赞比亚每天都有大量中国人乘机撤离。在公司的统一部署下，赞比亚分公司迅速成立新冠疫情防控小组，稳定员工情绪，建立防控应急机制。

得益于中材国际的平台优势，杨厚建带领着贸易团队逐步建立起了完整的采购、物流、保税、清关、销售的大宗商品贸易体系，并在市场竞争中站稳了脚跟。

2020 年有一段时间，每当从杨厚建办公室路过，同事们不时总能听见他温声细语的劝导的声音，同事们倒也见怪不怪，大家都知道是杨厚建大女儿即将参加中考，他原本早早就跟女儿约定好要回去陪她参加中考，但由于疫情和工作原因，他只能再次爽约。大家闲聊说到这个话题的时候，他满面愁容，摇着头说：“真没招，女儿跟我怄气也只能通过电话安慰安慰。”嘴里说着现在孩子到了叛逆期，怄气也很正常，但是他眼里却掩饰不住对女儿的疼爱和亏欠。对一个在工作中能直面各种挑战和困难的男人来说，无暇顾及家人大概是他最大的遗憾吧。

每个星期，杨厚建与团队都会组织晚间茶话会，分享外出调研和客户拜访的经验，提出工作中遇到的问题并讨论解决办法。他们时常能在轻松活跃的气氛中发散思维，一场头脑风暴后，对现行工作便有了更佳的执行方案，对未来发展也有了更好的创新想法。2021 年，分公司新承接 Mpande 工业园生产运营项目，为杨厚建在赞比亚的第一个 10 年画上一个圆满的“逗号”。

2023 年，杨厚建将带着他对赞比亚分公司贸易、多元工程、新产业投资等领域工作的深入思考和清晰规划，继续秉持实干为要、勇于创新的精神，带领团队奋勇拼搏，为分公司发展壮大贡献自己的力量，为公司海外发展继续发光发热。（中材国际所属苏州中材）

经过多年发展历练，我始终对公司饱含热爱与感激之情。在未来工作中我仍将保持锐意进取的精神面貌，践行“团结、担当、创新、奋进”的实干作风，不断提升自我，增长才干，回馈公司，成就不平凡的人生！

Striving for Excellence in a Pioneering and Innovative Manner

Yang Houjian

Joined CNBM in 2000

The General Manager of SINOMA International Engineering Co., Ltd. (Zambia Branch)

"I am just an electrical engineer, not an expert on trade." when visiting the client in 2021, Yang Houjian replied to the compliment from the person in charge of a large mining area. Under the leadership of SINOMA (Suzhou) Construction Co., Ltd. (SINOMA (Suzhou)), the Zambia branch has adhered to the principle of making friends with partners while doing projects in order to establish the enterprise reputation. During the pandemic, he overcame price fluctuations, logistics retardation and other adverse factors in a well-organized manner and got unanimous praises from clients and partners. Yang Houjian said humbly, "We are united in striving for excellence and innovation. With our joint efforts, the Zambia branch has achieved great success."

When Yang Houjian was the person responsible for the Zambia branch, the Dangote EPC&M project was in the handover stage. As the company put forward the "246+" overseas development idea, there was an urgent need for the branch to break new ground to achieve its development goals. After repeated investigation and careful planning, and with the approval of the company, the branch decided to seize the opportunity of selling cement to start the trade business. Facing the unknown area, based on the SINOMA brand and local resources and contacts accumulated by the branch, he led the team to contact and visit leading enterprises in various industries, sought advice from them modestly, and guided the branch to gradually develop its trade business from scratch. According to other colleagues of the branch, what Yang Houjian impressed the team most is "he always travels at night" in the early days of business development. In order to provide clients with better services, Yang Houjian required meticulous management of the trade process by referring to the construction management mode, so he had to visit every point of supply and purchase, and confirm the route, product quality and operation of various supply and logistics links in person. He often went on a business trip for several days, eating and resting in the car.

During his investigation and research in the Democratic Republic of the Congo, Yang Houjian accompanied a client on a field trip to a coal mine in a mountain 300 kilometers away from the city. At that time, he can't speak local language, the road was rugged, and there were no supplies midway. At night, when it rained heavily, the local driver was too scared to move on the roads which are all full of holes and steep cliffs. And if they were trapped in the wild, the consequences would be terrible. However, Yang Houjian threw himself into the breach, drove the car in the dangerous section with a length of more than 30 kilometers by virtue of excellent driving skills and good psychological quality, and finally made it to a shabby church left over from colonial times. Everyone felt a sense of relief. After settling down in the church without water and electricity, he had already fallen asleep with his clothes on before everyone finished their food.

In March 2020, the first case of COVID-19 was detected in Zambia, and then the pandemic quickly spread to all corners of the country. Facing the pandemic, a lot of Chinese people were evacuated from Zambia by air every day. Under the unified deployment of the company, the Zambia branch quickly set up a pandemic prevention and control team, stabilized employees' emotions, and established an emergency response mechanism for prevention and control.

Thanks to the platform of SINOMA International, Yang Houjian and his trading team gradually set up a complete commodity trading system of procurement, logistics, bond, customs clearance and sales, and gained a firm foothold in market competition.

In 2020, whenever passing by Yang Houjian's office, colleagues could always hear his gentle voice of patient persuasion from time to time. They were not surprised, and they all knew that his eldest daughter was about to take the high school entrance exam. Originally, Yang Houjian planned to accompany his eldest daughter, but he had no choice but to break the appointment due to the pandemic and work. When chatting with colleagues and mentioning this, he looked worried and shook his head, saying that he didn't know what to do and he could only console his angry daughter by phone. He mentioned that it was normal for children to be angry during the stage of rebellion, but colleagues could sense his love for his daughter in his eyes. For a man who can face all challenges and difficulties in his work, being too busy to take care of his family is probably his biggest worry.

Every week, Yang Houjian and his team organize evening tea parties, share their experiences in investigation and visiting clients, put forward problems encountered in their work, and discuss solutions. They tend to think big in a relaxed and lively atmosphere. After brainstorming, they will generate a better implementation plan for the current work and a better innovative idea for the future development. In 2021, the branch undertook the new production and operation project of Mpande Industrial Park, marking a successful milestone in Yang Houjian's first decade in Zambia.

In 2023, Yang Houjian will continue to adhere to the practical and innovative spirit, lead his team to work hard in a modest manner, contribute to the development and expansion of the branch. He will also devote himself to the overseas development of Zambia branch by virtue of his deep thinking and clear planning in such fields as trade, diversified engineering, new industry investment and other fields.

Personal Insights Through years of working, I have always felt passionate and gratitude towards SINOMA. From now on, I will keep forging ahead with determination. By laying emphasis on unity, ambition, innovative development, and fully living up to my responsibility, I will persist in elevating myself and contributing more to the company, thus leading to an extraordinary life.

爱拼才会赢

周有均

1993 年加入中国建材

现任苏州中材生产运维中心高级经理

1993 年，刚刚毕业的周有均加入了苏州中材。那时候，闽南歌曲《爱拼才会赢》正风靡一时，也深深地影响着他。在 28 年的一线工作生涯中，他从一名普通员工成长为项目经理，是认真、尽职、精诚的品质令他脱颖而出。他始终以高度的责任感和强烈的事业心对待自己的业务工作，经过多年打拼，周有均把自己磨砺成了一名“一专多能”的复合型人才。

在主抓现场施工期间，他凭借自己多年积累的施工经验和扎实的技术功底，大胆采用新的施工方法，将专业化的技术能力、良好的企业形象展现在业主面前，赢得了良好的口碑。他参与建设的越南福山 5000t/dPC 总承包工程获得了“中国建设工程鲁班奖（境外工程）”，阿联酋 UCC10000t/d 安装工程获得集团科学技术进步特等奖。

在 2011 年开始的南非项目建设过程中，业主对施工过程中的安全控制尤为严苛。作为安全经理，周有均积极学习当地安全法规，对安全工作严抓细管，无论是在矿山取料口，还是在窑尾框架和熟料库，都能见到他的身影，这段工作经历也为他积累了难能可贵的专业知识与实战经验。

2013 年底，周有均被派往伊拉克卡尔巴拉（拉法基）水泥厂技改项目。再次面对复杂多变的安全局势以及高难度技改等问题，他以积极主动的姿态接受挑战，带领团队根据节点任务制订计划、周密部署，每天深入现场进行检查落实，牢牢把控每个项目节点的进度，如期完成两条生产线的技改任务，用行动向业主展示了苏州中材不畏艰难、攻坚克难的铁军精神，赢得业主信赖，获得高度赞誉。

2017 年起，周有均开始从事生产运营管理工作，他利用业余时间不断充实自己在生产管理方面的专业知识，提升管理水平。通过不断学习和理解“三精管理”，在设备精细化管理方面，进一步降低了设备维护和维修的成本。在全员精益化管理方面，通过激发员工的积极性和主观能动性，不断提高生产的技术保障能力、提高设备运转效率。他所在的项目创造了

水泥熟料连续 3 年增产的记录，不断刷新历史新高，不仅为公司取得了良好收益，也提升了苏州中材在伊拉克市场的口碑和竞争力，为公司的高质量发展作出了积极贡献。

在生活中，周有均以与人为善的心态对待每一个人，他利用业余时间及时了解项目部每一位员工的思想动态，力所能及地帮助他们解决工作和生活中的实际困难，做好“双稳”工作，稳定了员工队伍。在他看来，“每一位员工不远万里来到异国他乡，唯有爱心和善意才能聚力成城”。

在非常特殊的环境中，他以“拼”的精神“赢”得尊重和认可，以扎实的业绩为公司高质量发展添砖加瓦。在新征程中，坚守奉行着“爱拼才会赢”的信念，周有均和他的团队以建材追梦人的风采勇立潮头、砥砺前行。

（中材国际所属苏州中材）

进入苏州中材工作，是我一生中非常荣幸的事情。28 年来，我亲历了公司的发展与壮大，同时我也不断成长。我将继续坚守初心，努力工作，为公司“十四五”时期高质量发展贡献力量。

No Pain, No Gain

Zhou Youjun

Joined CNBM in 1993

The Senior Manager of SINOMA(Suzhou) O&M Center

Zhou Youjun joined SINOMA(Suzhou) Construction Co., Ltd. in 1993 as a fresh graduate. The southern Fujian song No Pain, No Gain was hitting the market and deeply influenced him. In his 28-year career at the front line, he stood out for his conscientiousness, dedication and sincerity, climbing the corporate ladders from an ordinary employee to a project manager. With a high sense of responsibility and achievement, he has made constant progress in the cause. After years of hard work, Zhou Youjun has grown into an interdisciplinary talent.

During the on-site construction, he boldly adopted new construction methods by virtue of his accumulated experience and solid technical knowledge over years, thus showing professional ability and a high-efficient corporate image to the employer, and winning a great reputation. The 5,000t/d PC general contracting project in Phuoc Son, Vietnam he participated in won the "China Construction Engineering Luban Prize (Overseas Project)" and the UCC 10,000t/d installation project in UAE won the Group's Special Prize of Science and Technology Progress Award.

During the construction of the South Africa Project, which was launched in 2011, the employer has exposed a particularly strict safety control over the process. As a Safety Manager, Zhou Youjun took an active role in learning local safety regulations and employed severe measures to manage safety work. He could be seen anywhere, from the mine dump position and kiln tail frame to the clinker silo. The process has also accumulated valuable professional knowledge and practical experience for him.

At the end of 2013, Zhou Youjun was dispatched to Karbala (Lafarge) Cement Plant Technical Upgrading Project in Iraq. Again, he faced a complex and volatile security situation as well as high-difficulty technical transformation. With courage and confidence, he positively rose to the challenges, leading the team to make plans and careful deployment according to node tasks, inspecting and implementing the details on site every day, and firmly controlling the progress of each node. By doing this, he and his team completed the technical upgrading tasks of two production lines on schedule and demonstrated the iron troop spirit of SINOMA(Suzhou) to overcome difficulties with actions. Moreover, he has alleviated the employer's worries, gained trust and won praise.

Zhou Youjun has been responsible for production and operation management since 2017. In his spare time, he has been continuously learning professional knowledge in related fields to improve his management level. By learning and implementing "three-pronged fine management", he has further reduced the cost of equipment maintenance and repair. Meanwhile, he continued to improve the technical support ability of production and equipment operation efficiency by stimulating the enthusiasm and self-motivation of employees. His projects have increased the output of cement clinker for three consecutive years, constantly reaching new heights. Besides remarkable profits for the company, this move has also enhanced its reputation and competitiveness in the Iraq market, making positive contributions to the high-quality development of the company.

In a difficult environment, he has won respect and recognition with his "endeavoring" spirit and contributed to the company's high-quality development with marvelous performance. Embarking on the new journey , Zhou Youjun and his team, as dream chasers in SINOMA International, have prepared to stand at the forefront of the time with an unwavering will to forge ahead.

Personal Insights Working in SINOMA(Suzhou) is a great honor in my life. Over the past 28 years, I have witnessed the development and growth of the company, which made me grow at the same time. I will continue to stick on my original aspiration and work hard to contribute to high-quality development of the company's "14th Five-Year Plan".

如“螺丝钉”一般坚守在岗

李良辉
2018 年加入中国建材
现任邯郸中材缅甸万宏项目经理助理

李良辉，现任邯郸中材缅甸万宏项目经理助理。自入职以来，他一直奋斗在项目建设一线。他爱岗敬业，锐意进取，作风严谨，执行力强，工作配合度高，是领导的好助手，是同事的好伙伴，凭借工作中出色的表现，多次获得集团和公司的优秀员工称号。他说，这些荣誉就是努力最好的回报，也是让他不断奋勇向前的动力。

李良辉是个 90 后，一毕业便加入了邯郸中材大家庭，如今已是第五个年头。入职伊始，他怀着一颗“初生牛犊不怕虎”的炽热之心，主动申请加入了缅甸旦多淼项目，他说：“与其说缅甸旦多淼项目是我工作学习的地方，不如说这个境外项目是我的‘战场’。”

身为一名土建技术员，他先后参建了缅甸旦多淼二线排洪沟工程、三线地勘及临建工程、缅甸仰光粉磨站地勘及临建工程。缅甸三线项目临建施工前，仅施工方案就画了十几份，他在一次次的自我否定中追求完美，一直画到满意为止。

在缅甸仰光粉磨站项目做地勘时期，每天天色微亮，李良辉便从宿舍匆匆赶往 30 公里外的地勘场地。白天顶着接近 40℃的高温和暴晒，他仔细在现场记录地勘数据。晚上回到住所，他再将所有白天采集到的数据录入电子表格中，做好施工记录，每次工作结束都已经是深夜。农村小伙儿吃苦耐劳的精神在他身上发挥得淋漓尽致，再加上师傅的“传帮带”，李良辉在业务上快速成长，在极短的时间就熟悉并掌握了大部分一线施工的流程和技术要领。

2019 年 8 月，李良辉开始正式负责缅甸旦多淼三线土建工程管理、缅甸旦多淼燃煤电厂二线土建及安装管理工作。因为属地管理技术人员母语为缅语且第二语言为英语，英语还不错的李良辉欣然接受了帮助新来的属地员工学习、适应公司文化的任务，帮助解决他们在生活和工作中遇到的各种问题。新员工给项目部注入了新鲜的血液，李良辉也从徒弟变成师父，当初从自己师父身上学到的技能，如今他

也倾囊相授，由于表现突出，他与他的徒弟还被评为邯郸中材 2020 年“优秀师徒”。

作为缅甸子公司团支部书记，李良辉在工作和生活中以身作则，紧密联系青年团员，发扬艰苦奋斗、扎根一线的新时代革命精神。在缅甸子公司团支部的带领下，项目青年员工将学习的知识更好地应用到实际工作中，在不断学习和实践中提升了发现问题、解决问题的能力。2020 年，缅甸子公司团支部荣获“中材国际五四红旗团支部”的荣誉称号。

2019 年 8 月的一天早晨，李良辉所在项目的人，两两一组张贴宣传条幅，与他同组的缅籍员工在张贴时不小心滑倒，掉进了排洪沟中。由于前几天刚刚下过雨，排洪沟中水流比较急，这名员工掉下去的时候已被冲出几米远了。面对这种突发状况，李良辉来不及思考，迅速跳进水里将人一把捞起，幸运的是，被救的人并无大碍，大家虚惊一场，而李良辉因此受了轻伤，手机也报废了。有人说他是英雄，他笑笑说：“‘英雄’不敢当，当时自己心中只有一个念头——救人，其他的没多想，后来回想起来心里才有些后怕。”

“独在异乡为异客，每逢佳节倍思亲。”入职以来接连 3 个春节，李良辉都是在项目部度过的。他说：“其实我也很想家，想念父母亲，想念家乡的山山水水，可我更爱项目部这个和睦的大家庭。一想到还有很多跟我一样，过年期间仍坚守在岗位上的兄弟姐妹们，我就浑身充满了干劲儿。”

入职 5 年，李良辉始终坚守岗位，就像一颗“螺丝钉”，紧紧地守护着自己平凡的岗位，一刻也不放松，他用汗水和智慧践行着新时代青年的使命与担当。（中材国际所属邯郸中材）

个人体会

我参加工作后便选择扎根建设现场，就像一颗“螺丝钉”，紧紧地守护着自己平凡的岗位。我愿意继续将满腔热血投入工作中，团结和带领同事一起深耕一线，为公司的发展贡献微薄之力，祝愿公司越来越好。

A Man Dedicated to His Job

Li Lianghui

Joined CNBM in 2018

The Assistant Project Manager of SINOMA Handan Myanmar biomass fuel power plants project

Li Lianghui is the Assistant Project Manager of SINOMA Handan Myanmar Wanhong New Energy Comprehensive Multi-Energy Complementary Project. Since he joined the company, he has been working at the frontline. As a dedicated, enterprising and meticulous man with strong execution and readiness to cooperate, he is a good assistant to leaders and a good partner for colleagues. He has been recognized several times as the "Excellent Employee" by the branch company and SINOMA because of his outstanding performance. As he said, these honors are the best reward for his hard work and the driving force that encourages him to keep forging ahead.

Li Lianghui, a young man born in the 1990s, has joined the company for five years since he graduated from university. He had a strong passion for his work and volunteered to join the company's Than Taw Myat cement project in Myanmar. He said, "Than Taw Myat project is not so much a place where I work and study but a 'battlefield' for me."

As a civil engineering technician, he participated in Line 2 drainage ditch project and Line 3 prospecting and temporary facilities project of Than Taw Myat cement project in Myanmar, and prospecting and temporary facilities project of the cement grinding station in Yangon. Before the construction of Line 3 temporary facilities project was started, he designed and revised over ten construction plans until he finally got the most satisfactory plan.

When he was a prospector in the project of a cement grinding station, Li Lianghui rose from bed at dawn and hurried to the prospecting site about 30 kilometers away from his dormitory. In the daytime, he meticulously recorded all prospecting data regardless of the scorching sun and high temperature. At night, he entered all collected data in the spreadsheets as the part of construction records. He always worked far into the night. He is a perfect example of a tough and hardworking young man with rural background. What's more, the company's mentorship helped him grow fast in business and get acquainted with most of the frontline construction processes and technical essentials in a short time.

In August 2019, Li Lianghui started to take charge of Than Taw Myat Line 3 civil engineering project, and Line 2 civil engineering and installation project of Than Taw Myat coal-fired power plant. Since the local managerial and technical staff members all speak Burmese and English, he, a fluent English speaker, was pleased with the task of being a "guide" for the new local technicians. He helped the newcomers learn and become adapted to the company's culture, and solved various problems in their life and work. After the new employees breathed new life into the company, he changed from an apprentice to a master. He shared with his apprentice all he had learned from his master. Because of his outstanding performance, he and his apprentice were honored as the company's 2020 Excellent Master and Apprentice.

As the secretary of the Youth League branch in the company's Myanmar subsidiary, he set a good example in both life and work. He forged close ties with members of the Youth League and carried forward the revolutionary spirit for this new era - working diligently amidst hardships and pumping all efforts into frontline work. Under the leadership of the Youth League branch, the young employees of Project Department could make better use of their new knowledge in work and they learned how to discover and solve problems through their constant study and practice. The Youth League Branch of Myanmar subsidiary was recognized by the title of "May 4th Red-Flag Youth League Branch of SINOMA International".

On one morning in August 2019, the Project Department, assigned each team of two employees to put up publicity banners. A Burman employee of Li Lianghui's team, unexpectedly slipped and fell into a drainage ditch which had swift torrents because of heavy rain several days before. And the Burman employee was instantly swept away. In the face of this emergency, Li Lianghui waited for no time to jump into the water and got his colleague

out of danger. Luckily, the Burmese was not injured, but Li Lianghui was slightly wounded and his mobile phone had to be discarded. He was praised as a hero, but he smiled and replied, "I'm nothing of a 'hero'. The only thing in my mind was to get him out of water. Nothing else flashed through my mind. But I now find it's rather dangerous."

As a poem of Tang Dynasty said, "All alone in a strange land, I miss my family all the more on each festival day." Since he joined the company, Li Lianghui had spent the Spring Festival far away from home for three consecutive years. He said, "Frankly, I really miss my family, miss my parents, and miss my hometown. But I also love Project Department. It's a happy family for me. The moment I find many colleagues are still sticking to their posts during the Spring Festival, I am instantly filled with enthusiasm."

In his five-year engagement with the company, Li Lianghui has been dedicated to his daily job, like a "screw", and fulfilled his mission and responsibility as a young man of this new era.

Personal Insights After I joined the work, I chose to take root in the construction site, just like a "screw", to guard my ordinary position tightly. I am willing to continue to devote myself to my work, unite and lead my colleagues to work together in the front line, and contribute to the company's development. Wish the company a better future.

忠于职守 甘于奉献 助力建设“非洲之星”

巴塞纽·特克莱耶苏斯·斯泰胡

2021年加入中国建材

现任苏州中材埃塞莱米万吨线项目安全工程师

苏州中材埃塞莱米日产万吨水泥熟料生产线项目被称为“非洲之星”，是非洲首条万吨线项目。巴塞是苏州中材埃塞莱米万吨线项目所在地的本地人，所学专业为安全管理，于2021年7月大学毕业后加入苏州中材埃塞莱米万吨线项目部，参与了项目前期准备、市场调研、属地员工管理及安全管理等工作。

巴塞是属地员工委员会的主要负责人，他经常自豪地表示：“我在中企工作，我为SINOMA服务。”巴塞在工作中踏实努力、勤奋好学，结合大学所学到的安全专业理论知识和在现场学到的实践经验，从简单的工作开始做起，始终坚持“干一行，爱一行”的理念。

由于他表现突出，责任心较强，他目前主要负责对外协调、属地员工的管理及安全管理工作。在工作中，他始终以《中材国际安全作业防护标准》为准绳，对现场的各项安全工作坚持高标准、严要求。他平时积极向领导、同事学习，发现问题及时请教，以“俯下身、多观察、多动脑、多动手、多学习”的态度，努力工作，任劳任怨，很快地熟悉了项目部的情况，较好地融入团队当中，充分了解到一名专职安全员的职责和责任，为以后的工作奠定了基础。同时他利用工作之余，刻苦钻研业务知识，努力提高业务水平，认真践行中国建材集团的“三精管理”。

巴塞日常会给当地入场新员工做入场安全教育，且对现场的安全标准化进行实时监督，有时会解决一些安保方面的问题。在现场与我们交流时，他经常会说：“安全为天，质量第一，学无止境，我一定要做好本职工作，保护好每一位工友。”每周及每月巴塞都会主动与安环科其他成员一起进行现场的安全大检查以及各

个专项检查工作，并定期组织当地员工学习相关安全知识，让每个员工知道如何辨识危险源，还会通过相关理论的学习，掌握如何控制危险源，以降低施工现场事故的发生率。在巴塞的支持和带动下，施工现场安全态势保持良好，能够做好安全文明施工，属地员工的安全生产意识也得到了极大地提升。

巴塞除了做好安全管理工作外，也负责协调和地方政府的关系、办理相关政府审批文件、解决属地员工的各种纠纷等。

践行国际化发展战略需要更多像巴塞这样的外籍员工，巴塞脚踏实地、肯学肯干的工作精神未来将会感染更多的属地员工加入 SINOMA 的大家庭，助力公司国际化发展取得更大突破！（中材国际所属苏州中材）

个人体会

能够成为 SINOMA 的一员是我的荣幸，SINOMA 是一个积极向上的公司，我喜欢和 SINOMA 同事一起工作。在 SINOMA 工作期间，我学到了很多，从项目安全管理到 SINOMA 的企业文化，从博大精深的中国文化到 SINOMA 的“家”文化，SINOMA 的各个方面吸引着我，希望有机会去 SINOMA 总部看看。

Dedicated to the Construction of the "African Star"

Baseznew Tekleyesus Sntayhu

Joined CNBM in 2021

The Safety Engineer of SINOMA (Suzhou) Ethiopian Lemi 10,000t/d Cement Clinker Production Project

The SINOMA (Suzhou) Ethiopian Lemi 10,000t/d Cement Clinker Production Project is called "African Star", and it is the first 10,000t/d cement clinker production project in Africa. Base is a local, specializing in safety management. After graduating from university in July 2021, he joined the Project Department and participated in the project's preliminary preparation, market research, local employee management and safety management.

Base is the main person in charge of the local employee committee, and he often proudly says to other people that he works in a foreign company of SINOMA. Base works hard, diligent and studious. Combining the theoretical knowledge learned in the university and the practical experience learned in the field, he starts from the simplest work and loves his job. Due to his outstanding performance and strong sense of responsibility, he is currently responsible for external coordination, management of local employees and safety management. During the work, he always takes the "SINOMA International Safety Operation Protection Standard" as the guideline, and insists on high standards and strict requirements for all safety work on site. He usually actively learns from the leaders and colleagues, and consult and solve problems promptly. With an modest attitude, Base worked hard with observing, thinking and learning. He quickly became familiar with the department and integrated into the team, fully understood the responsibilities of a full-time security officer, laying the foundation for future work. At the same time, he took advantage of his spare time to study business knowledge assiduously, strive to improve his business level, and earnestly practice the management regulations of the group company.

Base will provide on-site safety education for new local employees on a daily basis, supervise the real-time safety standardization on site, and sometimes solve some security problems. He would often say: “Safety is paramount, quality comes first, and learning is endless. I must do my job well and protect every worker.” He will take the initiative to conduct on-site safety inspections and various special inspections with other colleagues every week and every month. He regularly organizes local employees to learn relevant safety knowledge, so that each employee knows how to identify danger sources and how to identify the source of danger to reduce the incidence of accidents on the site. With the support and drive of Base, the safety situation at the construction site has always been good, safe and civilized construction can be done well, and the safety awareness of local employees has also been

greatly improved.

In addition to safety management, Base is also responsible for coordinating the relationship with local governments, handling relevant government approval documents, and various disputes among local employees. The international development strategy needs more foreign employees like Base. Base's down-to-earth, willing to learn and hard-working spirit will inspire more local employees to join the SINOMA family in the future, helping the company achieve greater breakthroughs in its international development.

Personal Insights It is my honor to be a member of SINOMA. SINOMA is a positive and energetic company. I like working with SINOMA colleagues together. I have learned a lot while working in SINOMA. From project safety management to SINOMA's corporate culture, from the profound Chinese culture to SINOMA's "home" culture, all aspects of SINOMA attract me. I hope that I have the opportunity to visit SINOMA's headquarter one day.

与 SINOMA 携手同行 创造美好世界

伊马卡瓦尔·富兰克林

2011 年加入中国建材

现任苏州中材尼日利亚 Obajana5 线项目土建工程师

我的名字叫伊马卡瓦尔·富兰克林，来自尼日利亚的 EDO 州。我于 2011 年 2 月加入 SINOMA，现任科吉州丹格特水泥 Obajana5 线土建工程师。我在埃多州奥奇理工学院获得了土木工程技术专业的学位。

在加入中材国际之前，我曾在 Marubeni 西非工程有限公司（MEWAL）工作，该公司是一家日本公司。我的工作经历拓宽了我在土木工程建设领域的知识，这使我能够更好地履行职责。

回顾在中材国际工作的时光，有很多的小插曲，我曾有过犹豫，不过最终都更加坚定了我和中材国际一起走下去的决心。一开始加入公司的时候，由于办公室的土建工程师基本都是中国人，我作为仅有的一名当地工程师有很多的不适应，主要是语言沟通存在着一些障碍。但随着时间的流逝，中国人的勤劳、专业的工作态度慢慢地感染了我。工作让我成长很快，曾经有分包单位想花高薪雇用我，面对这种诱惑，我当时有所心动，但是中国主管长远的眼光使我意识到，在中材国际我会有更好的发展前途。事实证明了他们所说的是对的，我在中材国际工作期间并没有出现过因分包商撤场带来的工作中断的情况，更难能可贵的是公司给我的薪资待遇也逐步提高，这更加坚定了我与 SINOMA 同行的信念。每次想起来我都庆幸自己当时做了留在中材国际的正确决定。

工程建设是一个受时间限制且具有挑战性的工作，如工程设计、项目管理、施工、材料数量和评估、测量等。我的工作一直是在现场，主要工作内容是确保现场能够按照设计施工，在施工阶段负责分包商和业主之间的沟通工作，我在施工过程中如果发现图纸中有任何问题要及时向主管报告。我会在脑海中牢记项目时间表和在施工的各个阶段要完成的目标，并用各种工程软件跟踪和监测工作进度，通过电子邮件和电话定期汇报工作，使公司主管了解项目的进展情况。

我和团队、分包商以及业主之间一直保持着良好沟通。我也和中国同事建立了深厚的友谊，我们总是相互学习。因为我的英语说得比较地道，中国主管经常让我带一些新来的中国同事，跟他们练习英语口语，他们都有很好的英语基础，只是平时说的比较少，在我的引导下，他们很快可以顺畅沟通，也可以独立与业主沟通协调现场的施工细节。在日常工作交流中，我发现自己慢慢地对中文产生了浓厚的学习兴趣，中国同事也会耐心地教我一些常用的中文词汇，特别是公司组织的中文工坊培训极大地帮助了我，让我学到了更多中文和专业技能，这都有利于我和中国同事进行工作上的互动。在专注于现场土建施工的同时，有时我还负责现场安全，协助项目部做好现场安全管理工作。

我非常感激中材国际给我提供的工作机会，使我能够在履行职责的过程中学到很多，不错的收入也使我能够幸福地生活。感谢各位中方同事让我接触到土木工程领域的方方面面，感谢公司带给我的成长，我将继续努力工作，为公司发展贡献自己的力量。（中材国际所属苏州中材）

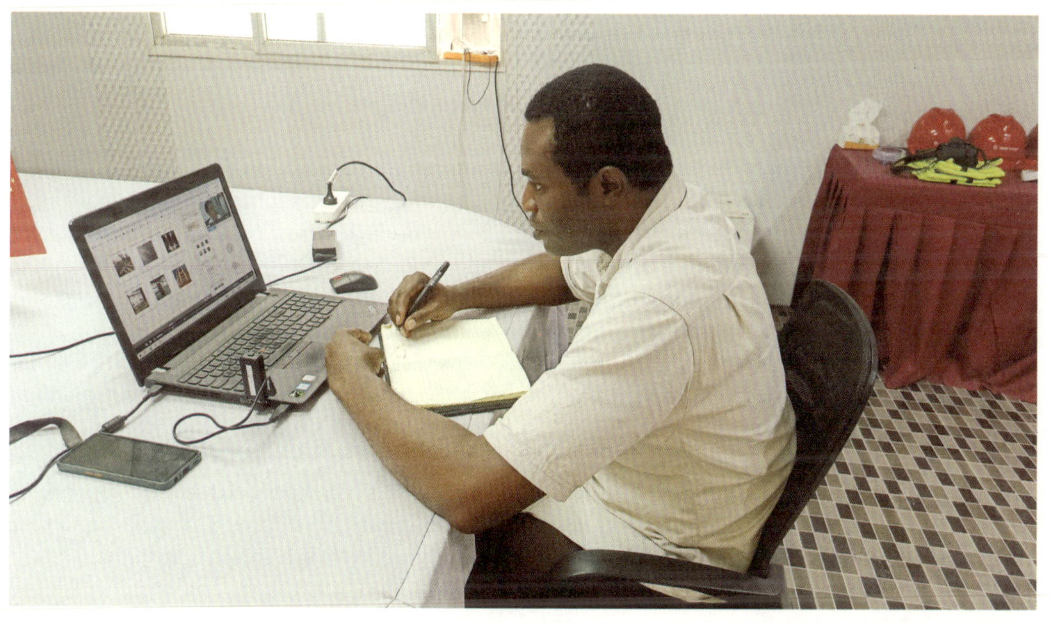

个人体会

12 年来，我由一个名不见经传的土建技术员成长为一名优秀的属地化土建工程师，这都得益于公司对我的辛勤栽培和领导对我的谆谆教导。在未来的岁月中，我将同 SINOMA 共命运、同呼吸，竭尽所能帮助公司培养更多的本土化人才，助推公司国际化发展迈上新台阶。

Create a Better World with SINOMA

Imakavar Franklyn

Joined CNBM in 2011

The Civil Engineer of SINOMA (Suzhou) Nigeria Obajana Line 5 Project

I am Imakavar Franklyn from EDO State, Nigeria. I joined SINOMA in February 2011. I am currently a civil engineer of Obajana 5 Line of Dangote Cement in Koji State. I bagged HND degree in civil engineering technology from Auchi Polytechnic.

Before joining SINOMA, I worked with Marubeni Engineering West Africa Limited, a Japanese company which specialize in the construction of power plant across the world. The past twelve years working with SINOMA has broaden my knowledge in the field of civil engineering construction, which better enables me to discharge my duties.

Looking back at the time when I worked in SINOMA, I hesitated, but finally I went on with SINOMA more firmly. At the beginning, when I joined the company, as the civil engineers in the office were basically Chinese, I had a lot of discomfort as the only local engineer. However, as time passed, the hardworking and professional attitude of Chinese people infected me. Work makes me grow rapidly. Some subcontractors once tempted me with higher salary, but the long-term vision of my Chinese supervisor made me realize that I would have more stability and development in SINOMA. Indeed, during my time at SINOMA, there was no interruption of work caused by the withdrawal of subcontractors, and my salary also gradually increased. Now every time I think about it and realize how right my choice was at that time.

Industrial construction is a time-limited and challenging task, such as engineering design project management, construction, material quantity and evaluation, surveying etc. I am always on the site to ensure clarity, mediate between sub-contractor and client and report any discrepancy in the drawing to my Chinese supervisor. I will keep the project schedule in mind and the goals to be achieved in each stage of construction. I will also be able to track and monitor the progress of the work using various engineering software and report to my Chinese supervisors via email and phone to keep them informed of the progress of the project.

I have good communication with the team, subcontractors and the owner. I have built a strong friendship with my Chinese colleagues and we always learn from each other. Because my English is more authentic, my Chinese supervisor often asked me to teach some new Chinese colleagues and practice oral English with them. They all have good English foundation, but usually speak less. Under my guidance, they can soon communicate smoothly and communicate independently with the owner

to coordinate the construction details on site. The Chinese colleagues are also very patient in teaching me some common Chinese vocabulary, especially the technical training organized by the company has also helped me a lot to learn more Chinese and professional skills, which is beneficial to my interaction with Chinese supervisors at work. While focusing on the civil construction, I am also responsible for site safety and assist the project department in site safety management.

I am very grateful for the job opportunity provided by SINOMA, which enables me to learn a lot in the process of performing my duties, and the good income enables me to live happily. I would like to thank all the Chinese supervisors for giving me the chance to learn all aspects of the civil engineering field, and I would like to thank the company for the growth brought to me. I will continue to work hard and contribute my strength for the development of the company.

Personal Insights Over the past twelve years, I have grown from an unknown civil engineering technician to an excellent localized civil engineer. This depends on the considerate cultivation of the company and Chinese colleagues' earnest teaching. In the years to come, I will share the fate and breath with SINOMA, and do my best to help the company cultivate more localized talents and push the company's nationalization business to a new level.

巴基斯坦“老铁”

沙凯博·阿赫迈德·赛迪科
2017 年加入中国建材
现任邯郸中材巴基斯坦子公司外事主管

老铁一词来源于方言中的“铁哥们儿”，是对哥们儿的别称，形容亲近、牢靠、值得信任、像铁一样坚固的关系。邯郸中材巴基斯坦子公司也有一位这样的“老铁”。

沙凯博·阿赫迈德·赛迪科，巴基斯坦籍，2012 年毕业于英国格拉摩根大学工程管理专业，理工类硕士研究生，毕业后有近 5 年从事石油天然气勘探和 EPC 项目建设方面相关工作经验。2017 年 2 月，他加入邯郸中材巴基斯坦子公司，岗位为外事主管，主要负责公司在巴基斯坦的物流清关、协助子公司中国团队市场拓展经营和地方事务处理等工作。入职公司 5 年来，他多次获得优秀员工称号。

沙凯博在协助物流清关工作中，顺利地完成了巴基斯坦各批次的物资清关，保证了现场施工的有序推进。他在银行交单审核过程中积极采取措施，对各项疑问做出了合理解释并妥善加以处置，积极与银行沟通汇率问题，尽一切可能降低子公司的当地成本。

在协助子公司中国团队市场拓展经营方面，沙凯博参与了巴基斯坦部分项目的市场经营和合同谈判。疫情期间，市场经营尤其困难，为了避免交叉感染，除了会议期间必须佩戴防护用品外，还要做到全程不吃不喝、不上厕所，开会一坐就是一天，对人的体能也是一种挑战。在这样的情况下，他利用在英语方面的优势，协助子公司团队对英文合同条款进行审核，协助子公司新签订施工合同 6 份，完成了年度经营指标。在收取进度款、税费、扣款证明等方面，他积极配合，使得各项目得以及时收款，解决了子公司的资金压力。

沙凯博始终专注于市场经营与开拓，利用施工信息化手段，全面在当地公共媒体平台宣传公司市场业绩、经营理念。使公司在行业内市场认可度逐渐提高，使公司品牌被绝大多数巴基斯坦水泥业主所认可。

在地方事务处理方面，沙凯博积极配合财务人员与地方税务局、财税审计团队等进行协作，确保了各项业务的顺利完成。子公司在公司注册事宜上，沙凯博与相关部门充分沟通，

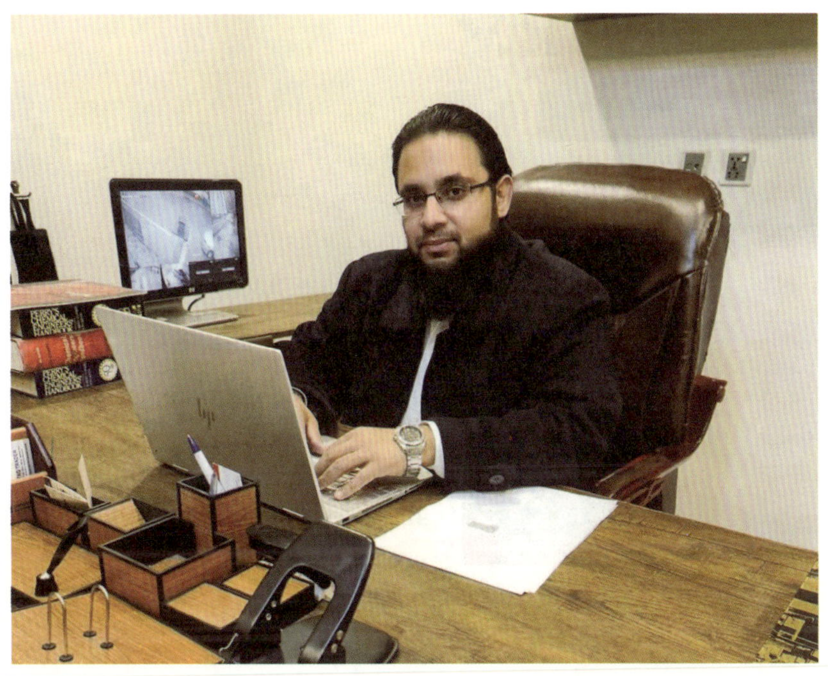

确保了各项资料的提供和完善，为公司的下一步运作提供了完整的资料支持；当年子公司收到地方税务局 3 份税务检查通知单，他积极配合财务人员与主管机关沟通，顺利完成了当年度的税务检查，并提出整改意见和建议，不遗余力地发挥自身优势为公司发展建言献策；在年度财税审计过程中，他负责与审计团队沟通答疑，顺利完成了当年的审计检查工作，为年度所得税汇算清缴提供了完整的申报支持。

沙凯博对待工作认真负责，爱岗敬业，积极服从公司的各项工作安排，与同事相处融洽，善于合作，业务知识扎实，高效率、高质量的工作表现得到了子公司上下的一致认可。

谈到未来，这位“老铁”笑着说：“我会一直在邯郸中材干到退休。”

（中材国际所属邯郸中材）

我热爱我的工作，我对工作感到很满足。我工作认真负责，积极服从公司的各项工作安排，与同事相处融洽，善于合作。未来我会与邯郸中材共同成长。

Pakistan's "Buddy"

Shakaib Ahmed Siddiqui

Joined CNBM in 2017

The Foreign Affairs Director of SINOMA Handan Pakistan Co., Ltd.

The term "iron brotherhood" derives from the dialectal expression "buddy," which signifies a deep bond of trust, solidity, and unwavering companionship. SINOMA Handan branch in Pakistan also shares such a profound connection, embodying the essence of this "brotherhood."

Shakaib Ahmed Siddiqui, a Pakistani, completed his studies at the University of Glamorgan, UK, in 2012, specializing in engineering management and earning a master's degree in science and engineering. Following his graduation, he amassed nearly five years of experience in the field of oil and gas exploration and EPC project construction. In February 2017, he joined SINOMA Handan branch in Pakistan, assuming the role of Foreign Affairs Supervisor. His primary responsibilities encompass logistics and customs clearance operations within Pakistan, as well as provide support to the Chinese team in expanding the market and handling local affairs. Over the course of his five-year tenure with the company, he has been recognized multiple times as an "Excellent Employee".

In his role overseeing logistics clearance, Shakaib has demonstrated great proficiency by successfully facilitating the customs clearance of numerous material shipments in Pakistan. His efforts have played a crucial role in ensuring the smooth and efficient progress of construction projects on-site. During the audit of bank bills, he displayed proactive problem-solving skills by providing thorough explanations and addressing various inquiries in a professional manner. Additionally, he actively engaged with the bank to discuss exchange rate matters, striving to minimize costs for the company.

While supporting the Chinese team in market development and operations for the subsidiary, he actively participated in market operations and contract negotiations for several projects in Pakistan. The outbreak of the Covid-19 presented significant challenges to market operations. In addition to wearing protective gear during meetings to prevent cross-infection, he had to endure the entire process without eating, drinking, or taking restroom breaks. Moreover, he demonstrated exceptional physical endurance, sitting in meetings for an entire day to meet tight deadlines. Utilizing his strong English language skills, he played a vital role in reviewing the terms and conditions of English contracts, assisting the subsidiary in successfully signing six new construction contracts and achieving the annual operational target. Additionally, he actively cooperated in facilitating the collection of payments, taxes, fees, and deduction certificates. His diligent effort has enabled timely payment collection for various projects and alleviated the financial burden on the subsidiary.

He has consistently prioritized market operations and growth as the core of his business strategy. Leveraging cutting-edge construction information technology, he has effectively disseminated comprehensive market performance and business principles through local public media platforms. This concerted effort has led to a progressive elevation of the CNBM/SINOMA brand's standing within the Pakistani construction industry. Consequently, the majority of cement owners in Pakistan now acknowledge and appreciate the superior quality and timely construction progress consistently delivered by CNBM/SINOMA.

Regarding local affairs management, Shakaib has established proactive collaboration between the finance team and local authorities such as the tax office and financial and tax audit teams. This synergy ensures the seamless execution of all operations. In 2021, in terms of subsidiary company registration, he engaged in extensive communication with agents, guaranteeing the provision of comprehensive information and offering valuable support for future operations. Throughout that year, the subsidiary company received three tax inspection notices from the local tax bureau. His proactive approach facilitated effective communication between the finance team and the relevant authorities, leading to the successful completion of the tax inspections and the submission of recommendations for improvement. He diligently utilized his expertise to provide valuable advice and suggestions for the company's development. During the fiscal audit, he assumed the responsibility of liaising with the audit team, addressing inquiries, and successfully completing the audit inspection This ensured the fulfillment of all filing requirements and provided substantial support for the timely remittance of annual income tax.

Shakaib demonstrates a profound sense of responsibility and professionalism, exhibiting a genuine passion for his role and a strong commitment to his work. He consistently adheres to the company's work arrangements and displays excellent rapport with colleagues, fostering a cooperative and harmonious work environment. His robust understanding of business practices and efficient and high-quality performance garners unanimous recognition from the company.

Looking ahead, this "buddy" expresses his dedication with a smile, stating, "I am committed to remaining a part of SINOMA until my retirement."

Personal Insights I love my job and I feel very satisfied with my work. I am serious and responsible for work, actively obey the company's work arrangements, get along well with colleagues, and good at cooperation. I will grow together with SINOMA Handan.

在海外一线绽放别样青春

邓拓科

2019 年加入中国建材

现任中建投巴新公司金贝店店长

5 月的金贝潮湿闷热，只有清晨的海风能吹来丝丝凉意，伴着缓缓升起的朝阳，邓拓科开始了一天的工作。简短的晨会结束，他的下一项工作就是巡店。总占地约 9000 平方米的金贝店由内场展厅、外场、仓库和办公区域组成，邓拓科从巡查展厅入手，检查价格标签、货物和宣传片展示，确保商品和重物的尖锐边角没有超出货架。

这是邓拓科在海外 4 年来每一天的“打开方式”。从马当店到金贝店，日复一日的勤奋工作锻炼了他坚毅的品质，他学会在细节中把控质效，时时处处做有心人，善于反思，勤于落实，在平凡的岗位上一次又一次绽放光芒。

近两年，巴布亚新几内亚兴起智能手机普及热潮。为在马当区域快速铺开手机板块业务，抢先占领市场份额，邓拓科带领外籍员工迅速行动，在较短时间内完成了店内的基础设施翻新优化工作。他悉心招募手机板块专职员工，为他们组织专业的知识培训，强化了售前售后服务质量。在品牌宣传方面，邓拓科借助线上社交平台大力进行产品推广，使品牌传播力和影响力得到提升。一分耕耘，一分收获，2020 年马当店手机板块销售额同比增长 800%。

巴新公司筹备开设哈根新店时，需要计算机制图完成平面设计，此时具有制图基础的邓拓科主动请缨，他不怕累、不怕难，与施工地现场人员进行远程沟通以获取基础信息，连续两个月牺牲休息时间完成了精准的店面设计平面图，为哈根店面合理布局、高效铺货奠定了重要基础。

2021 年，邓拓科被派往金贝店，挑起该店日常运营管理的重担。前期积累的工作经验、思考感悟在新环境中经受住了考验，他有条不紊地部署分店大小事务，着力发展和巩固新旧客户资源，严格把控产品线，带领新入职的同事共同成长，其间金贝店业绩始终保持平稳上升。勤勉敬业的邓拓科成为广大海外青年的学习榜样。

新冠疫情的暴发给巴布亚新几内亚疾病防

控体系带来了巨大挑战。关键时刻，邓拓科毫不退缩，严格落实巴新公司防疫小组的安排部署，第一时间制定门店防疫措施并督促落实。在培养员工防控意识的同时，他组织人员及时采购生活和防疫物资，做好防疫工作的后勤保障，为员工提供力所能及的医疗帮助，在抗疫战斗中体现出青年人的责任和担当。

每逢中秋节，邓拓科都会与当地员工一同分享公司总部发放的慰问月饼，以小派对的形式，向外籍员工讲解中国中秋节的由来和精彩的传说，大家共同感受中华文化的丰富内涵。除了向当地员工介绍中国文化，他还积极融入当地文化，热心参与筹备巴布亚新几内亚独立日等庆祝活动，体验当地的民族文化与风土人情，在文化交流中增进友谊。

邓拓科还热心公益事业。2022 年，金贝政府对果蔬集散市场进行翻新改造，商户们不得不露天摆摊，需要忍耐长时间的暴晒。细心的邓拓科向公司申请给当地政府捐赠 40 个帐篷，帮助商户度过市场改造的艰难时期。帐篷虽小，情谊深重，当地政府和居民为此表示衷心感谢。短短两年时间，邓拓科已收获了众多当地人民的喜爱，他相信，国相交，民相亲，只要用心就能架通两国人民的友谊桥梁。

邓拓科始终在工作岗位上发扬着艰苦奋斗的精神，在实践中不断提升自我。在未来的旅程里，他将满怀信心与希望，继续保持昂扬风貌，在海外一线绽放青春梦想。（中建投巴新公司金贝店）

国相交，民相亲，只要用心就能架通中国与巴布亚新几内亚两国人民的友谊桥梁。在未来的旅程里，我将继续在工作岗位上发扬艰苦奋斗的精神，在实践中不断提升自我，满怀信心与希望，保持昂扬风貌，在海外一线绽放青春梦想。

Bloom a Different Kind of Youth Overseas

Deng Tuoke

Joined CNBM in 2019

The Branch Manager of BNBM PNG LTD Kimbe Branch

Kimbe is humid and hot in May, and only the sea breeze in the morning can bring a little bit of coolness. With the slowly rising sun, Deng Tuoke started his daily work. The brief morning meeting is over, and the next job is to patrol the branch. The Kimbe branch, covering a total area about 9,000 square meters, consists of an infield exhibition hall, an outfield, a warehouse and an office area. Deng Tuoke started by inspecting the exhibition hall, checking price tags, goods and promotional video displays, and ensuring that goods and heavy objects are inside the shelf.

This is Deng Tuoke's daily work in the past four years overseas. From the Madang branch to the Kimbe branch, his hard work day after day has tempered his perseverance. The caring person, good at reflection, diligent in implementation, shines in his ordinary position.

In the past two years, there has been an upsurge in the popularization of smart phones in Papua New Guinea. In order to quickly seize the market share first, Deng Tuoke led the foreign employees to completed the renovation and optimization of the branch's infrastructure in a relatively short period of time. He recruited full-time employees in the mobile phone sector, organized professional knowledge training for them, and strengthened the quality of pre-sales and after-sales services. In terms of brand promotion, Deng Tuoke vigorously used online social platforms to improve brand transmitting power and influence. No pains, no gains. In 2020, the sales of mobile phone in Madang branch increased by 800% year-on-year.

When the company was preparing to open a new branch in Hagen, it needed computer graphics to complete the design. At this time, Deng Tuoke, who has a basic level of graphics, took the initiative. He was not afraid of being tired or difficult. He communicated with the construction site personnel remotely to obtain basic information. He has no rest time for two consecutive months and finally completed the accurate branch design, laying an important foundation for the rational layout and efficient distribution of Hagen branch.

In 2021, Deng Tuoke was sent to Kimbe branch to take on the burden of daily operation and management. The work experience accumulated in the early stage have withstood the test in the new environment. He deployed his work methodically, focused on developing and consolidating customer resources, strictly controlled the product lines, and led new colleagues to grow together. During the

period, the performance of Kimbe branch has maintained a steady increase. Diligent and dedicated, Deng Tuoke has become a role model for overseas youth.

The outbreak of COVID-19 epidemic has brought huge challenges to Papua New Guinea's disease prevention and control system. At the critical moment, Deng Tuoke did not flinch, strictly implemented the arrangement and deployment of the company's epidemic prevention team, and immediately formulated branch epidemic prevention measures and supervised the implementation. While cultivating employees' awareness of prevention and control, he organized personnel to purchase living and epidemic prevention materials in a timely manner, and provide employees with medical assistance, playing youth's responsibilities in the fight against the epidemic.

Every Mid-Autumn Festival, Deng Tuoke will share the mooncakes distributed by the company with local employees, explain the origin of the festival and wonderful legends to foreign employees in the form of small parties, and feel the rich connotation of Chinese culture together. In addition to introducing Chinese culture to local employees, he also actively integrates into the local culture, enthusiastically participates in the preparation of Papua New Guinea Independence Day and other celebrations, experiencing the local culture and customs and enhancing friendship through cultural exchanges.

Deng Tuoke is also enthusiastic about public welfare. In 2022, the Kimbe government renovated the fruit and vegetable distribution market. Merchants had to set up their stalls in the open air and endure long periods of exposure to the sun. Deng Tuoke applied to the company to donate 40 tents to the local government to help merchants tide over the difficult period of market transformation. Although the tents are small, they contain deep friendship. And the local government and residents expressed their heartfelt thanks for this. In just two years, Deng Tuoke has gained the love of many local people. He believes that the friendship between people can be established with sincerity.

Deng Tuoke has always carried forward the spirit of hard work, and constantly improved himself in practice. In the future, he will be full of confidence and hope, continue to maintain a high-spirited demeanor, and bloom his youthful dream overseas.

Personal Insights The friendship between China and Papua New Guinea can be established with sincerity. In the future, I will continue to carry forward the spirit of hard work, and constantly improve myself in practice. I will be full of confidence and hope, continue to maintain a high-spirited style, and bloom my youthful dream overseas.

与公司一起成长的优秀主管

查理·詹姆斯

2015 年加入中国建材

现任中建投瓦努阿图维尔克有限公司物流主管

我叫查理·詹姆斯，来自瓦努阿图恩古纳岛的一个村落，我是村落的酋长，同时也是中建投瓦努阿图公司维拉店的一名物流主管。我在维拉店工作了 11 年，切身感受到加入瓦努阿图公司大家庭的幸运，为能够在这里不断进步成长、充分展示自我而感到自豪。

目前我主管物流部门，团队有 22 名员工，我们每天要做好货物运输、仓储、配送、车辆管理等工作，为瓦努阿图很多交通不便的海岛提供免费的送货服务，这项服务使我的同胞们能够更方便地采购建筑材料，岛民的生活变得更加便利。在领导和同事的帮助下，经过我的不懈努力，我的业务技能和管理水平不断提高，团队的凝聚力、战斗力越来越强，感谢公司给我提供的成长平台。

公司参与和支持我们国家多个重大项目建设，我也参与其中，对此我深感自豪，其中支持建设洛岛项目让我记忆尤为深刻。洛岛是瓦努阿图北部托雷斯群岛的一部分，该岛屿被大量海礁包围，大型船只无法靠岸卸货。为了确保所有物品及时运送到项目地点，在当时没有码头和必要设施帮助的情况下，我们站在礁石群中间的海水中，排成长队，人工接力搬运货物，最终我们团队克服了恶劣的送货条件，夜以继日、保质保量地完成任务，让洛岛项目成为公司展示“竭诚为客户服务”的名片，当地人更加确信我们是一家值得信赖的公司。

我的家乡是瓦努阿图恩古纳岛上的一个小村落，我是村子里的酋长，平时负责管理村子事务。2015 年，一场飓风——帕姆（Pam）袭击了瓦努阿图，风速达到了每小时 250 公里，整个维拉港市被洪水淹没。我的村子里有很多

房屋被飓风摧毁，村民们遭受巨大的损失，甚至无处安身。灾难发生后，公司第一时间向我们伸出了援助之手，捐赠水泥和建筑材料，帮助我们建造房屋。现在我的村庄已经建设得越来越好，村民不再担心雨季台风的侵袭，大家对瓦努阿图公司充满感激。

我很高兴能够在公司工作，这份工作改善了我的生活，改变了我的人生。在这里我也非常开心能够拥有一群善良、踏实、真诚、能干的同事，我们的情谊愈加深厚。我相信中国与瓦努阿图人民的友谊坚固如铁，并将永远延续下去。（中建投瓦努阿图维尔克有限公司）

作为公司的物流与安全主管，随着公司的快速发展，我也在不断地积累经验、学习与成长。我们的公司一直在参与和支持瓦努阿图很多项目的建设，这些项目帮助我的国家发展得越来越好，我也为能亲自参与这些项目而感到自豪。

Outstanding Supervisor of Logistics Department Who Grows up with Wilco

Charlie James

Joined CNBM in 2015

The Logistics Supervisor of Wilco Limited

My name is Charlie James and I come from a village in Vanuatu called Nguna, where I am the village chief. I'm also a logistics manager at the Wilco's Vila Hardware branch. I have been working here for 11 years and feel fortunate to be part of the Wilco Limited family. I'm proud to be able to grow and develop here and show my true self.

Currently, I am in charge of the logistics department with a team of 22 employees. We are responsible for transportation, warehousing, distribution, vehicle management, and other tasks every day. We provide free delivery services to many islands in Vanuatu that have inconvenient transportation. This service enables my compatriots to purchase building materials more conveniently, making their lives easier. With the help of my leaders and colleagues and my persistent efforts, my business skills and management level have continuously improved. The cohesion and combat effectiveness of the team have become stronger and stronger. I am grateful to the company for providing me with a growth platform.

Wilco has participated in and supported many major projects construction in our country, and I have also been involved. I am deeply proud of this, and supporting the construction of the Lo Island project is particularly memorable to me. Lo Island is part of the Torres Islands in northern Vanuatu, and the island is surrounded by large amounts of reefs, making it impossible for large ships to anchor and unload cargo. To ensure that all items were transported to the project site in a timely manner, without the help of docks and necessary facilities at the time, we stood in the seawater of the reef group and formed a queue to manually transfer goods through manual relay. Finally, our team overcame the harsh delivery conditions, completed the task day and night with high quality and quantity, making Lo Island project become Wilco's business card to display their sincere customer service. Locals are more convinced that our company is trustworthy.

My hometown is a small village on Nguna Island in

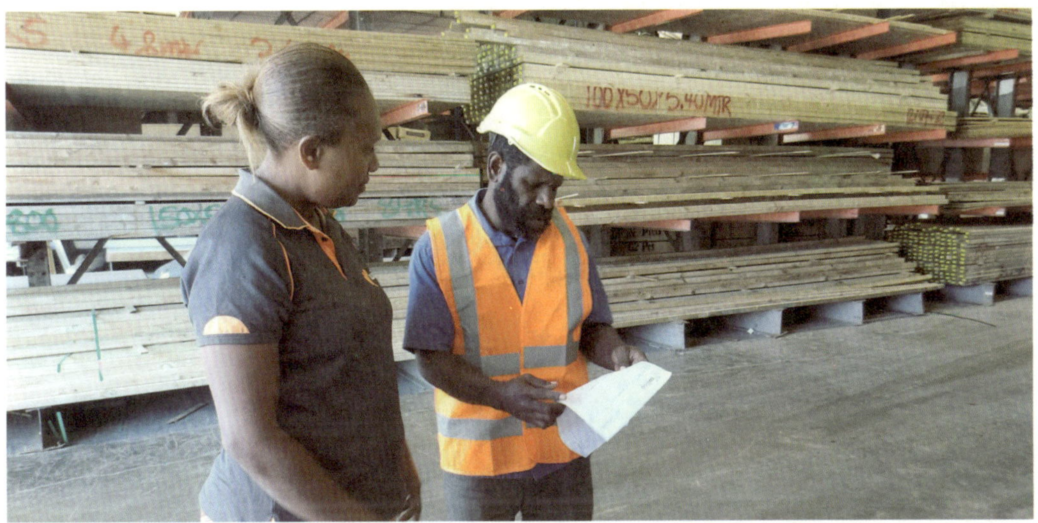

Vanuatu, and I am the village chief responsible for managing village affairs. In 2015, the hurricane Pam hit Vanuatu with wind speeds of up to 250 kilometers per hour, flooding the entire Port Vila city. Many houses in my village were destroyed by the hurricane, and the villagers suffered significant losses with nowhere to go. After the disaster, Wilco immediately extended a helping hand to us by donating cement and building materials to help rebuild our homes. Now my village is being built better and better, and we no longer have to worry about the impact of typhoons during the rainy season. The villagers are full of gratitude towards Wilco Limited.

I am glad to be working in Wilco, which has improved my life and changed my destiny. I am also very happy to have a group of kind-hearted, down-to-earth, sincere and capable colleagues here, and our friendship has become even stronger. I believe that the friendship between China and the people of Vanuatu is as strong as iron and will last forever.

Personal Insights As the logistics and security supervisor of the company, I have been constantly accumulating experience, learning, and growing with the company's fast development. Wilco has been actively participating in and supporting many projects in Vanuatu, which have improved the development of my country. I am proud to have been able to participate in these projects personally.

逐梦 CTF　与阳光共舞

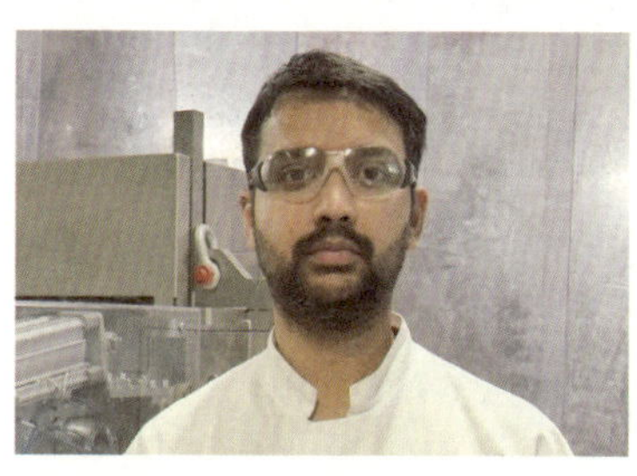

塞格尔·白图勒

2019 年加入中国建材

现任中国建材工程子公司 CTF Solar 研发工程师

我非常高兴和自豪，被邀请分享在中国建材集团的所属公司 CTF Solar 的工作经历。我是塞格尔·白图勒，自 2019 年 4 月以来，一直在 CTF Solar 工作。在这 4 年的工作中，我积累了丰富的工作经验，这些经验使我不断成长。

一份新工作的开始就像是开学的第一天。对我来说， CTF Solar 就是我职业生涯的第一所“学校”，这里有新的环境、新的同事，还有无数的探索和学习的机会。

CTF Solar 的一个优势是它的国际环境。我的同事来自世界各地，他们分享的经验和故事使这个地方成为一个充满活力的工作场所。这种充满多元文化的环境不仅具有包容性，而且还形成了持久的友谊纽带。

对我来说，CTF Solar 有很多东西需要学习。该公司为员工提供了提高技能的机会，像我这样的应届大学毕业生能够从新手转变为各自技术领域的专家。我们不局限于 CTF Solar 的一个具体任务，工作的动态性质鼓励我们跨

不同领域持续学习，这突出了在 CTF Solar 员工具有广泛的学习机会。

除了日常工作，CTF Solar 还鼓励和支持员工进一步学习和发展。无论是学习新语言还是参加技术课程，公司都十分重视员工的持续学习。在学习和工作的同时，娱乐活动也同样

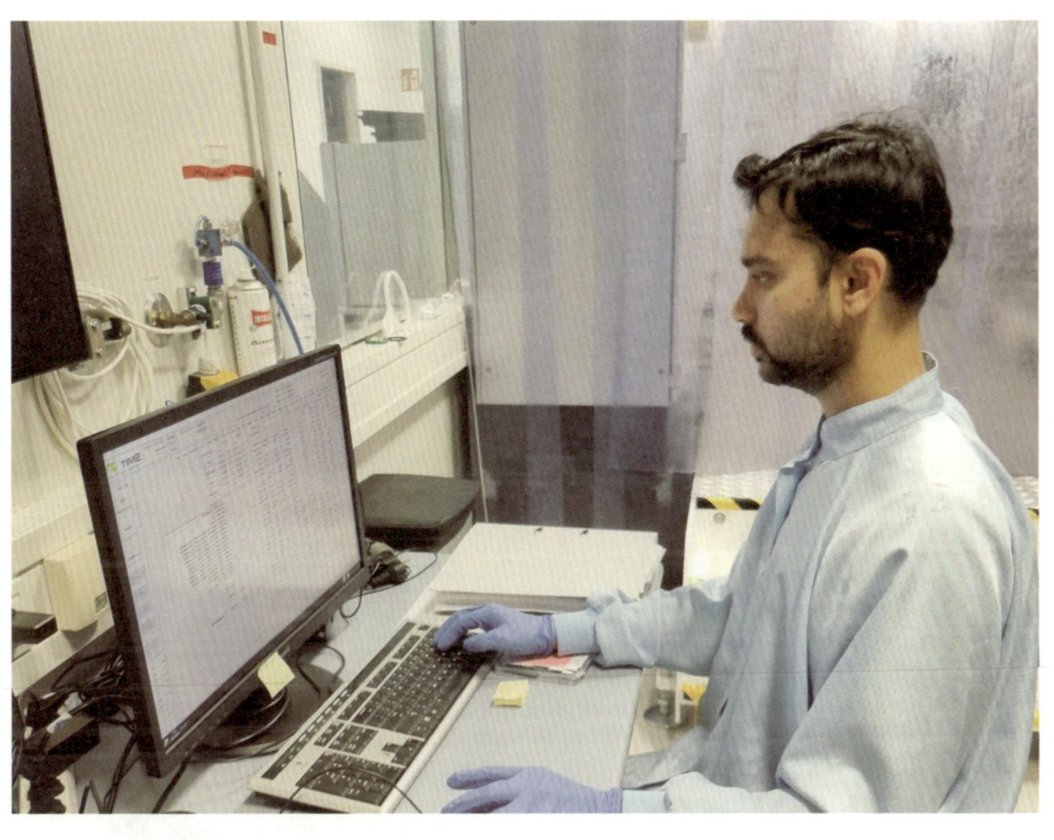

重要，例如，公司会举办小型运动会或烧烤活动，通过这些活动，我提高了人际交往能力，对技术有了深刻的认识和理解。

在我任职期间，CTF Solar 一直致力于质量研究和技术开发。在短短 4 年里，我见证了公司的茁壮成长，公司拥有了最先进的设施、工具，特别是有着杰出的技术和管理专家团队。因为拥有如此强大的团队和设施，CTF Solar 公司一直保持着高质量发展。随着公司继续生产高质量的太阳能电池，并将尖端技术运用到我们的生产过程中，我相信，在中国建材集团的支持下，CTF Solar 将成为太阳能行业的领跑者。（中国建材工程子公司 CTF Solar）

个人体会

我很高兴能成为公司的一员，为绿色能源理念在全球的推广作出贡献。我们目前尚未从太阳能中开发 1% 的能量，太阳能的开发和利用是我们的主要任务，我很高兴 CTF Solar 以此为目标，并正在尽最大努力为绿色能源事业作出贡献。

Fulfil Dreams at CTF Solar

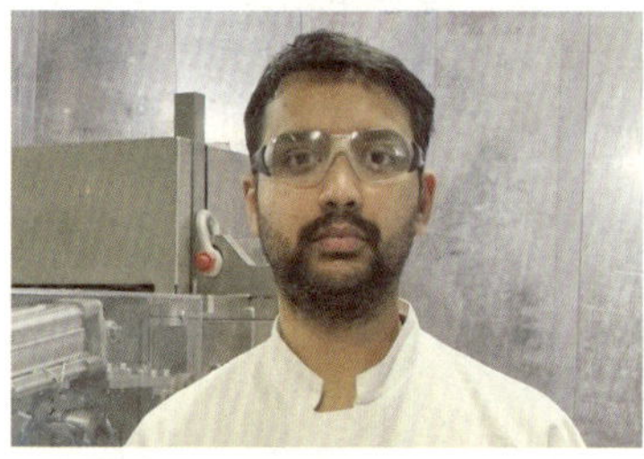

Sagar Baitule

Joined CNBM in 2019

The R&D Engineer of CTF Solar

It's my pleasure and pride when asked to share the experiences of working here at CTF Solar, a part of CNBM. I am Sagar Baitule working at CTF Solar since April 2019. Over the course of these four years, I have had the pleasure of gathering a wealth of experiences that have shaped my professional growth.

Beginning a new job feels like the first day of school. In my case, CTF Solar was that first "school", offering a new environment, new colleagues, and countless opportunities for exploration and learning.

One of the standout aspects of CTF Solar is its international environment. With colleagues hailing from all corners of the globe, the diversity of experiences and stories shared enriches our workplace. This multicultural environment not only fosters a sense of inclusivity, but also forms strong bonds that outlast employment terms.

For me, there's an abundance to learn at CTF Solar. The company presents the opportunity for substantial growth, allowing fresh university graduates, like myself, to transform from novices into technological experts. Our work is not limited

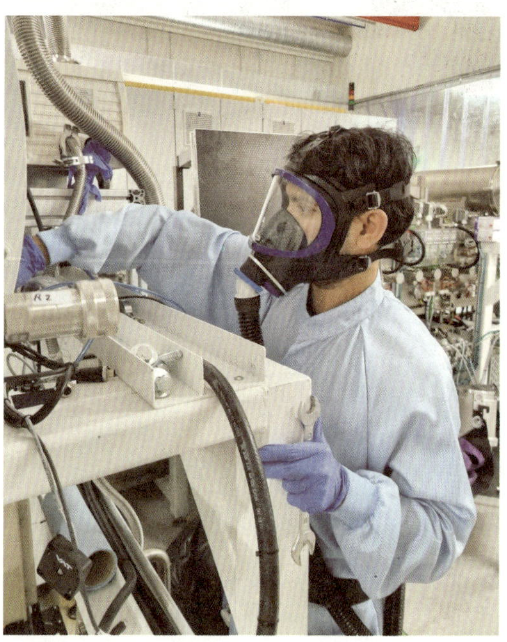

to their specific tasks at CTF Solar, but spans different fields, which highlights the broad learning opportunities at CTF Solar.

Beyond daily tasks, CTF Solar also encourages and supports further educational development. Whether it's learning new languages or enrolling in technical

certificate courses, the company values employees' continuous learning. Alongside working and learning, equal importance is given to recreational activities, such as sports day or grilling events. Through these activities, I have improved my interpersonal skills and have a deep knowledge and understanding of technology.

During my employment, CTF Solar has remained committed to quality research and technology development. In just four years, I have witnessed the company's significant growth, demonstrated by its state-of-the-art facilities, tools, facilities, and most importantly, its team of technical and management experts. With such a robust team, CTF Solar's growth trajectory shows no signs of plateauing. As the company continues to produce high-quality solar cells and use this cutting-edge technology in the production process, I am confident that CTF Solar, with CNBM's support, will well become a leading company in the solar industry.

Personal Insights I am glad that I am a part of the company which is contributing to the global promotion of green energy. We are not even taping 1% of the energy we receive from sun and the development and application of solar energy is our main task. I am happy that CTF has that goal in mind and is trying its best to contribute to the green energy cause.

高温下的挑战与突破

李佳佳

2008 年加入中国建材

现任中国建材工程玻璃工程国外事业部高级工程师

冬季的神州大地飞雪飘扬，地冻天寒，人们喜气洋洋，迎接新年的到来。而我的心情却十分的复杂：公司安排我到沙特项目出差驻场，而我要如何安排一家回老家过年，此刻的我还是希望过完年再去现场，毕竟由于疫情，全家好几年都没有回过老家了。然而 1 月 6 日接到公司驻场的通知后，我还是说服了家人，毅然收拾好行李，乘坐 1 月 9 日的航班到达沙特项目施工现场。

一到现场，我顾不上 30 多小时的奔波劳累，立即投入培训及与业主、管理公司的对接工作中。虽然我的工作是质量管理，但由于没有经验可循，也没有项目可参考，对我以及项目部而言，沙特项目是一个巨大的挑战。我有些迷茫，身处茫茫戈壁，眼前一望无际的荒漠难免给人一种孤独的感觉。玻璃工厂驻场工作艰难、繁重。虽然我知道累是不可避免的，也有不怕苦、不怕累的思想准备。但我时常问自己：有没有累出效率？累出创造？累出智慧？累出成长和发展？

面对新的挑战，虽然我也查阅了一些文章，收集了一些文件资料，但是外方一系列质量新名词把我所有的准备都打破了。好在大学期间我的英语还行，跟业主及监理公司的沟通不存在大的障碍，在了解对方所需后，我认真查询相关资料，对比国标及外方标准的差异，并及时作出反馈，同时学习外方较好的管理经验，经过磨合、配合、适应等过程，终于将一个一个难题顺利地解决。近半年时间我得到了较好的锻炼，不知不觉提高了自己解决各类问题的能力。现在的我工作已是游刃有余，工作之余，我还和同事一起踢足球、聚餐等，增进了彼此的友谊。

配合好业主及管理公司的工作后，项目经理还安排我兼任管道设备的安装、调试、测试工作，通过现场对管道的安装、探伤检测、打压、吹扫、清洗等工艺流程及方案的实施，我不断地学习图纸、相关专业技术知识并了解现场改造的实际情况，引导安装公司利用现场条件，文明有序施工，使业主和监理要求与国标施工基本一致，避免出现大的失误和纰漏，造成不

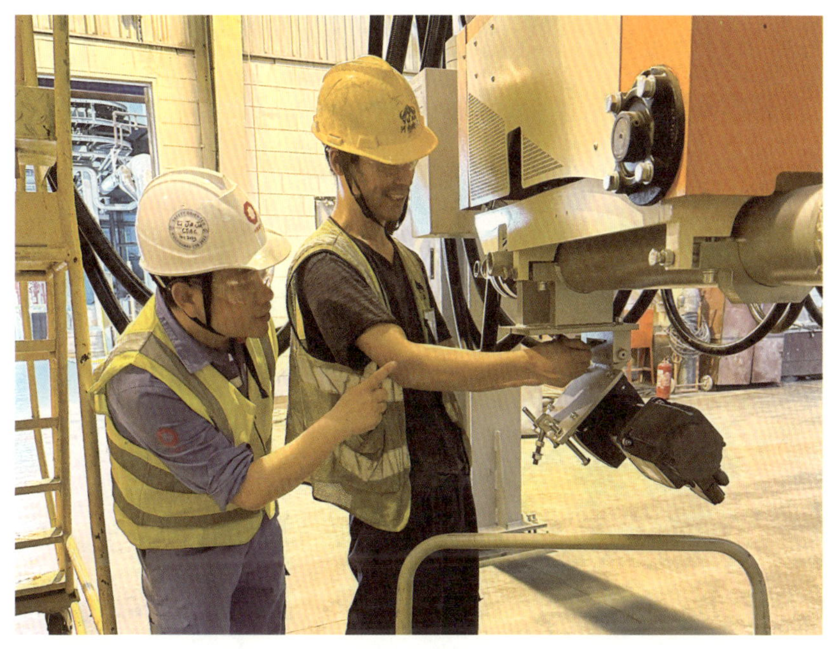

可挽回的损失，给公司和个人造成不良影响。与工人长时间的接触，我发现遇到任何事情，站的高度不一样，格局就不一样，处理事情的方法和所得到的结果也会不一样。因此，要学会换位思考，经常站在对方的角度考虑问题，会让自己不断改进工作方式，增强责任意识，促使自己更好地解决问题，避免矛盾，提高工作效率。

回顾近半年的工作，来时的困惑、迷茫、孤独现在已经淡去，取而代之的是热火朝天的干劲。我们的项目正在做最后的冲刺，面对40—50摄氏度的高温天气，整个项目团队没有退缩，也不能退缩，只能勇敢向前，闯出一片新天地。伴随着工程进度的不断加快，汗水不断浇灌着这片熟悉而又陌生的土地，相信我们的付出定能开出绚烂的花朵，结出丰硕的果实。

现在的我接触到的人和事比过去多，也比过去复杂。经过这次驻场工作，自己已经可以独当一面，可以说不负青春，不枉此行。我既然选择了这项工作，就应该积极、热情地干下去，做到“干一行，爱一行，专一行，精一行”。

（中国建材国际工程集团有限公司）

不知不觉我已经驻场将近半年了，经受住了恶劣气候和繁重工作的双重考验，收获了独立、自信以及游刃有余的处事方法，使自己快速成长起来，所有的付出和挥洒的汗水都是值得的，未来我将不负青春，建功立业。

Challenges and Breakthroughs under High Temperature

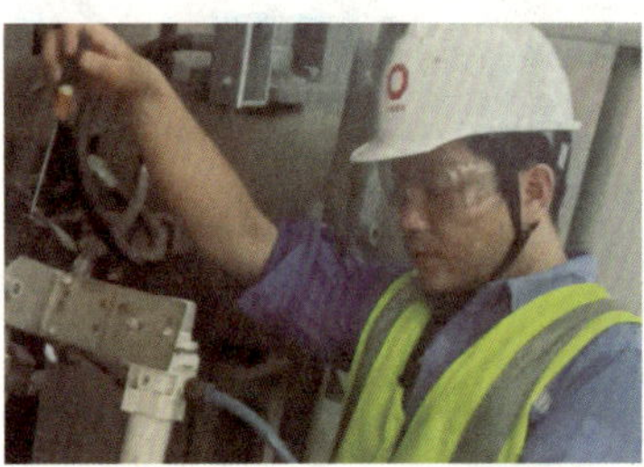

Li Jiajia

Joined CNBM in 2008

The Senior Engineer of CTIEC Overseas Glass Engineering Department

The snowy landscapes of China in winter are bitter cold, yet filled with joy as people look forward to the coming New Year. My feelings, however, was complex, as the company assigned me to a project in Saudi Arabia while my family planned to return to our hometown for the New Year. Having not returned home for a festive reunion in years due to the COVID-19 pandemic, I hoped I could go to the project site after the New Year. Nevertheless, I persuaded my family after received the company's assignment on January 6th, packed my luggage, and took a flight on January 9th to reach the site.

Upon arrival, I threw myself into work immediately despite more than 30 hours of travel. My responsibilities included training, liaising with the owner and management company. As a quality manager with no reference or prior experience, I faced a formidable challenge. The vast, lonely desert intensified my feelings of uncertainty. The job on-site at the glass factory is tough and demanding. I often asked myself – is it worth? Does work make me more efficient, creative, intelligent, growing and developing?

Faced with these new challenges, I was initially overwhelmed by unfamiliar quality jargon. However, thanks to my decent English skills in college, I did not face major communication barriers. After understood the requirements, I diligently researched related material, identified differences between domestic and foreign standards, provided prompt feedback, and gradually solved each problem in turn. Over the past six months, I've improved my problem-solving skills considerably. Now, I'm quite comfortable with my role. In my spare time, I attend football matches and dinner with my colleagues, which strengthens the friendship between us.

In addition to coordinating with the owner and the management company, the project manager also assigned me to oversee the installation, debugging, and testing of pipeline equipment. Through constant learning, adjusting to the actual situation on site, and guiding the installation company to conduct civilized and orderly construction, I managed to align the work with the owner and supervisor's requests and national construction standards, thus avoiding major errors and omissions that could cause irreparable damage.

Looking back at the last six months, the confusion, disorientation, and loneliness I felt when I first arrived have faded, replaced by a fiery passion for my work. Even under the high temperature of 40-50 degrees, the project team is not shrinking back, but

courageously pushing forward, creating a new world in this familiar yet strange land. I'm confident that our hard work will blossom into brilliant results.

Now I come into contact with more people and things than in the past, but also more complicated. Although I can't claim to have mastered every aspect of this on-site work, I believe that it was a worthwhile journey, that I have lived up to my youthful potential. I remind myself that as a young person, I should have the ability and courage to shoulder responsibilities. Since I chose this job, I should continue with positivity, passion, specialization, and dedication.

Personal Insights As time flies, I find myself having been on site for nearly half a year. I've withstood the dual challenges of harsh weather conditions and heavy workloads, gaining independence and confidence. The adeptness in handling affairs, attained in such a short span of time, has enabled rapid personal growth. I consider it an honor to contribute to the Belt and Road Initiative. Every effort made and sweat shed is worthwhile, embodying the spirit of youth, making achievements, and striving to be a model CTIEC employee.

中哈工程师交流的纽带

白凯

2017 年加入中国建材

现任中国建材工程哈萨克斯坦分公司员工

白凯于 2017 年 11 月入职中国建材国际工程集团有限公司哈萨克斯坦分公司，成为奥尔达玻璃总承包项目部的一员。他参与了该项目建设的全过程，担任过现场翻译、土建工程师、采购协调专员等职务，是总承包项目部任职时间最久的属地员工。从 2017 年至今，白凯伴随着奥尔达玻璃项目工程建设的推进不断积累、不断成长，在工作岗位上尽职尽责，做出了优异的成绩。

白凯出生在哈萨克斯坦塔拉兹市，2013—2017 年曾在北京工业大学留学，所学专业为土建。中国的留学经历不仅为他的工作打下了坚实专业基础，而且也使得他能够更加深入地了解中国的文化，增强了跨文化交流能力。

初入项目部，白凯的主要工作是现场翻译。哈萨克斯坦的成长经历和中国留学经历使他能够在哈语、俄语和中文三种语言间熟练切换。项目上有相当一部分土建工程由哈萨克斯坦本地分包单位实施，语言沟通的障碍和文化的差异使得总包管理难度较大。担任现场翻译时，白凯每天穿梭于工程建设现场的各个角落，哪里有翻译需求哪里便有他的身影，他成为中哈两国工程师沟通的纽带。

在担任现场翻译的同时，他也充分利用自己土建专业的背景协助中方工程师解决施工过程中遇到的技术问题，并在实践中慢慢积累经验。刚开始，由于没有玻璃厂工程建设的相关经验，他会向项目部其他工程师积极请教。同时，利用自己语言的优势，他能够准确传达相关方的观点和诉求，以灵活的方式协调处理施工过程中遇到的问题，保障工程建设的顺利推进。

随着对工程建设各个环节的熟悉和了解，白凯又参与到工程采购环节，主要负责现场工程物资的接货。项目大部分公用工程设备材料的采购均在哈萨克斯坦进行，大到变压器机柜、冷却塔，小到电缆螺栓，采购门类多、涉及物资庞杂。白凯负责的接货环节牵涉大量细节性工作，他跟踪货物的运输和交付情况，做好信息沟通以及内部汇报，他与各家供货商沟通协

调，确保货物顺利交付，他对到场的货物进行验收并交接给施工单位，保证货物的安全和完整性。

过去几年间，一座崭新的现代化浮法玻璃生产线拔地而起，奥尔达玻璃项目也见证了白凯的辛勤付出与个人成长。正如白凯所说，奥尔达玻璃项目是他职业生涯的起点，在这里他接触到各式各样的分包商，参与到玻璃厂工程建设的各个环节。与此同时，他与现场各专业工程师打成一片，工程技术知识得到积累，专业技能也得到了锻炼和提升。

"我所参与的玻璃厂已于去年 10 月正式建成，作为哈萨克斯坦第一条现代化浮法玻璃生产线，这里的日日夜夜对我而言都具有特殊的意义。能够参与这样的大型项目，我感到非常荣幸。未来我也会继续在自己的岗位上发光发热"，白凯如是说。（中国建材国际工程集团有限公司哈萨克斯坦分公司）

个人体会 多年来的现场工作锻炼了我协调问题、解决问题的能力。自从来到玻璃厂工作，我明显能够感受到生活水平在不断提升，日子也越过越好。能够参与哈萨克斯坦第一条浮法玻璃生产线这样的大型项目我倍感荣幸。未来，我也会继续在自己的岗位上发光发热，不断努力。

The Link between Chinese and Kazakh Engineers

Bai Kai

Joined CNBM in 2017

The Translator of CTIEC Kazakhstan branch

Bai Kai joined CNBM Kazakhstan branch in November 2017 and became a member of the Alda Glass Project. He participated in the entire process of project construction and held positions such as on-site translator, civil engineer, procurement coordination specialist, etc. He is the longest serving local employee in the Project Department. Since 2017, Bai Kai has been continuously accumulating and growing with the progress of the construction of the Alda Glass Project, fulfilling his duties and achieving excellent results in his work.

Bai Kai was born in Taraz, Kazakhstan. He studied at Beijing University of Technology from 2013 to 2017, majoring in civil engineering. The experience of studying in China not only laid a professional foundation for him, but also enabled him to have a deeper understanding of Chinese culture and enhanced his cross-cultural communication skills.

As a newcomer to the Project Department, Bai Kai's main job was on-site translation. The growth experience in Kazakhstan and the experience of studying in China have enabled him to proficiently switch between Kazakh, Russian, and Chinese. A considerable portion of the civil engineering projects are carried out by local subcontractors in Kazakhstan, and language communication barriers and cultural differences have significantly increased the difficulty of general contracting management. When serving as an on-site translator, Bai Kai shuttles around every corner of the construction site every day, where there is a translation demand, his presence is there, becoming a communication link between engineers from China and Kazakhstan.

Meanwhile, he also fully utilized his background in civil engineering to assist Chinese engineers in solving technical problems encountered during the construction process, and gradually accumulated experience in practice. At the beginning, due to his lack of experience in glass factory construction, he would actively seek advice from other engineers in the project department. At the same time, utilizing the advantages of language, he can accurately convey the views and demands of relevant parties, coordinate and handle problems encountered during the construction process in a flexible manner, and ensure the smooth progress of engineering construction.

With the familiarity and understanding of the engineering construction process, Bai Kai has also participated in the engineering procurement process, mainly responsible for receiving on-site engineering materials. Most of the procurement of public engineering equipment and materials for the project is carried out in Kazakhstan, ranging from transformer cabinets and cooling towers to cable bolts. There are many procurement categories and materials involved. Bai Kai is responsible for the receiving process, which involves a lot of detailed work. He tracks the transportation and delivery of goods, communicates information and reports internally. He communicates and coordinates with various suppliers to ensure the smooth delivery of goods. He also inspects and hands over the arrived goods to the construction unit, ensuring the safety and integrity of the goods.

In the past few years, a brand-new modern float glass production line has sprung up. The Alda Glass Project have also witnessed Bai Kai's hard work and personal growth. As Bai Kai said, the Alda Glass Project was the starting point of his career, where he came into contact with various subcontractors and participated in various stages of glass factory engineering construction. At the same time, he integrated with various professional engineers, continuously accumulating engineering and technical knowledge, and improving his professional skills.

"The glass factory I participated in was officially completed in October last year. As the first modern float glass production line in Kazakhstan, the days and nights here are of extraordinary significance to me. I am honored to be involved in such a large-scale project. I will continue to shine in my post in the future, "said Bai Kai.

Personal Insights Years of on-site work have honed my ability to coordinate and solve problems. Since I started working on the site, I feel that living standards are constantly improving and life getting better and better. This is the first float glass production line in Kazakhstan, and I am honored to participate in such a large-scale project. In the future, I will continue to shine and strive in my post.

赴阿联酋的最美逆行者

苏海荣

2017 年加入中国建材

现任中材节能工程分公司采购部采购经理

2021 年夏季，国内的新冠肺炎疫情逐渐得到控制，海外疫情却呈蔓延之势。面对疫情，仍然有人选择坚守原地，他们坚守平凡初心，像一粒粒尘土，随处可见，更像一盏烛光，在平凡岗位上闪耀光芒。

在疫情暴发初期，我选择返回项目部，驻扎在拉斯海马酋长国距阿曼边境 10 公里的项目现场。因为此时项目正处于最紧张的时期，所以我选择与项目部的同事一起并肩作战。我也问过自己：不害怕吗？怕，当然我也很怕。我可以选择疫情过后再返回现场，但是考虑到现场的需要，我决定在大年初八准时启程，跨越 6000 多公里，回到工作岗位。勇敢不是无所畏惧，而是明明畏惧，却仍然勇往直前。

阿联酋作为中东地区第一个出现新冠肺炎确诊病例的国家，在 2020 年 3 月也进入了紧急防疫状态。我又紧急联系当地朋友帮忙采购项目部急需的防疫物资，以缓解项目部的燃眉之急，并主动申请成为项目部抗疫一线志愿者，积极投入项目现场疫情防控的战斗中。

作为现场的翻译，除了常规翻译工作、与业主的联络沟通、现场人员签证的办理、与当地供货商联系沟通现场材料采购等日常工作之外，我还摇身一变，成为项目上的一名“抗疫小卫士”。为了保证大家的安全，我不敢有一刻大意，工厂里、办公室里、班车上、宿舍里总是可以看到我要么拿着体温枪、要么拿着消毒瓶、要么拿着口罩分发给大家的身影。

作为一名现场翻译，我的本职工作也逐渐得到了大家的认可，业主甚至经常开玩笑地说我是“Engineer Su”。可是最初到现场的时候并不是这样的，我也实实在在地经历了一段非常艰难的时期。俗话说“隔行如隔山”，虽然我的岗位是翻译，但刚刚接触这个工作的时候，一大堆的专业词汇还是差点让我崩溃。我首先面临的问题就是口音不同，虽然项目是在阿联酋，但是业主的负责人却来自菲律宾、印度、巴基斯坦等多个国家。初到项目部的我既不了解项目的情况，也不了解专业术语，更听不懂五花八门的口音。更让人啼笑皆非的是，

当时身边的同事和分包商也来自五湖四海，各自都说着一口浓重的中国各地的方言，所以第一个星期，我不但听不懂英文，甚至连中文也听不懂。雪上加霜的是，第二个星期，现场经理说：“小苏，走，我们去清点工具和设备。”依稀记得现场经理说了一串设备和工具名称，我当时就傻傻地站在那里，连这些工具的中文名字都没有听过，要如何翻译呢？到现在回忆起当时的状态，我依然能清晰地感觉到那时每天的紧张、焦虑和巨大的压力。为了尽快熟悉本职工作，只要是项目部的同事去现场，我就跟着，不懂就问，主动去适应各种不同的口音。我非常感谢项目上的同事、业主和监理对我的包容和耐心，在他们的帮助下，我通过不断的学习，慢慢地积累经验。现在跟业主开会，哪怕他们说到一些比较生僻的专业单词，我也能立刻反应过来。“Engineer Su”的称号就是这么来的。

疫情面前，谁都无法置身事外。每一场特殊战斗，都需要一批英勇的战士；每一次生死搏斗，都会涌现一批无畏的勇士。作为项目经理助理和现场翻译，我也在自己的“战场”，和大家一起默默贡献着自己的微薄之力，我的工作虽然平淡，但我依然会骄傲地告诉大家——我是中国建材人！（中材节能股份有限公司）

个人体会 在海外工作的这6年，我最大的感受是，走出国门才知道祖国给了我们多大的底气和依靠。很多次在跟别人自我介绍的时候，在对方听到CHINA的时候都会对我竖起大拇指，每次看到这样的场景，我心中都无比自豪。

The Most Beautiful Warrior to the UAE

Su Hairong

Joined CNBM in 2017

The Purchasing Manager of Purchasing Department in SINOMA-ec Engineering branch

In the summer of 2021, the COVID-19 epidemic in China gradually came under control and improved, while the epidemic abroad continued to spread. Faced with the epidemic, some people chose to return to their home country, while others chose to stay put. They held onto their ordinary initial intentions, like specks of dust that could be found anywhere, and shone like a candle flame.

In the early days of the outbreak, I chose to return to the project site in Ras Al Khaimah, 10 km from the Oman border. This was because the project was in its most critical phase, so I decided to fight alongside my colleagues at the project site. I asked myself if I was not afraid, but of course, I was very scared. I could have chosen to return to the site after the epidemic had passed, but considering the needs of the project, I decided to set off on the eighth day of the Chinese New Year, crossing over 6,000 kilometers to return and hold my position at work. Bravery is not about having no fear, it is about knowing you are scared but still moving forward.

As the first country in the Middle East to confirm a case of COVID-19, the UAE also entered a state of emergency prevention and control in March, 2020. I urgently contacted local friends to help purchase protective equipment needed by the project, easing the urgent need. I also proactively offered to become a volunteer on the front line of the project's epidemic prevention and control battle.

As an on-site translator, in addition to the usual translation work, communicating with clients, handling visas for on-site personnel, and coordinating with local suppliers for material procurement, I also took on the role of a "COVID-19 prevention guard" on the project. To ensure everyone's safety, I could always be seen in the factory, office, shuttle bus, or dormitory, carrying a thermometer, a disinfection bottle, or distributing masks.

As an on-site translator, my primary job has gradually gained recognition from everyone, and the owner even jokes around and calls me "Engineer Su." But it wasn't like this when I first arrived on site. I also experienced a very difficult period. As the saying goes, "a different trade is like a different mountain." Although my position is as a translator, when I first started, a ton of professional terms almost made me collapse. The first problem I faced was accents. Although the project was in the United Arab Emirates, the owner's representatives came from multiple countries like the Philippines, India and Pakistan. When I first arrived at the project site,

I didn't understand the situation or the professional terms, and I couldn't even comprehend the variety of accents. What's more ridiculous is that my colleagues and subcontractors at the time also came from various places, each speaking a strong dialect. Thus, the reality for my first week was that I couldn't understand English or even Chinese. To make matters worse, during the second week, the site manager said, "Xiaosu, come with me. We're going to count the tools and equipment." I vaguely remember the site manager rattled off a list of tool and equipment names, and at the time, I just stood there dumbfounded. I hadn't even heard of these tools' names, so how could I translate them? Recalling my state at the time, I can still clearly feel the tension, anxiety, and immense pressure that I felt every day. In order to quickly get up to speed with my job, I followed any of the project's colleagues who went to the site, asked questions if I didn't understand something, and actively adapted to the owner's accent. I have to thank my colleagues on the project, the owner, and the supervisors for their tolerance and patience with me. With their help, by continuously learning and gradually accumulating experience, I can now attend meetings with the owner and even immediately understand rare specialized terms they use. That's how I attained the title of "Engineer Su."

No one can stand aside in the face of a pandemic. Every special battle requires a group of brave soldiers, and every life-and-death struggle produces a batch of fearless warriors. As an assistant project manager and on-site translator, I am also on my battlefield, silently contributing my small strength with everyone else. My work may seem ordinary, but I still want to use my professional dedication, selfless devotion, and hard-fought battles to proudly tell everyone that I am a person from China National Building Material Company.

Personal Insights During my six years of working overseas, my biggest feeling is that only when we go abroad can we know how much confidence and reliance our motherland gives us. Many times, when introducing myself to others like clients, partners and suppliers, that I am from "China", I always can receive their thumbs up, which makes me feel immensely proud.

“一带一路” 建材同行

赵云飞

2021 年加入中国建材

中国建材尼日利亚新材料有限公司生产主管

今年是“一带一路”倡议提出 10 周年。在过去的 3 年间，中国建材尼日利亚新材料有限公司在尼踏出的每一步、经历的每一个大事件都可以清晰地看到中尼员工忙碌的身影。中尼员工团结一致，心往一处想，劲往一处使，拧成一股绳，积极地投入各项工作中，助力公司深耕尼日利亚市场，实现高质量发展。尽管属地化员工的国别不同、肤色不同、岗位不同，但他们共同在中国建材尼日利亚公司实现了华丽转身。他们是中国建材尼日利亚公司发展壮大的见证者，是中材节能持续深化国际化布局，推动中尼友谊、文明互鉴的践行者，是集团“走出去”、积极响应“一带一路”倡议的参与者。

当清晨行走在鸟语花香、绿草如茵的厂区大道上，我总有一种溢于言表的喜悦；当穿行在灯火辉煌、洁净宽敞的车间厂房内，看着繁忙的景象，我为拥有这份工作感到自豪。2021 年年初，我很幸运地进入中国建材尼日利亚新材料有限公司，工厂正值紧张的建设阶段，项目推进、设备安装、岗位练兵等，充满生机与希望，我为能亲身参与公司的建设而倍感荣幸。在新岗位上，许多工作需要从“零”开始，建厂初期事情繁杂，人手不足，我作为生产管理员，除了做好现场的设备安装工作外，还积极参与材料的采购计划与设备清点工作。在试生产阶段，材料的调配要保证及时到位，分秒的耽搁都会造成生产线停摆。最令我难忘的是，去年 9 月中旬，硅酸钙板订单接踵而来，时间紧、任务重，我每晚加班加点赶进度，在保证完成任务的同时还要解决好设备运行及产品质量问题，协调好交货时间及解决更换备品备件的问题。

我在工作和生活中对自己高标准、严要求，提醒自己在任何时候都要起到模范带头作用，为公司发展凝聚正能量。我做事擅于厘清重点难点、找准方法，工作成果多次得到公司和部门领导的肯定和表扬。我的英文也是从“零”开始，当地同事教得乐此不疲，我学得废寝忘食。现在我的英语水平已经得到了大家的高度认可。

不锈之光，处处闪耀。我时常被身边那些

爱岗敬业、无私奉献、可亲可敬的同事们打动，微微星光使我备受激励和鼓舞。在中国建材尼日利亚新材料有限公司这艘航母上，我要做那颗最坚固、最优秀的螺丝钉，与公司共同远航！

看，蓝图已经绘就；听，号角已经吹响。满载希望与未来的航母正在破浪前行，让我们同舟共济，与企业共成长！（中国建材尼日利亚新材料有限公司）

个人体会 来到中国建材尼日利亚新材料有限公司这段时间，我一直努力学习硅酸钙板生产线的专业知识，已经成长为公司的业务骨干，我把自己的理想追求、事业奋斗融入公司的发展之中，在公司发展过程中贡献了自己的青春智慧和力量。

Walk Together with Building Materials

Zhao Yunfei

Joined CNBM in 2021

The Production Supervisor of SINOMA Nigeria Company Ltd.

This year marks the 10th anniversary of the "Belt and Road" Initiative. In the past three years, every step of SINOMA Nigeria Company Ltd. and every major event experienced in Nigeria can clearly see the busy figure of the company's staff. They are united, thinking and working towards the same direction to help the company deeply cultivate the Nigerian market and achieve high-quality development. Though the local employees have different nationalities, skin colors and positions, they are all witnesses to the growth of the company. They constantly promote the company to deepen its international layout, promote China-Nepal friendship and mutual learning of civilizations, and actively respond to the Group's "Going Abroad" Initiative and China's "Belt and Road" Initiative.

When walking on green grass factory avenue in the morning, feeling the sound of birds singing and the fragrance of flowers I always have a sense of joy. When walking through the brightly lit, clean and spacious workshop, looking at the busy scene, I feel proud of this job. At the beginning of 2021, I was lucky enough to join the company. The factory was in the tense construction stage: project promotion, equipment installation, post training and so on. I cherished the opportunity to personally participate in the company's construction. In the new position, many tasks needed to start from "zero". In the early stage of the factory construction, things were complicated and manpower is insufficient. As a production manager, I not only did a good job of on-site equipment installation, but also actively participated in the material purchase plan and equipment inventory. In the trial production stage, the allocation of materials to ensure timely in place, every second delay will cause the production line shutdown. What impressed me most was that in the middle of September last year, orders for fiber cement board came one after another. Due to tight time and heavy tasks, I worked overtime every night to catch up with the schedule to ensure the completion of the task. At the same time, I had to solve equipment and product quality problems, coordinate delivery and replace spare parts.

I set high standards and strict requirements for myself in work and life, and remind myself to play a role model and take the lead at any time to gather positive energy for the development of the company. I am good at clarifying the key points and difficulties and finding the right methods. My work achievements have been affirmed and praised by the company and department leaders for many times. My English also started from "zero". Local colleagues taught me with enthusiasm and patience.

I indulged all myself into this English learning even forgetting eating and sleeping, and now my English is highly recognized by everyone.

I am usually impressed and inspired by those selfless dedication, amiable and honorable colleagues. If the company is an aircraft carrier , I want to be the strongest and most excellent screw and fly with it.

See, the blueprint has been drawn; Listen, the trumpet has sounded. The aircraft carrier full of hope and future is breaking through the waves. Let us work together and grow together with our enterprises.

Personal Insights After joining in the SINOMA Nigeria, I have been working hard and learning the professional knowledge of fiber cement board production. Now, I have grown into the business backbone of the company. I put my ideal pursuit and career struggle into the development of the company, and contribute my own youth, wisdom and strength in the development of the company.

“我们都在努力奔跑，我们都是追梦人。”

怀揣梦想的海外建材人，在工作中积淀，在淬炼中成长。

他们，披荆斩棘，挥洒汗水，凝聚青年力量，共筑丝路梦想。

“We are all relentlessly pursuing our dreams, running with unwavering determination.”

CNBM's overseas employees, driven by their dreams, fortify themselves through practical experiences. They blaze the paths forward, rally the power of youth, and jointly build dreams along the Belt and Road.

探路追梦篇

THE ROAD TO REALIZING DREAMS

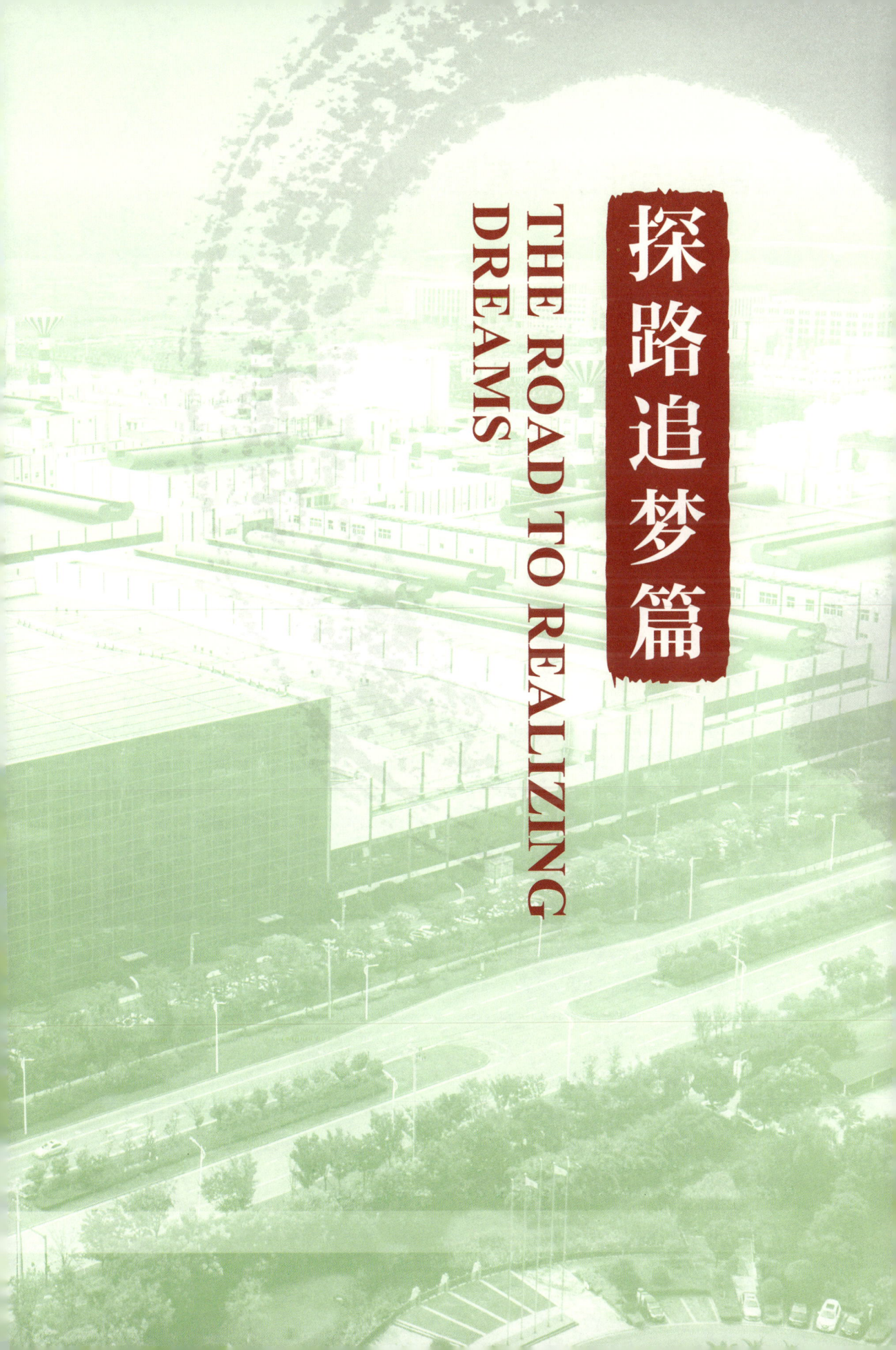

用智慧与汗水探索属地化经营之道

陈立新

2008 年加入中国建材

现任中国建材赞比亚工业园安全环保部副部长

赞比亚共和国是位于非洲中南部的内陆国家，大部分属于高原地区，风光旖旎。首都卢萨卡市是一个地道的非洲城市，面积开阔，布局简洁。从首都卢萨卡驱车沿东南方向行驶约 19 公里，在四周苍翠欲滴、丘陵绵延的小山谷里见到高耸的预热器和山谷入口处的标识，便可到达我工作了四年半的中国建材赞比亚工业园（以下简称“工业园”）——中国建材集团在海外投资建设的首个基础建材产业基地。

2018 年 3 月，为保证工业园顺利竣工投产，中材水泥有限责任公司充分发挥国内企业的人力资源优势，积极调动全级次企业派员赴赞支持，为只有国内专业经验的我们提供了赴海外历练实践的宝贵机会和平台。为响应国家“一带一路”倡议和央企“走出去”号召，在家人的支持下，我主动申请加入首批赴赞支持的队伍，投入如火如荼的项目建设和生产准备工作中，与海外的兄弟姐妹们一同为中国建材集团的国际化战略实施贡献自己的力量。

2018 年 7 月，这座综合性基础建材产业园正式投产，由中国建材集团旗下中材水泥有限责任公司在赞比亚投资设立的 Mpande Limestone Limited 负责工业园的建设及运营管理。在保驾工业园投产后，我又积极投身工业园的海外运营管理，运用自己在国内积累的专业知识和管理经验，使工业园的生产线可以在短时间内有条不紊地运转起来。

工业园运营初期，相较于国内成熟化、规范化的管理体系，在赞比亚搭建一套属地化的安全环保管理体系比想象的更加复杂。我深知问题从不会凭空消失，唯有积极应对。我从对当地相关法规懵懵懂懂的“小白”，一步步将习得的新知识转化成可应用于实际的管理体系，在查阅大量资料后，将自行翻译的常用法律规制梳理成册，并通过多角度、多途径学习了解当地相关法律后，借鉴在当地已发展成熟的企业的安全管理模式，与国内一级安全标准的部分内容融会贯通，逐步建立和完善适应于当地的安全管理体系制度，为安全生产夯实了基础。后续在实施过程中，以安全为目的，积极推进安全环保隐患排查整改，每周例会通报隐患内容和整改进度，不断提升整改完成率。在合规性经营方面，我牵头搜集、辨识安全环保法律法规 9 部，并参照修订、合并安全环保规章制度 36 项。同时，对接完成了电力保护审计、消防灭火器检验充装、环保基金审计等工作。一分耕耘，一分收获，通过摸索、学习、归纳、总结，以及与各部门的默契配合，工业园的安全环保体系从无到有，逐步完善，在提升企业管理成效的同时，为海外安全环保工作的开展积累了宝贵经验。

在赞比亚疫情暴发阶段，我与负责海外安全管理工作的战友们始终坚守在一线，严格按照上级要求，落实科学防疫的每一个环节，以实际行动确保了海外员工的生命安全与健康，实现了“生产、防控两不误”。其间，琼圭区卫生局医学博士 Dr.Kabungo 和琼圭区市议会 COVID-19 防控委员会主席 Mr.Aongola 先后莅临园区视察，现场了解园区的疫情防控措施和生产运营状况，对园区的防控成效高度认可，并对企业在疫情期间仍能保证正常运行表示赞赏。（中国建材赞比亚工业园）

个人体会

身为中国建材基础建材业务国际化发展团队中的一员，我深感使命光荣与责任重大，未来 10 年，我将继续与千万海外建材人一起乘风破浪，为打造具有全球竞争力的世界一流材料产业投资集团贡献更多力量！

Exploring the Path of Localized Management with Wisdom and Hard Work

Chen Lixin

Joined CNBM in 2008

Deputy Director of the Safety and Environmental Protection Department of CNBM Zambia Industrial Park

The Republic of Zambia is an inland country located in south central Africa, with most of its territory being highlands of breathtaking scenery. The capital city of Lusaka is a typical African city covering a vast area and with a simplified layout. About 19 kilometers southeast of the capital Lusaka, stand a towering preheater and a sign at the entrance of a lush and rolling small valley. It is the location of the China National Building Materials Zambia Industrial Park where I have worked for more than five years.

It is the first basic building materials industrial base established by China National Building Materials Group Corporation in overseas investment and construction.

In March 2018, in order to ensure the smooth completion and production of the industrial park, SINOMA Cement fully leveraged the domestic enterprise's human resources advantages and actively mobilized employees from all levels of the company to support the work in Zambia. This provided a valuable opportunity and platform for us who had accumulated professional experience in China to gain overseas experience through practice. In response to China's Belt and Road Initiative and the call for enterprises to "go global," and with the support of my family, I voluntarily applied to join the first team to support work in Zambia. I have been fully engaged in the intense project construction and production preparation work, contributing to the implementation of China National Building Materials Group's international strategy along with my overseas brothers and sisters.

In July 2018, the comprehensive basic building materials industrial park was officially put into operation. It was constructed and operated by Mpande Limestone Limited, invested by China National Building Materials Group's subsidiary, China National Building Material Company Limited in Zambia. After ensuring the successful production and operation of the industrial park, I actively participated in the overseas operation management of the park. With the knowledge and management experience I had accumulated in China, I helped the production line of the industrial park to operate smoothly and efficiently in a short period of time.

During the initial operation of the industrial park, compared to the mature and standardized management practices in China, it proved more complicated to establish a localized safety and environmental protection management system in Zambia. However, I knew that problems would not disappear on their own, so I proactively addressed them. Starting as a "novice" in terms of local regulations, I gradually transformed my newfound knowledge into an applicable management system. I collected and organized commonly used legal regulations by translating them and studied relevant local laws and regulations from multiple angles and sources. I also drew on the safety management practices of mature enterprises in the local area and incorporated aspects of China's first-level safety standards. Gradually, I established and improved an adapted safety management system to lay a solid foundation for safe production. In the follow-up process, we focused on fundamental safety and actively promoted the identification and rectification of safety and environmental protection hazards. We held weekly meetings to report on the content of the hazards and the progress of the rectification, continuously improving the completion rate of the rectification. In terms of compliance operations, we led efforts to collect and identify nine safety and environmental protection laws and regulations as well as revised or merged 36 safety and environmental protection rules and regulations. In addition, we completed tasks such as power protection audits, fire extinguisher inspections and charging, and environmental protection fund audits. With one step at a time, and through exploration, learning, summarizing and collaborating with various departments, the industrial park's safety and environmental protection system was built from scratch, gradually improving and contributing to the enhancement of enterprise management effectiveness. The process also accumulated valuable experience for the implementation of overseas safety and environmental protection work.

During the outbreak of the epidemic in Zambia, my fellow companions responsible for overseas safety management and I remained on the front line, strictly implementing every aspect of scientific epidemic prevention in accordance with superiors'

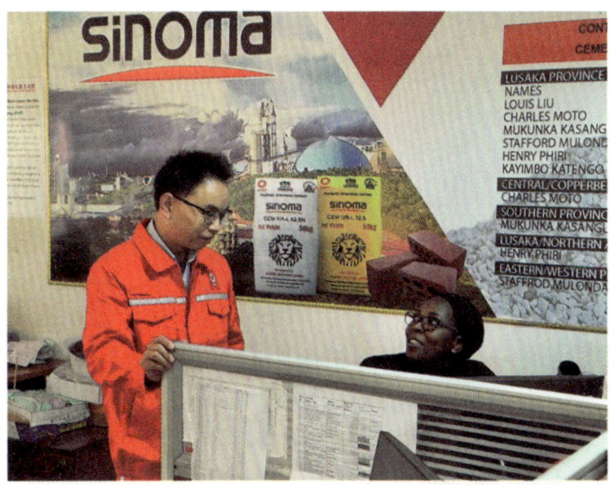

requirements. Through practical actions, we ensured the health and safety of overseas employees and achieved the goal of "production, prevention and control are not in conflict". During this period, Dr. Kabungo, a medical doctor from the Chongwe Health Bureau, and Mr. Aongola, Chairman of the Chongwe Council's COVID-19 Prevention and Control Committee, visited the industrial park to inspect the epidemic prevention and control measures and production operations. They highly recognized the effectiveness of epidemic prevention and control in the park and appreciated the enterprise's ability to maintain normal operations during the epidemic.

Five years have flown by. It's neither long nor short. As a permanent resident overseas, various challenges are always changing, but the original aspiration of deep cultivation, focus, and persistence remains unchanged. As a member of the international development team for China National Building Material 's basic building materials business, I deeply feel the noble mission and heavy responsibility. In the next ten years, I will continue to work with millions of overseas building materials personnel to forge ahead and contribute more to the creation of a globally competitive world-class material industry investment group!

Personal Insights As a member of the international development team for China National Building Material 's basic building materials business, I deeply feel the noble mission and heavy responsibility. In the next ten years, I will continue to work with millions of overseas building materials personnel to forge ahead and contribute more to the creation of a globally competitive world-class material industry investment group!

一名海外营销经理的北新造梦记

普罗斯佩·欧内斯特·豪尔
2018 年加入中国建材
现任北新建材工业（坦桑尼亚）有限公司营销部大区经理

“过去 5 年，我曾经的梦实现了。我有了值得尊敬的工作和收入，也组建了幸福的家庭。这一切都是从我加入坦桑北新开始的。”普罗斯佩·欧内斯特·豪尔谈及过往，感叹像梦一样。

2018 年，普罗斯佩加入了创建阶段的坦桑北新，成为北新建材最早的一批外籍员工。他是坦桑北新发展的见证者，也是北新建材国际化发展的亲历者。在这个过程中，他自己也从一名普通业务员，逐步成长为能够独当一面的区域经理，成为优秀的坦桑籍员工代表。

在工作中，凭借娴熟的谈判技巧、良好的沟通与协调能力，普罗斯佩积累了丰富的行业市场分析和开拓经验。他对营销工作有独特的思考和见解，尤其擅长维护大客户，负责的达市大客户销量在坦桑北新整体销量的占比接近 20%。

他乐于接受有挑战性的工作，坦桑尼亚重点大学本科的教育背景，让他除了能使用母语——斯瓦西里语外，还能熟练运用英语进行书写和交流，因此，他利用这个语言优势不断开发出口市场，使得卢旺达、刚果（金）等国家的出口销量在坦桑北新整体销量的占比接近 5%，对坦桑北新在辐射市场的产品推广和品牌影响力的提升作出了突出贡献。

普罗斯佩时刻保持激情、勇担重任，不仅在销售工作中快速成长为独当一面的核心骨干，而且发挥个人长项，主动承担了很多坦桑北新从初期设立到项目建设再到日常运行期间的其他各种工作。

2020 年年初，坦桑尼亚出台了新的工作签证制度。新制度对于非坦桑籍员工申请工作签的要求更加严苛，许多在坦的中资公司都出现了 20%—30% 的拒签率。

面对这种情况，普罗斯佩主动请缨为非坦桑籍员工办理工作签申请。他从网上下载了新的劳工和移民条例进行逐条学习、研究，然后又到坦桑尼亚投资中心拜访，了解申请工作签的注意事项。遇到不合理的拒签情况时，他带着申诉信到坦桑尼亚首都多多马，直接向坦桑尼亚劳工部部长反映情况。经过一次次的尝试、一次次的申请、一次次的争取，坦桑北新非坦桑籍员工，特别是

技术骨干都先后顺利拿到了工作签，有效稳定了坦桑北新生产经营团队，为生产经营和新线建设工作提供了有力保障。普罗斯佩用不畏挑战、敢打敢拼、勇于担当的实际行动生动诠释了建材人的精神，传递了北新力量，也给坦桑尼亚当地政府部门留下了深刻印象。

普罗斯佩发自内心地认同公司文化，一直以在坦桑北新工作为荣。他经常热情地向客户，向亲戚和朋友们介绍北新建材和坦桑北新。

他说："我周围的朋友都很羡慕我能在这样一家大型、规范的中资企业工作，因为他们看到了我的变化。我由一名普通业务员成为了大区经理，收入稳步提高，我还成功组建了家庭，实现了自己的短期人生目标。"

"我们坦桑尼亚有句谚语是'独行可以走得快，结伴才能走得远'。只有大家团结一心、共同努力，我们的公司才会越走越远，越来越好！我愿意和大家结伴而行、共同努力。"普罗斯佩认真地说。〔北新建材工业（坦桑尼亚）有限公司〕

坦桑北新是一个非常棒的公司，有着完备的制度、完善的质量控制体系、良好的福利待遇、公平的晋升机制等。我很珍惜自己的工作，也非常感谢我的领导和同事，让我们一起努力，相信我们的公司会发展得越来越好！

Prosper Ernest Haule: An Overseas Dream Maker at BNBM

Prosper Ernest Haule

Joined CNBM in 2018

The Regional Manager of the Marketing Department of of BNBM Building Materials Industry (Tanzania) Limited

"In the past five years, my dreams have come true. With a respectable job, a good income, I have built a happy family. It all started when I joined BNBM Tanzania." Prosper Ernest Haule reflects on his past, describing it as a dream-like experience.

In 2018, Prosper joined BNBM Tanzania at the stage of establishment, becoming one of the first foreign employees of BNBM. He witnessed the development of the company and experienced its expansion to the world stage. Throughout this process, he transformed from an ordinary salesperson to a capable regional manager, becoming an outstanding representative of the Tanzanian employees at BNBM.

Prosper is eager to take on challenging tasks. With an undergraduate education from a prestigious university in Tanzania, he is not only fluent in his mother tongue Swahili, but also proficient in written and spoken English. Leveraging this language advantage, he continuously explores export markets. As a result, the export sales from countries such as Rwanda and the Democratic Republic of Congo account for nearly 5% of BNBM Tanzania's overall sales, contributing greatly to the promotion of BNBM Tanzania's products and the enhancement of its brand influence in the target markets.

Prosper consistently maintains passion and willingly takes on major tasks. He not only rapidly grew into a backbone employee in the sales department but also showcased his diverse skills by voluntarily taking on various tasks throughout the establishment, project construction, and daily operation phases of BNBM Tanzania.

In early 2020, Tanzania introduced a new work visa system, which has stricter requirements for non-Tanzanian employees, resulting in a rejection rate of 20% to 30% for many Chinese-invested companies in Tanzania. Confronting this situation, Prosper took the initiative to handle work visa applications for non-Tanzanian employees. He downloaded and studied the new labor and immigration regulations meticulously, visited the Tanzania Investment Centre to understand the application process. He would also personally address unreasonable visa rejections by submitting appeals to the Minister of Labor in Dodoma, the Tanzanian capital. Through numerous attempts, applications and efforts, non-Tanzanian employees of BNBM Tanzania, especially technical experts, successfully obtained their work visas. This achievement effectively stabilized the production and operation team of BNBM Tanzania, providing strong support for the company's production and operation, and for the construction of new lines.

Prosper's unwavering determination, courage, and willingness to take on challenges vividly exemplify the spirit and strength of BNBM, leaving a deep impression on the local Tanzanian government authorities.

Prosper genuinely identifies with BNBM's corporate culture and takes great pride in working at BNBM Tanzania. He often enthusiastically introduces BNBM Tanzania and BNBM to his relatives and friends.

He says, "My friends around me admire that I can work in such a large and wellestablished Chinese-invested company, because they have witnessed my transformation. I have grown from an ordinary salesperson to a regional manager, with a steady increase in income. I have also successfully built a family and achieved my short-term life goals."

"In Tanzania, we have a saying that goes, 'Alone, you may travel fast, but together, you'll journey far'. Only when we are united and make joint efforts can our company go further and become better! I am willing to walk together and work hard with everyone." Prosper earnestly states.

Personal Insights BNBM Tanzania is a great company with a robust and thorough framework, a well-established quality control system, a good salary and welfare system, and a fair promotion mechanism. I cherish my work and feel grateful to my leaders and colleagues. I believe, with our concerted efforts, the company will continue to thrive!

跨越万里的另一种“浪漫”

张洪旭

2009 年加入中国建材
现任北新建材工业（坦桑尼亚）有限公司生产调度

刘彬

2009 年加入中国建材
现任北新建材中亚外资有限公司综合管理部主任

在北新建材有一对夫妻，他们跨越万里，一个在坦桑尼亚，一个在乌兹别克斯坦，遥遥相望，却守望相助，互相支持，互相鼓励，共同为北新建材的国际化发展奋斗，书写着属于他们的独特“浪漫”故事，他们就是坦桑北新张洪旭和中亚北新刘彬。

他，张洪旭，2009 年 3 月大学毕业后，作为最早的一批员工，加入了北新建材铁岭分公司，担任三控机长。他入职后，快速投入设备安装和调试工作，并将工作中学到的专业知识、遇到的问题和解决方法以及对工作的思考都及时记录下来，至今，这样的记事本已数不清有多少个。

她，刘彬，与张洪旭同年入职北新建材铁岭分公司，她见证了北新建材钻石 10 年的发展历程，更坚定了她想为公司贡献一份力的决心。踏实认真是她的品行，严谨敬业是她的特性，好学上进是她的个性，多次被评为“优秀员工”“三八红旗手”。在她的身上，可以清楚地看到优秀员工该有的模样。

就是这样本无交集的两个人，因北新而结缘，又在公司加快推进国际化战略落地的关键时期，勇于走出去。2022 年，因为工作需要，他们放弃了国内稳定的工作和家庭生活，张洪旭远赴坦桑尼亚，刘彬奔向乌兹别克斯坦。他们共同逐梦而行，开启海外“夫妻档”跨越万里的另一种“浪漫”。

张洪旭是一名优秀的技术人才，熟悉石膏板生产工艺和设备维修，曾多次参与国内的石膏板项目建设和技术改造工作。2022 年，他主动申请到北新建材坦桑尼亚石膏板厂工作，担任生产调度一职，负责生产线的运行、维护、改进和优化。他有丰富的生产管理经验和深厚的工艺技术功底，能够快速解决生产过程中遇到的各种问题，保证产品质量和生产效率。他不仅指导当地员工操作设备，还培训他们掌握技术知识和安全规范。

刘彬在中亚北新担任综合管理部主任一职，负责人力资源、行政、后勤等方面的工作。综合管理部各项工作事务繁杂，她凭借扎实的专业知识和灵活的应变能力，总是能够游刃有余的化解难题，高效地协调各部门之间的沟通和合作，为乌兹项目建设期间的正常运营提供了有力保障。她非常注重培养当地员工的专业素养和团队精神，通过组织各类活动增进中外员工之间的沟通和协作，营造了良好的工作氛围。

作为老员工，这对海外“夫妻档”心有灵犀地认识到“传帮带”不仅是一种义务，也是一种荣誉。

项目建设需要不断吸纳新员工，为尽快让新员工适应新环境，提高专业技能，增强团队凝聚力和战斗力，提升整个组织的效率和水平，需要发扬“传帮带”的精神。张洪旭分享自己的工作经验，帮助新人成长，不厌其烦地为新人讲解和示范，给他们创造实践的机会。刘彬传授工作方法，让新人快速进入工作状态，提高工作效率。

刘彬和张洪旭相隔万里，每天都通过电话或视频聊天，分享彼此的工作和生活，互相鼓励和支持。她告诉他，在管理食堂的同时，她也学会了做拉面；他告诉她，今天又教会了新徒弟一项技能。他说，奶奶打电话说孩子生病了找妈妈；她说，奶奶是世界上最好的奶奶，

有她在我放心。他们说，有时候也会感到孤独和辛苦；他们也说，虽然远隔万里无法相见，但他们始终肩并肩……

当夜幕降临，张洪旭和刘彬忙完一天的工作，打通了这条跨越万里的视频通话，几句问候、几句关心、几句鼓励，共同期盼着下一次相聚，这便是属于他们的另一种“浪漫”。〔北新建材工业（坦桑尼亚）有限公司、北新建材中亚外资有限公司〕

个人体会

张洪旭：我一毕业就进入了北新，十年如一日。我爱北新，所以北新哪里需要我，我就往哪里去。我希望自己的专业水平和过硬的能力能为北新的海外建设增砖添瓦。

刘彬：在北新工作多年，我已经将北新当成自己的家，为了家园更美好，我愿意努力，愿意奋斗，愿意到海外工作。我用尽能用的时间，努力学习新知识，提升各方面的能力。我会用实际行动证明北新的女人能顶半边天。

A Different Kind of "Romance" across Thousands of Miles

Zhang Hongxu

Joined CNBM in 2009

The Production Dispatcher of BNBM Building Materials Industry (Tanzania) Limited

Liu Bin

Joined CNBM in 2009

The Director of the General Management Department of BNBM Building Materials Central Asia

Within BNBM works a couple who are thousands of miles apart. One is in Tanzania, and the other is in Uzbekistan. They are separated by distance but stand by each other, offering support and encouragement. Together, they strive for the international development of BNBM, composing their unique "romantic" story. They are Zhang Hongxu from BNBM Tanzania and Liu Bin from BNBM Central Asia.

Zhang Hongxu, one of the earliest employees, joined BNBM Tieling branch as a control machine captain in March 2009. After entering the post, he quickly immersed himself in the process of equipment installation and commissioning. He diligently documented the professional knowledge he gained, the challenges he encountered, the solutions he found, and his reflections on the work. Until now, he has filled countless notebooks with such records.

Liu Bin, like Zhang Hongxu, joined BNBM Tieling branch in the same year. She witnessed the tenyears' Diamond development journey of BNBM and became even more determined to contribute to BNBM. She is known for her down-to-earth and serious attitude, meticulous dedication, and eagerness to learn and progress. She has been repeatedly recognized as an "outstanding employee" and a "March 8th Red Flag Bearer". One can clearly see the qualities of an excellent employee in her.

These two individuals, who initially had no connection, came together because of BNBM and ventured abroad during a crucial period of advancing the company's globalization strategy. In 2022, for the sake of work, they gave up stable work and family life in China with Zhang Hongxu going to Tanzania while Liu Bin heading to Uzbekistan. They embarked on a shared dream, opening a new chapter of "romance" as an overseas couple, spanning thousands of miles.

Zhang Hongxu is an excellent technical talent who is familiar with gypsum board production processes and equipment maintenance. He has participated in multiple domestic gypsum board projects and technical improvement works. In

2022, he proactively applied to work at BNBM's gypsum board plant in Tanzania, taking on the role of production scheduler. He is responsible for the operation, maintenance, improvement, and optimization of the production line. With his extensive production management experience and profound technical expertise, he can quickly resolve various issues encountered during production, ensuring product quality and efficiency. He not only guides local employees in operating equipment but also trains them to acquire technical knowledge and safety standards.

Liu Bin holds the position of Director of the General Management Department at BNBM Central Asia, being responsible for various aspects of work including human resources, administration, and logistics. The tasks of the General Management Department are complex, but with her solid professional knowledge and flexible adaptability, she is always able to handle challenges with ease. She efficiently coordinates communication and cooperation among departments, providing strong support for smooth operation during the construction of the project in Uzbekistan. She attaches great importance to developing the professional competence and team spirit of local employees. By organizing various activities, she promotes communication and collaboration between Chinese and foreign employees, creating a positive working atmosphere.

As veteran employees, the overseas couple understand the importance of "sharing knowledge and helping each other" and see it not only as an obligation but also as an honor.

The project construction requires more new employees. Therefore it is imperative to help them quickly adapt to the new environment, improve their professional skills, so as to enhance team cohesion and combat effectiveness and elevate

the overall efficiency and level of the organization. This requires the spirit of "sharing knowledge and helping each other". Zhang Hongxu shares his work experience and tirelessly assists newcomers, explaining and demonstrating tasks, and providing them with practical opportunities. Liu Bin imparts work methods, enabling newcomers to quickly get into the work pace and improve their efficiency.

Liu Bin and Zhang Hongxu, despite being thousands of miles apart, communicate with each other every day through phone calls or video chats, sharing their work and lives and giving support to each other. She told him that while managing the canteen, she also learned to make Hand-Pulled Noodles. He told her that he taught a new apprentice a new skill today. He mentioned that his mother called saying the kid was sick and looking for the mother. She replied that the mother-in-law is the best grandma in the world, and with the grandma taking care the kid, she is grateful. They admitted that sometimes they felt lonely and tired, but they also said that even though they are far apart, they are always shoulder to shoulder...

When the night falls, after a busy day of work, Zhang Hongxu and Liu Bin connect through a video call that spans thousands of miles. With a few greetings, caring or encouraging words, they create their own unique "romance", eagerly anticipating their next meeting.

Personal Insights Zhang Hongxu: I joined BNBM right after graduation from university and have been with the company over decade. I love BNBM, so wherever BNBM needs me, that's where I will go. I hope that my professional skills and strong abilities can contribute to BNBM's globalization.
Liu Bin: After working at BNBM for many years, I consider it my home. I am willing to strive and make efforts to make my home even better. I use all available time to study and enhance my abilities in various aspects. Through practical actions, I prove that women at BNBM can hold up half the sky.

坚守匠心的海外项目筑梦人

杨承文
2021年加入中国建材
现任北新建材中亚外资有限公司海外项目经理

杨承文，北新集团建材股份有限公司高级工程师。1996年，他进入石膏板行业，逐步了解行业标准和工厂建设以及运营。2021年，他投身中亚北新乌兹项目。3年来，他努力克服疫情等重重困难，从项目环评、设计、报建、土建开工建设到项目全套设备到达接收、安全存放、安装调试，直至顺利投产，一直坚守在一线。一路走来，踏平坎坷、甘苦自知，对于献身的这份事业，他发自内心地感到光荣与自豪。

深耕石膏板行业27年来，杨承文积累了丰富的工作经验，利用自己的专业技能为中亚北新乌兹项目的顺利推进和投产作出了重要贡献。他不仅精通国内外各种石膏板先进工艺装备和前沿技术，还熟知石膏板项目建设的全周期重大节点。他结合乌兹别克斯坦当地项目建设方面的标准和规范，主动作为、敢于作为，大大提高了项目建设效率。他曾成功解决多个技术难题。例如，项目建设中的天然气、高压供配电、消防工程等在建项目的工程图纸设计、施工和验收，为公司节省了大量的成本和时间。

杨承文是北新建材国际公司海外项目经理，在海外项目建设领域有着丰富的行业经验和卓越的业绩背景。他曾参与和主持设计过多个重大石膏板项目的建设和管理，如泰国GPMAN项目、越南Vinafrit项目、德国可耐福以及其他国家多条石膏板生产线建设等。

他不仅具备专业的技术能力和管理水平，还具有高度的敬业精神和良好的职业道德。他多次在海外项目中克服困难，解决问题，保证工程质量和进度，赢得了公司领导和当地政府的高度赞誉。

他不仅是公司的优秀员工，也是同事们的好榜样。他积极参与公司的各项活动，帮助培训新员工，传授经验、推动成长，有力提升了团队的凝聚力和协作力。

作为一名项目经理，同时也是一名高级工程师，杨承文在掌控全局的同时也专注做好每一个细节。

他常说：“标准很重要，标准是我们进入项目地国家石膏板市场的基础，只有符合当地

国家标准，我们生产出的产品才有意义，才能获得这个国家和人民的认可。”

在乌兹别克斯坦石膏板国家标准翻译版出来后，他逐字逐句地校对审查，不放过任何一个错误或不准确的地方。遇到不明白的，他仔细查阅资料，与中国标准和国际标准进行比对，和翻译员反复讨论，多次审查后才最终定稿。

又比如，拿回来一些外语资料，不需要翻译，一般大家大概知道了是什么意思后就放下了，但他总会拿起笔，在一些外语文件上标注主要内容。

他说："好记性不如烂笔头。不标注，时间一长都忘记了，反而降低了工作效率。而且标注后还方便其他不懂外语的人看，何乐而不为呢？”在后来的工作中也证明，小小的标注能给工作带来很大的便利。后来同事们纷纷向他学习，养成了标注中文的习惯。

他热爱工作，认真坚守在工作岗位。同时，他也坚持良好的作息和饮食习惯，保持着健康的体魄。每天准时起床锻炼，按时吃早饭，坚持多喝水，尤其爱喝苦瓜水。他有着终身学习的理念，一有时间就会看书、研究图纸、翻看公众号、关注行业内新闻等。他乐观向上，每次见到他的时候，他总是带着微笑，语调总是昂扬的，从不叹气，也从不抱怨，始终保持着积极的人生态度，他是一位有理想、有担当、有情怀的建材人。

（北新建材中亚外资有限公司）

个人体会 我热爱石膏板行业，我愿意用我几十年的技术和经验为中亚北新的建设和发展鞠躬尽瘁、保驾护航。我会以身作则、以厂为家，视同事为家人，团结并带领大家把中亚北新建设得越来越好，为中乌友谊贡献微薄之力。

The Dream Builder of Overseas Project with a Dedication to Craftsmanship

Yang Chengwen

Joined CNBM in 2021

The Overseas Project Manager of BNBM Building Materials Central Asia

Yang Chengwen is a senior engineer of Beijing New Building Materials PLC. In 1996, he entered the gypsum board industry and gradually gained knowledge about industry standards, plant construction and operations. In 2021, he dedicated himself to the BNBM CENTRAL ASIA's project in Uzbekistan. Over the past three years, he has overcome numerous challenges, including the COVID-19 pandemic, and has been actively involved in various project stages, including environmental assessment, design, construction application, construction, as well as acceptance, storage, installation, commissioning and production of the whole set of equipment. Throughout the journey, he has faced and conquered obstacles, been fully aware of the hardships and sacrifices involved, and taken great pride and honor in dedicating himself to his career.

With 27 years of deep involvement in the gypsum board industry, Yang Chengwen has accumulated extensive work experience. His expertise has played a crucial role in ensuring smooth progress and production of the BNBM CENTRAL ASIA's Uzbekistan project, especially during the challenging times of the pandemic. He not only possesses in-depth knowledge of advanced gypsum board technologies and equipment from home and abroad, but also has a deep understanding of critical nodes in the construction cycle of a gypsum board project. By reference to local standards and regulations in Uzbekistan, he has proactively and courageously taken initiatives, significantly improving construction efficiency. He has successfully resolved various technical challenges, including the engineering drawing design, construction, and acceptance of projects under construction such as natural gas, highvoltage power supply, and fire protection, saving substantial cost and time for the company.

Yang Chengwen is the overseas project manager of BNBM International, and he possesses rich industry experience and an outstanding track record in the field of overseas project construction. He has participated in and led the design and construction of multiple major gypsum board projects, including the GPMAN project in Thailand, the Vinafrit project in Vietnam, the Knauf project in Germany, and the construction of gypsum board production lines in other countries.

He not only possesses professional technical skills and management capabilities but also demonstrates a high level of dedication and good professional ethics.

He has overcome difficulties, solved problems, and ensured project quality and progress in numerous overseas projects, earning high praise from the company leadership and local governments.

He is not only an excellent employee of the company but also a role model for his colleagues. He actively participates in company activities and assists in training new employees, sharing his experience to promote their growth, which has effectively enhanced team cohesion and collaboration.

As a project manager, as well as a senior engineer, Yang Chengwen pays attention to every detail while overseeing the overall situation.

He emphasizes the importance of standards, stating that "standards are crucial as they serve as the foundation for us to enter the gypsum board market of the country where our projects are. Only by complying with the local national standards can our products gain recognition from the country and its people."

When the gypsum board national standards of Uzbekistan were translated, Yang Chengwen meticulously reviewed every word and sentence, not overlooking any errors or inaccuracies. If there was anything he did not understand, he would carefully consult reference materials, compare it with Chinese and international standards, discuss it with translators, and conduct multiple reviews before finalizing the version.

In addition, when he received foreign-language materials that didn't require translation, while others normally put them aside after having a general understanding, he would pick up a pen and annotate the main points on the documents.

He said, "A good memory is not as reliable as a pen. Without annotations, we tend to forget the content over time, which reduces work efficiency. Moreover, making important annotations also facilitates others who don't understand the foreign language. So why not?" Subsequently, it was proven that these small annotations brought great convenience to work. Colleagues followed suit and developed the habit of annotating in Chinese.

He loves his work so much that he even hopes to work non-stop for 365 days a year. At the same time, he maintains a healthy lifestyle as well as a good physical condition by adhering to good routines and dietary habits. He exercises regularly, eats breakfast on time, and drinks plenty of water, particularly enjoying bitter melon juice. He embraces lifelong learning and seizes any available time to read books, study drawings, and follow industry news on public platforms. He is optimistic and positive, always smiling and speaking with an upbeat tone. He never sighs or complains, maintaining a positive attitude towards life. And he is the very BNBMer of ideals, a sense of responsibility, and passion.

Personal Insights I love the gypsum board industry, and I am willing to dedicate my decades of technical expertise and experience to the construction and development of BNBM CENTRAL ASIA. I will lead by example and treat the plant as my home and the colleagues as my family members. Together, we will unite and strive to make BNBM CENTRAL ASIA better and contribute to the friendship between China and Uzbekistan.

融入“熔炉” 迸发光热

王大海

1994 年加入中国建材

现任中材国际（南京）一级工程师

王大海，在矿山专业设计岗位上默默奉献，工作是其生命中的重要部分。30 年前，当融入这个滚烫“熔炉”的时候，他做好了迸发光热的准备，用豪情激励着自己。同时，他也感受到了工作所赋予的使命，面对压力，义无反顾地直面现实，直至压力成功化解。

他就是中材国际（南京）的王大海，一名出色的矿山专业设计师。

王大海在设计中贯彻“绿水青山就是金山银山”理念，在行业率先开展绿色矿山方案设计及建设；主持了铜陵海螺、天瑞郑州、芜湖海螺万吨线等 200 多个建材矿山开采方案设计工作，完成数个建材矿山生态修复方案，以实际行动践行绿色矿山建设目标。

工作中，他紧跟科技发展前沿，作为主要研发人员，承担了公司数字化智能矿山系统的研发和应用，完成了云南易门大椿树、吴忠赛马数字化矿山系统的建设工作，显著提高了矿山的生产管理水平、资源的综合利用率和进厂矿石的稳定性，获得业主好评。目前，这一系统正在建材行业内进一步推广，以提高矿山智能化建设水平。

王大海一直不断学习应用新技术，在秭归项目第一次采用溜井平硐系统 + 大倾角皮带隧道，解决了特大高差（1000 米）矿石运输难题；在陆川项目率先采用无爆破法开采石灰石，避免了爆破开采产生的飞石、震动以及扬尘，大幅度提高了矿山开采的安全和环保水平。

他多次前往海外项目现场踏勘，用实际行动支持公司海外市场的开拓；作为矿山技术负责人，他先后承担了莫桑比克、安哥拉、印度尼西亚、津巴布韦、埃塞俄比亚、乌兹别克斯坦等多个国外项目设计工作。在津巴布韦项目现场考察期间，他和技术团队驱车几百公里，与业主一起爬山，踏勘现场，查阅图纸，讨论问题到半夜。业主表示，这个团队是自己见过的最专业的技术专家团队。业主纷纷竖起大拇指，对技术团队赞不绝口。

2020 年，全球新冠疫情蔓延，当公司征求他是否可以去海外出差时，王大海没有丝毫

犹豫就作出了肯定的答复，用行动诠释责任与担当。2020 年 10 月初，在举国欢庆、全家团圆的时节，他义无反顾地出发，成为疫情发生后公司派往海外的第一批技术团队的成员。

埃塞莱米镇矿区在山谷中，高差超过千米。大家顶着烈日，先下后上，行程开始没多久，王大海便依据丰富的经验提醒团队成员一定要控制饮水，尽量保留部分饮用水以备紧急情况。但由于天气炎热，有的成员还是很快就将水喝完了。返程到最后一段路，有一名成员口渴难耐，无法前行，他赶紧将省下来的半瓶水分给这位同事，同事感慨道："今天幸亏有他省下的半瓶水，要不然我就危险了。"

2021 年，王大海再次承担海外项目出差任务，对乌兹别克斯坦项目进行现场调研。已经连续两年中秋节、国庆节都在国外度过，无法看望百岁的奶奶，也无法与家人团聚，他虽然有不舍，但还是以工作为重，圆满完成海外现场各项工作。

新时代是奋斗者的时代，像王大海这样的工程技术人员，是科技成果落地的重要执行者。是他们，用智慧的头脑和勤劳的双手演绎了一个个奇迹；是他们，专啃"硬骨头"，让一个个困难成为提高技术和能力的动力，让一个个项目高质量完成。

从他们的经历中，每个人都能获得不一样的启发，我们要学习他们身上善于攻坚克难的优秀品质，练就一身"硬本领"，在一点一滴中完善，从小事小节上修炼，以实际行动学习、保持乃至赶超先进，在推动中材国际成为材料工业世界一流服务商的征程中发出自己的光和热。〔中材国际（南京）〕

个人体会 有幸成为中材国际的一员，我感到骄傲与光荣。个人的成长离不开公司的培养，我将把握机遇，不断学习，提高专业知识，推动矿山数字智能化发展，建设绿色矿山，实现"绿水青山就是金山银山"。

Immersed in the "Hot Melting Pot" to Emit Light and Heat

Wang Dahai

Joined CNBM in 1994

First-class Engineer in SINOMA (Nanjing)

Mr. Wang Dahai has made silent contributions in the field of mining design. His work is a significant part of his life. When he immersed himself in this "hot melting pot" 30 years ago, he was ready to burst into light and heat and inspire himself to grow stronger with passion. At the same time, he also embraced the sense of mission bestowed upon him by his work. Faced with pressure, he confronted difficult problems directly without hesitation until he successfully resolved them. Mr. Wang is an outstanding professional mining designer from SINOMA International (Nanjing).

Mr. Wang has implemented the concept of "Lucid waters and lush mountains are invaluable assets" in his design work. He took the lead in the industry to carry out the design and construction of green mines. He has led the mining design for over 200 building materials mines, including those of Tongling Conch Cement Plant, Tianrui Group Zhengzhou Cement Plant and Wuhu Conch 10kt/a cement production line, and completed several ecological restoration plans for building materials mines. He has implemented the green mine construction principle through practical actions.

In his work, he closely follows the forefront of technological development. As the main R&D expert of the company, he has undertaken the research and application of the company's digital intelligent mining system, and completed the construction of the digital mining system for Yunnan Yimen Dachunshu Cement Plant and Wuzhong Saima Cement Plant, significantly improving the production management level of the mines, the comprehensive utilization rate of resources and the stability of incoming ore, thus receiving praises from customers. At present, this digital system is being further promoted in the building materials industry to make mines more intelligent.

Mr. Wang has been continuously learning and applying new technologies. In the Zigui project, he, for the first time, adopted a chute adit system plus a large inclination belt tunnel, solving the problem of transporting ore in case of a huge height difference (1000 meters). In the Luchuan project, he took the lead to use the non-blasting method to mine limestone, avoiding flying rocks, vibrations and dust generated by blasts, which made the process of mining safer and more environmentally friendly.

He has visited overseas project sites multiple times and supported the company's overseas market development with practical actions. As the leader of mining technology, he has undertaken design work

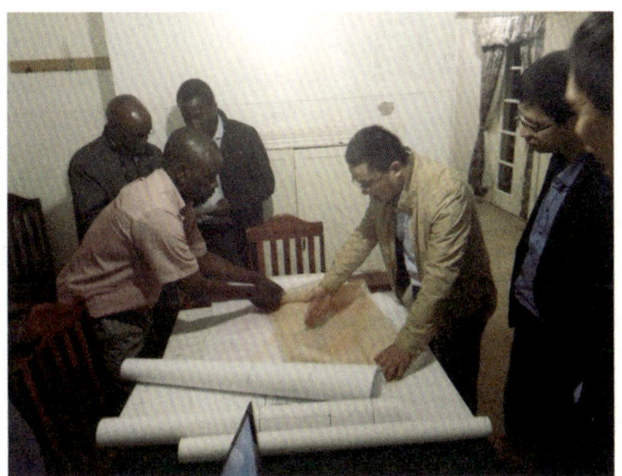

for multiple foreign projects in Mozambique, Angola, Indonesia, Zimbabwe, Ethiopia, Uzbekistan and other countries. During the on-site inspection of the Zimbabwe project, he and his technical team drove several hundred kilometers, climbed mountains with the owners, inspected the site, reviewed blueprints and discussed issues till midnight. The owners said that this technical team is the most professional technical expert they have ever met, and gave their thumbs up in praise of the team.

In 2020, the COVID-19 pandemic spread across the world. When the company asked him whether he could travel overseas, Mr. Wang gave a positive answer without hesitation, and interpreted his responsibility with actions. In early October, during the festival season of national celebration and family reunion, he set out without hesitation and became a member of the first technical team dispatched by the company after the outbreak of the pandemic.

The mining area in Lemi Town in Ethiopia is located in a valley, with an elevation difference of over 1000 meters. The team first went down to the valley and then went up to return to the office. They walked under scorching sun. No sooner after the journey had started, he reminded team members out of his rich experience to control the use of drinking water and try to keep water as much as possible in case of emergency. But due to the hot weather, some members quickly drank up the water. On the last leg of the return journey, one member was too thirsty to continue. He quickly distributed a half bottle of water he had saved to this colleague who urgently needed the replenishment. This grateful colleague said: "Thanks to the half bottle of water he saved today; otherwise, I would be in danger."

In 2021, he once again traveled overseas to conduct an on-site investigation on projects in Uzbekistan. In two consecutive years, he stayed abroad on the Mid-Autumn Festival and the National Day and was unable to see his 100-year-old grandmother and reunite with his family. Although he felt a little sad, he still placed his work on the first place and successfully completed all the on-site work.

The new era is the era for strivers. Engineering and technical personnel like Mr. Wang are important implementers in applying scientific and technological results into actual production. It is them who have made one miracle after another with their wise thinking and diligent hands. It is them who have been committed to solving difficult technical problems, making each difficulty a driving force for improving their skills and abilities, and enabling projects to be completed in high quality one after another.

From their experiences, everyone can gain different inspirations. We should learn their excellent expertise at overcoming difficulties, develop our professional skills, improve our qualities bit by bit, cultivate ourselves from small details. We should learn, catch up with and even surpass the exemplar individuals through practical actions, and emit our own light and heat on SINOMA International's journey towards a world-class service provider in the materials industry.

Personal Insights I feel proud to be a member of our company, especially during its rapid growth. I would take the chance to express my gratefulness to our company for its training and nourishing. Through further study to enrich my professional knowledge, I will promote the development of intelligent digital mining and build a green mine, realizing the goal of turning "lucid waters and lush mountains" into "invaluable assets".

敢啃“硬骨头”的一线指挥员

敬学宾

2003 年 6 月加入中国建材
现任成都建材院工程管理二部副部长
夏河祁连山技改项目调试总指挥

2020 年底，中国中材国际工程股份有限公司所属成都建材院运营调试经理敬学宾被授予“四川省劳动模范”荣誉称号。受此表彰的劳动模范和先进工作者都是千千万万奋斗在各行各业劳动者中的杰出代表，敬学宾正是其中一员。

“每当自己坚持不下去的时候，一看到老敬还在坚持，我就没有放弃的理由。”金杯银杯不如群众口碑，跟着敬学宾一起工作的同事们谈起他都要竖起大拇指。认识敬学宾的人，都说他质朴、刚毅、严谨、细致，是典型的技术专家型管理人员。生活中沉默少语，有点“佛系”，工作中扎实可靠、有条不紊，是他留给大多数同事的印象，但只要一遇到难题，他从来都是死磕到底。

自 2003 年入职以来，敬学宾长期坚守在工程总承包项目一线，先后参与了公司总承包的烟台东源、沙特 HCC、AJCC、TCC、埃及 GOE Arish 二期、埃及 GOE Beni Suef 六条线、云南滇西等项目的生产准备、调试运行、生产考核工作。

敬学宾回忆，刚入职时，自己对一些前沿技术和新型设备的了解不多。但他凭借着一股冲劲，每天在图纸、技术资料堆中和现场学习，把精力和心思都用在了他热爱的工作上。同时，他也凭借过硬的专业技术和丰富的生产调试经验，在项目调试过程中不断总结和积累各种技术参数，为项目顺利履约、公司水泥技术升级、装备研发提供了有力支撑。

“到了工作岗位后，调试过程中的任何一个细节搞不清楚都可能会出大问题，因此我在工作上养成了事无巨细、不弄明白不罢休的性格。”

“我们建材人，就是要沉得下心气，耐得住寂寞。”

敬学宾的经验与道理都很朴素，正是这样日积月累的经验与不服输的韧劲让他成了团队的中流砥柱。

作为迄今世界水泥行业规模最大和境外工期最短的总承包项目——埃及 Beni Suef 六条

日产6000吨水泥熟料生产线项目的调试总指挥，在远离祖国、远离亲人、漫漫黄沙、茫茫戈壁、条件艰苦的异国他乡，面对工期紧、调试任务重的六条生产线，他却沉稳镇定，带领团队“啃”起了这块“硬骨头”。他超前谋划，周密安排，突破常规，身先士卒，夜以继日，忘我工作，狠抓重点，攻克多项技术难关，确保了项目按期建成投产并完成六条生产线的考核，按时按质将“钥匙”交到了业主手里，如期取得了业主颁发的PTOC证书，极大地提升了公司在世界水泥行业的知名度和影响力，树立了中国建材集团境外工程建设良好的品牌形象。

由敬学宾担任调试总指挥建成的沙特HCC项目、埃及GOE Arish二期、埃及GOE Beni Suef项目均荣获中国建材行业优秀工程总承包一等奖。埃及GOE Beni Suef 6×6000T/D项目荣获中国建设工程最高奖——国家优质工程金奖。

榜样的力量是无穷的。近年来，中材国际所属成都建材院大力弘扬劳模精神、劳动精神和工匠精神，努力营造“劳动最光荣、劳动最崇高、劳动最伟大、劳动最美丽”的良好风尚。敬学宾为人谦逊，做出的成绩有目共睹，是公司涌现出来的先进代表。公司号召广大干部员工向敬学宾同志学习，学习他艰苦奋斗、敢于担当、勤于创造的品质，都能在自己的岗位上发光发热！（中材国际所属成都建材院）

个人体会 一滴水只有放进大海才永远不会干涸，没有公司的培养，就没有我的成长。我将在公司提供的广阔发展平台上勤耕不辍、蓄力前行，努力在本职岗位中发光发热，为公司高质量发展贡献力量。

A Front-line Commander who Dares to Bite the Bullet

Jing Xuebing

Joined CNBM in June 2003

The Vice Director of Engineering Management Department No.1 of CDI and the Commander in Chief of Commissioning of Xiahe Qilianshan Upgrading Project undertaken by CDI

At the end of 2020, Jing Xuebin, Operation and Commissioning Manager of Chengdu Design Research Institute of Building Materials Industry Co., Ltd. ("CDI") affiliated to SINOMA International Engineering Co., Ltd. ("SINOMA International"), was awarded the honorary title of "Model Worker in Sichuan Province". He is one of the outstanding representatives of thousands of workers from all walks of life who are commended as Model Workers and Advanced Workers.

"Whenever I feel that I cannot hold on, there is no reason to give up when I see Mr. Jing, still striving on." Nothing is as good as the public praise from the masses. Jing Xuebin's colleagues always give him big thumbs up when talking about him. According to those who know him, he is down-to-earth, resolute, rigorous and meticulous. He is a typical technical expert manager. He is not good with words outside of work but holds a "down-to-earth and reliable" manner at work. This is the impression he leaves to his colleagues. Whenever he encounters difficulties, he always fights to the end.

Since his induction in 2003, Jing Xuebin has been working at the front-line of EPC projects for years and has successively participated in the preparation, commissioning, operation and production assessment of six lines, including Yantai Dongyuan, Saudi Arabia HCC, AJCC, TCC, Egypt GOE Arish Phase II and Egypt GOE Beni Suef Line, as well as the company's projects in Western Yunnan.

Jing Xuebin remembered that when he joined the company, he knew little about cutting-edge technologies and new equipment. But with a strong impetus, he kept on studying the blueprints, technical data piles and on-site work everyday, devoting all his energy and time to the job. Meanwhile, he continuously reflected and accumulated various technical parameters in the project with professional technology and abundant experience in production and commissioning, which provided strong support for the smooth fulfillment of the project as well as the upgrading of the company's cement technology and equipment R&D.

"Once at work, it may cause big trouble if we cannot figure out details in the commissioning process. Thus, I have cultivated a meticulous personality that never stops until making clear each and every detail in a down-to-earth manner."

"We CBMlers need to calm down and endure the loneliness."

Though simple as his experience, it is such steady accumulation and unyielding tenacity that have forged the spirit of the team.

As the Commissioning Commander-in-Chief of Egypt Beni Suef Six 6,000t/d Cement Clinker Production Lines Project, the largest EPC project in the world's cement industry with the shortest overseas construction period so far, Jing Xuebin has always kept calm in the face of difficulties such as the heavy task of completing six production lines within 18 months at the same time. With challenges such as living and working in a foreign country far away from home and boundless deserts, he led the team to "bite" the "bullet". He planned ahead, made meticulous arrangements and thought out of the box. He spearheaded in work day and night, emphasized tackling technical difficulties one after another, guaranteed the completion and operation of the project on schedule and the assessment work of six production lines, handed over the "keys" to the employer on time with high quality, and obtained the PTOC certificate issued by the employer. All these efforts have greatly enhanced the company's popularity and influence in the cement industry across the globe, and established an impressive brand image for CNBM's oversea engineering projects.

The Saudi Arabia HCC Project, Egypt GOE Arish Phase II and Egypt GOE Beni Suef Project completed by Jing Xuebin and his team in which he acted as the Commissioning Commander-in-Chief, had won the first prize of the National Excellent General Contracting Award of China's Building Materials Industry. Also, the Egypt GOE Beni Suef 6×6000T/D Project won the National Quality Engineering Gold Award, the highest award in China's construction industry.

The power of role models is infinite. In recent years, Chengdu Design Research Institute of Building Materials Industry Co., Ltd. affiliated to SINOMA International Engineering Co., Ltd. has vigorously carried forward the spirit of model workers, laborers and craftsmen, and striven to create a favorable environment where laborers are the most glorious, noblest, greatest and most beautiful people. Being modest, Jing Xuebin has made remarkable achievements, who is an representative among them. The Company calls on leaders and employees to learn from Jing Xuebin! That is, leaders and employees shall learn from his qualities of hard work, sense of responsibility and diligence in creation.

Personal Insights **Just like a drop of water will never dry up when it is put into the sea, i will never really grow up without the cultivation and training from my company. With the wide platform provided by my company, I will work devotedly to achieve progress and strive to shine in my job, so as to make contribution for high-quality development of company.**

周裕的海外十五年

周裕

2008 年 7 月加入中国建材
现任成都建材院埃及 Canal Sugar 日产 5700 吨白糖精炼厂施工项目和配套石灰窑总包工程项目副经理

成都建材院埃及 Canal Sugar 糖厂工程建设项目技术经理周裕，是公司国际化发展战略的践行者，也是公司深耕海外、多元发展的重要开拓者。十五年来，周裕一直奋斗在海外工程项目建设一线，转战中亚、西亚、非洲等多地，坚忍不拔，辛勤工作，为公司的海外业务发展开拓市场，用自己的实际行动坚守着海外一线耕耘者的初心与梦想。

随着成都建材院海外业务的不断扩展，项目管理人员出现短缺。2010 年，刚刚参加工作两年的周裕主动请缨，从工艺设计人员向项目管理人员转型。面对语言不通、缺乏海外项目管理经验等困难，他没有按部就班地等任务、听安排，而是主动学、踏实干，凭着一股不服输的韧劲和强烈的责任心，短短两个月时间，便能和外方流利沟通交流，独立承担起了分管区域的工艺技术和现场管理工作。从此，他笃定前行，足迹遍布哈萨克斯坦、沙特、埃及等国家的多个一线项目，在技术难题最集中、沟通难度较大的技术岗位上兢兢业业、任劳任怨，为多个海外项目成功建成投产倾注了心血和智慧。

埃及 Canal Sugar 糖厂项目是公司进一步开拓埃及市场、实施多元化经营战略的重点项目。该项目是公司首次总承包的糖厂工程建设项目，全新的课题，新工艺、新技术，既无历史经验可循，又无成功案例借鉴。该项目包含一个世界最大储存能力的白糖储库，由地上直径 124 米、高 40 米的混凝土薄壳穹顶和地下直径 124 米、深度 70 米的漏斗状混凝土仓两部分组成，复杂的地质结构给漏斗的结构设计和施工带来了巨大的挑战。周裕毅然受命，担任该项目技术经理，分秒必争地开展技术攻关工作，带领项目部团队严格选择地勘单位，通过筛分、直剪、岩石单轴抗压、点荷载试验等室内试验以及标贯、旁压、坑探等现场试验，得到了大量的试验数据，为复杂地质结构分析参数的合理性提供了保障。

众所周知，保持砂层开挖的稳定性是施工单位非常棘手的问题，为此，他带领团队查阅大量资料，刻苦钻研旋喷机具，并与设备商反

复讨论，最终试验出了适用于项目砂层的高压旋喷参数，为砂层开挖找到了科学、稳定、安全的措施。

解决了设计、开挖问题之后，几十万方的土方外运对工期和成本的控制又是另一个挑战。他坚信办法总比困难多，带领本土化的埃籍技术团队，积极咨询，与分包商沟通，反复论证，将土方外运的时间控制到了最短，制定最佳实施方案，获得了业主和监理的高度认可。

周裕作为项目核心骨干，顾全大局，以身作则，目前已连续 9 个月坚守在埃及糖厂项目一线。3 个月前，周裕的女儿在成都出生了，他错过了见证女儿呱呱坠地的美好时刻，也无法陪伴照顾刚生产的爱人。长期奋斗在海外，家人始终是他心里最柔软的部分，他始终心怀愧疚。谈起刚出生 3 个多月的孩子，他一脸幸福，笑着说：“在奋斗的岁月里，孩子一直是我努力向前的不竭动力，我想努力成为更好的自己，为孩子做出表率和榜样。”

从大学时代的优等生到现在独当一面的项目技术经理，对周裕来说，这是努力奋斗的结果，也是一路成长的收获。职业生涯的每一步成长，都留下了他力学笃行、勤耕不辍的足迹。在他眼里，未来还有很长的路要走，他将继续满怀激情投入到工作之中，在海外一线拼搏奋斗，为公司的伟大事业和宏伟梦想贡献力量。

（中材国际所属成都建材院）

从懵懵懂懂的大学毕业生到独当一面的项目技术经理，我一路成长。我将继续扎根海外项目一线，为公司国际化发展贡献力量。

Mr. Zhou Yu's Fifteen Years Overseas

Zhou Yu

Joined CNBM in July 2008

The Deputy Project Manager of Construction Project for Canal Sugar 5700TPD Beef Sugar Factory and Associated Lime Kiln EPC Project undertaken by CDI in Eygpt

Mr. Zhou Yu, a technical manager of the Egyptian Canal Sugar Factory construction project of Chengdu Design & Research Institute of Building Materials Industry Co., Ltd. ("CDI" or "the company" for short), is a practitioner of the company's international development strategy and an important pioneer of the company's overseas and diversified development. Over the past fifteen years, Mr. Zhou has dedicated himself to working on the frontlines of engineering construction abroad, venturing into various regions such as Central Asia, West Asia and Africa. With unwavering determination and diligent efforts, he has promoted the company's overseas business and remained committed to the initial aspirations and dreams of those who toil on the overseas frontlines through his own practical actions.

With the continuous expansion of CDI's overseas business, there was a shortage of project management personnel. In 2010, Mr. Zhou, who had just graduated from college two years ago, voluntarily stepped forward and transitioned from a process designer to a project manager. Faced with difficulties such as language barriers and the lack of experience in overseas project management, he did not wait for help. Instead, he took the initiative to learn and work diligently. With an indomitable resilience and a strong sense of responsibility, he was able to communicate effectively with foreign partners in just two months, and independently took on the process technology and on-site management work in his assigned area. From then on, he embarked on a steadfast journey, leaving his footprints in various frontline projects across countries such as Kazakhstan, Saudi Arabia, and Egypt. He worked diligently and tirelessly in technical positions that posed the greatest technical challenges and communication difficulties. His dedication and wisdom contributed to the successful completion and operation of multiple overseas projects for CDI.

The Egyptian Canal Sugar Factory project is a key project for the company to further explore the Egyptian market and implement a diversified business strategy. This project is the first sugar factory construction project generally contracted by the company, presenting entirely new challenges in terms of technology and processes. The construction of the project has neither historical experience to follow nor successful cases to learn from. It includes the construction of a white sugar storehouse with the world's largest storage capacity. The storehouse consists of a concrete thin-shell dome above ground, which is 124 meters in diameter and 40 meters high, and an underground funnel-shaped concrete depot, with a 124-meter diameter and a 70-meter depth. The complex geological structure posed a huge challenge to the structural design and construction of the funnel-shaped depot. Mr. Zhou was appointed as the technical manager of the project. He raced against time to carry out technical research work. He led the project team to strictly select detailed geological exploration units and obtained a large amount of test data through indoor tests, such as screening, direct shear, uniaxial rock compression and point load tests, as well as on-site tests such as standard penetration, pressuremeter test and pit exploration, providing genuine geological structure analysis parameters.

As is well known, solving the stability of sand layer excavation is a very difficult problem for construction units. Therefore, he led his team to consult a large amount of literature, diligently studied rotary spraying equipment, and repeatedly discussed with equipment manufacturers. Finally, they obtained the high-pressure rotary spraying parameters suitable for the project sand layer through tests, and found scientific, stable and safe measures for sand layer excavation.

After the design and excavation problems were solved, transporting hundreds of thousands of cubic meters of earthwork posed another challenge to the construction schedule and cost control of the project. He firmly believed that there are always more solutions than difficulties. He led a localized Egyptian technical team to actively

As the core member of the project, Mr. Zhou actively responded to the call of the superior and the company's party committee, took the overall situation into consideration, and set an example for other employees. As of now, he has been on the frontline of the Egyptian Canal Sugar Factory project for nine consecutive months. Three months ago, Mr.

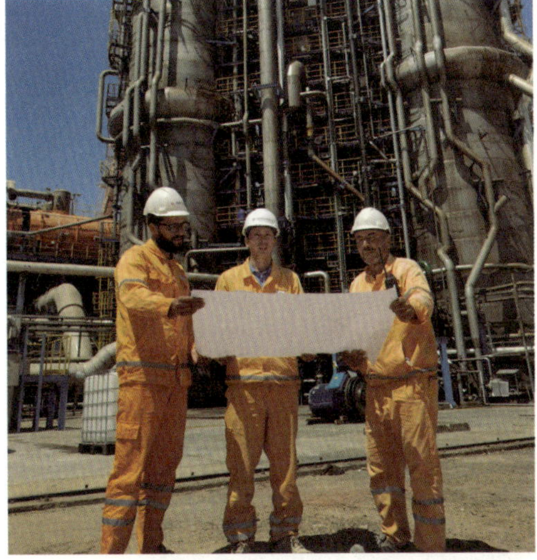

Zhou's daughter was born in Chengdu, China. He regretted missing the wonderful moment of her birth and was unable to accompany and take care of his wife who had just given birth to a child. After having worked overseas for a long time, he has always felt guilty for his family. Speaking of his daughter who was just born over three months ago, he looked thrilled, saying smilingly: "In the years of hard work, my daughter has always been an inexhaustible driving force for me to strive forward. I want to strive to become a better myself and set an example for her."

For Mr. Zhou, who has grown from an excellent student in college to the leading technical manager of the project, this is the result of his hard work and also a harvest along his growth path. Every step in his career growth has left behind his footsteps of diligent learning and perseverance. In his eyes, there will still be a long way to go in the future. He will continue to devote himself to his work with passion, work hard on the frontlines overseas, and contribute to the great cause and grand dreams of the company.

Personal Insights All the way from a college graduate who didn't really know where to go to a competent project technical manager, this is what I have achieved and what the company has brought to me. I will continue to work at the front-line of overseas project, and to expand the territory for the company's international development.

一心热爱 SINOMA 的阿卜杜拉

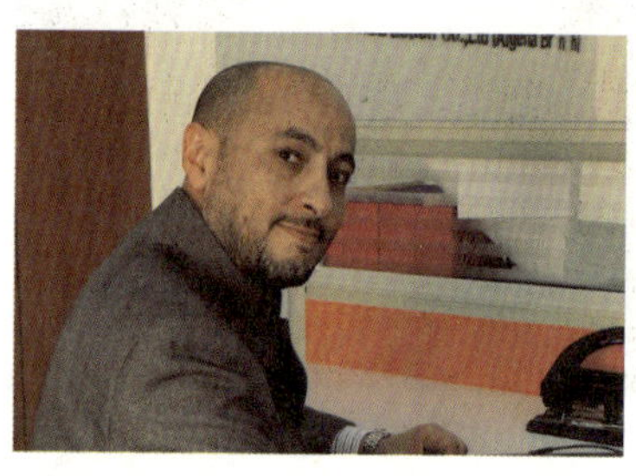

阿卜杜拉·阿瑞比

2017 年加入中国建材

现任中材建设阿尔及利亚公司商贸供应链经理

阿卜杜拉·阿瑞比于 2017 年 4 月 1 日入职中材建设阿尔及利亚公司，是目前阿尔及利亚公司效力时间最久的属地员工之一；历任阿尔及利亚公司物流助理、物流工程师、商贸供应链经理职务；曾被评选为 2018 年度中材建设有限公司优秀外籍员工，连续多年被评为阿尔及利亚公司优秀属地员工。

2022 年是油脂制取项目重新启动谈判的关键一年。面对物流工作出现的新问题，在每次的物流专题会议中，阿卜杜拉均积极协调，运用专业、扎实的物流海运知识，从国际贸易术语的权责划分到目的港清关过程的具体详细程序，从船公司方面的文件流转到海关部门的工作流程，他不断攻克难关，推动项目重新启动。

随着中材建设阿尔及利亚公司业务开展和区域一体化管理的推进，各项目物流工作均由阿尔及利亚公司承担，阿卜杜拉·阿瑞比作为物流工程师义无反顾地承担起物流工作的责任。在阿尔及利亚，各省份海关在政策执行上存在不同程度的偏差，由于公司项目在不同的省份，尤其是临时进口机具设备受不同海关监管。因此，项目结束后，这些临时进口机具需要及时进行相应的海关备案处置，否则将面临被阿尔及利亚政府罚没的风险。阿卜杜拉·阿瑞比不辞劳苦，与新婚妻子分别，奔波于各海关之间，从首都 ALGIERS 海关到摩洛哥边境附近的 BECHAR 海关；从港口城市 ORAN 海关到戈壁滩上的 BISKRA 海关，这些地方均留下了他奔波的身影和坚实的足迹。

他经常是周日披星出发，周四戴月而归，就连他新婚妻子也调侃道：“是我嫁给了你，而你嫁给了 SINOMA 了吗？”经过反复沟通协调和专业论证，阿卜杜拉·阿瑞比与各地海关建立起高效的沟通渠道，顺利完成了公司临时进口机具转关手续。在这场长期的沟通协作过程中，各省海关官员也真实感受到 SINOMA 这家工业工程公司专业、担当、守信的风采。

2022 年，阿尔及利亚公司开始推动以项

目为载体支撑产业发展，逐步实现从经营项目向经营市场的转变。阿卜杜拉知责于心，担责于身，履责于行，在工作中，站在前、冲在前、干在前，先后拜访了 20 多家水泥厂，中材建设当年新增客户较上年增长 950%，并与各水泥厂建立起良好合作关系。截至目前，各项工作开展顺利，阿卜杜拉·阿瑞比也赢得了客户的高度赞扬。

一砖一瓦绵绵用力，一针一线久久为功。阿卜杜拉·阿瑞比经常激励身边的同事："我们要认真做事，认真做人，SINOMA 给了我们一个展示自我的平台，我们要与 SINOMA 一起成长，为 SINOMA 的发展和我们阿尔及利亚的发展添砖加瓦。"（中材国际所属中材建设）

个人体会

阿卜杜拉说："2022 年 12 月，在沙特阿拉伯举行的中阿联盟峰会上，关于'一带一路'倡议的讲话让我备受鼓舞，我决心积极响应这一倡议：促进中国和阿拉伯国家文化融合和文化交流，尤其是与阿尔及利亚之间的文化交融。很荣幸，我将是见证者和参与者。我爱中国，我爱 SINOMA。"

A Passionate Supporter of SINOMA, Abdellah

Abdellah Aribi

Joined CNBM in 2017

Business and Supply Chain Manager

Abdellah Aribi became a member of the SINOMA Algeria Company on April 1st, 2017, marking the beginning of his enduring tenure as one of the company's most longstanding local employees. Throughout his journey, he has assumed various roles including logistics assistant, logistics engineer, and Business and Supply Chain Manager. In 2018, Abdellah Aribi's exceptional contributions were acknowledged when he was honored as an outstanding foreign employee by SINOMA Construction Co., Ltd. Furthermore, he has consistently demonstrated exceptional performance as a local employee of the Algeria company, earning recognition for several consecutive years.

The year 2022 is the key year for restarting the negotiation of Oil Extraction Project. Facing new problems in logistics, Abdellah step up coordination on good grounds in every logistics meeting, using his professional and solid knowledge of logistics and shipping, from the division of rights and responsibilities of Incoterms to the specific and detailed procedures of the customs clearance process at the port of destination, and from the flow of documents from the shipping company to the workflow of the customs department, he constantly overcame the difficulties, and pushed forward the restarting of the project.

As SINOMA Construction Algeria Company expanded its operations and implemented regional integrated management, the Algeria company took on the responsibility of managing logistics for various projects. Abdellah, as a dedicated logistics engineer, readily embraced this role without hesitation. Algeria's customs policies exhibit varying degrees of deviation across different provinces. Given that the company's projects are situated in diverse provinces, particularly when importing temporary equipment, they are subjected to distinct customs regulations and oversight. Consequently, upon project completion, it becomes imperative to promptly register these temporarily imported equipment with customs to mitigate the risk of confiscation by the Algerian government. Abdellah displayed unwavering commitment, even leaving behind his newlywed wife, as he tirelessly traversed between multiple customs offices. He navigated the ALGIERS customs in the capital, ventured to the BECHAR customs near the Moroccan border, journeyed to the ORAN customs in the port city, and ventured further to the BISKRA customs located amidst the desert. His relentless efforts and steadfast determination are evident in the indelible marks he left behind.

Frequently embarking on journeys that commenced

on Sundays and concluded on Thursdays, Abdellah's commitment was such that even his recently married wife humorously questioned married wife joked that he married SINOMA like she married him. Thanks to persistent communication, coordination, and adept showcases of his expertise, Abdellah managed to establish streamlined communication channels with customs offices across different regions. As a result, he successfully executed the necessary customs clearance procedures for the company's temporarily imported equipment. Throughout this extensive process of interaction and collaboration, customs officials in various provinces came to genuinely recognize SINOMA as an industrial engineering company embodying professionalism, responsibility, and unwavering integrity.

In 2022, as SINOMA Algeria Company embarked on promoting industrial development through project support, there was a gradual shift from project management to market management. Abdellah exemplified dedication and leadership, wholeheartedly embracing his responsibilities. He undertook a remarkable journey, Abdellah is aware of his responsibility, takes it on himself and carries it out. He stood at the front, rushed to the front, and worked at the front in his work, and visited more than 20 cement plants one after another. SINOMA's new customers in the year increased by 950% compared with the previous year. Furthermore, strong and cooperative relationships were established with each cement plant. As of now, all operations have proceeded seamlessly, garnering significant acclaim and appreciation from the esteemed customers.

Abdellah consistently serves as a source of inspiration for his colleagues, frequently reminding them of the importance of hard work, diligence, and ethical behavior. He emphasizes that SINOMA has provided them with an exceptional platform to demonstrate their capabilities. It is their collective responsibility to progress alongside SINOMA in Algeria, contributing to the growth and development of both the company and the nation.

Personal Insights Abdellah said: "The China-Arab States Summit was held in Saudi Arabia in December 2022, and President Xi Jinping's address about The Belt and Road Initiative encouraged me. I am determined to respond positively to this initiative: to promote cultural fusion and cultural exchanges between China and the Arab countries, in particular with Algeria. I am honored to be a witness and a participant. I LOVE CHINA, I LOVE SINOMA."

周立东的坚守与奉献

周立东

2000 年加入中国建材

现任中材建设总监、塞内加尔公司总经理

2000 年，周立东毕业后即加入中材建设。他在兢兢业业工作的 20 多年里，有 15 年都在境外，如今的他担任阿尔及利亚 ZAHANA 项目经理。他的职业生涯伴随着工程总承包模式的萌芽、成长和成熟，从“走出去”“站稳脚”，到“塑品牌”，再到“创一流”，他把青春献给了海外工程项目建设，生动诠释了建材人的担当、敬业、奉献的精神。

ZAHANA 项目合同执行难度大，当地雨季漫长，地质条件极其复杂，场地狭小，老厂生产灰尘污染严重，生产环境恶劣。周立东周密部署，提前策划，精心组织，强化项目关键节点，精耕细作挖掘潜力，牢牢把控项目进度和质量，带领全体员工奋力拼搏，确保了项目安全、优质、高效的实施。项目建设高效推进，被当地人称赞为“中国速度”。

2020 年 1 月 12 日，周立东正在国内处理工作，新冠肺炎疫情暴发，他意识到航班可能会停运，立刻改签机票返回项目部，奔赴项目一线。

阿尔及利亚疫情暴发前，周立东提前谋划，做好疫情防控宣传工作，避免人员密切接触，对在场的员工每日进行体温测试并记录其数据，发放消毒液和口罩，加强员工食堂的卫生管理，注重办公公共区域管理。为增强项目部人员免疫力，细心的他特地安排增加食堂蛋白质食品供应量，以提高大家的身体素质。

疫情下的项目建设总是面临各种困难。2020 年 3 月份，受疫情影响工厂停工，周立东多方协调，在意外受伤的情况下，依然同员工一起守在现场，保护建筑、设备等资产安全，并多次夜间巡查现场。受疫情影响，项目部调试备件无法如期到达，业主原材料供应出现短缺。面对困难，他仍然保持豁达乐观的心态，积极制订应对措施，化解难题、掌控大局，7 个月未曾回国休假，始终坚守一线。

ZAHANA 项目进展时间节点是 2 月 3 日，ZAHANA 项目实现回转窑一次性点火；

2 月 7 日，该项目成功生产第一批熟料；

2 月 14 日，回转窑产量达标至满产；

2月15日，水泥磨顺利生产出第一批水泥；

2月19日，生产出袋装水泥；

5月4日，该项目顺利取得了安装完成证书；

5月22日，回转窑点火；

5月24日，窑投料生产；

6月13日，完成TPI和性能测试，各项关键指标均高于合同要求，得到了业主的认可。

项目建设过程中，项目无一人感染新冠病毒，员工情绪稳定，积极乐观。

2020年4月12日，周立东的孩子突发疾病住院，身在异国他乡的他特别希望能陪陪孩子，公司领导也劝他回国陪护。但是，为了保证项目建设，他毅然决定坚守岗位。“阿国疫情正在蔓延，现场可能会有很多突发情况，这里还有100多号人需要我，现在是稳定人心和项目收尾的关键时期，我要守在一线”周立东说。6月4日，他的孩子历经17个小时终于完成手术。“这17个小时，是我人生中最忐忑不安的17小时，手术时间比预期多了很长时间。”他说。他是公司的员工，是一线的项目经理，也是一名普通的父亲，说到这一幕时，他不禁眼眶湿润。

周立东表示，在孩子住院期间，公司给予了很多关心和帮助，协调医院、住院陪护、解决实际困难，他深深感受到了公司大家庭的温暖。“这个大家庭中的爱将永远铭记在我和我的家人心间。作为公司的一员，我将牢记初心和使命，继续加倍努力工作，完成好公司交给我的任务，用实际行动践行使命与担当，为公司的持续发展贡献应有的力量！”他说。

（中材国际所属中材建设）

个人体会　我热爱中材建设，我愿意用我二十几年的工作经验为中材建设在塞内加尔属地化经营鞠躬尽瘁，积极做好属地化市场开拓和产业发展工作，团结和带领塞内加尔公司员工把塞内加尔市场建设得越来越好。

Mr. Zhou Lidong's Dedication and Commitment

Zhou Lidong

Joined CNBM in 2000

Director and General Manager of SINOMA CBMI CONSTRUCTION SUARL

In 2000, Mr. Zhou Lidong graduated from college and then joined CBMI Construction Co., Ltd. ("CBMI" or "the company" for short), which is a subsidiary of SINOMA International. During his over 20 years of dedicated work, he spent 15 years overseas. Now, he serves as the project manager of ZAHANA project in Algeria. His career has been closely intertwined with the emergence, growth and maturity of the engineering, procurement, and construction (EPC) model. He has personally witnessed the entire globalization process, evolving from "going global", "establishing a solid foothold overseas" to "shaping international brands" and then to "creating world-class enterprises". He has dedicated his youth to the construction of overseas engineering projects for the company, vividly embodying the responsibility, professionalism and dedication of SINOMA International employees.

The implementation of the ZAHANA project contract is difficult. The geological conditions of the project site are extremely complex, and the site area is small. The old factory generates severe dust pollution, and its production environment is harsh. The rainy season there is too long. Mr. Zhou carefully deployed, planned and organized the construction of the project. He strengthened the key nodes of the project, meticulously tapped into the potential of the project, firmly controlled the construction schedule and quality of the project, and led all employees to work hard to ensure the safe, high-quality and efficient implementation of the project. The construction progress of the project has been praised by locals as "China Speed."

On January 12, 2020, Mr. Zhou was dealing with work in China when the COVID-19 broke out. He immediately anticipated potential flight cancellations and rescheduled his plane ticket to return to the project site in Algeria, going back to the frontline of his post.

Before the outbreak of the pandemic in Algeria, Mr. Zhou planned in advance to carry out pandemic prevention and control. He requested workers to avoid close contact with each other. He organized personnel to conduct daily temperature tests on workers on site and record their test data, distributed disinfectant and masks to workers, strengthened the hygiene management of the canteen, and paid attention to the management of office and public areas. In order to strengthen the immunity of project employees, he increased the supply of protein-rich food in the canteen to improve employees' physical fitness.

On February 3rd, the ZAHANA project achieved one-time ignition of the rotary kiln;

On February 7th, the first batch of clinker was successfully produced;

On February 14th, the output of the rotary kiln met the requirement and reached full capacity;

On February 15th, the cement mill successfully produced the first batch of cement;

On February 19th, bagged cement was produced;

On May 4th, successfully obtained the installation completion certificate;

On May 22nd, the rotary kiln was ignited;

On May 24th, the kiln was put into production;

On June 13th, TPI and performance testing were completed, and all key indicators were higher than the contract requirements and were recognized by the owner.

By now, no one in the project has been infected with COVID-19, and the project team is united, stable, positive and optimistic.

On April 12, 2020, Mr. Zhou's child was hospitalized due to a sudden illness. Mr. Zhou, who was staying in a foreign country at that time, hoped to accompany his child very much, and the company's leaders also advised him to return to China. However, in order to ensure the construction of the project, he resolutely decided to stick to his position. "The COVID-19 is spreading in Algeria, and there may be many uncertain factors on site. There are

still over 100 people here who need me. This is a critical period for stabilizing people's mindsets and completing the project, so I need to stay on the frontline," said Mr. Zhou. On June 4, his child successfully underwent a 17-hour surgery. He said: "These 17 hours were the most anxious 17 hours of my life, and the surgery took much longer than expected." He was an employee of the company, a frontline project manager, and an ordinary father as well. When he mentioned this scene, his eyes were full of tears.

Mr. Zhou said that during the child's hospitalization, the company provided a lot of care and support in coordinating with the hospital, accompanying the patient in the hospital and solving practical difficulties for his family. He deeply felt the warmth of the company as a big family. He said: "The love in this big family will always be remembered in the hearts of me and my family. As a member of the company, I will keep in mind my original intention and mission, continue to work harder, complete the tasks assigned to me by the company, fulfill my responsibilities and duties with practical actions, and contribute my due strength to the continuous development of the company."

Personal Insights I love CBMI. I am willing to use my over twenty years of experience to do my best for the localized operation of SINOMA Construction in Senegal, and actively do a good job in localized market development and industrial development in order to unite and lead the Senegalese company employees to build a better Senegalese market.

创新焕发活力

张昊信

2006 年加入中国建材

现任中材海外环保与玻璃事业部副部长

无论是在安哥拉担任技术工程师还是在阿根廷勇挑重担，恪尽职守的张昊信总能深耕专业，见微知著，在较短的时间内完成工作目标。熟悉张昊信的人总会说，他是头脑活络的专业者，创新让他和他服务的对象焕发活力。

用心才能创新。任安哥拉 NC15 石油焦粉磨站项目经理时，面对一堆问题，张昊信总是独立思考，然后找出解决问题的方法和路径，再经过团队的合议，执行起来非常顺利，原本复杂的“疑难杂症”被顺利破解。NC15 石油焦粉磨站项目从设计、采购、加工制作，到运输、现场施工、调试和考核各环节，创造了公司在一年内完成海外粉磨站 EPC 项目的纪录。

在安哥拉 NCII 5000TPD 熟料生产线项目执行期间，张昊信被任命为熟料生产线技术经理、23MW 重油电站项目经理、调试负责人，承担设计管理、重油电站的项目管理、熟料生产线的调试和考核等核心工作。这些工作有的他没有涉足过，难免会有疑虑，该怎么办？唯有学习才能补短。工作之余，大家总会看到张昊信手捧业务书本苦啃，遇到不能工作的天气，他总是在现场办公室有针对性地向一些老技术人员、管理人员虚心请教，特别是重油发电领域的新知识。经过深入学习，有指向性地汲取精华，整个项目工程期间的各个节点工作都圆满完成。特别是在调试考核阶段，他编制性能考核方案，制订详细的考试实施办法，对生产参数进行调整，确保性能考核顺利通过。

担当激发创新。披坚持锐的张昊信接着又接手阿根廷 L’Amali 5000TPD 水泥生产线项目工作。经过充分调研，他提出的关于属地化建设的建议得到了公司的肯定。有了公司的支持，张昊信和项目团队就在土建、安装等方面进行属地化分包。中阿两国文化和思维不同，现场管理也就显得异常复杂，张昊信不惧困难，每天最早到达现场，充分协调业主、工会、当地土建分包、当地安装分包、中方技术指导的配合事宜，合理安排现场施工作业，使得项目现场秩序井然，有序推进。

正当阿根廷项目如火如荼地进行安装抢工

的关键时刻，在全球蔓延的新冠疫情波及阿根廷，项目一度停工 50 天。这次停工引起一系列连锁反应，工会谈判、防疫及复工方案、复工申请、复工生产、机具退租、现场维稳等问题相继出现。作为阿根廷项目现场核心管理团队成员，张昊信与项目团队并肩作战，通过 8 轮艰苦的工会谈判最终达成停工解决方案。停工期间，项目团队也丝毫不敢懈怠，制订项目复工及疫情防控方案，获得阿根廷政府以及业主颁发的复工许可。项目复工后，当地劳动力短缺，张昊信和团队创新思维，采取灵活的用工方式，巧妙地走出人员不足的困境，并通过与工程机械、材料租赁厂家的多轮谈判，降低或减免在疫情期间的租赁费用。这期间的艰辛和劳碌，非一般人所能承受，张昊信充分展示了建材人的综合素质和出众的危机管理能力，捍卫了公司的利益，确保了项目平稳推进，是项目顺利竣工并移交业主的核心力量。唯有牺牲多壮志，敢让岁月流金彩。

从来豪杰多奇魄，维新维能烛岁月。张昊信走在维新维能的创新之路上，我们有理由相信他的精神在二万公里之外的阿根廷绽放异彩——他的背后有强大的祖国，他的心里有深沉的大爱。

（中材国际所属中材海外）

感谢公司为我提供的发展平台，我会将所学的专业知识、积累的丰富经验服务于公司发展。我必须克服困难、勇挑重担、开拓创新，以必胜的信念完成公司交付的任务。

Innovation Endows Vitality

Zhang Haoxin

Joined CNBM in 2006

The Deputy manager of Environmental protection & Class engineering of SINOMA OVERSEAS

Zhang Haoxin worked as a technical engineer in Angola and took on heavy responsibilities in Argentina. He has always fulfilled his duties, deepened his expertise, and accomplished his work quickly. Why? Those who know him well will always describe him as a quick-witted professional whose innovations revitalize him and his clients.

Innovation requires concentration and diligence. When he was first appointed as the project manager of NC15 petroleum coke grinding station in Angola, Zhang Haoxin always thought independently about difficulties, and then found out the methods and paths to solve them. After consultation with the team, the original "headache" was successfully addressed with the joint efforts. The NC15 petroleum coke grinding station project has set a record. It is the company's first EPC overseas project that was completed within a year, notwithstanding its long process of design, procurement, processing and production, transportation, on-site construction, debugging and assessment.

The highest innovation requires the best ability to learn. During the NCII 5000TPD clinker production line project, Zhang Haoxin was appointed as technical manager of clinker production line, project manager of 23MW heavy oil power station and debugging leader, and took on the roles of design management, project management of heavy oil power station, debugging and assessment of clinker production line, etc. Of course, he had his doubts, since some of these jobs were new to him. What should he do? He could only make up for it by studying. After work, he could be seen slaving away at books. In case of a bad weather, he always consulted some old technicians and managers in the office. In particular, the new knowledge in the field of heavy oil power generation broadened his mind. He studied deeply and absorbed the essence with specific questions in mind. He successfully completed the work at all points throughout the project. Especially in the debugging and assessment stage, he prepared the performance assessment scheme, formulated detailed examination implementation methods, adjusted the production parameters, and ensured the smooth performance assessment.

Innovation requires responsibility. Persistent, Zhang Haoxin moved to Argentina to work on the L'Amali 5000TPD cement production line project. After full investigation, his proposal of localized construction was approved by the Company. Supported by the Company, Zhang Haoxin and the project team conducted localized subcontracting in civil

engineering and installation. Due to the differences in culture and thinking between China and Argentina, the site management was extremely complicated. Undaunted by it, he was the first to arrive at the scene every day. He fully coordinated with owner, trade union, local civil engineering subcontractor, local installation subcontractor, and Chinese technical director, and reasonably arranged the on-site construction, so as to promote the project in an orderly way.

At the critical moment when the Argentine project was in full swing, the global COVID-19 pandemic spread to Argentina, and the project was suspended for 50 days. This led to a series of ripple reactions as well as crises such as trade union negotiation, pandemic prevention and work resumption plan, work resumption application, production resumption organization, withdrawal of rent of machines and tools, on-site stability maintenance, etc. As a core member of the field management team of the Argentine project, Zhang Haoxin fought side by side with the project team, and finally reached a shutdown settlement agreement through eight rounds of arduous trade union negotiations. During the shutdown, the project team did not slack off. Instead, he worked out the project resumption and pandemic control plan, and obtained the resumption permit issued by the Argentine government and owner. After the project resumed, the local labor force was in short supply. Zhang Haoxin and his team thought creatively and adopted flexible employment methods to get out of the understaffed mess. Through several rounds of negotiations with construction machinery and material leasing manufacturers, they succeeded in reducing or waiving leasing fees during the pandemic. The hardships and struggles involved were beyond the endurance of ordinary men. Zhang Haoxin fully demonstrated outstanding overall quality and crisis management skills as SINOMA staff, defended the interests of the Company and ensured the smooth progress of the project.

Only reform and innovation can make brilliant years. Zhang Haoxin is on the road to reform and innovation. He has a strong motherland behind him and great love in his heart. Therefore, we can fully believe that his talent will shine in Argentina, 20,000 kilometers away from China.

Personal Insights I'm grateful that SINOMA can provide growth platform for my career, where I can devote my professional knowledge and abundant experience to assist the company's development. I have to devote all my strength, tackle all kinds of obstacles, overcome all the trouble with creative spirit to accomplish the task SINOMA grants to me.

开矿“先锋官”

陈川
2005 年加入中国建材
现为中材国际东非公司工程产业部员工

2005 年，四川小伙子陈川加入苏州中材，一直在机械工段工作。2018 年，敬业、专注的他被派遣到坦桑尼亚 DANGOTE 水泥厂，担任保产项目设备材料科科长。目前，陈川负责坦桑尼亚林迪石膏矿的开采、运输和销售工作。

近年来，中材国际（南京）大力实施“246+”发展战略，明确多元化、属地化两大发展方向，在非洲、东南亚、中东、中亚等四大片区，打造尼日利亚、坦桑尼亚、埃塞俄比亚、伊拉克、印尼、越南等六大基地。在坦桑尼亚，中材国际（南京）决定开发年产 10 万吨石膏矿产开采业务，为北新建材以及 DANGOTE 等核心客户提供石膏供应。

2019 年 8 月，在坦桑子公司的安排下，陈川只身一人来到了距项目部 200 多公里的林迪省 KIRANJERANJE 镇 MAKANGAGA 村，在一家中国地矿企业学习石膏矿开采技术。深入研习理论知识后，他很快进入了实操阶段。“和想象的完全不一样，石膏矿区一片荒芜，灌木丛生，什么生活设施、开采设施都没有，一切都要从零开始。”他说。

斯瓦希里语是当地的土著语言，官方交流也大多采用这种语言交流。对于日常多用英文交流的陈川来说，无疑加大了沟通难度。“我必须向向导学习语言，所以在寻找石膏矿的过程中有意识地让向导不厌其烦地说话，针对性地表述特定的名词和属性。我也做好记录，用英文标示清楚。”

天道酬勤。几个月下来，陈川在当地人的协助下，终于找到了有价值的矿石采地。“尽管这个矿区很小，但完全可以作为开展工作大本营了。”他说。接着，坦桑子公司从保产项目部大本营调来改装好的集装箱，既可当宿舍又可当办公室，一些生活物品和食堂厨具也随之备齐。“营地有了，食宿和办公不用担心了，找矿的劲头就更大了。”他说。

在荆棘和峻岭中寻找目标，除了眼睛，也需要可以丈量土地的脚板——这对陈川提出了新的要求。“眼睛向前看，脚板踩稳大地，具有中材国际发展潜力的流量才可以形成洪流。”

陈川实践着这句话，茫茫山野留下了他的足迹和身影。通往成功的道路上需要坚持和坚韧，功夫不负有心人，在公司的协助下，一座具有较大开采价值的矿山最终为公司所用。

陈川每天凌晨5点半出发去矿区，晚上9点才能回到营地，不可谓不辛苦。矿场确定后，从人员进驻，到开采设备的进场、石膏石的开采、运输、储存等，每一项工作都做到了然于胸。当时正好是雨季，整个矿区的安全、排水等也都需要他组织和实施。

步步为营，稳扎稳打。现在陈川的开矿队伍从当初的“独侠客”壮大到9人团队。和在设备材料科岗位一样，他把所能想到的工作都安排得井然有序。“林迪石膏矿今年采矿目标是2万吨，受疫情影响，7月份才开工，不过大家加班加点，现在已经采矿石4000余吨，创造利润10余万元人民币。发展的潜力和势头还在后面。”身为林迪石膏矿负责人的陈川对未来充满信心地说。

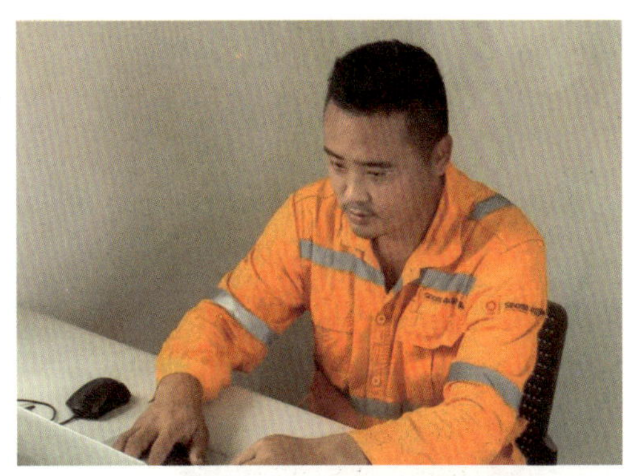

在远离城市的地方开辟一片新“矿区”，他本身就是一座“精神富矿”。他在那里已有一年了，他的青春也在矿区潜滋暗长、蓄力向上。他用他的热忱和坚守，把荒原打造成梦想，感动并激励着我们共同奋斗、并肩前行。（中材国际所属苏州中材）

个人体会

自从2005年进入苏州中材以来，18年间，我已经发生了翻天覆地的变化，但是，这样的变化不会停止，因为我前进的脚步从未停歇。在今后的工作中，我也会继续努力，为苏州中材贡献自己的一份力量！

A Pioneer in Mining

Chen Chuan

Joined CNBM in 2005

The Employee of SINOMA East Africa Co., Ltd. Engineering & Industry Management Dept.

In 2005, Chen Chuan, a young man from Sichuan Province, joined SINOMA (Suzhou) Construction Co., Ltd., "SINOMA (Suzhou)" for short. Since then, he has been working in the mechanical section of SINOMA (Suzhou). In 2018, due to his professionalism and dedication, he was dispatched to DANGOTE Cement Plant in Tanzania as the Head of the Equipment and Materials Department of the Production Guarantee Project. Currently, Mr. Chen is responsible for the mining, transportation and sales of the Lindi gypsum mine in Tanzania.

In recent years, SINOMA International (Nanjing) has vigorously implemented the "246+" development strategy, clarifying two major development directions, which are diversification and localization, and building six major bases of Nigeria, Tanzania, Ethiopia, Iraq, Indonesia and Vietnam in Africa, Southeast Asia, the Middle East and Central Asia. In Tanzania, SINOMA International (Nanjing) decided to develop a 100kt/a gypsum mining business to supply gypsum to core customers such as Beijing New Building Materials Co., Ltd. (BNBM) and DANGOTE.

In August 2019, under the arrangement of SINOMA International (Nanjing)'s subsidiary in Tanzania, Mr. Chen arrived alone at Makangaga Village of Kiranjeranje Town in Lindi Province, more than 200 kilometers away from the production guarantee project headquarters, to study gypsum mining technology at a Chinese geological and mining enterprise. After an in-depth study of theoretical knowledge, he quickly entered the practical operation stage. " It was completely different from what I had imagined. The gypsum mining area was a barren land filled with bushes and no living or mining facilities whatsoever. Everything needed to start from scratch."

Swahili is the native language for locals and most official communications. For Mr. Chen who frequently uses English for daily communication, this undoubtedly increases the difficulty of communication with locals and officials. He said: "I had to learn language from the guide, so in the process of searching for gypsum mines, I consciously made the guide speak patiently and express specific nouns and attributes in specific ways. I also made notes and clearly marked them in English."

Heaven rewards diligence. After several months, with the assistance of local people, Mr. Chen finally found valuable mineral mining sites. He said: "Although this mining area is small, it can

serve as a base for carrying out subsequent work." Subsequently, SINOMA International (Nanjing)'s Tanzanian subsidiary transferred modified containers from the headquarters to the campsite in the mining area. These containers could function as both dormitories and offices. Some daily necessities as well as the kitchen utensils for the cafeteria were also sent there. Mr. Chen said: "With the campsite, we don't need to worry about accommodation and office space any more, and our enthusiasm for finding mines grows stronger."

Searching for mines in thorns and steep mountains requires not only eyes but also feet that can measure the land. This poses new requirements for Mr. Chen. He said: "Only by looking forward with our eyes and stepping firmly on the ground with our feet can the development potential flow of SINOMA International form a torrent." Mr. Chen demonstrated this principle, leaving his footprints and shadows in vast mountains and fields. On the road to success, persistence and perseverance are necessary. Everything comes to him who works hard. With the assistance of the company, a mine with significant mining value was ultimately mined by the company.

Every day, Mr. Chen leaves for the mining area at 5:30 am and doesn't return to the campsite until 9 pm. He really works very hard. After the mining site was determined, he clearly planned everything, ranging from personnel entry to the entry of mining equipment, as well as the mining, transportation and storage of gypsum. It was the rainy season at the time, and he also had to organize and implement measures for the safety and drainage of the entire mining area.

Step by step, his mining team grew steadily. Now, his mining team has expanded from one person to nine. Similar to his role in the Equipment and Materials Department, he arranged for his team everything he could think of in an orderly manner. "The mining target of Lindi gypsum mine this year is 20,000 metric tons. Due to the impact of the pandemic, we didn't start production until July. However, everyone has worked overtime. We have now mined over 4,000 metric tons of gypsum, creating a profit of over 100,000 yuan. The potential and momentum for development will continue to grow in the future," said Mr. Chen, the head of Lindi gypsum mine. He is confident about the future.

Opening up a new mining area far from the city is a rich source of inspiration for him. He has been working there for a year. His youth has also been quietly growing and shining in the mining area. He has used his enthusiasm and perseverance to turn the wilderness into a dream, touching and inspiring us to work together and move forward together.

Personal Insights Since entering SINOMA (Suzhou) in 2005 18 years ago, I have undergone tremendous changes, and such changes will not stop, because my progress has never stopped. In the future, I will continue to work hard to contribute my own strength to SINOMA (Suzhou)!

争当转型先锋　磨砺运维尖兵

龚腾

1995 年加入中国建材

现为苏州中材伊拉克生产运营项目经理

冬去春来，10 年前种下的小树苗，终于成长为一片枫树林，成为伊拉克 SCP 水泥工厂里一道亮丽风景线。十多年的筚路蓝缕，中材国际在伊拉克开拓市场，从 EPC 工程总包到多元化工程，再到水泥厂保产运维，实现递进式发展。伴随而来的是众多优秀人员的脱颖而出，龚腾就是他们中的杰出代表。

来伊拉克前夕，龚腾是苏丹 ALSALAM 2500t/d 水泥厂安装工程项目经理，在完成合同任务后配合业主进行“保标”期间，帮助业主较好地解决了总承包方印度 Tk-II 公司的诸多问题，赢得了业主的高度信任，也促成了业主与公司签订的第一份按人工计费的保产合同。作为苏州中材第一位保产项目经理，龚腾深入生产一线，带领生产团队努力学习，克服设计、装备、备件供应短缺等重重障碍，仅用了两个月的时间，就将工厂的月度运转率从接手前的 52%，提高至 84%，树立了公司承接保产项目的信心。

2010 年，公司决定进行业务延伸，从单纯的 EPC 工程正式向保产运维领域进军，龚腾被任命为苏州中材伊拉克 SCP 保产项目部项目经理，然而这条路并非坦途，充满各种挑战和诸多未知。

上任伊始，龚腾与项目管理团队精心谋划，经讨论确定了“安全、优质、高产、低耗、环境优美”的生产指导方针，以及三部门三车间的分级分层管理组织结构。为解决生产技术骨干短缺的问题，他先后通过引进、借调、寻求外部支持等方式，为伊拉克 SCP 项目现场协调到多名有着 10 年以上生产经验的技术人员，搭建起了生产运营技术团队。磨合 4 个月之后，项目各项生产工作全面步入正轨，对后续保产运维工作的顺利拓展创造了先决条件。

队伍建设对任何一个企业来说都至关重要。先期的引进借调只能解决短期困难，而龚腾考虑更多的则是长期的人才培养和储备。自承接保产项目的第一天开始，新的人才培养计划也随即展开。苏州中材长年的工程建设，造就了一大批优秀工程技术人员，其中不乏在设备运行和生产保障方面的行家里手，而第一批保产人员就是从他们中考核选拔而来的。经过10余年磨砺，他们已经逐渐走向成熟，并陆续输送到公司其他保产运维项目中。

保产运维项目，其核心是确保生产线的稳定运行和水泥产品的质量稳定。除了需要有经验的生产技术人员把关，管理水平的提升更是新的挑战。在最初从事保产运维业务时，全公司对生产相关的核心数据、风险控制节点、容错纠错范围等的认识都比较模糊，这为生产运维工作的精确控制和全面把控造成了很大的障碍。针对现状，龚腾带领团队，从原料成分分析，到原料制备、存储、粉磨，再到入窑煅烧、冷却、输送，最后到水泥粉磨、包装等全部流程，进行了数据搜集整理。那段时间，龚腾几乎每时每刻都和他的保产团队一起，穿梭在各个生产车间，以求用最快的速度，掌握了解清楚各个环节的核心数据，并对数据进行分析汇总。在逐渐熟悉掌握各方面实际情况的基础上，龚腾带领保产团队从实际出发，制定各类操作规程、设备维护手册、各个车间和机组的监控办法、质量控制程序等，逐步建立健全生产管理办法、综合管理制度等，形成了一整套管理体系，为确保保产运维业务的体系化管理，以及在其他国家和地区推广该体系具有开创性的作用和意义。

多年励精图治，换来的是保产运维业务的蓬勃发展。目前，公司已包揽在伊拉克市场承建的全部6条水泥生产线项目的后续保产运维业务。

2020年初，新冠疫情横扫全球。在疫情初期，迅速出台一系列管控方案、应急预案，紧急成立疫情防控指挥部，并责成各个项目部成立应急指挥小组，全面实行封闭式管理，疫情防控成效显著。2020年中到2021年底，在一年多时间内，苏州中材在伊拉克境内的近千名中方员工，无重症感染者。与此同时，在包括新冠疫情、原材料价格大幅波动等极其困难、复杂的情况下，各保产项目部迎难而上，全部完成生产任务计划，实现产值和利润目标，获得了业主和公司的高度认可和赞许。

经营属地国家，深耕本土化市场，大力推进产业延伸，开创多元化经营新格局，在一系列改革创新浪潮中，龚腾及其团队精诚合作、奋力拼搏，争做时代转型先锋；锐意进取、矢志不渝，为公司发展长远谋划。在逆境中前行，十年磨一剑，淬炼磨砺出一支专业、奋进、朝气蓬勃的运维尖兵。（中材国际所属苏州中材）

个人体会 我自2010年投身伊拉克市场以来，带领团队服务公司发展大局，精诚合作、锐意进取，创建生产运维管理模式，为SINOMA品牌增光添彩。后续我将继续踔厉奋发，勇毅前行，加强学习，提升管理，助力公司的高质量发展！

A Pioneer of Transformation and O&M

Gong Teng

Joined CNBM in 1995

The O&M Projects Manager of SINOMA(Suzhou) In Iraq

As time goes by, the saplings planted a decade ago have grown into a maple grove, a beautiful sight at the Sulaymaniyah Cement Plant (SCP) in Iraq. Over the past decade or so, SINOMA International has expanded its footprint in Iraq, from EPC projects to diversified projects, and then to cement plant production support and operation & maintenance (O&M), achieving progressive development. Along the way, many outstanding people have come to the fore, and Gong Teng is an outstanding representative.

Before coming to Iraq, Gong Teng was the project manager of the ALSALAM 2500t/d cement plant installation project in Sudan. During the period of "bid maintenance" with the owner after completing the contract tasks, he solved many problems of the general contractor Tk-II, an Indian company, and won the owner's trust. He also contributed to the first production support contract on a pay-per-hand basis between the owner and the company. As the first production support project manager of SINOMA (Suzhou), Gong Teng inspected the production line and led a production team to study and overcome obstacles such as shortages of designs, equipment and spare parts. In only two months, he enhanced the monthly operation rate of the plant from 52% before his tenure to 84%, building the company's confidence to undertake production support projects.

In 2010, the company decided to expand its business from EPC projects to production support and O&M. Gong Teng was appointed as the project manager of the Iraq SCP Production Support Project Department of SINOMA (Suzhou). However, it was not a smooth ride, and full of challenges and unknowns.

At the beginning of his tenure, Gong Teng and the project management team carefully planned and determined the production guidelines of safety, high quality, high yield, low consumption and environmental friendliness through discussion, as well as an organizational structure featuring hierarchical management by three departments and three workshops. To cope with the shortage of production technicians, he coordinated a number of technicians with more than ten years of production experience for the Iraqi SCP project through personnel introduction, secondment and seeking external support, and built a production and operation technical team. After four months of running-in, the production of the project was fully on track, creating a prerequisite for the smooth expansion of subsequent production support and O&M.

Team building is crucial to any enterprise. The introduction and secondment of personnel at an early stage can only solve difficulties in the short term, while Gong Teng is more concerned about long-term talent training and reserve. From the first day of the project, a new talent training program was launched. After years of engineering construction, SINOMA (Suzhou) has built up a large number of excellent engineering and technical personnel, many of whom are experts in equipment operation and production support, and the first batch of production support personnel were selected from them through assessment. After more than ten years of practice, they have gradually matured and been successively sent to other production support and O&M projects of the company.

The core of production support and O&M projects is to ensure the stable operation of production lines and the stable quality of cement products. These projects need to be supervised by experienced production technicians, and improving management is a new challenge. At the beginning of the production support and O&M business, the company had a vague understanding of production-related core data, risk control nodes, scopes of error tolerance and correction, etc. which caused great obstacles for the accurate and comprehensive control of production and O&M. In view of this, Gong Teng led his team to collect and organize the data of the whole process from the analysis of raw material composition, to the preparation, storage and grinding of raw materials, to calcination in kilns, cooling and transportation, and finally to cement grinding and packaging. During that time, Gong Teng spent almost every minute with his production support team. They shuttled around workshops so as to grasp the core data of each link as quickly as possible, and analyze as well as summarize the data. With a gradual grasp of the reality of all aspects, Gong Teng led his team to prepare operating procedures, equipment maintenance manuals, monitoring methods of each workshop and unit, and quality control procedures based on the actual situation. They have gradually established and improved production management methods and comprehensive management systems, and built a management system, which has been playing a pioneering role in ensuring the systematic management of the production support and O&M business and promoting it in other countries and regions.

Years of hard work has created a booming production support and O&M business. At present, the company has contracted the production support and O&M business of all six cement production lines in Iraqi.

The company taps with local markets in the countries in which it operates, vigorously promotes industrial extension, and creates a new pattern of diversified business. In a series of reform and innovation, Gong Teng has sincerely cooperated with his team, striving to be the pioneer of transformation. He has forged ahead with determination and made long-term development plans for the company. In the face of adversity, ten years of trials and endeavor have trained a professional, enterprising and vigorous O&M team.

Personal Insights Since I devoted to the Iraqi market in 2010, upholding the concept of serving the company's overall development, I've led the team to cooperate closely and forge ahead. We successfully created the management model for the operation & maintenance business and added luster to the SINOMA brand. In the future, I'll continue to work hard, move forward with determination, enhance learning and improve management to assist the company's high-quality development!

豪情抒写奋进诗

叶飞
2003年加入中国建材
现任苏州中材埃塞俄比亚莱米万吨线项目经理

“等不起”的紧迫感、“慢不得”的危机感、“坐不住”的责任感，成为叶飞的“三感”工作状态。2003年至今，叶飞一直在项目生产第一线，“三感”意识越来越浓厚，成为他积极投身项目建设的原动力。现在的叶飞已经成为埃塞莱米万吨线项目经理，除了日常的管理工作，他和他的团队秉承“创新、绩效、和谐、责任”核心价值观，彰显“特别能吃苦、特别能战斗、特别能攻关、特别能奉献”的中材“铁军”风采，书写了一曲不负青春的奋进诗章。

疫情的3年间，叶飞一直坚守在越南项目现场。“心中想着项目，唯独没有自己”成为他的工作写照。在越方政府抗疫政策允许下，他先后参与组织越南蓝河四号粉磨站、大洋一期及大洋二期项目的建设。众所周知的原因，使得各个方面受限：厂家服务人员出境受限，物资匮乏及各种防疫措施的约束不一而足。如何破解这些难题，唯有创新和有限的突破。叶飞和团队人员与厂家服务人员线上沟通，在线下与当地政府联络，最终克服了重重困难，从而使项目按时保质完成。“每一个项目现场都有他的足迹，每一个生产车间都有他的身影，每一个难题的解答都有他的智慧。”他的团队这样评价他。他也因过硬的专业能力和高品质服务水准，为每个余热发电项目交付工作都画上了圆满的句号，赢得业主的高度认可和信赖。

扎根一线20年，练就过硬本领，方能翱翔。在闲暇之余，叶飞总能利用一切时间学习和总结，“九层之台，起于累土”。慢慢地就理解“高度影响一切”的箴言真理。当然，这也给他带来了直接的影响：在管理上用“真”，在服务上求“精”，在工艺上寻“新”，从“细”上着眼，从“精”上下功夫。如《激光雷达料位计在水泥厂料仓监测中的应用》等高质量论文也频频刊发在专业期刊上，使他获得同行与业主的尊重与信任。

“纸上得来终觉浅，绝知此事要躬行。”此言不虚，要想解决现场的问题，不到现场是无论如何也解决不好的。叶飞之所以能够赢得大家的尊重，除了精湛的专业知识外，还有他

一贯的“三感”姿态。到现场，展现思想，回来订计划，慎而又慎，牢牢记着每一个进度的节点，做到“胸中有丘壑”。特别是在各余热发电项目解决多处技能难题时，他以积极主动的工作态度、富于创新和敢于挑战困难的品格，如期完成越南宁平余热发电、蓝河粉磨站、大洋一期投产及大洋二期的节点工作，用行动向外界展示了苏州中材不畏艰难的“铁军”精神。

鱼和熊掌不可兼得，选择海外事业，意味着要一心扑在工作上，难免疏忽对家庭的照顾。离家3年的他，在2022年年底终于踏上了回国之旅，但是大年初二，在与家人相聚20天之后，又再次经历离别。2023年2月份，他接到调令前往苏州中材埃塞莱米万吨线项目任项目经理一职，他义无反顾，又踏上万里之外的埃塞，埃塞莱米万吨线项目对他来说是要面对一个陌生的工作环境。他通宵达旦，经过一周时间，了解、熟悉、掌握项目现状，分别从合同、图纸、进度、质量、安全、成本、物流等各方面紧密部署、详细规划、责任到岗到人。目前苏州中材埃塞莱米万吨线项目在他的带领下正高质量地推进建设中，在不久的日子后，一首豪情万丈的新时代乐章将在遥远的非洲大地上奏响——中材国际的奋进诗章也将在“叶飞们”的手上镌刻成丰碑。

20年来，叶飞一心扑在工作上，兢兢业业，他没有华丽的修饰，没有惊天的壮举，没有煽情的故事，但他将自己的青春岁月无私地奉献在基层一线。一方天地之间，他用责任与担当将“SINOMA”的品牌扎根于他涉足的每一片土地上。

“除了专业和精神，品质闪耀在内心”，这句话是他的座右铭。（中材国际所属苏州中材）

个人体会 我会以身作则，团结并带领大家在管理上用“真”，在服务上求“精”，在工艺上寻“新”，从“细”上着眼，从“精”上下功夫，用责任与担当将“SINOMA”的品牌扎根于我涉足过的每一片土地上。

Write a Poem of Hard Work with Passion

Ye Fei

Joined CNBM in 2003

The Project Manager of SINOMA(Suzhou)'s Ethiopian Lemi 10000t/d Cement Clinker Production Project

Ye Fei's working consists of "three senses", namely the sense of urgency that can't be delayed, the sense of crisis that can't be mitigated, and the sense of responsibility that can't be evaded. Since 2003, Ye Fei has been working at the frontline of various projects. The increasing awareness of his "three senses" has become the driving force for his active involvement in those projects. Today, Ye Fei is the project manager of the 10K-ton production line project in Lemi, Ethiopia. In addition to daily management tasks, he and his team uphold the core values of "innovation, performance, harmony, and responsibility". They demonstrate the abilities to endure hardships, fight difficulties, tackle challenges, and dedicate themselves, showing the "Iron Army" spirit of SINOMA. Together they write a poem about youth and hard work.

During the three years of the rampant epidemic, Ye Fei insisted on the Vietnam projects. "Thinking about the projects all the time, but never about personal life" has become a portrait of his work. Under the permission of the Vietnamese government's epidemic prevention policy, he successively participated in the construction of Vietnam Song Lam No. 4 Pulverizing Station, Ocean Group Phase I and Ocean Group Phase II projects. For well-known reasons, all aspects of the projects were hampered. The manufacturers' service personnel were restricted from leaving the country. There was a shortage of supplies. And they were bounded by various epidemic prevention measures, etc. The only way to solve these problems was to make limited breakthroughs using innovation. Ye Fei and the team members communicated with the manufacturers' service staff online and liaised with local authorities offline. Finally, they overcame numerous difficulties and completed the projects on time with high quality. "His footprints can be found at every project site. His figure can be seen in every production workshop. And his wisdom lies in every solved problem," this is how his team describes him. He has also received praise and trust from the clients due to his professional skills and high-quality service, which brought every WHP project to a successful end.

Rooted in the frontline for 20 years, Ye Fei has gained superb skills, like a bird soaring high in the sky. Ye Fei surely is a person who keeps learning and becomes better. In his spare time, he always uses every moment to learn and summarize. As he gradually increases his knowledge like building a tower, he slowly comes to understand the proverb "height affects everything". In turn, this has brought him direct changes and results. He uses his experience in management work and strives for excellence in service. He also seeks innovation in craftsmanship. He focuses on details and works hard to improve his knowledge and skills. He has published many high-quality papers in various journals, such as "Application of Laser Radar Level Sensor in Cement Plant Silo Monitoring", which have brought him value and honor as well as respect and trust from his peers and clients.

It is true that action is the key to true understanding. It is impossible to solve the problems that occur on site without being there. Ye Fei gains everyone's respect not only because of his superb professional knowledge, but also due to his unswerving "three senses" attitude. He goes to the site and shows his ideas. Then he returns to make plans. He needs to be extremely cautious and memorize every progress point. That's how he gets a well-thought-out plan. It is worth mentioning that he has solved many technical problems on various WHP projects. With his proactive work attitude, innovative personality and the courage to face challenges, he has completed many projects on schedule, including the Vietnam Ninh Binh WHP project, Song Lam Pulverizing Station, Ocean Group Phase I production and Ocean Group Phase II. He shows the world the fearless "Iron Army" spirit of SINOMA (Suzhou) with his actions.

You can't have your cake and eat it too. Choosing to work abroad means focusing wholeheartedly on work and lack of time to spend with the family. After working abroad for 3 years, Ye Fei finally embarked on a journey back to China at the end of 2022. However, on the second day of the Lunar New Year, after spending only 20 days with his family, he once again set off on a journey. In February 2023, he received an order to go to SINOMA (Suzhou) as the project manager of the 10K-ton production

line project in Lemi, Ethiopia. Without hesitation, he embarked on a journey to Ethiopia thousands of miles away. Upon arriving at the location of the project, he found himself in an unfamiliar working environment. He worked day and night and spent a week learning the current state of the project. Then he made detailed plans of the project in various aspects such as contracts, blueprints, progress, quality, safety, costs, and logistics. He also assigned tasks and responsibilities to specific positions and personnel. Today, under his leadership, the SINOMA (Suzhou) 10K-ton production line project in Lemi, Ethiopia is under construction with high quality. Soon, a passionate melody of a new era will be heard on the vast land of Africa. The SINOMA International's poem of hard work will also be carved into a monument by the hands of people like Ye Fei.

In the past 20 years, Ye Fei has devoted himself to his work diligently. His position has no glamorous embellishments. Nothing about his work is earth-shattering or sentimental. However, he has selflessly dedicated his youth to the frontline far away from home. Being a man of responsibilities and commitment, he has planted the SINOMA brand on every piece of land he visited.

"Apart from professional spirit, quality shines from within," is his motto.

Personal Insights I will lead by example, unite and lead team members to do the management work with full sincerity, strive for perfection in service, seek innovation in craftsmanship, focus on details and pursue excellence, so as to make the SINOMA brand root in the places I have been.

开疆拓土的“领头羊”

尼勒・切威

2021 年加入中国建材
现任中材国际赞比亚分公司清关主管

2022 年对中材国际赞比亚分公司来说是特殊的一年。这一年，赞比亚分公司继续开拓市场，在恩多拉正式拥有了自己的保税库，也有了属于自己的公司驻地。保税库成立伊始，一切都是全新的领域，海关区保税库的划分及申请、清关资质的申请等，都需要专业人才的介入，而尼勒・切威正是这方面的人才，他利用自己的专业知识和深耕多年的工作经验，成功助力分公司成立了现有的保税库并完成了一般清关资质的申请。

尼勒・切威于 2021 年加入中材国际赞比亚分公司，在进入分公司前曾在 SDV 与博洛雷国际物流公司工作过 13 年，积累了丰富的清关经验。同时，对国际贸易和物流业也颇为了解。进入赞比亚分公司后，他在清关贸易部门独挑大梁，承担着清关方面的各项任务，从进口到出口的各环节都严格把关，保证货物清关的顺利进行。

2022 年，中材国际赞比亚分公司成立自己的保税库后，水泥、煤炭、建材等跨境贸易量急剧增加，相应的业务量也大大增加，尼勒・切威作为清关业务的主力兵，自然承担着不小的压力，忙得经常没时间休息。在办公室，他常常凳子都没坐热，一个电话过来，就又要外出处理事情。虽然后来也陆续招了几名当地员工分担压力，但遇到复杂问题，他还是要亲自处理。虽说能者多劳，但劳需有度。因此，一般的事情公司都会选择交给其他人来做，尽量给他减负，避免给他安排超负荷的任务。

工欲善其事，必先利其器。既然是跨境贸易，就免不了要和政府部门打交道，尤其是税务部门。而尼勒・切威之所以能游刃有余地处理工作上的难题，除了多年积累的工作经验和过硬的专业能力之外，还在于他积极与当地政府沟通对接，除了工作期间的见面外，还会定期与他们保持电话联系，让工作能更顺利地开展。

即使工作繁忙，尼勒・切威也不忘抽空阅读来提升自己，尤其是不断地阅读相关的专业材料与法律文件，以持续更新自己的知识库，

保持对工作的敏感度。此外，在入职的两年期间，尼勒·切威还抓住一切机会参加政府举办的论坛会议以及到其他同行公司进行参观学习，这为他处理工作难题提供了不少新的方法和观点。他曾向分公司建议，希望公司可以定期对新入职的当地员工开展专业知识方面的培训，毕竟人员业务水平参差不齐，在工作沟通时容易产生误解，或者造成不必要的损失。公司在采纳建议后，各部门在工作效率上都有了显著提升。

尼勒·切威作为清关业务的“领头羊”，虽有着其他员工所不具备的专业知识和业务能力，但却一直不骄不躁，对其他人的疑问总是耐心解答，在他人遇到困难时总会悉心提供帮助。

具备专业能力和优良品德的员工正是一个企业发展壮大所需要的，中材国际海外分公司需要更多像尼勒·切威这样的“领头羊”，带领属地化员工一起开拓市场，走向更广阔的天地！（中材国际所属苏州中材）

个人体会 我很高兴能加入中材国际这个大家庭，它让我看到了人生不一样的可能，也给我的人生带来了非凡的意义。在这里，我们团结一心，一起面对挑战，攻克难题，让我在得到锻炼的同时也深深爱上了中国和中国文化。非常庆幸能在中材国际工作，希望中材国际会越来越好，一起加油吧！

A Leader in Expanding Territory

Nile Chewe

Joined CNBM in 2021

The Customs Clearance Supervisor of SINOMA International Engineering Co., Ltd. (Zambia Branch)

2022 is a special year for the Zambia Branch of SINOMA International. In this year, the Zambia Branch continued to expand its territory, officially owned its own bonded warehouse in Ndola, and also had its own company residence. At the beginning of the establishment of bonded warehouses, everything was a brand new field. The division and application of bonded warehouses in customs areas, the application for customs clearance qualifications, and so on, all required the intervention of professional talents, urgently requiring a transformation from scratch. Nile Chewe is a talent in this field, and he used his professional knowledge and years of work experience to successfully assist the branch company in establishing the existing bonded warehouses and completing the application for general customs clearance qualifications.

Nile Chewe joined the Zambia branch in 2021. Prior to joining the branch, he worked at SDV and Bolore International Logistics for 13 years, accumulating rich experience in customs clearance. At the same time, he also has a good understanding of international trade and logistics industry. After entering the Zambia branch, he took on the responsibility of the customs clearance and trade department, undertaking various tasks related to customs clearance. He strictly controlled all aspects, from import to export, to ensure the smooth progress of goods customs clearance.

In 2022, after the establishment of its own bonded warehouse by the Zambia branch of SINOMA, the cross-border trade volume of cement, coal, building materials, and other materials has sharply increased, and the corresponding business volume has also greatly increased. As the main force of customs clearance business, Nile Chewe naturally bears a lot of pressure, often too busy to rest and has to go out to handle things at a call's notice. Although several local employees were gradually recruited to share the pressure later, he still has to personally handle complex problems whenever they show up. Although the skilled person tends to share more, the workload needs to be controlled. Therefore, the company usually chooses to entrust other people to do the general tasks, trying to reduce his burden and avoid overloading him with work.

If you want to do good work, you must first sharpen your tools. Since it is cross-border trade, it is inevitable to deal with government departments, especially tax departments. The reason why Nile Chewe can handle work with ease is not only due to his years of accumulated work experience and strong professional abilities, but also due to his relationship management between government departments. In addition to meeting with them during work, he also regularly maintains phone contact with them to ensure a smoother work process.

Even though he is busy with work, Nile Chewe never forgets to take time to read to improve himself, especially by constantly reading relevant professional materials and legal documents to continuously update his knowledge base and maintain sensitivity to work. In addition, during his two-year tenure, Nile also seized every opportunity to participate in government organized forums and conferences, as well as visit and learn from other peer companies, which provided him with many new methods and perspectives when dealing with work. He once suggested to the branch company that professional knowledge training should be held regularly for new local employees. After all, the professional level of each person was uneven, and misunderstanding and unnecessary losses were easy to occur in work communication. After adopting the suggestions, the company has significantly improved communication and efficiency among various departments.

As a leader in customs clearance business, Nile Chewe, although possessing professional knowledge and skills that other employees do not possess, has always been calm and patient in answering other people's questions, and always providing assistance when others encounter difficulties.

Employees with professional abilities and excellent moral character are exactly what a company needs for its development and growth. SINOMA's overseas branch needs more leaders like Nile Chewe to lead localized employees to expand their territory and expand into a broader world!

Personal Insights I am really happy to be a member of SINOMA, which has provided a different path for me and brought an extraordinary meaning to my life. United as one, we face challenges and conquer difficulties together. Through working with my Chinese colleagues, I has gained many valuable skills and fell in love with China and Chinese culture. In the end, I just want to say that I really appreciate to work for SINOMA. Wish the best for SINOMA. Good luck.

我与 SINOMA 一同建设尼日利亚最大炼油厂的故事

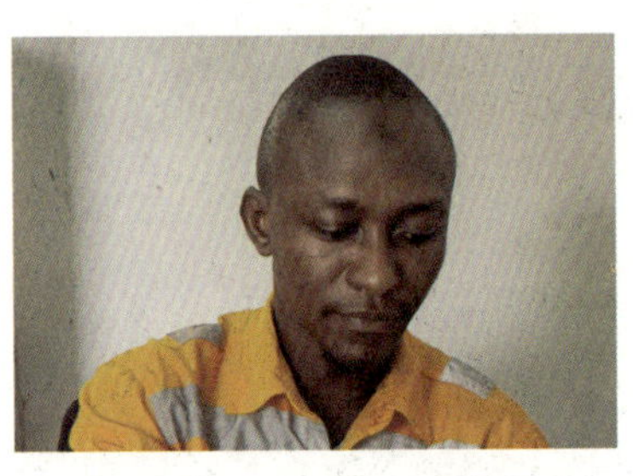

穆罕默德－奥瓦尔·托伊布

2020 年加入中国建材

现任苏州中材尼日利亚炼油厂项目土建工程师

我叫穆罕默德－奥瓦尔·托伊布，来自尼日利亚西南部，目前在 SINOMA 尼日利亚 Dangote 炼油厂项目工作。

2019 年，我以二等荣誉（高年级）毕业于奥松州立理工学院土木工程师专业，毕业后我立即找到了一份尼日利亚公司 (BB & J 建筑公司) 的工作，该公司从事住宅房地产开发和装修，在那里我工作了将近两年。

2020 年底，我接到本科时期朋友的电话，他在 Dangote 炼油厂项目工作，介绍我来担任土木工程师的工作，我把我的简历转发给他帮我提交，几周后我被邀请参加面试，幸运的是，在参加面试的很多人中，我是少数几个通过面试的人之一。

工作的第一天，为了帮助我适应工作，公司安排了一位中国土木工程师直接指导我的工作。尽管我有一位中国导师，但由于存在着沟通障碍以及炼油厂建筑结构复杂、工地路线繁杂等问题，一开始工作的开展有点困难。

我担心我可能需要很长时间来适应这个工作环境，因为我周围的大部分人都是中国人，只有少数当地的工程师。但我的担心很快就消除了，因为和我搭档的中国工程师综合能力非常全面并且很友好。

除了学习专业技能，我开始在办公室和施工现场主动向我的中国同事学习一些中文单词，以提高我在工作中的沟通能力。

经过两周的试用期，我被安排负责一个车间的厂前区施工工作，厂前区工作包括油罐区、管枕、T 型支架基础、泵站、污水池 / 地下油池和地面硬化。在此期间，我接触了很多以前工作中没有接触过的东西，比如从图纸中提取坐标、如何在现场有效地执行和监督，最终我能够监督和顺利移交很多结构工作面给机电团队。

这个项目给我带来了很多挑战，比如图纸问题、现场协调工作、如何确保达成计划的混凝土方量目标、如何确保现场混凝土按图纸施工以及检查钢筋下料单等。管枕的建造给我们带来了挑战，因为有些管枕线与地下管道的坐标相冲突，尽管困难重重，最终我都能将所有的工作任务完美交付。

此外，我还通过积累经验增长了作为工程师需要必备的技能，在使用 MS excel 方面发挥了自己的特长，如做工程量清单（B.O.Q）、对每月在现场完成的工程进行测量（RA 账单）、保存工作的证明文件、与顾问公司 EIL 和 Dangote 炼油厂业主一起检查和确认有关工程量等，我的工作能力得到很大提升。

此外，在项目结束时，我还坚持每月核对所有的工程量清单，以确定是否少报或多报了工程量或遗漏了现场的工程，这为正确记录、检查和平衡工程成本以及纠正检查过程中的错误奠定了基础。

对于这次工作的转型，我心怀感恩，感谢公司给我工作的机会，证明了我可以应对复杂的工作。在与 SINOMA 共同成长的这些年里，我积累了很多经验，也收获了足以满足家庭需求的回报，我期待在公司的新项目中工作，继续发挥我的优势，为客户提供优质的精品工程。（中材国际所属苏州中材）

个人体会 在 SINOMA 工作的这些日子，是我人生当中最充实的一段时光，不管是在工作上还是在生活上，我都得到了很大的提高。很高兴能够参与如此伟大的工程建设当中，感谢中国同事们给我的帮助和支持，我将努力做得更好，为公司在尼日利亚的发展作出新的贡献。

My Story with SINOMA to Build the Largest Oil Refinery in Nigeria

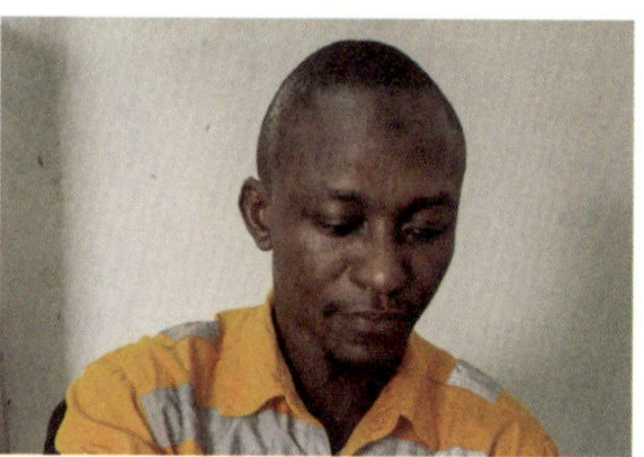

Muhammed-awwal Toyyib

Joined CNBM in 2020

The Civil Engineer of Nigeria LEKKI Oil Refinery Installation Project of SINOMA(Suzhou)

My name is Muhammed-awwal Toyyib from southwest part of Nigeria (OYO STATE). I currently work with SINOMA Company Dangote Oil Refinery Nigeria.

I graduated from Osun State College of Technology, Osun State in 2019 with a second class honors (upper division). After graduation, I secured an employment of a Nigeria residential estate development & renovations company where I worked for almost 2 years.

In late 2020, I received a call from a friend back in College who was working with SINOMA Dangote Refinery, saying that there was an vacancy for engineer at his work place. I forwarded my curriculum vitae and was invited for an interview after a few weeks. Fortunately, I was one of the few who passed the interview.

On my first day, in order to help me settle down, a Chinese civil engineer was assigned to me as my guide. Despite the fact that I had a Chinese mentor, the work was a little bit tough at the start because of communication barriers and the complicated structures as well as complex routes in the construction sites.

Initially, I was afraid that it would take a long time for me to get used to the working environment because most of the people around me in the department were Chinese and only a few local engineers. But my worries soon disappeared since the Chinese engineer I was partnered with was very sound and friendly.

In addition to learning professional skills, I started learning some Chinese words from my Chinese colleagues to improve my communication in office and particularly at site.

After two weeks of probation, I was put in charge of a section in offsite work, which includes tank farms, pipe sleepers, T-supports, pump station, OWS/UG pits and pavement. During work, I was exposed to so many new things, such as extracting coordinates from blueprints, executing and supervising on site. Eventually, I was able to supervise and hand over many structure works to the mechanical and electrical team.

The project brought so many challenges like drawing issues, site coordination work, ensuring the proposed volume of concrete target, quantifying the concrete to be cast as per the issued drawings, ensuring compliance to all the safety rules by the

workers at site, checking the bar bending schedule and so on. The construction of the "Sleepers" particularly gave us a set back because some of the sleeper lines clashed with the coordinates of the underground pipes and needed to be buried first by the mechanical agency before the pipe sleepers installation. Despite the difficulties, all the issues were managed perfectly and works delivered on schedule.

Additionally, I further accumulated experiences as an engineer and developed my skills of MS Excel, such as doing Bill of Quantity (B.O.Q), making monthly measurements (RA Bills) sheets, keeping documents of the job, checking and confirming the scale of engineering, to name a few. My abilities were enhanced greatly during the process.

Moreover, I keep checking the lists of work done every month at the end of the project, in order to determine whether less or more work had been claimed or omitting. This gave room for proper documentation, checking and balancing production costs as well as correction of potential mistakes.

I am thankful to the company for giving me the opportunity to work and proving my ability to cope with the complexity of the job. I have gained experiences over the years working with SINOMA and I have been able to cater for my needs and my family. I'm looking forward to working on a new project with the company, so that I can continue to give my best to deliver quality works to our clients.

Personal Insights The days of working at SINOMA have been the most fulfilling period of my life. I have grown both in work and in life. I am happy to be able to participate in such a great project. I would like to thank my Chinese colleagues for their help and support. I will try my best to do better and make new contributions to the development of the company in Nigeria.

海外市场探路者

陈金泉

2013 年加入中国建材
现任中国中材海外科技发展有限公司沙特 YAMAMA 项目部副总经理兼商务部副部长

十载风雨少年书，一身戎装海外路。陈金泉自 2013 年入职中材海外公司以来，一直奋斗在海外现场一线，10 年间先后参与了阿联酋 ABMC 项目、刚果（金）PPCB 项目、阿根廷 L'Amali 二线项目以及 2023 年刚刚启动的沙特 YAMAMA 项目。10 年来，他一直勤勉克己、任劳任怨，面对困难从不退缩，成为公司年青一代的模范先锋，为公司这 10 年来的海外项目执行、属地化经营和国际化进程作出了积极贡献。

千淘万漉虽辛苦，吹尽狂沙始到金。2014 年，PPCB 项目刚启动，刚果（金）便暴发埃博拉病毒，加之该国常年疟疾盛行，项目一线商务人员紧缺。陈金泉了解情况后，义无反顾地加入了刚果（金）PPCB 项目现场一线。刚果（金）PPCB 项目施工条件异常艰苦，而且物资匮乏，码头装卸能力和运输路况都非常落后，清关、免税等工作更是困难重重，令人望而生畏。在此种艰苦的环境下，从 2014 年到 2017 年，作为商务经理的他，虽然多次感染疟疾，却始终以项目工期和进度为重，多次主动延缓休假，在项目关键时期发挥了重要作用，非常出色地完成了整个项目的物流清关和进度款收汇等相关工作，为项目的顺利推进奠定了坚实基础。

乘风破浪会有时，直挂云帆济沧海。2017 年 8 月，阿根廷 L'Amali 项目启动。作为公司在南美首个最大的单体 EPC 项目，该项目具有重要的战略意义。因此，在项目人员规划上，优先考虑具有丰富项目经验的员工。陈金泉毫不犹豫地接受了公司的委派，作为项目商务经理，深入该项目现场一线。“定谋略，常思变，以退为进，步步为营”。阿根廷项目的施工，全部分包给当地公司，这是公司属地化经营的一次重大尝试。在项目的执行过程中，他遇到了难以想象的困难。其中，对商务管理的挑战，尤为突出。复杂的免税和清关、大量的当地采购、中途引进 4 家土建分包、经济危机、法令变更、疫情、频繁的合同变更、索赔与反索赔等问题时有出现，而且谈判难度异常

之大，这些平时只出现在合同条款中的事件几乎都出现在了这次项目上，使他面临着巨大的商务管理压力。由他主导的商务组在公司领导的带领下，勇挑重担，积极主动联合费控、土建、安装、财务及相关法律顾问等，严格按照公司的“大谋略”，坚定地以维护公司利益为大方向，排兵布阵，多次在危机中寻求机会，突破常规，另辟蹊径，在业主过于强势的情况下，以退为进，一步一个脚印，步步为营，顺利解决了当地分包的索赔，并及时通过索赔的方式解决了项目所需的现金流短缺问题。2022 年初，该项目在克服了上述的种种困难后最终顺利移交，且整个项目的所有商务工作，包括索赔与反索赔等，也均在预期内完成。

前进的步伐从未停止。2022 年，阿根廷 L’Amali 项目结束后，在经过短暂的休憩后，陈金泉又踏上了沙特 YAMAMA 项目的征程。该项目为全球首个万吨线拆迁项目，其难度和挑战实属空前。作为公司商务部副部长兼项目副总经理的他，也必将会砥砺前行，不忘初心，为公司在沙特甚至整个中东地区的属地化经营继续作出贡献。（中国中材海外科技发展有限公司）

在过去的 10 年里，我紧跟公司战略步伐，不断在海外 EPC 项目中锤炼自己，从一名普通的商务人员到现在具备独立管理能力的优秀商务经理。我将继续在海外市场中深耕发展，为公司的海外项目执行和属地化经营添砖加瓦。

The Overseas Pathfinder

Chen Jinquan

Joined CNBM in 2013

The Deputy General Manager of YAMAMA Relocation Project and Deputy Manager of Commercial Department of SINOMA Overseas

For the past decade, Chen Jinquan has been a devoted and steadfast presence on the front lines of overseas operations. Since assuming his role in 2013, he has actively participated in prestigious projects such as the UAE ABMC project, the Congo-Kim PPCB project, the Argentina-L'Amali second-line project, and the recently launched Saudi YAMAMA project in 2023, where he will now be based as a resident. Throughout his journey, Chen Jinquan has exemplified unwavering diligence, selflessness, and a resolute commitment to his labor duties, never succumbing to complaints or setbacks. His courage and trailblazing spirit as an overseas representative have positioned him as a role model for the younger generation within the company. Furthermore, his steadfast efforts over the past decade have made significant contributions to the successful implementation, territorial operations, and internationalization of the company's overseas projects.

Amidst the challenges and adversities, Chen Jinquan embraced the opportunity to turn difficulties into triumphs. In 2014, as the PPCB project was launched in the Democratic Republic of the Congo, an Ebola outbreak and a prevailing malaria epidemic plagued the country, exacerbated by a scarcity of commercial personnel on the front lines. Unfazed by the circumstances, Chen Jinquan made an unwavering commitment to join the PPCB project site in the Congo, becoming an integral part of the team. The construction conditions in Congo were exceptionally arduous, marked by limited availability of materials, outdated transportation routes, and daunting customs clearance and tax exemption processes. Undeterred by these adversities, Chen Jinquan served as the commercial manager, persistently focused on project timelines and schedules. Between the period of 2014 and 2017, despite suffering from recurring bouts of malaria, he willingly postponed his leave multiple times, playing a pivotal role during critical stages of the project. He ensured smooth logistics clearance and maintained steady progress throughout the project, laying a solid foundation for its advancement.

Like a ship navigating through turbulent waters, Chen Jinquan fearlessly embraced the challenges that came his way. In August 2017, the launch of the L'Amali project in Argentina marked SINOMA International's first single EPC project in South America, carrying significant strategic importance. Recognizing the project's significance, the company prioritized the assignment of personnel with extensive project experience, and Chen Jinquan eagerly accepted the role of project business

manager, joining the project site's front line. The Argentine project, with its localization efforts subcontracted to local companies, posed a major endeavor for the company. The project implementation encountered unprecedented difficulties and presented substantial challenges to business management. Complexities such as tax exemptions, customs clearances, substantial local procurements, the involvement of four civil works subcontractors, economic crises, legislative changes, outbreaks of Covid-19, frequent contract alterations, and claims and counterclaims became the norm, creating immense pressures in business management. These challenges were unlike anything typically encountered in other projects, and they demanded exceptional negotiation skills and resilience. Throughout the project implementation, under the leadership of the company, Chen Jinquan and his dedicated business team bravely shouldered heavy responsibilities. They actively integrated fee control, civil works, installation, finance, and legal advisory services, aligning their actions with the company's formulated "grand strategy." Their unwavering focus remained on safeguarding the company's interests, seeking opportunities amidst crises, breaking free from routine approaches, and forging new paths. Despite facing significant resistance from the project owner, they made steady progress, gradually resolving local subcontractor claims and addressing cash flow requirements through timely claims. In early 2022, after overcoming the aforementioned difficulties, the project successfully reached a smooth handover, and all commercial aspects, including claims and counterclaims, were closed within expectations.

Pressing forward while staying true to our initial aspirations, the march of progress never ceases. Following the conclusion of Argentina's L'Amali project in 2022, and after a brief interlude, Chen Jinquan now embarks on a new endeavor—the YAMAMA project in Saudi Arabia. This groundbreaking initiative, encompassing the world's first 10,000-ton line demolition project, presents unparalleled difficulties and challenges. As the company's Vice Minister of Commerce and Deputy General Manager of Projects, Chen Jinquan remains resolute in his commitment to forge ahead, unwavering in his dedication to the company's expansion in Saudi Arabia and the broader Middle East region.

Personal Insights The realization of overseas development strategy demands an esteemed team with international vision and advanced management capability. During the past ten years, I have had the honor to steadily follow such development strategy of the company and continuously forged myself in those EPC Projects from a normal commercial engineer to an independent and good commercial manager. It is my determination to unswervingly deepen my contribution to the overseas market and make all due effort to witness and facilitate the further international and localization development of the company.

年逾花甲的销售经理

阿米莉亚·丹尼斯·博思玛

2019 年加入中国建材

现任中国建材国际南非公司销售经理

为响应“一带一路”倡议，围绕中国建材集团国际化战略布局，2018 年集团在南非开始探索发展海外仓模式，2019 年 1 月，南非约翰内斯堡海外仓正式运营，开始了东南部非洲市场开拓。

南非海外仓运营初期，资金与人员十分紧张、产品采购和销售的渠道尚未打通，客户短缺，市场经验不足、社会治安不稳定、生活环境不适应等困难接踵而至。此时的南非公司，急需一个熟悉当地市场、业务能力全面的属地员工打开局面。阿米莉亚·丹尼斯·博思玛就是在这时加入南非团队的。

出生于 1961 年的阿米莉亚，进入公司时已年近六十，在国内这已是退休的年纪，但是阿米莉亚却每天都激情饱满，全身心投入工作。

南非公司起步之初，人手十分紧张，每个人都身兼数职，既是销售也是采购，既要负责前端清关，也要负责产品入库。阿米莉亚做事细心负责，公司将销售单据管理交由她负责，她每天都要处理几百页的销售单据，进行归档、管理，从未出现过差错。为有效做好仓库盘点，每天下班后，阿米莉亚都带着几个年轻同事，加班加点梳理货物，更新盘点台账，做到数目账本日日清。阿米莉亚以公司为家，高度的责任心也影响着其他属地化员工，在她的培养下，仓库团队力量日益强大。

2020 年，新冠疫情暴发，既是机遇，也是挑战。也正是因为疫情，南非当地很多竞争对手无法工作，国内竞争工厂无法到南非拜访客户。此时，南非团队借助强大的供应链资源优势，备齐产品种类，陆续引入离网逆变器、铅酸电池等产品，保障供货充足，成功发展了大量优质稳定的客户，不断提高市场影响力和占有率。

近 5 年来，南非公司的业绩连续实现爆发式增长，从几百万、上千万、一个亿到超过十个亿，南非海外仓完美地诠释了什么是“从无到有，从有到优，从优到精”。而阿米莉亚的 2022 年个人销售业绩也达到 2.49 亿兰特（约为 0.9 亿人民币），为公司超额完成业绩目标

作出了重要贡献。

目前，南非海外仓已搭建起以约翰内斯堡为总部，开普敦、德班和伊丽莎白港为分仓的“1+3”市场布局，仓储规模达 3 万平方米，围绕分布式光伏 + 储能等新能源产品链进行分销及服务，并为客户提供属地化的售后服务，形成以南非为核心，辐射津巴布韦、赞比亚、博茨瓦纳、纳米比亚等周边区域国家的发展格局。

海外公司在经营的过程中，属地员工建设对公司的发展很重要。属地员工通常都更加通晓当地的对接方式，不存在文化隔阂的问题，使很多难题可以迎刃而解。因此中建材海外在属地人才队伍建设方面不断加大力度，吸引和培育当地的高质量人才。

在南非公司起步阶段，由于属地化员工紧缺，阿米莉亚向公司推荐了自己女儿香农 · 雷 · 凯特。经过严格的考核，香农于 2020 年 2 月正式加入南非团队，成为一名行政人员。进入公司后，香农也继承了她母亲认真负责、敬业忠诚的品格，在工作中不抱怨、不推诿，脚踏实地，遇到困难想方设法去解决，得到大家充分认可。

随着公司发展规模不断扩大，南非团队也不断壮大。目前南非团队共有员工 145 人，其中属地化员工 127 人，属地化占比达 87%。

现如今，公司“一带一路”建设已经到了深耕厚植、精雕细琢的关键阶段，海外仓也逐渐成为中国制造走出去的新驿站、贯通融让不同经济文化的友谊桥梁。在属地化战略部署下，阿米莉亚依靠敬业的精神，始终以公司利益为先，通过不断的实践，提升自我优势，拉紧与公司互联互通纽带，共同融入经济全球化大潮中，走出一条互利共赢的康庄大道。（中国建材国际南非公司）

个人体会 得益于公司属地化战略，入职后我从事过销售、业务账款对账、仓库盘点等工作。公司就像一个大家庭，在这里我深切感受到了和谐融洽的公司文化氛围，感谢公司给予了一个很好的发展平台，我在这里获得了良好的职业发展，我很自豪在 CNBM 工作。

A Sales Manager in Her 60s

Amelia Denise Bothma

Joined CNBM in 2019

Sales Manager of China National Building Materials International South Africa Company

In order to implement President Xi Jinping's high-quality development plan on promoting the joint construction of the "Belt and Road", and center on the international strategic layout of CNBM,the Group began to explore the development of overseas warehouse models in South Africa in 2018 and the overseas warehouse in Johannesburg, South Africa was officially opened In January 2019.

In the initial stage of the development of the South African Company, both the funds and personnel were very tight. Problems such as channels for product procurement and sales had not been opened, the shortage of customers, the lack of market experience, the instability of social security, and the unsuitable living environment and other difficulties followed one after another. The Company urgently needed a local employee who was familiar with the local market and had comprehensive business capabilities to kick start projects. And this was when Amelia Denise Bothma joined the team.

Amelia, who was born in 1961, was nearly 60 years old when she joined the company. In China, this is the age of retirement, but Amelia is full of passion every day and devotes herself to her work.

At the beginning of the South African Company's start-up, the manpower was very tight, and each person took on several roles in sales and procurement, not only in front-end customs clearance but also in product storage. She is meticulous and responsible in her work, and the company entrusted her with the management of sales documents. She processed, archived and managed hundreds of pages of sales documents every day with zero mistakes. To effectively carry out warehouse inventory, after getting off work every day, Amelia took a few young people to work overtime to sort out the goods, update the inventory ledger, and clear the account book every day. Amelia is the head of the company, and her high sense of responsibility also affects other local employees. Under her training, the warehouse team is becoming stronger and stronger, overcoming difficulties and seizing the big market in South Africa.

The epidemic that began in 2020 was both an opportunity and a challenge. It is precisely because of the epidemic that many local competitors in South Africa could not work, and domestic competitive factories could not visit customers in South Africa. At this time, the South African team took advantage of the strong supply chain resources to prepare a complete range of products and successively

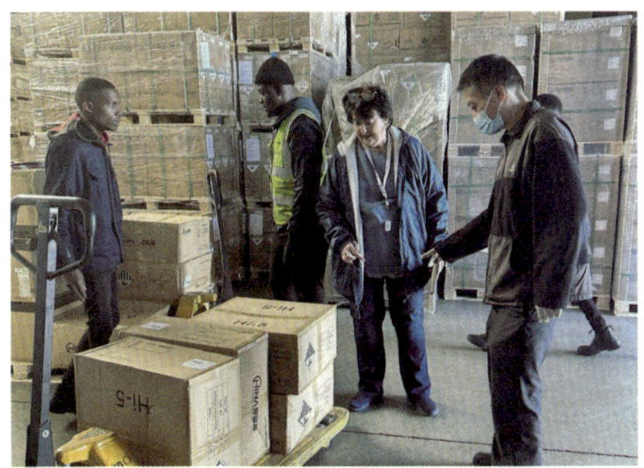

introduced off-grid inverters, lead-acid batteries, and other products to ensure sufficient supply, successfully developing many high-quality and stable customers, and continuously increased market influence as well as the Company's market share.

Over the past five years, the performance of South African Company has continuously achieved explosive growth, from a few million, tens of millions, and 100 million to more than 1 billion. It has been a journey from excellent to outstanding! And Amelia's personal sales performance in 2022 also reached 249 million rands (approximately 90 million yuan), which had made an important contribution to the Company's exceeding performance goals.

At present, the overseas warehouse in South Africa has established a "1+3" market layout covering 30 thousand square meters, with Johannesburg as the headquarters and Cape Town, Durban, Port Elizabeth as the sub-warehouses. The new energy production chain provides distribution and service, and provides customers with localized after-sales service, forming a development pattern centered on South Africa and radiating to neighboring countries such as Zimbabwe, Zambia, Botswana, and Namibia.

In the process of operating an overseas company, the development of local employees is very important. The local employees are usually more familiar with the local working methods, and there is no cultural barrier, so many problems can be easily solved. Therefore, the Company has continuously increased its efforts in the construction of local talent teams, attracting and cultivating local high-quality talents.

In the initial stage of the South African Company, due to the shortage of localized employees, Amelia recommended her daughter, Shannon Leigh Kate, to the company. After a rigorous assessment, Shannon officially joined the South African team in February 2020 as an administrator. After entering the Company, Shannon also inherited her mother's serious, responsible, dedicated, and loyal character. She never complains or shirks at work. She is also down-to-earth, and always finds ways to solve difficulties, which is fully recognized by everyone.

The team has continued to grow with the continuous expansion of the Company's evergrowing scale. At present, the South African team has a total of 145 employees, including 127 local employees, accounting for 87% of the total personnel.

Nowadays, the "Belt and Road" Initiative has reached a critical stage of deep cultivation and meticulous craftsmanship. Overseas warehouses have gradually become a new station for Chinese manufacturing to go global, and a bridge of friendship that connects different economies and cultures. Under the localization strategy, Amelia relies on a dedicated spirit and always prioritizes the Company's interests. Through continuous efforts and practice, she enhances her own advantages, tightens the connection with the company, and integrates into the tide of economic globalization, walking out a mutually beneficial and win-win path.

Personal Insights Thanks to the Company's localization strategy, I was able to join the South African Company team. After joining the company, I have worked in sales, business account reconciliation, warehouse inventory, and other related fields. The company is like a big family, where I deeply feel the harmonious atmosphere of the company. I am grateful to the company for providing a good platform for self development. I have achieved good career here, and I am proud to work here.

勇于亮剑　做中东市场的“李云龙”

李伟峰

2007 年加入中国建材

现任中国建材国际阿联酋公司总经理

2007 年加入中国建材大家庭的李伟峰，至今已在海外工作十余个年头，先后在中建材约旦 NCC 项目部、埃塞 DMC 项目部、阿曼分公司、埃塞分公司、阿联酋公司等工作过。他善于处理工作中的难题，把大家经常吵架拍桌子的会议室变成了静心处理问题的“阿拉伯咖啡厅”；他洽谈业务，“选承包商我们只认中国建材”是业主方给出的评价；他与员工相处，“峰哥能和大家打成一片，有啥事都敢跟他说。”大家如是说。

2020 年 10 月，李伟峰被任命为中国建材国际阿联酋公司（以下简称“阿联酋公司”）总经理。刚接手时，阿联酋疫情严重，员工居家办公，公司面临连年下滑的业绩、银行授信额度骤降以及高额逾期账款等问题。但他毫不退缩，怀揣着中国建材人的荣誉感，坚定地踏上改革之路。

李伟峰上任后，并未急于实施新策略，而是深入了解公司影响发展问题的根源。他发现员工信心不足，有些人甚至对未来的工作感到迷茫。为此，他组织业务骨干一起观看了关于我国第一颗原子弹研发试爆的影片《横空出世》，每位员工观影后都发表了自己的感想：如何完成不可能完成的任务。受到影片的启发，李伟峰制订了阿联酋公司的精神口号：勇于创新，向“做不了”说“不”。这个略显怪异的口号引导着每个员工的行动，帮助公司解决了一个又一个的困难。

在树立起大家信心的同时，一个亟待解决的问题是公司现金流不足，他组织领导班子开始制定新的绩效体系。首先，开展业务主题月激励活动。活动一开展，就取得了显著成效，在活动前两个月，公司的月均营业收入增长了 28.13%，实现了扭亏为盈。其次，制订月度绩效考核制度、逾期账款催收临时制度和超额利润奖励制度等，确保针对实际问题采取切实有效的措施，并跟随公司发展动态调整。

经过一系列的调整，阿联酋公司确立了“自营 + 共享”海外仓的发展战略，其海外仓并成功入选首批国家级国际营销服务公共平台，

获得了中国公共海外仓标准化 A 级（最高级）认证。公司率先提供新能源整车和零部件的分销寄售服务，并与上游车企、制造商以及下游渠道经销商合作，致力于打造中国新能源汽车在中东地区的基地。2022 年，阿联酋海外仓的营业收入同比增长 109%，净利润同比增长 26%。

在业务开拓方面，李伟峰强调主动推动业绩增长，包括开发新业务和新客户。在财务方面，获得与业务发展匹配的授信额度是职责所在。风险控制方面，其责任是提高优劣客户辨别能力，进行风险评级，并使用风控工具实现公司年度目标。采购方面，公司秉持大采购理念，和资源提供商建立与集团建设世界一流建材企业目标一致的合作伙伴关系。

除了内部发展，公司也没有忽视对外宣传。李伟峰争取到了阿联酋中国跨境电子商务协会的支持，成功挂牌阿联酋海外仓，并得到迪拜王室、中国发改委南方国合中心、中国贸促会、河南省商务厅以及深圳市坪山区等大力支持。迪拜王室、阿布扎比王室和吉布提政府的代表也来到公司访问，李伟峰向他们积极介绍中国建材集团，提升公司在海外的品牌形象。阿联酋公司多次登上《绿洲报》《鼎新传媒》等当地知名媒体，宣传公司与各类市场主体合作发展的理念。

为了使阿联酋公司能够尽快进入良性发展轨道，李伟峰连续 17 个月没有与家人团聚。他有一儿一女，他的妻子说，当儿子出生时，他正坚守在中建材埃塞的岗位，未能亲眼见证儿子的出生，现在儿子已经两岁了，他还没有为孩子庆祝过一次生日。作为父亲，他感到有些不称职。但他全心全意地投入工作，相信阿联酋公司的蓬勃发展中必然包含着属于他家人的一份荣耀！（中国建材国际阿联酋公司）

在中国建材任职 17 年，中国建材人的荣誉感一直激励着我，我坚持践行岗位责任。中东与中国关系处于历史最佳时期，迪拜团队将继续践行勇于创新、向“做不了”说“不”的公司精神，为集团发展作出更大贡献，谱写共建“一带一路”高质量发展新篇章！

Brave and Decisive, the "Li Yunlong" of the Middle East Market

Li Weifeng

Joined CNBM in 2007

General Manager of CNBM UAE

Li Weifeng, who joined the CNBM family in 2007, has been working overseas for more than ten years. He has worked in CNBM Jordan NCC Project Department, Ethiopia DMC Project Department, Oman Branch, Ethiopia Branch, CNBM UAE, etc. He had dealt with work challenges, turning the conference room where people often quarreled and slapped tables into an "Arab café" where problems were quietly dealt with. He had negotiated business, and "We only choose CNBM as our contractor " was the evaluation given by the owner. He gets along with his staff. "Brother Feng can get along with everyone, and we won't hesitate to tell him anything."

In October 2020, Li was appointed as the General Manager of China National Building Material Group FZE (Hereafter referred to as "CNBM UAE "). At that time, the pandemic was serious in the UAE. Employees were working from home, and the company was facing problems such as declining sales production for years, plummeting bank credit lines, and high overdue accounts. However, he didn't flinch at all, with the sense of honor of a CNBMer, he stepped firmly on the road of reform.

After taking the seat, Li did not rush to implement the new policy. Instead, he explored into the root causes of the company's developmental issues. He discovered that employees lacked confidence, with some even feeling lost. To address this, he watched a film called "Atomic Bomb" with key business personnel. After the film, each employee shared their thoughts and feelings. Inspired by the film, Li formulated the team's motto: "Be courageous in innovation, say no to 'impossible'." This slightly unusual slogan guides the actions of every employee and helps the company overcome one difficulty after another.

While building up everyone's confidence, an urgent issue to address was the company's cash flow. Li organized the leadership team to develop a new performance system. Firstly, they implemented incentive activities based on monthly business. These activities yielded significant results within the first two months, with a 28.13% increase in average monthly revenue and a turnaround from losses to profits. Secondly, they established monthly performance assessment, overdue account collection measures, and excess profit reward systems to address specific issues effectively, and adjusted according to the company's development dynamics.

After a series of adjustments, the UAE Overseas Warehouse has established a "self-operated +

shared" development strategy. It was successfully selected as one of the first national-level international marketing service public platforms and obtained the highest-level A-grade certification for China's public overseas warehouse standardization. The company took the lead in providing distribution and consignment services for new energy vehicles and parts, collaborating with upstream vehicle companies, manufacturers, and channel distributors, aiming to create a base for Chinese new energy vehicles in the Middle East region. By 2022, the UAE Overseas Warehouse's operating revenue increased by 109% year-on-year, and achieved a net profit by 26% year-on-year.

Corporate culture is the soul of a great company. To create a distinctive culture, he promotes the learning of the group's culture and national policies within the CNBM UAE, displaying the essence of the group's culture in the exhibition rooms. Innovation is the core value of CNBM Group and the core of the corporate culture to be shaped in the CNBM UAE. The company emphasizes the importance of proactively identifying and overcoming challenges, which is the innovation culture of the UAE company.

In terms of business development, Li proactively creates pressure for performance growth, including developing new business and new clients. On the financial side, obtaining credit limits that match with business development is a responsibility. In risk control, the responsibility is to enhance the ability to distinguish between good and bad customers, conduct risk rating, and use risk control tools to achieve the company's annual goals. In procurement, the company upholds the concept of large-scale procurement and establishes cooperative partnerships with resource providers that align with the goal of building a world-class building materials enterprise.

In addition to internal development, the company has not neglected external promotion. Li secured the support of the UAE China Cross Border E-Commerce Association, successfully listing the UAE overseas warehouse, and received strong support from government such as the Royal Family of Dubai, the China Development and Reform Commission Southern Cooperation Center, the CCPIT, Henan Provincial Commerce Department, and the Pingshan District of Shenzhen City, etc. A number of senior officials such as representatives from the Royal Family of Dubai, the Royal Family of Abu Dhabi and representative of Djibouti Government also visited the company. Li actively introduced CNBM Group and enhanced CNBM's brand image overseas. The CNBM UAE has appeared on well-known media such as Middle East Chinese Newspaper and Dingxin Media for many times to promote the company's concept of cooperation and development with various market players.

In order to enable the CNBM UAE to enter a healthy development track as soon as possible, Li has not reunited with his family for seventeen consecutive months. He has a daughter and a son. His wife said that when their son was born, he was sticking to his post in Ethiopia project and could not witness the birth of their son. Now his son is two years old, and he has not celebrated his birthday once. As a father, he felt somewhat incompetent. He puts his heart and soul into his work and believes that the prosperity of the CNBM UAE also contains a glory belonging to his family!

Personal Insights In my 17 years of service at CNBM, I have been motivated by a sense of honor to fulfill my responsibilities. The relationship between the Middle East and China is at the best time in history. The Dubai team will continue to embody the spirit of innovation and reject the notion of "impossible." We will strive to make greater contributions to the Group's growth, and write a new chapter in the high-quality development of the "Belt and Road" Initiative!

奋斗的青春最美丽

张钰昇

2018 年加入中国建材

现任中建投巴新公司莫港建材店店长

在我们海外公司，一批批中建投青年将热情和汗水播撒在海外热土，张钰昇正是这些青年奋斗者中的一员。这位 1995 年出生的福建小伙在工作中一直冲锋在前，干劲十足，2021 年带领门店实现业绩逆势上涨，并获得“中央企业优秀共青团员”荣誉称号。

张钰昇敢于应对工作中的挑战，为了开拓市场，他与销售团队来到西不列颠岛坎德里安特区，由于该地区偏远落后，条件艰苦，是市场开拓的“空白地带”。他带领团队克服重重困难，深入一线考察，成功挖掘当地政府和企业客户，也成功搭建了双方长期合作的桥梁。客户深情地说：“此前我们从未见过任何供应商来到这里，中建投巴新公司是第一个，你们好样的！”通过日复一日的磨砺成长，张钰昇成长为一名高效专业的门店经营能手。

新冠疫情对这里薄弱的疾病防控体系发起了巨大挑战。关键时刻，张钰昇毫不退缩，严格落实公司防疫小组的安排部署。戴口罩、勤洗手、测体温，这些基本的防疫举措店内已重复了不下千遍。他组织及时采购生活和防疫物资，做好防疫工作的后勤保障；安排司机团队，为离家远的员工提供出行帮助，最大限度降低密集传播的可能性；每日派专人跟进员工及其家人的身体状况，提供力所能及的医疗帮助和答疑解惑，让疫情里的紧张忙碌与温暖关爱并存，在抗疫战斗中发挥青年人的责任和担当。

在做好疫情防控的同时，店面也要高效运营。他带领员工全面翻新门店基础设施，优化店面展示，客流显著提升；配合布局小米之家生态产品，大幅增加门店市场份额；加班加点处理客户的需求和反馈，获得客户的一致好评。一分耕耘，一分收获，他所在门店当年客单价同比提高 23.87%，销售总额同比上涨 9.49%。

做新时代的奋斗者，奋斗的青春最美丽。今年已经是张钰昇在公司工作的第五个年头，他说：“海外工作生活中的酸甜苦辣余味绕心头，感谢家人、朋友、同事逆境中给予我力量，顺境中为我敲警钟，奋斗的青春永不落幕，让我们继续加油！”

在距离祖国 6260 公里的巴布亚新几内亚，我们年轻的巴新中方团队，蓬勃的青春与国家“一带一路”倡议、中国建材集团国际化战略同频共振，让奋斗的青春色彩更加绚烂。奋斗，是青春的底色！（中建投巴新公司首都建材店）

个人体会

古之立大事者，不唯有超世之才，亦必有坚忍不拔之志。正如中建投巴新公司嘹亮的口号所说，“建设更好的未来”，多彩的生活，需自己的双手去打造，人生的道路，需自己的双脚去探索。

Striving of the Youth is the Most Beautiful

Zhang Yusheng

Joined CNBM in 2018

The Branch Manager of BNBM PNG LTD Pom Hardware Branch

In our overseas companies, batches of young people from China Construction Investment have spread their enthusiasm and responsibility to overseas. Zhang Yusheng is the epitome of these young strivers. This Fujian guy born in 1995 is full of energy. In 2021, his team achieved a performance increase against the downward trend, and won the honorary title of "Excellent Communist Youth League Member of Central Enterprise".

Zhang Yusheng dared to meet the challenges in his work. In order to expand the market, he and his sales team came to the Candrian District of West Britain. Due to the remoteness and backwardness of this area and the difficult conditions, it is a "blank area" for market development. His team overcame many difficulties and went deep into the frontline inspection, successfully found local government and corporate customers, and successfully built a bridge for long-term cooperation between the two parties. The customer said affectionately, "We did not see any supplier come here before. BNBM is the first one. BNBM good". Through daily hard work and growth, Zhang Yusheng has become an efficient and professional branch management expert.

The epidemic had posed a huge challenge to Papua New Guinea's weak disease prevention and control system. At the critical moment, Zhang Yusheng did not flinch and strictly implemented the arrangements and deployments of the Papua New Guinea company's epidemic prevention team. Wearing masks, washing hands frequently, and taking body temperature, these basic epidemic prevention measures have been repeated no less than a thousand times in the branch. He organized the timely purchase of living and epidemic prevention materials to provide logistical support for epidemic prevention work. He arranged a team of drivers to provide travel assistance for employees far away from home, minimizing the possibility of transmission. He followed up physical conditions of employees and their families everyday, providing medical help and answering questions as much as possible, providing warmth and care despite the busy epidemic prevention work, and giving full play of the responsibility of young people in the fight against the epidemic.

While doing a good job in epidemic prevention and control, the branch must also operate efficiently. He led the staff to comprehensively renovate the branch infrastructure, optimize the branch display, and significantly increase the customer flow. He resolutely implemented the iron processing factory and cooperated with the layout of Mi Home's ecological products, which greatly increased the branch's market share. He worked overtime to deal with customer needs and feedback, and won the unanimous approval of customers' praise. No pains, no gains. The unit price of his branch has increased by 23.87% year-on-year, and the total sales volume has increased by 9.49% year-on-year.

To be a striver in the new era, the striving youth is the most beautiful. This year is Zhang Yusheng's fifth year working in Papua New Guinea. He said, "The ups and downs of overseas work and life linger in my heart. I am grateful to my family, friends and colleagues for giving me strength in adversity. Prosperity is a wake-up call for me. The strive of youth will never end. Let's keep going!"

In Papua New Guinea, which is 6,260 kilometers away from the motherland, our young Chinese team resonates with the country's "Belt and Road" construction and China National Building Material Group's internationalization strategy, making the youthful color of striving more brilliant. Striving is the foundation of youth.

Personal Insights Those who achieved major accomplishments in ancient times not only had talents beyond the world, but also had the will to persevere. Just like PNG's loud and clear slogan, "Building the Better Future". A colorful life needs to be built with one's own hands, and the road of life needs to be explored by one's own feet.

行劳神不倦　奋斗趁年华

黎江涛

2016 年加入中国建材

现任中建投瓦努阿图维尔克有限公司维拉店店长

黎江涛说：“我出生在湖北的一个小山村，打小就是穷人的孩子。正是因为公司给了平台，让我能够充分发挥，展现才能，才有了自己的小家，我尤其珍惜海外的工作机会。”

在中建投巴新公司工作期间，由于海外业务拓展需要，员工经常要紧急支援其他外岛门店，中建投巴新公司每家门店几乎都出现过黎江涛的身影。

2018 年，他临时接到出差外岛的任务，因为时间仓促，来不及打包行李，他顺手塞了两件工服进背包，这一走就一直没有机会回去，这就是他经常戏说的“两件工服打天下”的故事。

同事们也都因此笑称他为“自由人”“革命的一块砖，哪里需要哪里搬”。“自由人”的称号蕴含着他不断打磨学习的耐心、不断开拓市场的决心，以及为了公司发展不退缩的初心。

2019 年，黎江涛调至中建投瓦努阿图维尔克有限公司任维拉店店长，在新的工作环境下面临更多挑战。2020 年，长期奔波的他患上了结石，面对身体不适，他对工作没有半分怠慢，始终坚守心中的信念，奋战在工作一线。

2021 年，瓦努阿图经济持续下滑，公司业务遭到冲击，黎江涛积极寻求突破口，拓展合作对象，推出沥青搅拌机、水泥搅拌机、地板革等新产品，弥补产品线的空白；通过水泥单品批发量的骤增，全面引爆市场，维拉店业绩逆势上扬，销售额同比增长 11.94%。

身处海外，黎江涛也不忘弘扬中华传统美

德，积极投身慈善事业，中瓦人民相互守望、互帮互助。台风过后桑托岛受灾严重，瓦努阿图维尔克有限公司及时捐赠，他加班至深夜，做好物资调拨，主动参加社区建设，尽心尽力帮助学校、医疗部门等机构渡过难关。面对疫情的严峻形势，他始终在前线督促和鼓励员工做好疫情防控及疫苗接种工作，用真情和友爱增进互信友谊，为共建和谐温馨的员工大家庭贡献自己的力量。

行劳神不倦，奋斗趁年华。黎江涛至今已坚守海外 6 年多，并通过自己的努力在武汉安家。他的故事是我们奋斗在海外一线有志青年的真实写照，吃苦耐劳，默默耕耘，用双手创造属于自己的幸福生活。（中建投瓦努阿图维尔克有限公司）

个人体会 非常荣幸能够加入中建投瓦努阿图维尔克有限公司的大家庭，在海外工作的 6 年多里，一步步从运营经理成长为店长，我收获很多。“与公司共同进步”是我的座右铭。面对公司新的发展战略，我将通过不断的学习，使自己成长为助力公司海外开拓的优秀人才。

Seizing the Day with Diligence and Hard Work

Li Jiangtao

Joined CNBM in 2016

The Branch Manager of Wilco Limited Vila Hardware Branch

"I was born in a small rural village in Hubei Province. As a child of poor parents, I took on responsibilities at an early age. It is precisely because my company has provided me with a platform that I am able to fully display my talents and create my own life. I especially cherish the opportunity to work abroad." says Li Jiangtao.

During his time working for BNBM, due to the need to expand overseas business, employees frequently had to rush to support other outer island branchs. Almost every branch in BNBM has seen Li Jiangtao's presence.

In 2018, he was called upon to go on a mission to an outer island at short notice, leaving no time to pack his luggage. He quickly put two sets of work uniforms into his backpack and left without ever returning. This became the story behind his frequent jokes about "two sets of work uniforms carrying him forward."

His colleagues also nicknamed him the "free man", as he constantly sharpened his skills, expanded the market, and remained true to his original intentions of contributing to the company's development.

In 2019, Li Jiangtao was transferred to the Vila Branch as the banch manager. In this new environment, he faced even more challenges. In 2020, the long-term exhaustion resulted in calculus. Despite his physical discomfort, he never wavered in his faith and fought tirelessly on the front lines of his work.

In 2021, Vanuatu's economy continued to decline and the company's business was affected. Li Jiangtao actively sought opportunities to break through and expand partnerships by introducing new products such as asphalt mixers, cement mixers, and floor tiles. By filling in the blank product line, sales of cement individual units surged dramatically, setting off a full-blown market boom. The Vila Branch's performance rebounded, with sales increasing by 11.94% year-on-year.

While working overseas, Li Jiangtao never forgets to vigorously promote traditional Chinese virtues and actively participates in philanthropic activities. China and Vanuatu people look out for and help each other. After the cyclone in Santo, Vanuatu was severely damaged. Vila Branch timely donated money. And Li Jiangtao worked overtime until late at night to distribute materials. He actively participated in community building, made every effort to implement humanitarian assistance to schools,

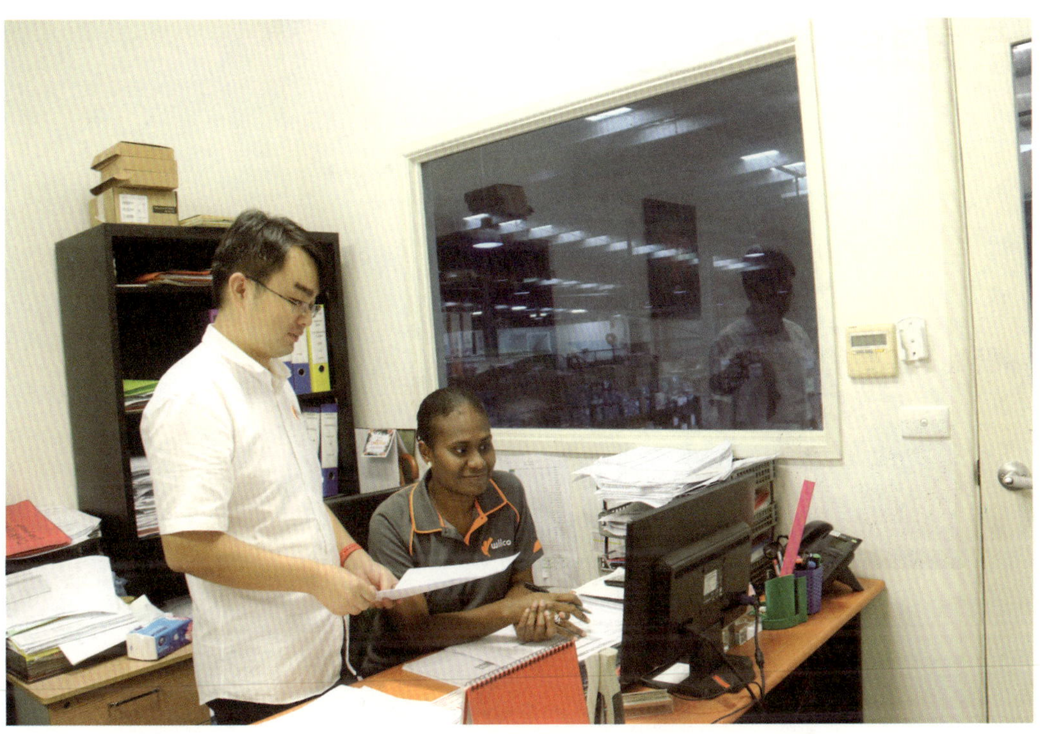

medical departments and other institutions. In the face of the severe situation of the Covid-19, he was always on the front line to urge and encourage employees to do a good job in Covid-19 prevention and vaccination. By using sincerity and friendship, they enhanced mutual trust and friendship, and contributed their own strength to build a harmonious and warm home together.

Seizing the day with diligence and hard work. Li Jiangtao has been working overseas for over six years now, having established a family in Wuhan through his own efforts. His story is a true portrayal of the hardworking young people who aspire to work abroad. They endure hardships, quietly cultivate their skills, and use their hands to create their own happy lives.

Personal Insights It is a great honor to be a part of the Vanuatu family! Over the past six years of working overseas, I have grown from an Operation Manager to a Branch Manager step by step, and gained a lot. "Progress together with the company" is my motto. In the face of the new development strategy, I will continue to learn and improve, making myself an excellent talent to assist company's overseas expansion.

点亮非洲热土上的光

张啸

2012 年加入中国建材

现任中材高新市场部业务经理

为响应国家“一带一路”倡议，中材高新与特变电工联合承建莱索托王国 70MW 光伏工程 EPC 建设项目，旨在解决当地电力紧张问题。张啸作为在火力发电和光伏发电均有丰富经验的老电力人，新冠疫情初期便身先士卒，前往非洲热土，开启一段基建之旅，一去便是两年之久。从一期开工、并网发电，到如今二期稳步推进，他见证了莱索托这个拥有丰富清洁能源的国家从时常断电到如今在非洲版图上第一次用耀眼光芒的绿电永久点亮万家灯火，他内心颇感欣慰和自豪。

2015 年，一下飞机，张啸就被接到了“国中国”——南非包围之中的高山王国莱索托，映入他眼帘的除了荒芜的土地便是人们殷切的眼神。当地业主代表急切地用手向远处画了个圈，项目的原始选址地已初步确定，这次的主要任务虽然是调研该国发展光伏项目建设的可行性，如勘探系统接入条件、初步勘测设计、提供技术支持服务等，但他已然能感受到当地人对改变电力紧张现状的急迫感。

2021 年 6 月，张啸被正式派往莱索托，作为项目经理负责此次光伏发电建设项目 EPC 工程管理、设备采购、技术支持以及运维监督工作。

据他回忆，刚到营地，看到一排排崭新的白色板房有序地矗立在带有铁丝网的高大红砖围墙内，一片片待平整的丘陵、小洼地和分布在场区各处零星且色彩不一的机械设备，以及三五成群推着小斗车的非洲兄弟时，如何面对接下来无数的晨暮交替还不得而知，但他深知从那一刻起，真正的考验开始了。

尽管远离故土和家人，在境外开展项目枯燥乏味，但既然接受了工作安排就不能“掉链子”。张啸快速融入项目团队，了解现场工序、人力机械配置情况、工程进度计划，并推动项目朝预定目标前进。他认为，自己代表中材高新驻海外现场，必须以高度负责任的态度全力以赴，树立央企海外良好形象。

项目虽按计划进行，但国际环境变幻莫测，对于传统施工分包单位来说，在现有模式下弊

端逐步显露。

对此，张啸根据现场施工计划，把握项目进度总体方向，利用自身多年行业技术优势和经验，合理规划设备堆放和开箱检查及进出场地安全管理工作，并主动协助完成电站接入系统分界点的设置方案。在完成电气安装初步单体调试阶段后，由于他全面熟悉国家及光伏行业标准规范，于是结合自身运维管理经验，编制完成本该由合作方负责的项目运维大纲和运维细则，并将其作为后期招标运维技术规范书，满足了对外主合同要求并得到了领导的称赞。

受疫情冲击，货运费上涨、光伏产品和变电设备无法按期到港等不利因素的影响，经历了定预案、被推翻、再修改以及不停反复停工、施工，张啸积累了宝贵的项目管理经验，也提高了应急处置能力。如今，莱索托光伏一期30MW项目已成功并网，获得了莱索托政府的高度评价："为莱索托点亮了希望之光"。莱索托是南部非洲发展共同体成员国，这个高山之国享有"非洲水塔"的称号，拥有丰富的太阳能和水利资源，在建的二期项目以及未来承建的项目完成后，莱索托有望从目前的能源输入国转变为绿色电力输出国，可源源不断地供应清洁绿色能源到南非、博茨瓦纳等周边国家。

（中材高新材料股份有限公司）

个人体会　海外建设有苦有累，非洲驻扎有得有失，但愿以我所长，见证一个又一个拔地而起的光伏工程丰碑，让阳光点亮这片热土上的美好未来，同时我将深耕非洲市场，为集团在海外再建一个"中国建材"贡献更大力量。

Light up the African Soil

Zhang Xiao

Joined CNBM in 2012

The Business Manager of the Marketing Department of SINOMA Advanced Materials Company

In response to the country's "Belt and Road" Initiative, SINOMA took the lead to jointly construct a 70MW photovoltaic project with TBEA in the Kingdom of Lesotho, aiming to solve its power shortage problem. As a veteran electrician with extensive experience in both thermal and photovoltaic power generation, Zhang Xiao was the first to embark on his journey to Africa at the beginning of the epidemic to build infrastructure, which lasted for two years. He witnessed the process from the first phase of construction and connection to the grid, to the now steadily progressing second phase. He is very pleased and proud to see that Lesotho, a country rich in clean energy, has been able to permanently light up the lights with dazzling green electricity for the first time in Africa. And the achievement has been built from scratch with frequent power cuts.

The first time Zhang Xiao went to Lesotho in 2015, he was transported to the mountain kingdom surrounded by South Africa, thus the name of the "country in a country", as soon as he got off the plane. What he saw was not only the barren land but also people's eager eyes for light. The representative of the local owner eagerly drew a circle in the distance with his hand, and the original site of the project was initially determined. Although the main task was to investigate the feasibility of developing photovoltaic projects in the country, such as access conditions for exploration systems, preliminary survey and design, and providing technical support services, their sense of urgency in relieving the tight demand for electricity was already felt.

In June 2021, Zhang Xiao was sent to Lesotho as the project manager, responsible for the EPC engineering management, equipment procurement, technical support and operation and maintenance supervision of the photovoltaic power generation construction project.

He recalls that when he first arrived at the camp and saw the rows of new white cubicles standing in an orderly fashion within a tall red brick fence with barbed wire, the hills and hollows to be levelled, colourful machinery scattered all over the site, as well as the groups of African brothers pushing their little carts, he didn't know how to face the countless shifts that would follow. But he did knew the real challenge had begun.

Although far away from his homeland and family, and facing boring work of carrying out projects overseas, he accepted the work arrangement and could not drop the ball until the last minute. He quickly integrated into the project team, got to know the site procedures, manpower and machinery allocation, the project progress plan, and pushed the project forward towards the intended goal. He believed that he had to do his best in a highly responsible manner to establish a good image of the enterprise overseas.

Although the project was carried out according to the plan, the international environment was unpredictable, and the disadvantages of the existing model were gradually becoming apparent for traditional construction subcontractors.

In this regard, according to the site construction plan, Zhang Xiao used his rich technical advantages and experience in the industry to grasp the overall direction of the project progress, and rationally planned the equipment stacking, unpacking inspection and the safety management of entering and leaving the site, and actively assisted in completing the setting scheme of the demarcation point of the power station access system. After completing the initial monomer commissioning phase of electrical installation, he completed the project operation and maintenance outline and rules using his knowledge and experience of the national and photovoltaic industry standards and specifications, which could be used as the guide for more biddings in the future. It greatly met the requirements of the external main contract and was praised by the leadership of the consortium.

After more than 700 days in Lesotho, with adverse factors such as the epidemic, the increase of freight charges, the failure of on time arrival of the photovoltaic products and power transformation equipment, etc., Zhang Xiao was enabled to accumulate valuable project management experience and improve the emergency handling ability after countless overturns and revisions of the plan and repeated stoppage and construction. Today, the first phase of the 30MW PV project in Lesotho has been successfully connected to the grid, which has been unanimously recognized by the government of Lesotho. The project has been appreciated as “the light of hope for Lesotho”. Known as the "Water Tower of Africa," this alpine country is a member of the Southern African Development Community (SADC). It has abundant solar and water resources and is expected to transform itself from an energy importer into a green electricity exporter with the completion of the second phase of the project, which is currently under construction, and future projects. It will continuously supply clean and green electricity to South Africa, Botswana and other neighboring southern African countries.

Personal Insights Overseas construction has its hardships, and there are gains and losses in Africa. But I hope to use my strengths to witness one after another rising monuments of photovoltaic projects so that the sunlight can light up a bright future for the country. And at the same time, I will continue developing the African market to contribute more to the Group's overseas construction of another "CNBM"overseas.

电瓷小将的海外开拓记

张冰

2018 年加入中国建材

现任中材电瓷国际贸易部业务员

北美、南美、欧洲等地区是中材江西电瓷电气有限公司（以下简称中材电瓷）主导产品特高压纯瓷棒型产品的主要海外销售市场。张冰自 2018 年起作为中材电瓷国际贸易部的一员，在加拿大致力于特高压电瓷海外市场开发，在开拓业务的同时，为企业建立了良好的国际形象。

M 公司坐落在加拿大魁北克省希尔布鲁克的一个以法语为主语言的小镇上，是工业区内规模最大的公司。该公司的采购负责人，是一位早期移民到此的越南裔长者，张冰曾多次向他提出接洽拜访的请求，但他总是找种种理由避而不见。尽管如此，张冰并没有因此感到沮丧，也从未想过放弃。

经过反复思索，张冰想到了一个看似不相关但能接近他的方式。镇上有越南米粉店，该店是这个小镇上唯一的越南餐馆。他猜想，"家乡胃"应该是每个异乡人思乡之情的最好体现。于是，张冰开始了"等待"计划，一等就是一个月，终于有一天，在米粉店里等到了这位采购负责人，那一刻，张冰心中的兴奋和激动无法用言语来形容。他知道，机会来了。

在采购负责人等餐的时候，张冰主动上前与他打招呼。起初，他似乎有些警惕，但张冰并没有因此退缩，而是尽可能地保持友好和亲切的态度，与他聊些日常的话题，再逐渐将话题引向工作，并询问他对中国供应商的看法。在交流的过程中，张冰发现他明显对中国制造业存在着一些偏见。于是他决定改变策略，没有过多地谈论中材电瓷的产品，反而介绍起了中国制造业的现状，如中国近年来在制造业方面取得的巨大成就，以及政府推行的高质量发展战略等。

在接下来的日子里，张冰开始陆续接到对方的电话，询问中材电瓷产品的细节，以及索要样品。每次通话，张冰都耐心地回答他的问题，并详细讲解中材电瓷产品的优点和特性。每一次交谈，张冰都能感觉到他对中国制造商的信心在增加，经过几个月的努力，张冰成功地从他手里获得了第一份订单。时至今日，中材电瓷已成为 M 公司的主要供应商。

张冰说："这些年感触最深的是，除了中材电瓷的产品更新迭代提高竞争力外，采用因地制宜的销售手段和打破西方对中国的固有认知是实现海外市场成功的关键。"

一方面，创新销售的思维和方法是企业拓展海外市场的重要手段。销售人员不仅要了解并熟悉目标市场的消费需求和习惯，还要主动寻找和创造机会，建立和维护良好的客户关系。另一方面，尽管中国的制造业在过去几十年里取得了令人瞩目的成绩，但一些海外国家对中国制造业的认知仍停留在过去，这种认知不仅限制了我国制造业在海外市场的发展，也影响了我国品牌的形象。张冰深刻感受到，主动讲好中国经济发展的故事、中国人民奋斗圆梦的故事、实事求是地展现中国制造业实力是建立起良好沟通的前提和基础。

2023 年，恰逢"一带一路"倡议提出 10 周年。10 年来，越来越多的国家和地区通过"一带一路"倡议，与中国共享发展机遇。10 年间，无数中国人为"一带一路"建设添砖加瓦，作为奋斗在一线的海外工作者，张冰感到无比骄傲和自豪。

张冰说："唯实创新行致远、踔厉奋发向未来，唯有奋斗才能创造美好未来。我要继续讲好中国故事，讲好中材电瓷产品和服务的故事，努力为世界电力行业贡献力量，为中国建材集团海外建设添砖加瓦。"（中材江西电瓷电气有限公司）

个人体会 海外市场开拓要建立在具有强大竞争力的产品基础上，更重要的是要因地制宜，同海外客户建立良好的沟通和交流机制，同时要向外宣传和展示我国制造业的品牌形象，这才是制胜法宝。

Porcelain Pioneer and His Journey Overseas

Zhang Bing

Joined CNBM in 2018

Salesman in the International Trade Department of SINOMA Electric Porcelain

Overseas markets such as North America, South America, and Europe are major markets for SINOMA Insulator and Electricity Co., Ltd (referred to as "SINOMA Insulator" hereafter). Its leading product, extra-high voltage porcelain post insulators, accounts for over 30% of the company's market share. Since 2018, Zhang Bing, as a member of SINOMA Insulator's International Business Department, has been dedicated to the development of the overseas market for extra-high voltage insulators in Canada. He has been working to establish a positive image for the company and the country.

M Company is located in Sherbrooke, a predominantly French-speaking town in the province of Quebec, Canada. It is the largest company in the industrial area. The procurement manager of the company is the person Zhang Bing has been trying to connect with after several attempts. He is an elderly Vietnamese immigrant who settled in the town early on. Zhang Bing has made multiple requests to meet and establish contact with him, but he always found various excuses to avoid it. However, Zhang Bing did not feel discouraged and never gave up on this potential customer.

Zhang Bing came up with an apparently unrelated but convenient way to approach him. There was a Vietnamese noodle shop in town, the only Vietnamese restaurant in the small town. He speculated that "homeland cuisine" would be the best embodiment of homesickness for every foreigner. So Zhang Bing started his "waiting" plan. After waiting for a whole month, he finally spotted the procurement manager at the noodle shop. In that moment, Zhang Bing couldn't describe the excitement and thrill with words. He knew that the opportunity had come.

When the procurement manager was waiting for his food, Zhang Bing took the initiative to greet him. At first, he seemed somewhat wary, but Zhang Bing did not retreat. Instead, he maintained a friendly and approachable attitude, engaging in casual conversations and gradually shifting the topic towards work. He inquired about the procurement manager's views on Chinese suppliers. However, during the course of their conversation, Zhang Bing noticed his clear biases and prejudices against Chinese manufacturing. Zhang Bing decided to change his strategy and refrained from discussing SINOMA Insulator's products. Instead, he introduced the current state of Chinese manufacturing, highlighting the tremendous achievements China has made in the manufacturing

industry in recent years and the government's high-quality development strategy.

In the following days, Zhang Bing started receiving calls from the procurement manager, inquiring about the details of SINOMA Insulator's products and requesting samples. Each time, Zhang Bing patiently answered his questions and explained the advantages and features of SINOMA Insulator's products. The more conversations were made, the more evident that the procurement manager's confidence in Chinese manufacturers was growing. After several months of effort, Zhang Bing successfully secured the first order from him. Today, SINOMA Insulator has become a major supplier for M Company.

"The most profound realization over the years has been that, in addition to SINOMA Insulator and Electricity Co., Ltd.'s product updates and iterations to improve competitiveness, adopting localized sales strategies and challenging Western perceptions of China are the key to achieving success in overseas markets.", Zhang Bing says.

On one hand, innovative thinking and methods in sales are crucial for expanding into foreign markets. It is important not only to understand and familiarize oneself with the consumer demands and habits of the target market, but also to actively seek and create opportunities while establishing and maintaining good customer relationships. On the other hand, despite the remarkable achievements of China's manufacturing industry in the past few decades, some overseas countries still hold outdated perceptions of Chinese manufacturing, which not only limit the development of China's manufacturing industry in overseas markets but also affect the image of Chinese brands. Zhang Bing deeply feels the need to proactively tell the story of China's economic development and the Chinese people's struggle to achieve their dreams, presenting the true strength of China's manufacturing industry which is the premise and foundation for establishing good communication.

Since 2016, SINOMA Insulator has experienced rapid development, with total revenue increasing by 120% by the end of 2022. The proportion of direct and indirect exports has increased from 24% to 48%. The revenue target for 2023 has increased by 200% compared to 2016 and has already achieved over half of the target by mid-year. These impressive achievements would not have been possible without the efforts of every SINOMA Insulator employee.

Zhang Bing said that "Only through practical innovation can we achieve long-term success, and only through diligent efforts can we create a better future. I will continue to 'tell the story of China' and share the story of SINOMA Insulator's products and services. I will strive to bring tangible value and impact to the global power industry and contribute to the overseas development of China Building Materials Group."

Personal Insights In the process of expanding into international markets, besides focusing on product innovation, iteration, and improving core competitiveness, adopting location-specific and non-traditional methods of communication and breaking Western stereotypes and biases towards China's manufacturing industry are the keys to success.

海外员工成长记

宋炯生

1990 年加入中国建材
现任秦皇岛玻璃工业研究设计院有限公司经营部副部长

2017 年 10 月，作为项目经理的宋炯生来到了新德里。他虽身经百战，海外管理经验丰富，但迎接他的仍是全新的挑战。这是秦皇岛院首个境外多子项指导安装的总包浮法玻璃工程项目，而印度国内没有专业的玻璃熔窑、锡槽安装砌筑队伍，且禁止外国劳务进口；货运时效、语言沟通和异国环境等多方面的不确定性因素给项目的进程带来了巨大的挑战。

面对重重困难，宋炯生不禁陷入了沉思，内心也充满了焦虑；但他始终坚信，凭借秦皇岛院深厚的技术底蕴、扎实的专业水平、先进的装备和丰富的海外经验，一定能让中国“洛阳浮法玻璃工艺”在南亚次大陆结出硕果！

2017 年 8 月 8 日，窑炉砌筑开始；2017 年 12 月 17 日，窑炉点火。短短 4 个多月的安装时间里，宋炯生带领项目组成员克服了来自工作、生活中的重重困难：当地施工队不懂安装，宋炯生就从最基础的看图和砌筑教起，把木料都锯不直的小工培养成了行家里手；语言不通，宋炯生就挤出时间，给大家突击培训英语，运用肢体语言、以物指代等各种方法；饮食不便，宋炯生就提出了“自力更生，不劳动者不得食”的口号，带头做饭。那个烟火缭绕的厨房、时不时前来偷食的猴子成了每个人记忆中不可磨灭的印记。

每一个工段、每一项任务都能看到宋炯生奔波的身影：从组织施工图设计、统筹海运发货到土建监理、窑炉锡槽砌筑、设备电气的安装调试、试生产、达产达标，宋炯生以他在科研、设计、建设、生产多个领域的专业素养推动项目不断进行。

每逢佳节，宋炯生总是发动项目组成员，一起动手准备团圆饭；对业主外聘的中国籍技术人员，宋炯生本着同胞之谊在工作、生活中多次予以帮助。施工队长说：“宋工，你放心，我们都是中国人，绝不会给中国人丢脸。”掷地有声的话语令他不禁潸然泪下。就这样，在大家的共同努力下，2017 年年底，总包浮法玻璃工程项目整体安装完成，顺利点火。

曙光将至，而任务依旧繁重。2017 年 12

月 17 日，项目举行点火仪式。此时距预定的投产时间仅有不到一个月，却要完成设备安装、系统调试等一系列复杂、艰难的任务，这意味着每一个人都必须全力以赴、加班加点。此时，忙碌的宋炯生每日辗转难眠，他的睡眠时间极短，依旧随时处理来自业主、施工队的各种问题。长久的高强度工作使他日渐消瘦，疲惫到在等待就餐时就会悄然入睡。

功夫不负有心人。2018 年 1 月 16 日凌晨 6 点，GP 项目终于成功引板，欢呼和喜悦的气氛洋溢在整个现场，业主当场赞扬宋炯生和秦院团队——“你们团队太棒了！你们把不可能的事情变成了可能的事”而此时，宋炯生已患上尿结石，但他仍带病坚持工作，直至春节后，待项目稳定后方才回国治疗。在印度的一年，劳累的工作和艰苦的生活使他减重 40 斤，他却仅以一句“印度是个减肥的好地方”轻轻带过。

2018 年，GP 项目的正式运营给业主带来了显著的社会、经济效益，成为中国“洛阳浮法玻璃工艺”技术在印度的一个靓丽的标志，也为秦皇岛院打开印度市场发挥了巨大推动作用。2020 年，项目获评“2020 年度建材行业优秀工程设计二等奖”，为宋炯生和项目组多年来的辛勤付出画上了一个圆满的句号。

像宋炯生一样的建材人有很多。从 2004 年乌克兰“无产阶级”玻璃厂 350t/d 浮法总包开始，将近 20 年的时间里，秦皇岛院先后有近千人投身到海外建设的浪潮中，为中国“洛阳浮法玻璃工艺”走向世界而奉献着。

（秦皇岛玻璃工业研究设计院有限公司）

虽然离开印度已 5 年，但忆起那段轰轰烈烈的日子，依旧感慨万千。他表示：项目的一次次历练不仅能增添员工的阅历和经验，更能实现新一代建材人的成长和秦院精神的传承。希望有着 70 余年历史的秦院在“一带一路”的进程中“老树发新枝”，再创辉煌！

A Growth Story of Overseas Staff First Arrival in New Delhi

Song Jiongsheng

Joined CNBM in 1990

The Deputy/vice Director of the Business Department of QGRDI

In October 2017, Song Jiongsheng arrived in New Delhi as the project manager. Despite his rich experience in overseas management, he faced lots of new challenges. This was QGRDI's first overseas turnkey float glass project with multiple sub-projects to guide the installation, and there were neither professional glass melting furnace and tin bath installation nor masonry teams in India, and the import of foreign labour was prohibited. Various uncertainties such as local workers' installation level, shipments timeliness, language barrier and foreign environment also posed huge challenges to the project process.

In the face of these difficulties, Song Jiongsheng was deep in thought and filled with anxiety. However, he was convinced that with QGRDI's profound technical background, solid professionalism, advanced equipment and rich overseas experience, he would be able to make "Luoyang Float Glass Process" bear fruit in the South Asian subcontinent!

On 8 August 2017, the masonry of the furnace began. On 17 December 2017, the furnace started heating up. In just four months, Song Jiongsheng led the project team overcome many difficulties on work and life. The local construction team did not know how to install, so he taught them the most basic skills, and trained junior workers who could not even reading the wood straight into becoming experts. With the language barrier, Mr Song made time to give everyone English training, using various methods of communication such as body language and object referencing. When food supply was not guaranteed, Mr Song put forward the slogan of "self-reliance and no food for those who do not work" and took the lead in cooking. The smoky kitchen and the monkeys that came to steal food from time to time became indelible marks in everyone's memory.

Song Jiongsheng could be seen running around in every section and every task: from organizing the design of the construction drawings, coordinating the shipments, to the supervision of the civil construction, the masonry of the furnace, the installation and commissioning of the equipment and electrical machines, the trial production, and the achievement of the production standards. Mr Song used his professionalism in many fields of scientific research, design, construction and production to push the project forward.

The overseas life has witnessed the friendship among all Chinese on site. On each festival, Mr Song always mobilized all project team members to prepare dinner together. For the owner's external Chinese technicians, Mr Song helped them many times in their work and life in the spirit of compatriot friendship. And when the construction team leader told him that "Mr Song, rest assured. We are all Chinese, and we will never let you down!" He was touched to tears. With the joint efforts of everyone, the overall installation of the float glass project was completed and successfully heated up at the end of 2017.

The dawn is coming, but the task is still heavy. On December 17, 2017, the project held a heating up ceremony. It was less than a month before the scheduled commissioning time, but it had to complete a series of complex and difficult tasks such as equipment installation and system commissioning, which means that everyone must go all out and work overtime. Song Jiongsheng was so busy that he couldn't sleep. His sleep time was extremely short, but he still dealt with various problems from the owner and the construction team at any time. Long and intense work made him thinner and so tired that he fell asleep quietly while waiting for dinner.

The effort payed off. At 6 a.m. on January 16, 2018, the GP project finally successfully launched the board. The atmosphere of cheers and joy filled the place, and the owner praised Mr Song and our team on site - "Your team is fantastic and made impossible to possible"! At this time, Mr Song had already suffered from urolithiasis, but he still persisted on working until after the Spring Festival. Finally, he returned to China for treatment after

achieving stable production. In a year in India, his tiring work and hard life made him lose 40 pounds, but he brushed it aside with "India is a good place to lose weight".

In 2018, the official operation of the GP project brought remarkable social and economic benefits to the owner, which became a beautiful symbol of "Luoyang Float Glass Process" in India, and also played a great role in promoting the opening of the Indian market in QGRDI. In 2020, the project was awarded the "Second Prize for Excellent Engineering Design in the Building Materials Industry in 2020 ", which brought a successful end to the hard work of Mr Song and the project team over the years.

There are still many people in QGRDI like Mr Song. Starting from Ukrain 350t/d Float Glass Production Line in 2004, in nearly 20 years, nearly 1,000 people in QGRDI have devoted themselves to the wave of overseas construction, fighting and dedicating to "Luoyang Float Glass Process" to the world.

Personal Insights Although he has been away form India for 5 years, those vigorous days are still unforgettable experience for him. He says that through the experience of the project, it can not only increase the experience of employees, but also realize the growth of a new generation of QGRDI and the inheritance of the spirit of QGRDI . He hopes that QGRDI, which has a history of more than 70 years, will create glory again in the process of "Belt and Road" Initiative .

不忘初心 热血筑梦

李承翰
2015 年 10 月加入中国建材
现任中建材国际贸易有限公司复合材料部项目经理

许多年之后，面对千奇百怪的客户询盘，和神态各异的外国面孔，我依然会想起，2015 年 10 月 12 日的那个早上。秋高气爽，万里无云，一名 24 岁的青年雄赳赳气昂昂，怀着无限憧憬走进中建材国际贸易有限公司（以下简称中建材国贸）。故事从这里开始。

2017 年，我单枪匹马带着公司电脑和样本册，踏上了飞往越南河内的航班。越南是一个发展很快的国家，也是一个充满未知的国家。刚下飞机我就恍如隔世，这是越南的首都机场呢，还是老家南阳的城市机场？等我坐出租车到达市区后，看到周边低矮的民居建筑，路边拿着篮子兜售水果饮料的老奶奶时，我再次迷茫了：我是不是回到我们县城出差了？

有次拜访客户时，出租车司机却怎么也找不到客户的公司。尽管他是一名本地司机，车上安装了 GPS 地图，途中还不停打电话问路，我们仍然在“未知”中前进。当司机又一次停在了一片荒芜的三岔路口去问路的时候，我忽然有种“古道西风瘦马，断肠人在天涯”的苍凉感。

终于安全抵达客户公司，虽然这位当地司机并不熟悉环境，我仍拜托他在门口等我谈判出来。因为他走了，我就找不到车子回酒店了。在这样充满未知挑战的条件下，我仍每天拜访 3 位客户。功夫不负有心人，很快我与当地最大的几家经销商建立起联系并开展合作，把越南的客户数量和订单量翻倍了。

假如你觉得越南的出差是最辛苦的，那我会说：这个结论下早了。2018 年，我们部门只有 1 个菲律宾客户，于是我又开启新的任务线。

菲律宾的枪支毒品、治安乱象在国际上一直备受关注。在出发前一天，我唯一的客户发来一张冲锋枪的照片，对我说：“我的朋友，来的时候穿上防弹衣，我带着武器去接你。”我当时非常震惊，赶紧跑去商场买了一件真皮马甲带上飞机。当然，它没有派上用场，因为马尼拉太热了。

到了菲律宾，我发现每个公司、商店、宾

馆门口都会有保安，每个保安都携带枪支武器。没有公司内部的确认，我就被持枪的保安请到门外等待。这个场景，让我想起在战争中前去谈判的使者：即使外面大雨滂沱，台风在 2 个小时后就要来了，我也只能安静地在堡垒外面等待。

就在这样的条件下，我的菲律宾客户数量从 1 个变成 10 多个，中建材国贸成为菲律宾进口中国玻纤最大的供应商之一，在当地有了较大品牌影响力，客户采购也指明中建材产品优先。

经过不懈努力，我的业务成绩有了不小的突破。2019 年个人订单利润约 339 万元，2020 年达到 240 万元，2021 年达到 412 万元。2017—2022 年成交新客户和激活休眠客户 61 个，生效订单 704 个。

在集团推动国际化的进程中，中建材国贸凭借在玻纤行业 20 多年来的深耕细作以及团队成员的共同扶持成长，一直稳坐玻纤产品出口量贸易商领先的行业地位，并为集团内部企业提供出口服务增值，促进互利共赢。正是更多的中建材青年投身海外，不畏艰险，才成就了中建材国贸业务往来遍布 160 多个国家、客户数量超过 2500 个的骄人成绩。

一个个建材人不畏艰险，投身贸易；以星星之火，铸就燎原之势。

一群群建材人脚踏实地，精益求精；打造“国之大材”，服务“国之重器”。

一代代中国青年不忘初心，牢记使命，乘帆远航，披荆斩棘。

最后，我用一首诗歌与各位优秀的中建材青年共勉：

相信不屈不挠的努力，

相信战胜死亡的力量，

相信未来，热爱中建材。

（中建材国际贸易有限公司）

加入中国建材大家庭，我学习了很多，也成长了很多。中建材国贸完善的国际化培训体系和风控体系为我们开拓国际市场保驾护航，集团内部协同为我们的业务提供强大后盾。我们一定不负组织嘱托，为集团公司国际化战略添砖加瓦！

Upholding Original Aspiration and Building Dreams with Passion

Li Chenghan

Joined CNBM in 2015

The Project Manager of the Composite Materials Department of CNBM International Corporation

Years have passed, and when faced with various inquiries from customers from diverse backgrounds and foreign faces with different expressions, I still recall vividly that morning of October 12th, 2015. The sky was clear and crisp, and I, a 24-year-old young man full of vigor and high spirits, walked into CNBM International Corporation with boundless aspirations. And thus began my story.

After rigorous training, I ultimately faced a defining moment. In 2017, I set off for Hanoi, Vietnam, carrying a laptop and a product catalogue. Vietnam is a land of rapid development and also great unknowns. Stepping off the plane, I felt as if I had been transported to a different world. Was this truly the airport in capital Hanoi, or had I mistakenly arrived at the city airport back in my hometown of Nanyang? My confusion only grew as I rode in a taxi and gazed at the low-rise residential buildings and elderly women selling fruit and drinks along the roadside. I couldn't help but wonder if I had returned to my hometown.

During a visit to a Vietnamese client, my taxi driver failed to locate the company's premises. Despite being a local driver and having GPS installed in the car, he continuously made calls to ask for directions and we found ourselves wandering in the realms of the "unknown". As the driver once again stopped at a deserted crossroads to inquire about the location, I suddenly felt a strong sense of desolation.

After finally arriving safely at the client's company, I asked the local taxi driver, who was unfamiliar with the area, to wait for me at the entrance. Because if he left, I would not be able to get a ride back to hotel. Despite facing such unknown challenges, I continued to visit three clients each day. My perseverance paid off, as I soon established contacts with several of the largest local distributors and conducted cooperation. Finally, I successfully doubled the number of Vietnamese clients and orders.

If you think that business trips to Vietnam are the toughest, I would say that conclusion was made prematurely. In 2018, our department had only one Philippine client, so I was entrusted with the critical mission of expanding our market presence in the region.

The issues of firearm proliferation, drug problems, and public safety concerns in the Philippines have garnered significant attention on the international stage. On the day before I departed for the trip, my client sent me a photo of an assault rifle and said: "My friend, wear a bulletproof vest, and I will pick you up with my weapons." I was shocked and quickly bought a leather jacket for the trip. However, it proved to be unnecessary given the heat in Manila that rendered the vest impractical.

Upon arrival, I immediately noticed armed security personnel stationed outside every company, store and hotel entrance. Without proper identification, I was directed to wait outside by the armed guards. This scene reminded me of a negotiator in a war zone: Even in the pouring rain and the imminent arrival of a typhoon in two hours, the negotiator had to patiently wait outside the fortress.

With these challenging conditions, our client base in the Philippines grew exponentially from a mere one to over ten, positioning CNBM International Corporation as one of the largest suppliers of Chinese fiberglass imports in the Philippines. CMAX has become a well-known brand in the local market, and customers specifically request products from CNBM International Corporation.

Through unwavering diligence, my business achievements have soared to new heights. In 2019, my personal order profit was about 3.39 million yuan, 2.4 million yuan in 2020, and 4.12 million yuan in 2021. From 2017 to 2022, I successfully dealt with 61 new and dormant clients, leading to 704 effective orders.

In the pursuit of internationalization, CNBM International Corporation has established itself as a leading fiberglass product exporter and trading company, thanks to over two decades of unwavering dedication to the industry and the staunch support of its formidable team. This success has also added value to the CNBM by offering export services, creating mutual benefits and win-win scenarios. The persistence and willingness of more young

CNBM personnel to venture abroad in the face of challenges are key contributors to the exceptional achievement of CNBM International Corporation with business operations spanning more than 160 countries with more than 2,500 clients.

One after another, the fearless CNBM International Corporation staff dive into the world of trade, igniting a prairie fire with each tiny spark of effort.

CNBM professionals commit themselves to excellence, pursuing it with unwavering efforts to forge monumental works that serve the nation.

Generation upon generation of Chinese youth recall their original aspirations, remaining true to the mission and setting sail under the Party's guidance to discover new lands.

In conclusion, I'd like to share an inspiring poem with all the young CNBMers:

Believe in tenacious, unwavering endeavor,

Believe in the power that conquers death,

Believe in the future and love CNBM forever.

Personal Insights My time with CNBM has been a tremendous learning and growth experience for me. The comprehensive international training and risk control systems provided by CNBM International Corporation have paved the way for our success in expanding into international markets, while the internal collaboration within the group has served as a sturdy backbone for our business operations. We are fully dedicated to meeting the company's expectations and making significant contributions to CNBM's internationalization strategy!

星光不问赶路人 唯以奋进致青春

陶伟

2012 年加入中国建材

现任中建材国际贸易有限公司钢材事业部卷板部部门副经理

陶伟，2012 年大学毕业后加入中建材国际贸易有限公司，10 年间，他从腼腆青涩的外贸新人成了坚强可靠的业务骨干，他描画着自己的梦想蓝图，将青春融入公司的发展事业中，与公司共同成长，共同进步。

陶伟入职后进入了钢材事业部。钢材是大宗类基础建材，交易订单额动辄上千万元，行情天天变化，操作订单须时时处处谨慎小心。他主攻南美市场，为与客户保持“热联”，经常忙到凌晨一两点才下班；出差国外时白天走访客户，晚上联系报价，每天只能睡四五个小时。虽然是零起点，但功夫不负有心人，陶伟凭借突出的外语优势和敢想敢拼的工作劲头，短短两年时间就成交了 14 个新客户的订单，信心大增的同时，他把目光投向了更远处。

2016 年，陶伟开始接触中美洲的主流市场——巴拿马，该国对卷板类钢材产品需求非常大，但市场竞争异常激烈，业内普遍认为，这里是钢厂的天下，但贸易商很难分得一杯羹。陶伟凭借实战经验和前期市场数据分析，从询盘、试订单到正式订单，逐步与当地几个主要客户建立了合作关系。近些年，他与这些客户合作日益稳固，中建材国贸不仅在巴拿马站稳了脚跟，更发展为当地卷板类钢材主要供应商之一，“CNBM”也成为当地广为人知的品牌。

成功没有独家秘诀。陶伟正是凭着持之以恒的韧劲和真诚服务的理念，才赢得客户的信任和青睐。2012 年，在广交会上成交的哥斯达黎加客户是他的第一个客户，至今仍是公司的金牌客户。从 2013 年起，他坚持为一位潜在的秘鲁客户每周更新价格，7 年不曾间断。终于在 2021 年取得实质性进展，该客户连续签订了两个大订单。

天道酬勤，凭借骄人的业绩，在 2018 年至 2019 年，陶伟被评为“中国建材集团青年岗位能手”；在 2021 年，他获得“中建材进出口有限公司优秀员工”的荣誉，并以个人完成的 1400 多万元销售利润为中建材国贸首次

进入集团“亿元俱乐部”作出突出贡献。

作为落实集团“走出去”战略的重要平台，中建材国贸准确把握新形势下共建“一带一路”的总体要求，在国际化道路上不惧挑战，风雨兼程，笃定前行，彰显中国制造的实力，不断加强“CNBM”品牌在“一带一路”国家和地区的推广。

外贸通商自古是国际交往的重要桥梁，作为身居一线的业务员，陶伟深知排头兵的重要性，他坚持扎实做好本职工作，认真践行公司构建全产业链的外贸综合服务平台战略。通过夜以继日地攻坚克难，以陶伟为代表的建材人正一点一点地把“CNBM”这个品牌推向世界，不断促进国内与“一带一路”沿线国家和地区的市场相通、产业相融。他们以朴素生动的方式，向世界讲述中国的发展故事；他们以脚踏实地的奋斗，书写新时代中国青年的风采。

我们正走在一条充满希望的道路上。我相信，只要我们相向而行，心连心，不后退，不停步，我们终能迎来路路相连、美美与共的那一天。在筑造中国梦的伟大过程中，需要有成千上万个像陶伟这样的一线人员精耕细作，不畏艰难，甘于奉献。“路漫漫其修远兮，吾将上下而求索”，作为重任在肩的建材人，我们将矢志不渝为早日实现“中国梦”贡献自己的青春力量！（中建材国际贸易有限公司）

作为一线国际贸易业务员，我们应该扎实做好本职工作，推动“CNBM”品牌在“一带一路”国家和地区的推广与发展，助力北新集团成为有行业影响力的现代数智供应链集成服务商的战略愿景。

Embracing Youthful through Unwavering Effort

Tao Wei

Joined CNBM in 2012.

The Deputy Manager of the Coil Department of the Steel Division of CNBM International Corporation.

Tao Wei joined CNBM International Corporation in 2012 after graduating from university. Over the past decade, he has transformed from a shy and inexperienced foreign trade newcomer to a strong and reliable business backbone. During the process, he has been drawing his own blueprint for his dreams while also dedicating his youth to the development of the company, progressing together as one.

After joining the company, Tao Wei became a member of the steel department and dealt with the bulk building material. With trading orders often exceeding tens of millions of yuan and the market constantly fluctuating, handling orders requires the utmost care and attention to detail. Tao focused on the South American market and worked late until one or two in the morning to stay connected with clients. While on business trips overseas, he spent his days visiting clients and his nights following up on quotes, sleeping only four to five hours each day. Despite starting from scratch, his unwavering dedication and exceptional language proficiency allowed him to close deals with 14 new clients in just two years, boosting his confidence and inspiring him to set sights even further.

In 2016, Tao began to explore Panama market, which is the major market in Central America with a high demand for steel products, particularly coils. Despite the intense competition in the market and widespread industry belief that it was dominated by steel mills and trading company could hardly get a market share, Tao persevered. Drawing from his practical experience and analyzing early market data, he gradually established cooperative relationships with several key local clients, from initial inquiries and trial orders to final contracts. Over the years, these partnerships have solidified, cementing CNBM International Corporation's position as one of the major suppliers of coil steel in Panama, with the "CNBM" brand becoming widely recognized within the local market.

There is no one secret to success. Tao Wei's unwavering persistence and dedication towards sincere service have enabled him to win the trust and appreciation of his clients. His first client from Costa Rica, secured during the 2012 Canton Fair, remains the company's most valued client. Since 2013, Tao Wei has consistently updated prices for a potential client from Peru on a weekly basis, without interruption for seven years. This unwavering commitment finally bore fruit in 2021, when this client signed two substantial contracts in succession.

Through hard work and outstanding achievements, Tao was recognized as a "Young Expert in CNBM" in the 2018-2019 fiscal year. In 2021, he was honored with the title "Outstanding Employee of CNBM Import and Export Co., Ltd", having contributed more than 14 million RMB in sales profits, which also enabled the company to become a member of the "Billion Yuan Club" within CNBM.

As an essential platform for implementing the "Going Global" strategy of CNBM, CNBM International Corporation accurately grasps the overall requirements of building the Belt and Road Initiative under new circumstances. The company has faced challenges with determination and progressed through difficulties to showcase the strength of China's manufacturing, constantly strengthening its presence in countries and regions along the Belt and Road.

International trade and commerce have always played a crucial role in facilitating international relations. As a front-line salesperson, Tao deeply understands the importance of this position. He insists on executing his work with excellence and diligently implementing CNBM International Corporation's strategy of "constructing a comprehensive foreign trade service platform across the entire industry chain". Overcoming obstacles day and night, CNBM International Corporation staff, with Tao as the representative, are gradually pushing the "CNBM" brand out into the world. They work tirelessly to promote market connectivity and industrial integration with countries and regions along the Belt and Road. They narrate the story of China's development to the world in a simple yet vivid way, while their steadfast efforts depict the outstanding capabilities of Chinese youths in the new era.

President Xi Jinping once stated that "We are walking on a path full of hope. I believe that as long as we walk hand in hand, move forward together, and never stop or retreat, we will finally reach the day when we are all connected and share common prosperity." In the magnificent process of realizing the Chinese Dream, we need thousands of dedicated frontline workers like Tao Wei, who are unafraid of difficulties and willing to make contributions. As noted by the poet Qu Yuan, the road ahead is long and arduous, yet we are determined to explore with a pioneering spirit. The Belt and Road Initiative is a logical extension of the great Chinese Dream. As members of CNBM International Corporation, we carry a great responsibility on our shoulders. We are committed to serving the construction of the BRI and contributing our youth towards achieving the "Chinese Dream" as soon as possible.

Personal Insights As frontline international trade professionals, we must diligently and effectively fulfill our responsibilities, driving the development of the "CNBM" brand within these regions. This will also assist Beijing New Building Materials Public Limited Company in achieving its strategic objective of becoming an influential service provider of smart and digitally intelligent integrated supply chains. It is also the most direct and effective way for us to participate in the construction of the Belt and Road Initiative.

坚守是一份责任，更是一份担当。

深耕一线的海外建材人，以恒心守望初心，用平凡铸就不凡。

他们，不惧骄阳，不畏热浪，恪守工匠初心，谱写丝路华章。

Perseverance embodies a sense of responsibility and a dedicated commitment.

CNBM's overseas employees keep their original aspirations with perseverance and make extraordinary achievements in ordinary posts.

Undeterred by any weather, they work diligently and embody the true spirit of craftsmanship, crafting an extraordinary chapter in the saga of the Belt and Road Initiative.

一路坚守篇

FORGING AHEAD WITH UNWAVERING PERSEVERANCE

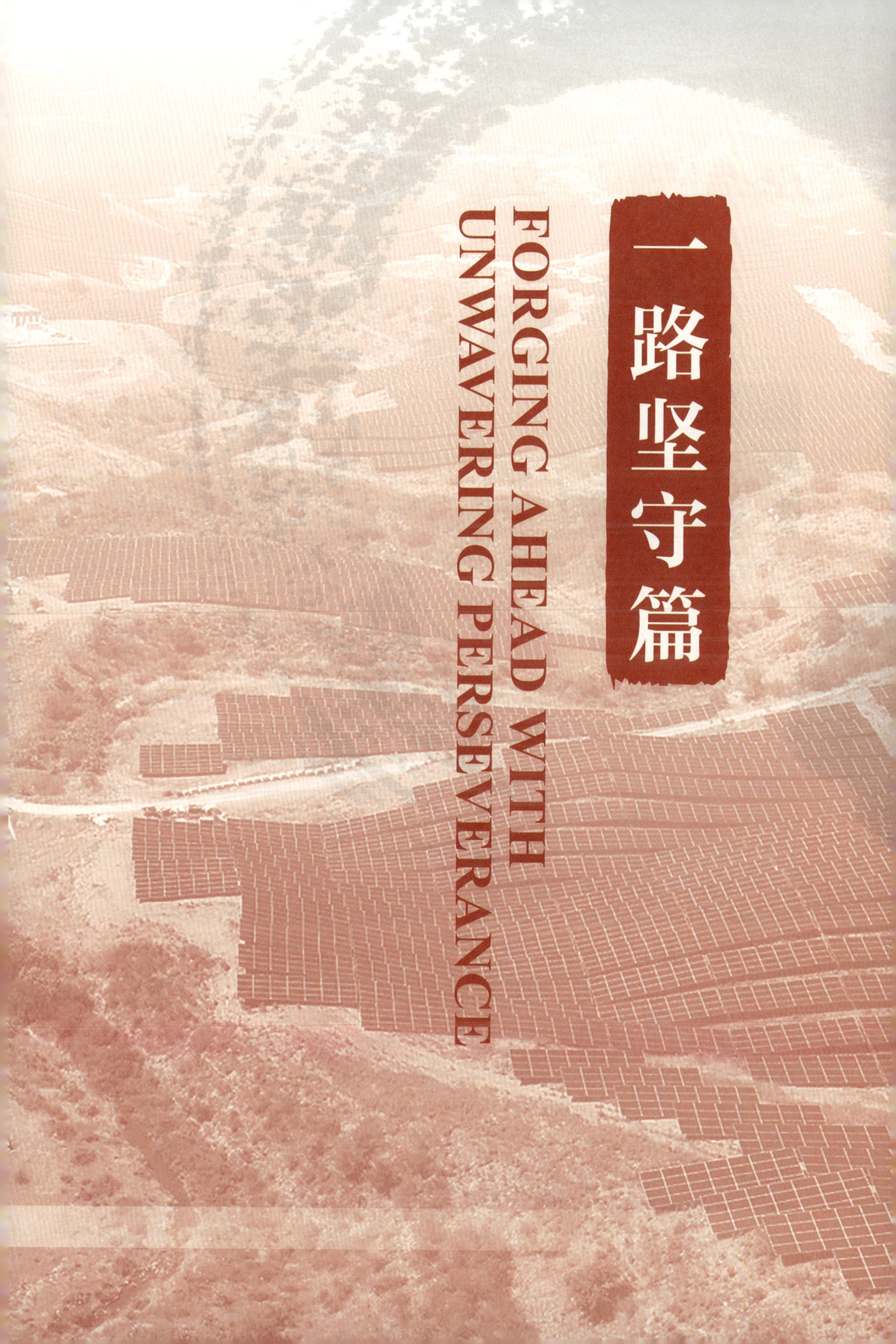

85 后技改能手立足海外坚守责任

曹旭

2008 年加入中国建材

现任中国建材赞比亚工业园安全环保部主管

2018 年，曹旭积极响应中国建材集团国际化发展号召，主动申请远赴海外，加入中国建材赞比亚工业园的运营管理工作中。在新的起点上，从跑现场到中控，再到公司安环主管，5 年多光景一晃而过。

2018 年 3 月，曹旭到达异国他乡赞比亚，面对新奇的环境，曹旭需要尽快去适应和熟悉，同时，他深知自己作为第一批进入现场的试生产人员，首要任务便是熟悉同事和生产工艺，为将来更好地领导工作打好基础。每天他都和小伙伴们拿上图纸跑现场，积极联系设备厂家和调试人员，不断与同事交流学习，增长理论知识，2018 年 5 月试生产工作顺利进行。

在 2019 年调入安环部后，他充分调用在国内多次参加“一级安标”建设的经验，在安环管理前辈不辞辛劳的基础上，持续推动安环工作标准化，完善现场安环状况。在本地员工和外包单位员工安环意识远低于国内、且赞比亚安环形势复杂程度远高于国内的情况下，他直面问题，以合规合法化建设为目标，找重点、定计划，从最基础做起，持续推动安环体系的建设，取得了有目共睹的成效。

他不懂就问、不会就学，正视自己的不足，从点滴做起，积极应对复杂的安环形势以及 2020 年暴发的新冠疫情，始终保持一颗临危不惧的平常心，按部就班，一步步推动安环防疫工作顺利进行。合法合规化是安环工作的核心，他从零开始，查阅资料，自行翻译常用且重要的法律法规，一条一条地学习，时常与本地人咨询一些不成文的本地安环管理规定，从多个角度了解赞比亚安环法律法规。在这个近四百人的公司里，他每周组织本地安环经理和安环主管会议，以提高他们的工作积极性、责任感、规范性、专业化为重点内容，从本地经理和主管开始，一层一层地传导下去，引导本地员工，同时，定目标、定计划、常沟通、同努力、共协作，将安环工作提高到一个新台阶，赢得了本地员工的赞誉。

“安全环保优先”是公司安环管理的理念，。合法合规化成了公司安环管理的核心，尤其是在境外，在公司领导的带领下，他积极动员各层级员工开展学习安环法律法规和风俗习惯、与本地人来往以及打交道时的注意事项等。在公司领导的支持下，他全力做好本地安环员工的管理工作，并发挥他们的模范带头作用，积极开展合法合规化自查自纠，以务实、高效的处事风格获得了公司领导的好评。

远赴海外，5 年多光景一晃而过，但责任和热爱一直常在。（中国建材赞比亚工业园）

作为安环部的一员，我全力做好本地安环员工的管理工作，并发挥他们的模范带头作用，积极开展合法合规化自查自纠，以务实、高效的处事风格获得了公司领导的好评。

A Post-1985s Technician Rooted Overseas with Responsibility

Cao Xu

Joined CNBM in 2008

The Supervisor of the Safety and Environmental Protection Department of CNBM Zambia Industrial Park

In 2018, Cao Xu actively responded to the call for national development of CNBM Group and voluntarily applied to go abroad to join the operational management work of CNBM Zambia Industrial Park. He has achieved rapid progress from being in the field, to central control, and then to his current position as a Safety and Environmental Protection Supervisor in just over five years' time from the new starting point.

Cao Xu arrived in Zambia in March 2018. He needed to adapt to the new and unfamiliar environment promptly. As one of the first on-site pilot production personnel, he knew that his top priority was to familiarize himself with colleagues and the production processes, and to solid foundation for his future work. Every day, he and his colleagues went to the site with the drawings in hand, contacted equipment manufacturers and commissioning personnel actively. He kept communicating and learning with colleagues to increase his theoretical knowledge. The pilot production work proceeded smoothly in May 2018.

After being transferred to the Safety and Environmental Protection Department in 2019, he fully leveraged his experience of participating in the "Grade-One Safety Standard" construction in China to continuously promote standardized safety and environmental management, and improve on-site safety and environmental conditions on the basis of the hard work of his colleagues. The safety and environmental awareness of local employees and outsourcing unit employees was far lower than that of China, and the complexity of the safety and environmental situation in Zambia was far higher than that in China. Facing these challenges, he focused on key points, made plans from the basics, continuously promoted the construction of the safety and environmental system, and finally achieved visible results.

Cao Xu never stopped learning and asking questions. Facing his own shortcomings, he started from the basics. He actively responded to the complex safety and environmental situation and the outbreak of the COVID-19 pandemic in 2020. For all this, he still remained calm in the face of danger. He steadily promoted the successful implementation of safety and environmental protection measures. He started from scratch, consulted relevant information, and translated key legal regulations. He learned from local people about the unwritten local safety and environmental management norms from different perspectives to understand the laws and regulations in Zambia. In the company of nearly 400 people, he organized weekly meetings with local safety and environmental managers and supervisors, focused on improving their work enthusiasm, sense of responsibility, standardization and professionalization. Starting with local managers and supervisors, and then to local employees, he guided them to set goals, plan, communicate regularly, and work together to elevate safety and environmental work to a higher level. He won the praise of local employees.

"Safety and environmental protection are the priority" is the philosophy of the company's safety and environmental management. Zambia adopts the legal system of the United Kingdom. Compliance and legalization are the core of the company's safety and environmental management, especially overseas. Under the leadership of the company's leaders, he actively mobilized employees at all levels to learn about safety and environmental laws and regulations, customs, and how to interact with local people and deal with related matters. With the support of the company leaders, he made every

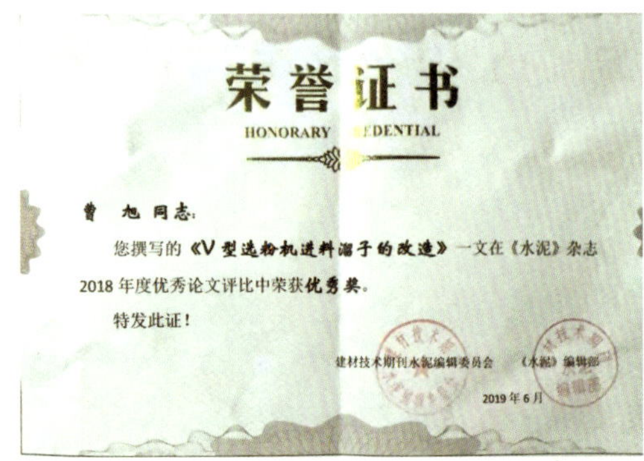

荣誉证书

HONORARY EDENTIAL

曾 旭 同志：

您撰写的《V型选粉机进料溜子的改造》一文在《水泥》杂志2018年度优秀论文评比中荣获优秀奖。

特发此证！

建材技术期刊水泥编辑委员会 《水泥》编辑部

2019年6月

effort to manage local safety and environmental employees, and encouraged them to play a leading role. He also actively carried out self-examinations and self-corrections among employees. His pragmatic and efficient style of doing things has won praise from company leaders.

Having spent more than five years overseas, his heart has always been full of responsibility and passion.

Personal Insights As a member of the Safety and Environmental Department, I do my best to manage local employees, and give full play to their exemplary and leading role, actively carry out self-inspection and self-correction. I have won praise from the company's leaders for my pragmatic and efficient handling style.

抓培训 促提升的海外一线“老兵”

裴新亮

2019 年加入中国建材

现任北新建材工业（坦桑尼亚）有限公司石膏板坦桑厂车间主任

裴新亮，从事纸面石膏板生产工作近20年，拥有丰富的生产和管理经验，是一名不折不扣的一线专家。他于 2019 年 5 月入职北新建材工业（坦桑尼亚）有限公司（以下简称“坦桑北新”。自入职以来，他积极参与旧生产线升级改造和新生产线建设，为坦桑北新打造过硬技术队伍和生产线建设工作作出了巨大贡献。

坦桑尼亚当地员工文化水平普遍偏低、操作能力较差，缺乏安全意识和风险辨识能力。作为车间主任，裴新亮在了解了相关情况之后，与生产团队积极探索实践，依据不同岗位制订培训计划，进而打造出了一套特有的“一带两训”员工管理模式，有力提升了当地员工队伍水平。“一带”为师带徒，“两训”分为基本技能培训（包括员工守则、三级安全教育）和专业技能、岗位技能培训。

裴新亮利用自己的语言优势和丰富的生产经验，全面参与坦桑尼亚当地员工的培养工作，着力提升坦桑尼亚当地员工的技能水平，满足新生产线的岗位要求。在员工能力提升培训过程中，裴新亮不断创新形式，把课堂搬到车间。中方员工利用检修时间在车间现场教学，仔细讲解各岗位操作技能，不断提升当地员工的实操水平，培养每位员工的多面技能，工作效率显著提升。在后期生产过程中，面对生产上各类突发情况，他对坦桑当地员工言传身教、倾囊相授，不断提高他们解决突发事件的应急能力，为实现减员增效、提升劳动生产率作出了重大贡献。

新冠疫情暴发初期，非洲医药短缺、航班熔断，坦桑尼亚当时没有相关疫情防控措施，坦桑北新的生产经营和新建生产线项目建设遇到了前所未有的挑战。一是疫情防控工作，二是原有老生产线的正常运营，三是新建生产线项目也要稳步推进，裴新亮以大局为重，服从公司安排，始终坚守工作岗位，两年半未回国休假，全身心地扑到坦桑北新的建设上来。由于客观原因，新线设备均要从国内进口，84 个集装箱近 2000 吨设备，裴新亮与留守的 10 名中方员工和 6 名当地员工一起，不顾日晒雨

淋，每天爬上集装箱进行挂钩固定、检查和卸货。他们平均每天卸货 100 多吨，同时，还要保证所有集装箱能及时卸货并还回。凭着一腔热血和精湛技艺，他们从未让坦桑北新产生过滞箱费用。

最终，2022 年 1 月，坦桑北新年产 1500 万平方米石膏板生产线顺利投产，生产能耗下降 36%，自动化程度及产品质量大幅提升，产品品质达到欧美国家标准，成为东非地区最大、最先进的石膏板生产线之一。该生产线的投产也使得作为本地化生产的坦桑北新产品质量和性能全面超过当地品牌和进口产品，实现了“本地化生产可全面替代进口”的目标。

北新建材通过输出先进产能，扎根“一带一路”建设，所取得的成果凝结了以裴新亮为代表的一批海外建设者的心血与汗水，为提升当地石膏板产业水平、规范当地石膏板产品标准作出了积极贡献。〔北新建材工业（坦桑尼亚）有限公司〕

个人体会

自 2019 年加入公司以来，我经历了老线生产、新线建设、试生产和正常投产，见证了公司各项工作的逐步完善与壮大。近 5 年的经历使我收获很多，坦桑北新的过去有我的参与，我倍感自豪。我坚信坦桑北新的未来会因我们共同的努力而更加辉煌。

A Frontline "Veteran" Overseas, Focused on Training and Promotion

Pei Xinliang

Joined CNBM in 2019

The Workshop Director of the gypsum board plant of BNBM Building Materials Industry (Tanzania) Limited

Pei Xinliang, with nearly 20 years of experience in paper-faced gypsum board production, possesses extensive production and management expertise, making him an unquestionable specialist at the front line. He joined BNBM Tanzania in May 2019 and has since actively participated in upgrading and transforming existing production lines, as well as establishing new ones, contributing significantly to the development of a highly skilled technical team and production line construction in BNBM Tanzania.

Local employees in Tanzania generally have lower levels of cultural literacy, limited operational abilities, and lack safety awareness and risk identification skills. As the workshop director, Pei Xinliang, upon understanding these issues, actively explored and implemented practical solutions with the production team. By designing tailored training programs for different positions, they developed a unique "OneGuidance and Two-Training" employee management mode, which effectively enhanced the skills of the local workforce. "One Guidance" represents the guidance of a mentor for apprentices, while "Two Trainings" refer to basic skills training (including employee codes of conduct and three-level safety education) and professional and job-specific skills training.

Utilizing his language advantage and extensive production experience, Pei Xinliang actively participated in the training of local employees in Tanzania, focusing on improving their skill levels to meet the job requirements of the new production line. In the training to improve employee capability, Pei continuously introduced new forms of training, such as bringing the classroom into the workshop. Chinese employees utilized maintenance time in the workshop for on-site teaching, carefully explaining operational skills for each position. This approach consistently elevated the practical skills of the local employees and cultivated their multiple skills needed in work, leading to a significant improvement in work efficiency. When faced with various unexpected situations during the production at later stages, he helped local employees improve their capability to handle emergencies by giving instructions and examples, thereby making a significant contribution to downsizing the staff and improving the labor efficiency.

During the initial outbreak of the pandemic, Africa faced a shortage of medical supplies and flight disruptions, and Tanzania had no specific measures for epidemic prevention and control, imposing unprecedented challenges to BNBM Tanzania's production and operation, as well as to new product

line construction. On one hand, there was the task of epidemic prevention and control, while on the other hand, the existing old production line needed to operate normally, and the construction of the new production line had to progress steadily. In front of all these challenges, Pei Xinliang followed the company's arrangements, steadfastly held his position and did not return home for vacation for two and a half years, dedicating himself entirely to the construction of BNBM Tanzania. Due to objective reasons, all the equipment for the new line, weighing nearly 2,000 tons loaded in 84 containers, was imported from China. Pei Xinliang, together with 10 Chinese employees and 6 local employees who stayed behind, climbed onto the containers to secure, inspect, and unload the goods every day, disregarding the weather. They unloaded more than 100 tons per day while ensuring that all containers were promptly unloaded and returned. With their passion and superb skills, BNBM Tanzania never incurred any demurrage.

Finally, in January 2022, BNBM Tanzania's production line with an annual output of 15 million square meters of gypsum board was successfully put into operation. The production energy consumption decreased by 36%, and the level of automation and product quality significantly improved, which met the standards of European and American countries, making it one of the largest and most advanced gypsum board production lines in East Africa. The operation of this line also allowed the localized BNBM Tanzania brand to comprehensively surpass other local and imported brands in terms of product quality and performance, achieving complete substitution of imported products through localized production.

Through the deployment of advanced production capacity, BNBM has firmly rooted itself in the construction of the Belt and Road Initiative. The achievements it has made are a testament to the efforts of a group of overseas builders, represented by Pei Xinliang, who have actively contributed to improving local gypsum board industry and standardizing local gypsum board products.

Personal Insights Since joining the company in 2019, I have experienced the production of the old line, the construction of the new line, the trial production, and the normal operation, and have witnessed the gradual optimization of various work in the company. I have reaped a lot in the past five years, and I am proud to have played a part in the development of BNBM Tanzania. The future of BNBM Tanzania will be even more brilliant with our concerted efforts.

敢打敢拼的坦桑北新销售尖兵

法迪利·维纳斯·琼维

2018 年加入中国建材

现任北新建材工业（坦桑尼亚）有限公司营销部大区经理

“真诚是最好的销售技巧。”法迪利这样认为。法迪利于 2018 年 6 月北新建材工业（坦桑尼亚）有限公司（以下简称“坦桑北新”）成立之初入职，现任坦桑北新营销部的大区经理。

他吃苦耐劳、踏实肯干，从事销售工作 10 余年，尝尽销售工作的酸甜苦辣，却始终一心扑在工作上，多渠道收集行业信息，敏锐察觉市场变化，高度关注客户需求、存在的问题及应对措施，积累了丰富的工作经验。他销售业绩突出，对坦桑尼亚市场和客户有深刻的理解。

2022 年，他深入空白地区破局坦桑尼亚西部湖区市场，为坦桑北新投产后产能得以迅速提升作出巨大贡献。2022 年坦桑北新销量实现大幅增长，与法迪利带领的销售团队做出的努力密不可分。在坦桑北新工作的 5 年间，他爱岗敬业、不畏艰难，出色地完成公司交派的各项任务。

坦桑尼亚是北新建材全球化的第一个生产基地，2018 年刚成立时，营销工作的开展还处于摸索阶段。法迪利凭借多年的销售经验、对建材行业的了解和对市场的敏锐度，协助公司制订销售制度、梳理发货流程、筛分优质客户、制订风控策略等，既保证了营销工作得以顺利交接过渡，又确保了坦桑北新的平稳发展。在这套制度的有效运行下，坦桑北新成立 5 年来一直保持着年末应收账款为零的佳绩。

2022 年 1 月，坦桑北新建设的东非地区规模最大、技术最先进的石膏板生产线之一的石膏板新线竣工投产，产品质量达到国际水平，它是北新建材坚定推进国际化战略道路上的里程碑，同时，产能较之前扩大了几倍，给坦桑北新的营销团队带来了更大挑战。

法迪利急公司之所急，身先士卒，冲在一线开拓空白市场。此时，正值坦桑尼亚的高温天气，烈日似火、酷暑难耐，他顶着高温跑遍了湖区 5 省，竭尽全力想把产品推销出去。经过他的不懈努力，坦桑北新在湖区已有稳定的 25 家客户，市场占有率增长 30% 以上。此外，他还带领着业务员成功开发了坦桑尼亚西部市场以及境外的乌干达和布隆迪等市场，攻克了一个个空白市场。产品一经投放市场，无论是外观平整度还是内在质量强度都很快得到了客户的广泛认可。

法迪利非常擅长维护客情关系，因为经常真诚地给予客户情感上的温暖和关怀，由此获得客户充分的信任。他对待客户可谓于细微处见真情，不嫌事小、不怕麻烦。不论是节假日的问候，还是日常的迎来送往，抑或是在客户生病时给予问候和关怀，他都能处理得当，甚至利用业余时间帮助客户的孩子补习功课，协助客户招聘员工，为客户的家人安排就医等，真正做到了先交朋友再做生意。

有一次，客户 SANYA 的卡车在提货返程的途中因为夜黑路滑发生了车祸，法迪利得到消息后，连夜赶到现场协助客户处理事故，帮忙叫救护车把司机送往医院，又联系交警到现场拍照保存证据，并且一直留在事故地点看守货物，直至客户 SANYA 赶到现场后才离开。客户非常感激他，事后专门到公司表达了谢意。直到现在，这位客户一直是坦桑北新的独家代理，这在坦桑尼亚的建材行业中非常少见。

法迪利踏实肯干、勤勉努力的工作态度，攻坚克难、敢拼敢干的工作作风，正是北新建材企业文化的体现，也带动了当地其他员工的工作热情，为中资企业与当地企业的合作搭建起了友谊的桥梁。〔北新建材工业（坦桑尼亚）有限公司〕

个人体会 我是一名穆斯林员工，自加入公司，我就被坦桑北新倡导的“人类命运共同体”的文化所吸引，公司非常尊重我们的文化和信仰，给予我们关怀，我们也会更加努力地工作，回报公司。我很自豪能够成为坦桑北新的一员，我会继续努力工作，取得更大的进步和成绩。

A Top-notch Marketing Staff in BNBM Tanzania Who Dares to Fight

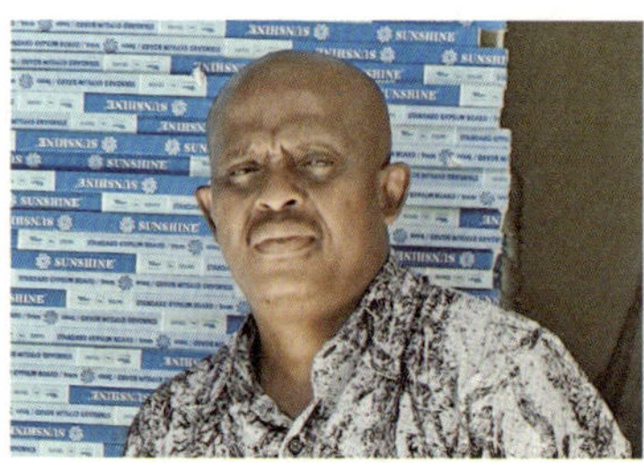

Fadhili Venus Chongwe

Joined CNBM in 2018

The Regional Manager of the Marketing Department of BNBM Building Materials Industry (Tanzania) Limited

"Sincerity is the best sales skill," said Fadhili. Fadhili joined BNBM Tanzania at its inception in June 2018 and currently serves as the Regional Manager of the Marketing Department of BNBM Tanzania.

He is diligent, practical and willing to work. He has been engaged in sales for more than 10 years, tasting the sweetness and bitterness of the profession. But he's been always devoted to his work, collecting industry information through multiple channels, keenly aware of market changes, and highly concerned about customer needs, problems and countermeasures. He has accumulated a wealth of working experience. He has an outstanding sales track record and a deep understanding of the Tanzanian market and customers.

In 2022, he found access to the maiden market in the western lake region of Tanzania, and made a great contribution to the rapid release of production capacity after BNBM Tanzania had been put into service. BNBM Tanzania achieved a significant increase in sales, an outcome partially attributable to the contribution of the sales team led by Fadhili.

During his five years of work in BNBM Tanzania, he has been dedicated to his job and completed all the tasks assigned by the company with excellence.

BNBM Tanzania marks the first production base of the group's globalization strategy. Back to its inception in 2018, seeking a way of marketing was at the fumbling stage. Thanks to years of sales experience, knowledge of the building materials industry and market acumen, Fadhili assisted the company in formulating sales systems, sorting out delivery processes, screening quality customers and formulating risk control strategies, thereby ensuring both a smooth transition of marketing work and a compliant and smooth development of BNBM Tanzania. Under the effective operation of this system, BNBM Tanzania has maintained zero accounts receivable in the five years since its establishment.

In January 2022, the new plasterboard line built by BNBM Tanzania, one of the largest and most technologically advanced in East Africa, was completed and put into operation with product quality reached international standards. It is marking a milestone in BNBM's firm promotion of its globalization strategy. At the same time, the production capacity was enlarged several times compared to the previous, which brought a greater challenge to BNBM Tanzania's marketing team.

Worrying about what had worried the company,

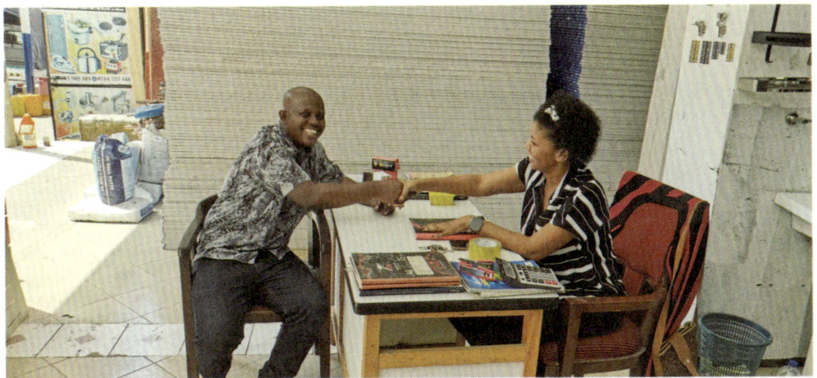

Fadhili blazed a trail in the maiden market. He ran around the five provinces of the lake region in the heat of the day in Tanzania, trying his best to sell the products. Through his unremitting efforts, BNBM Tanzania has owned more than 25 stable customers in the lake region, occupying a market share of more than 30%. In addition, he led his sales team to successfully develop the western market of Tanzania, as well as the markets of Uganda and Burundi, opening one new market after another. The quality of the products, whether the flatness of appearance, or internal strength, received wide recognition from customers upon their release to the market.

Fadhili is very good at maintaining customer relationships, as he often expresses sincere and warm care to his clients, thus gaining full trust from them. He treats his clients with true affection in the smallest detail, not complaining about the trivia and trouble. He sends greetings on holidays, keeps reciprocal courtesy, and shows care when clients are ill. He even spends his spare time helping his clients' children with their homework, assisting them in recruiting employees, arranging medical treatment for their families, etc. He is truly making friends before doing business. Once, the client SANYA's truck had a car accident on the way back from picking up the goods because of the slippery road at night. Hearing of the accident, he rushed to the scene at night to help deal with the accident, called an ambulance to take the driver to the hospital, contacted the traffic police to the scene to take pictures and preserve evidence, and stayed at the accident site to guard the goods until SANYA arrived at the scene. The client was so grateful that he came to the company in person afterwards to express his gratitude. Up to now, this client is the agent who only sale the product of BNBM Tanzania, a very rare case in the building materials industry in Tanzania.

Fadhili's down-to-earth, hard-working and diligent attitude, and his style of tackling difficulties and working hard embody the corporate cultures of BNBM, which drives the working enthusiasm of other local employees and builds a bridge of friendship for the cooperation between Chinese and local enterprises.

Personal Insights I am a Muslim employee. Since I joined the company, I was attracted by its corporate culture of "a human community with a shared future". The company respects our culture and beliefs and gives us care, and we will work harder to repay the company. I am proud to be part of the BNBM Tanzania, and I will continue to work hard to achieve more progresses and accomplishments.

异国他乡那段激情燃烧的岁月

吴平

2006年加入中国建材
现任巨石埃及公司总经理

伴随着中国巨石首个海外生产基地从无到有、从有到大，巨石埃及公司总经理吴平十年如一日，从埃及公司最初的工程建设到稳定生产，再到经营管理，他始终保持着不断将集团国际化事业向前推进的初心。

自2013年被派驻到巨石埃及公司，吴平先后参与了公司三条玻纤池窑生产线的工程建设。他主持仓库、包材、短切毡以及微粉等多个配套项目的建设，带领团队提前4年完成20万吨玻纤生产基地的建设，为巨石筑梦红海之滨倾尽全力。

2015年，年产8万吨玻纤生产线项目拉开建设的序幕，而其中66kv变电站的建设成为吴平至今难忘的项目。那时距离生产线点火时间不到20天，建设团队却发现电缆终端接口部件跟电缆无法匹配。这个部件是定制件，没有现货，要从中国发货，如此一来，根本无法在预计点火时间成功点火。

吴平顿时不知所措，只得将情况向上级领导汇报，得到上级“点火时间不能推迟，要不计一切代价解决”的命令后，他和其他同事反复与供货方沟通，终于让他们将原来半个月的工期赶在4天内加班加点完成。

靠着吴平和其他同事的不懈努力，变电站通电问题终于得到了解决。随后，项目组夜以继日、加班加点，最终在6月16日，66kv变电站全线通电，玻纤生产线建设胜利点火投产。

2016年，巨石埃及二期项目建设如火如荼地进行，但新线的生产作业还不稳定。为了全心工作，吴平将家人提前接到了埃及，此时，已经怀孕几个月的妻子由于不适应当地的气候和环境，身上出现很严重的湿疹。吴平既要协调跟踪工程建设，又要忙着恢复、稳定生产，每天下班后还要带妻子去一百多公里外的开罗看病，然后当天晚上再返回公司，继续工作。

6月，孩子在开罗医院出生，为了不耽误工程建设的进度，他把仅住了三四天院的妻子接回公司，一边照顾妻女一边又投身项目建设中。为了纪念那段难忘的岁月，他给女儿取名吴恺洛，谐音“开罗”。

2022 年，巨石埃及公司新线投产，年设计产能达到 32 万吨，在海外打造了一家优秀公司。而吴平也将在无边的戈壁上，背靠祖国，如“定海神针”一般，守护着巨石埃及这颗“一带一路”上的璀璨明珠。

（巨石埃及公司）

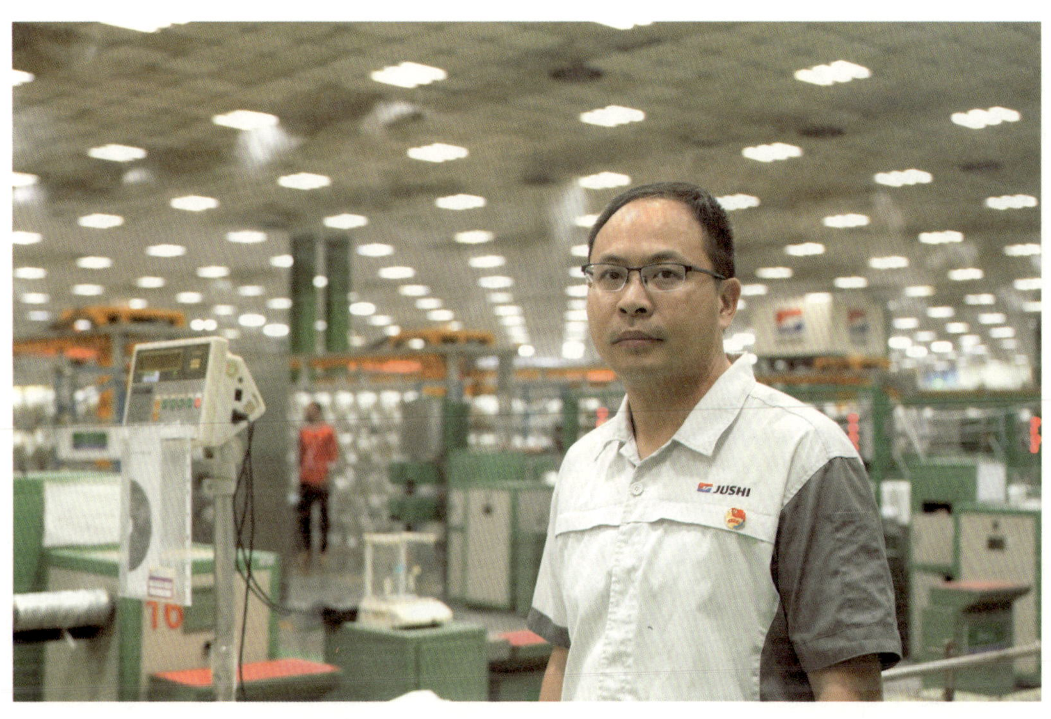

个人体会 工作 10 年来，我们巨石埃及不负众望、不辱使命，实现预期、超出预期，比想象中更努力、更坚韧、更闪耀。目前巨石埃及已经建成 4 条生产线，成为“一带一路”上一颗璀璨的明珠，我由衷地感到高兴。

The Passionate Years in a Foreign Country

Wu Ping

Joined CNBM in 2006

The General Manager of Jushi Egypt

Accompanied by the first overseas production base of China Jushi, Wu Ping, the General Manager of Jushi Egypt, has maintained his original intention of continuously advancing the internationalization of the company from the initial engineering construction to stable production and business management for 10 years.

Since being stationed at Jushi Egypt in 2013, Wu Ping has participated in the construction of three glass fiber tank furnace production lines. He presided over the construction of multiple supporting projects such as warehouses, packaging materials, short cut mat, and powder. He led the team to complete the construction of a 200,000-ton fiberglass production base four years ahead of schedule, making every effort to build a dream for Jushi on the Red Sea.

In 2015, the construction of an 80,000 ton/year fiberglass production line project began, and the construction of a 66kV substation has become an unforgettable project for Wu Ping. At that time, the ignition time of the production line was less than 20 days, but the construction team found that the cable terminal interface components could not match the cable. This component was a customized item and there was no stock available. It needed to be shipped from China, so it couldn't be successfully ignited at the expected time.

Wu Ping suddenly didn't know what to do, and had to report the situation to his superiors. After receiving an order that the ignition time should not be postponed and resolved at all costs, he and other colleagues repeatedly communicated with the supplier, working overtime within 4 days to complete the original half-month project.

Thanks to the unremitting efforts of Wu Ping and other colleagues, the power supply problem in the substation had finally been solved. Subsequently, the project team worked day and night and rested on site when tired. Finally, on June 16th, the entire 66kV substation was electrified, and the construction of the fiberglass production line was successfully ignited and put into operation.

In 2016, the construction of the second phase of the Jushi Egypt project went on in full swing, but the production operation of the new line was still unstable. In order to work wholeheartedly, Wu Ping had already taken his family to Egypt. At this time, his wife, who had been pregnant for several months, had severe eczema due to climate and environmental discomfort. He not only needed to coordinate and track the construction, but also was busy restoring and stabilizing production. Every day after work, he also took his wife to Cairo, more than 100 kilometers away, to see a doctor, and then returned to the company by evening.

In June, his child was born at the Cairo Hospital. In order not to delay the progress of the project construction, he took his wife back to the company who had only stayed in the hospital for three or four days, taking care of her and his child while also participating in the project construction. To commemorate that unforgettable time, he named the child Wu Kailuo, homophonic for "Cairo".

In 2022, Jushi Egypt's new line was put into operation, with an annual designed production capacity of 320,000 tons, creating an excellent industrial model overseas. Wu Ping will continue to guard the Jushi Egypt, one of the shining projects under the "Belt and Road" Initiative.

Personal Insights Over the past decade of work, Jushi Egypt has lived up to expectations and fulfilled the mission, achieved and exceeded expectations, working harder, more resilient, and more shining than we had imagined. At present, four production lines have been built in Jushi Egypt, which has become a shining project under the "Belt and Road" Initiative. And I am sincerely happy for that.

公用系统的安全守门员

穆罕默德·侯赛因

2015 年加入中国建材

现任巨石埃及公司公用车间副经理

“宝剑锋从磨砺出，梅花香自苦寒来。”他追随公司一路走来，一直默默无闻，虽经历风雨无数，却始终不离不弃。敬业，在他的身上得到了最完美的诠释，他就是侯赛因。

2015 年，侯赛因加入巨石埃及公司，从普通的工程师一步步成长为公用工程部主要负责人。在 7 年的时间里，他不断提升自身专业技术水平，积极创新管理方法，使埃及公司的公用系统一直处于平稳运行的状态。

作为埃及公司的一员老将，公司哪里有困难、有需要他就出现在哪里，在停电等紧急突发事件中他永远冲在第一位。侯赛因说：“工作时默默无闻，但是容不得丝毫差错，每位员工上岗前都要经过一定时间的安全培训。”

侯赛因深知安全生产是企业的生命线，他的安全意识也来自一次极其凶险的经历。虽过去多年，但他清楚地记得自己刚进公司时和一位老员工进行室内墙壁插座更换工作时的情景。他们接到通知后，拿了两把工具，直奔房间，按部就班地先将电源总开关漏保掰开，随后开了一下照明灯，灯并没有亮，他们便立马开工。

当他将墙壁插座打开准备逐根拆开导线时，刚接触到一根导线，顿时一股刺、麻、酸、胀、痛的感觉袭其右手臂，多亏身边的老员工以其多年的经验将他一脚踢开，加之脚下为实木地板才让他能及时抽回手臂，脱离危险。经过自己的亲身经历，他深知这个职业的危险性，所以他每次在公司看到其部门员工工作时，他都要抽查这位员工的工具、服装，有时还会随机提问一些安全问题。

2022 年，他围绕公司方针目标，在水、

电、气等节能减排项目上作出突出贡献。在日常管理中确保污水处理系统稳定运行，污水处理达标率 100%，保证其处理达标后有效回收利用；在空压机、制冷机的运行管理上创新思路，有效降低电耗，用电量较 2021 年下降 10 个百分点。

作为埃及公司公用工程部的负责人，他善于学习，勤于创新，以持续不断的激情积极投身到他热爱的工作事业中，锲而不舍，自强不息。他是埃及公司本土化推进过程中的一面旗帜，是埃及当地员工的优秀榜样。（巨石埃及公司）

个人体会

巨石埃及公司为员工提供了多种班车选择，让我们没有通勤的后顾之忧，还根据员工家到公司之间的距离，发放不同等级的交通补贴，这让我感到十分温暖。同时，来自中国的师傅言传身教让我学到了很多，我对自己的前途充满信心。

Security Goalkeeper for Public Systems

Mohamed Hussein

Joined CNBM in 2015

The Deputy Manager of Utility Department

April showers bring May flowers. Since joining the company, he has experienced countless difficulties, but he has never given up. He is Hussein, always dedicated to his profession.

In 2015, Hussain joined in Jushi Egypt and gradually grew from an ordinary engineer to the main leader of the department in seven years. He continuously improved his professional and technical level and actively innovated management methods to keep the public system of Jushi Egypt on a stable operation state.

As a veteran of Jushi Egypt, wherever there are difficulties and needs, there must be his presence. He always takes the lead in emergency events such as power outages. Hussein says that no mistakes are allowed and that every employee must receive safety training before starting work.

Hussein clearly knows that safety production is the lifeline and business line of enterprises, and his safety awareness also comes from his extremely dangerous experience.

Although many years have passed, he also remembers when he first joined the company, he was working with a veteran employee to replace indoor wall sockets. After receiving the notice, they took two tools and headed straight to the room. They followed suit by first turning off the leakage protection of the main power switch, and then turn on the lighting. But the light did not turn on, then they immediately started work.

When he was about to take apart the wall socket and begin to take apart the wires one by one, he felt a tingling, sour, swollen, and painful sensation on his right arm as soon as he touched one of the wires. Thanks to his partner kicking him away immediately, he was able to quickly retract his arm and escape from the danger. Through his own personal experience, he was well aware of the dangers of this profession. So, every time he sees employees working, he will randomly check their tools, clothing, and sometimes even ask some questions about safety in production.

In 2022, he made outstanding contributions in energy-saving and emission reduction projects such as water, electricity, and gas. In daily management, he ensured the stable operation of the sewage treatment system which achieved 100% sewage treatment standards, and ensured effective recycling and utilization after water treatment meets the standards. He brought out innovative ideas

in the operation and management of air compressors and refrigerators, effectively reducing electricity consumption by 10 % compared to last year.

As the Deputy Manager of Utility Department, he is good at learning, diligent in innovation, and actively participates in the work with continuous passion. He perseveres and strives for self-improvement. He is a banner in the localization process of Jushi Egypt and an excellent role model for local employees.

Personal Insights Jushi Egypt provides employees with a variety of shuttle bus options, which makes us have no worries about commuting. It also provides different levels of transportation subsidies based on the distance between employees' homes and the company, which makes me touched. At the same time, the Chinese supervisor has taught me a lot through words and deeds, and I am confident in my future.

建功海外显担当　毅然坚守谱华章

杨峰

2002 年加入中国建材

现任中材国际（南京）产业发展部副部长

杨峰，现任中材国际（南京）产业发展部副部长。他参加工作 20 余载，原是总图专业技术骨干，工作兢兢业业、精益求精，深得领导和同事的信任与好评。2019 年底，在公司开拓海外产业的关键时期，他积极响应号召，主动请缨，奔赴尼日利亚，挑起尼日利亚产业园前期筹备的重任。

初到园区，场地大部分是灌木林和沼泽地，尼日利亚每年从 5 月份开始就进入长达近半年的雨季。在雨季来临前，他必须完成场地清表、测量地形、施工图设计、场地平整等一系列工作，才能保证后续工作按计划进行。时间紧，任务重，杨峰顶着烈日踏勘现场，冒着大雨了解场地排水情况，为园区规划收集第一手资料。园区地形四周高中间低，尼日利亚雨季持续近半年，如何在雨季排水通畅，保证园区不受内涝，是当务之急。杨峰根据现场收集到的第一手资料，与设计团队、子公司相关人员及施工单位多次讨论，3 天时间就迅速敲定了园区的排洪方案，如今排洪系统已成功经受住连续 3 个雨季的洗礼与考验，俨然成为园区一道美丽的风景线。

筹备工作刚刚起步，所有工作只能由他一

人承担。2020 年 8 月底，彩石瓦厂计划带料调试，需要做好供电和供气保障。杨峰一边与 Power Gas 公司进行供气谈判，一边组织人员进行发电站设备调试，与此同时，还组织安装人员进行管道安装与检测，并对当地员工进行天然气卸车安全培训。经过 72 小时连续奋战，终于实现天然气站和发电站的正常运行，保证了彩石瓦厂如期带料调试。

2020 年以来，新冠疫情暴发，经济和医疗都欠发达的尼日利亚形势更是异常严峻。杨峰同志按照集团和公司的防疫政策和要求，结合尼日利亚政府及产业园的实际情况，制订了符合园区实际情况的防疫策略，从物资储备到网格化管理，从进出人员检查到定期消杀等工作，事无巨细，组织得井井有条。与此同时，杨峰对"墙内、墙外"安全问题也给予了高度重视，通过定期组织安全巡检、安全培训、自查风险源等举措，强化安全意识，增强风险识别能力，夯实应急处突水平，使中外员工的生命安全得到了保障。杨峰同志一手抓防疫，一手抓建设，疫情期间物价飞涨，施工单位要求涨价，他积极与施工单位沟通交流，保证各项计划顺利推进。

为了园区建设，杨峰有两年多时间没有与家人共度春节，全身心扑在一线。不忘初心，牢记使命，杨峰同志凭借一片赤诚热血奋战在公司海外产业项目中，以"舍小家，为大家"的奉献精神毅然奔赴海外，勇担责任、不畏风险、冲锋在前，为中材国际（南京）的国际化、属地化贡献力量。〔中材国际（南京）〕

个人体会 顺应时代之呼声，响应公司之召唤，在中材国际融入全球之策的背景下，我积极投身于公司国际化发展的浪潮之中。未来，我将继续以梦为马，不负韶华，为公司扩展国际疆域及本土深耕献一己之力。

Overseas Achievements Show Commitment and Perseverance

Yang Feng

Joined CNBM in 2002

The Deputy Director of Industrial Development Department of SINOMA Nanjing

Yang Feng is the Deputy-director of Industrial Development Department of SINOMA (Nanjing), has been working for more than 20 years. As a professional and technical backbone, he works conscientiously and strives for perfection, winning the trust and praise of leaders and colleagues. At the end of 2019, during the critical period when the company was developing overseas market, he responded positively to the call and volunteered to go to Nigeria to take up the heavy responsibility of preparation work of the industrial park in Nigeria.

When he first arrived at the industrial park, most of the site was shrubland and swampy land, and the rainy season in Nigeria which lasted for nearly half a year begins from May every year. Before the rainy season, a series of work such as site clearance, topography measurement, construction plan design and site leveling had to be completed to ensure that the subsequent work would be carried out as planned. Time is tight, and the task is heavy. Yang Feng visited the site under the hot sun, braved heavy rain to understand the drainage situation of the site, and collected first-hand information for the planning of the park. The topography of the park is high all around and low in the middle, so how to drain the park smoothly in the rainy season and ensure that the park is not flooded is a top priority. Based on the first-hand information collected on site, Yang Feng discussed with the design team, relevant staff of the subsidiary company and the construction unit for many times, and quickly finalized the main drainage plan in 3 days. Now the drainage system has successfully withstood the baptism and test of 3 consecutive rainy seasons and has become a beautiful scenery of the park.

At the preliminary stage, all the work could only be undertaken by Yang Feng himself. At the end of August 2020, the color stone tile factory is scheduled to commission with materials, and the park needs to guarantee power supply and gas supply. Yang Feng negotiated with Power Gas for gas supply while organizing personnel for power station equipment commissioning, and organizing installers for pipeline installation and testing, while training local employees on gas unloading safety. After 72 hours of continuous struggle, the natural gas station and power station operated normally and ensured that the color stone tile factory was commissioned with materials as scheduled.

Since 2020, the epidemic has been raging worldwide, and the situation in Nigeria, where the economy and medical care are less developed, is even more severe. Yang Feng, in accordance with the epidemic prevention policies and requirements of the Group and the company, led the staff to formulate an epidemic prevention strategy in line with the actual situation. From material stockpiling to grid management, from inspection of personnel to regular disinfection, everything was organized in an orderly manner. At the same time, Yang Feng also attached great importance to the safety issue, through regular safety inspections, safety training, self-inspection of risk sources to strengthen the safety awareness of the staff, enhance the ability to identify risks, and consolidate the level of emergency response, so that the life and safety of Chinese and foreign employees in the park are guaranteed. During the epidemic period, prices soared and the construction unit requested for price increase. He actively communicated with the construction companies to ensure the progress were promoted as planned.

For the construction of the industrial park, Yang Feng did not spend the Spring Festival with his family for more than two years, and devoted himself to the front line. With the spirit of "sacrificing the small family for the everyone", Yang Feng is determined to go abroad, take the responsibility, brave the risks, and take the lead, contributing to the internationalization and localization of SINOMA Nanjing.

Personal Insights In response to the call of the times and the appeal of the company, and following SINOMA International Engineering Co., Ltd.'s global integration strategy, I actively participate in the wave of international development of the company. In the future, I will continue to be motivated with passion and spare no efforts in the company's expansion of international territory and deep cultivation in the local area.

疫情面前的逆行“市场人”

周华

2004年加入中国建材

现任中材国际(南京)非洲设计研发中心副主任、中材国际(南京)市场营销中心区域经理

他，既没有轰轰烈烈的事迹，也没有惊人的壮举，他只是一名兢兢业业、勤勤恳恳地在平凡的工作岗位上做好本职工作、刻苦钻研专业技术、不断提升自己岗位技能和专业水平的市场经营人员。

他，始终以“敢于担当、勇于开拓”的精神作为自己的行动指南，爱岗敬业、甘于奉献、一步一个脚印，扎实开拓海外市场。

他，默默奉献、任劳任怨，没有豪言壮语。但是，他在疫情面前，毫不退缩、勇担职责、践行使命。

唯其艰难方显勇毅，唯其笃行方显珍贵。他就是中材国际南京公司驻东非市场代表——周华。

2020年2月21日，新冠疫情暴发不久，带着忐忑和家人的担心，国际市场一部东非市场代表周华踏上了非洲市场经营的征途。

飞行途中，周华严格按照公司疫情期间的管控要求，全程佩戴口罩，减少不必要的接触。迪拜机场繁忙依旧，佩戴口罩的大部分是中国人。当时外国人对新冠病毒传染性毫不上心，反而对佩戴口罩的人投以异样的眼光。

一路的焦虑飞行，他终于抵达坦桑尼亚达累斯萨拉姆国际机场。坦桑入境管理部门在飞机降落的不远处临时设置了体温检测、登记管理关口，但管理人员力量偏少，导致旅客长时间排队等候，入境耗费3个多小时。

抵达坦桑分公司驻地后，周华首先接受分公司14天的自我隔离。在十几平方米的宿舍内，他的生活与工作交织在一起。他白天与当地业主、分公司工作人员进行远程会议，夜晚与国内同事沟通工作进展。隔离期间他坚持锻炼身体，提高自身免疫力。14天的隔离，他

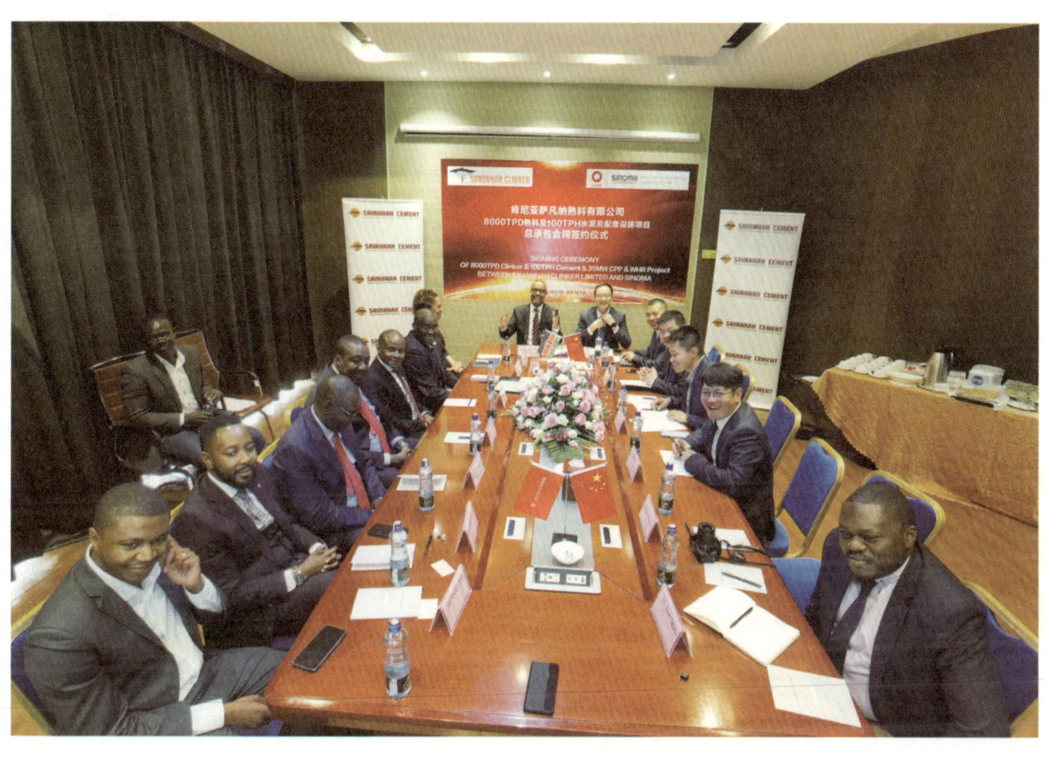

就在这样充实的工作与生活中度过了，隔离期过后又投入到忙碌的工作中。

随着疫情的蔓延，周华前往埃塞、肯尼亚和莫桑比克的计划只好搁置，但在坦桑市场的开拓持续进行。集团北新建材石膏板项目继续推进，星皓粉磨站项目用地确认和现场考察顺利进行，配合分公司承接紧挨北新建材石膏板项目的方钢管工厂项目。周华结合公司海外“246”发展思路，做好前方调研和后方技术储备。他先后调研了烧石灰项目、加气砌块项目、彩钢板项目、工业厂房项目等多元化投资和市场开拓发展情况。

坦桑最大的工程项目 Rufiji 水电大坝的子项工程已经顺利完成合同谈判及签约。

2020 年 6 月，受疫情影响，坦桑尼亚与肯尼亚已断航，周华克服重重困难，通过陆路驱车前往肯尼亚见，最终到了客户，赢得了客户的尊重和信任。2022 年 12 月 1 日，坦桑分公司成功与客户签约萨凡纳 8000t/d 熟料水泥生产线项目。〔中材国际（南京）〕

个人体会

中国国际贸易的快速发展和中材国际的快速国际化，给了我们机会和舞台。我希望能在这个舞台上继续为提升 SINOMA 品牌的国际影响力贡献力量。

Zhou Hua: A Marketing Hero Brave Coronavirus Risk

Zhou Hua

Joined CNBM in 2004

The Deputy Director of African Design R&D Center of SINOMA Nanjing

The Regional Manager of Marketing Center of SINOMA Nanjing

Zhou Hua hasn't made spectacular deeds or amazing feats, but he is a market person worthy our high regards. He works an ordinary job but has been doing it conscientiously and diligently. Industriously studying state-of-the-art technologies, he constantly improves his professional skills and level.

Following the "daring and pioneering" spirit, he loves his job and is willing to contribute. Step by step, he has been working to develop overseas markets in a solid way.

He is a man of quiet dedication and hard work. Speaking no grand word, he has braved coronavirus risk, shouldered his responsibilities and fulfilled his missions without second thoughts.

Only in hard times can courage and perseverance be manifested, only through solid action can rare qualities be demonstrated. That speaks who he is -- Zhou Hua, the representative of East African Market of SINOMA International Nanjing.

At the beginning of 2020, the COVID-19 epidemic just broke out. Although his family was worried, Zhou Hua embarked on his journey to the African markets.

Strictly following the company's requirements, Zhou Hua wore mask and made minimum contacts with others throughout his flight. At the busy Dubai airport, most Chinese travelers wore masks regardless of the strange eyes of foreigners who had no ideas of the pandemic.

After an anxious flight, he finally arrived at Dar es Salaam International Airport in Tanzania. The Tanzanian Immigration Management Department set up a temporary check station to detect temperature and manage registration. Due to the inadequate staff, it took him more than 3 hours to entry the country.

Upon his arrival at the Tanzanian branch, Zhou Hua was quarantined for 14 days. In a dormitory of about 10 m^2, his life and work were intertwined. He had online meetings with local owners and the branch company during the day while making communications with colleagues in China on their work at night. In this tight space, he kept working out to improve his immunity. In spite of insolating from others, the 14 days was fulfilling. Once it was over, he devoted himself to his busy work.

As the pandemic ravaging more countries in the world, Zhou Hua stopped his plans of travelling to

Ethiopia, Kenya and Mozambique. He spared no efforts to develop Tanzania markets. He advanced BNBM gypsum board project, visited the site of Xinghao GU project, and cooperated with the Tanzanian branch to undertake square steel pipe factory project which is close to BNBM gypsum board project. By referring to SINOMA International Nanjing's 246 Overseas Development Concepts, he made investigation and survey while studying applicable technologies. He had investigated the investment and market opportunities for various projects, such as lime burning project, aerated block project, color steel plate project and industrial plant project.

The sub-project of Rufiji Hydropower Dam, Tanzania's largest engineering project, has successfully signed.

In June 2020, the flight between Tanzania and Kenya was cut off. Overcoming various difficulties, Zhou Hua drove to Kenya. He met the clients in the face of the severe pandemic situation at that time, winning their respect and trust. On 1st December, 2022, he successfully signed a contract for the 8,000t/d clinker cement production line project in Savannah.

Personal Insights The rapid development of China's international trade and the rapid internationalization of SINOMA have given us the opportunity and the stage. I hope to continue to play a role in increasing the international influence of the SINOMA brand on this stage.

扎根项目一线的实践者

杜晓雷

2011 年加入中国建材

现任天津水泥院乌兹 WKCP 项目部副经理

在戈壁、在荒滩、在河谷、在高原……有这样一群人——他们以工程项目为阵地，不惧艰难险阻、不辞劳碌辛苦，不驰于空想、不骛于虚声，踏踏实实奋斗，默默奉献光热，以实际行动彰显奋斗者的责任与担当。在这个优秀的团队中，有一名阳光乐观、浑身洋溢着正能量的年轻人，他就是天津水泥院乌资 WKCP 项目部副经理杜晓雷。

2011 年研究生毕业后，杜晓雷便坚定了到项目现场工作的念头。在天津水泥院建筑设计研究所工作期间，他专注于学习专业结构图集，认真汲取图集涉及的每种结构形式、做法和现成经验，将所学的结构工程专业知识与结构设计工作紧密结合，不断提升设计能力和业务水平。

自 2012 年 4 月，杜晓雷便一直在项目现场拼搏着、奉献着，先后参与了贵州荣盛、马来西亚 YTL 煤磨改造、马来西亚 HUME 二线、埃及 GOE 油改煤等 20 余个国内外重点 EPC 工程项目建设工作，至今已度过近 12 个春秋。

在埃及 GOE 油改煤项目中，杜晓雷担任土建主管，负责土建和资料管理工作。他为了赶工期，白天参与正常土建工作，晚上投身繁杂的资料收集整理。穆斯林斋月期间，他多次去找当地土建分包的管理人员，“晓之以理，动之以情”协调工人工作，获得了分包商的理解与配合，圆满完成项目建设，并且提前 10 天完工。辛勤的付出终有回报，最终该项目提前一个月取得 PAC 证书，受到业主的肯定。

永登祁连山 1#2# 煤磨改造项目的土建施工贯穿冬季，当地气温零下 20 摄氏度。为了减少冬季施工对质量和工期的影响，他积极制订施工方案，采用了最经济有效的暖棚法，确保了混凝土的质量，克服改造项目中诸多不利条件，制订具体方案改造管道，推进改造子项建造，使旧管沟新建、旧管沟管道拆除、桩基施工有序进行，最终节约工期约 10 天。

就是这样，从一个项目到另一个项目，从国内现场到国外现场，他从一名大学生到现在的项目部副经理，工地就是他的家，公司就是

他的舞台，他在这个舞台上奋力起舞，在项目上飞扬青春。

一分部署，九分落实。作为天津水泥院乌兹别克斯坦 7500TPD 熟料水泥生产线咨询管理服务项目的项目副经理，他始终注重打造高效项目管理团队，强调务实化管理，定期总结工作完成情况，提出问题，解决问题，赢得了业主的高度赞扬。

在新冠疫情面前，他与当地政府协调沟通，建立联防联控、互帮互助的疫情防控机制，发动项目部成员采购防疫物资，强化防疫宣传，引导中方职工和当地员工进行科学防疫，做好常态化疫情防控工作，定期组织开展疫情防控应急演练，最终实现项目部的中方员工无一人感染新冠病毒。

在德上坚守、在能上提高、在勤上着力、在绩上见效，杜晓雷用实际行动诠释了央企员工在海外生产经营过程中的责任和担当，让自己的青春在天津水泥院这个广阔天地发光发热、尽情绽放。（中材国际所属天津水泥院）

个人体会 不驰于空想、不骛于虚声。我将带领项目团队在德上坚守、在能上提高、在勤上着力、在绩上见效，用实际行动诠释央企员工在海外生产经营过程中的责任和担当，让自己的青春在天津水泥院这个广阔天地发光发热、尽情绽放。

A Dedicated Professional Strived in the Frontline

Du Xiaolei

Joined CNBM in 2011

The Deputy project manager for WKCP project of SINOMA-TCDRI

Amidst the vast Gobi, desolate wastelands, river valleys and high plateaus, there is such a group of people - they perceive engineering projects as their calling, not afraid of difficulties, obstacles and hard work, strive steadily, dedicate silently, using practical action to show the responsibility of the strugglers. In this excellent team, there is a young man who is sunny and optimistic and full of positive energy. He is Du Xiaolei, the Deputy Project Manager of SINOMA-TCDRI.

After completing the graduate school in 2011, Du Xiaolei firmly decided to work on the project site. Throughout his tenure at the SINOMA-TCDRI's Architectural Design Institute, Du Xiaolei dedicated himself to the meticulous study of structural professional drawing sets. He diligently absorbed the invaluable experiences within each completed drawing set, seamlessly integrating his theoretical knowledge of structural engineering with practical structural design work. Continuously striving for growth, he consistently honed his design abilities and elevated his proficiency in the field.

Since April 2012, Du Xiaolei has diligently and wholeheartedly contributed to project sites, actively engaging in the construction of over 20 significant EPC projects both domestically and internationally. These projects include Guizhou Rongsheng, Malaysia YTL coal mill transformation, Malaysia HUME second line, Egypt GOE oil-to-coal conversion and more. Du Xiaolei has devoted nearly 12 years to these endeavors, experiencing countless seasons of growth and progress.During the Egypt GOE oil-to-coal project, Du Xiaolei assumed the role of Civil Construction Supervisor, overseeing and managing civil construction activities as well as data management. To adhere to the project's strict timeline, Du Xiaolei actively engaged in regular civil construction work during the day while wholeheartedly dedicating his nights to the intricate task of data collection and organization. Throughout the Muslim month of Ramadan, Du Xiaolei made multiple visits to the local civil construction subcontracting managers to coordinate the working hours of workers. Through his exceptional communication skills, he garnered the understanding and cooperation of the subcontractors, resulting in the project's successful completion a remarkable 10 days ahead of schedule. The perseverance and dedication bore fruit as the project successfully obtained the Provisional Acceptance Certificate (PAC) one month ahead of the scheduled deadline. This outstanding achievement received high praise and affirmation from both the project owner and the military authorities involved.

The civil construction of the Yongdeng Qilianshan 1#2# coal mill renovation project persisted throughout the winter season, enduring harsh temperatures of approximately -20 °C. To mitigate the adverse effects of winter construction on quality and schedule, he proactively devised a comprehensive construction plan. Implementing the most efficient and cost-effective warming shed method, he ensured the concrete quality and effectively addressed the uncertainties that arose during the renovation project. By formulating a detailed pipeline renovation plan and expediting the construction of the renovation sub-top, he facilitated simultaneous progress in the new construction of the old pipe trench, removal of the old pipe trench, and pile foundation construction. This strategic approach resulted in a remarkable time-saving of at least 10 days in the construction schedule.

Transitioning from one project to another, traversing both domestic and international sites, he has embarked on a remarkable journey, evolving from a college student to the esteemed position of Deputy Manager in the Project Department. The project sites have become his home, and the company serves as his stage. With unwavering dedication, he dances tirelessly on this stage, infusing the essence of youth into every project, embodying the spirit of passion and ambition.

Deployment is important, but implementation is even more crucial. In his role as Deputy Project Manager for the consulting management service project of the 7,500TPD clinker cement production line at the SINOMA-TCDRI in Uzbekistan, he consistently prioritizes the establishment of a highly efficient project management team. With a strong emphasis on practical management, he conducts regular reviews of completed work, identifying and

resolving challenges to enhance technological proficiency, civil construction standards, and overall management capabilities. These efforts have garnered immense acclaim from the project owner, attesting to his commendable performance.

Facing the COVID-19 pandemic, he proactively coordinated and communicated with the local government, establishing a collaborative mechanism for prevention, mutual support, and epidemic control. Mobilizing members of the project department, he facilitated the procurement of necessary epidemic prevention supplies and intensified awareness campaigns. Through guidance and training, he ensured that both Chinese workers and local employees implemented scientific and effective measures for epidemic prevention and control. Regular monitoring and emergency preparedness drills were conducted, leading to a significant achievement — none of the Chinese employees in the project department were infected.

With unwavering determination, continuous improvement, and diligent effort, Du Xiaolei exemplifies the values of responsibility and dedication for employees of Chinese enterprises rooted overseas. Through his practical actions, he has dedicated his youth to the vast world of the SINOMA-TCDRI.

Personal Insights Do not indulge in fantasies. I will lead the project team to uphold integrity, strive for excellence, emphasize diligence, and achieve targets, exemplifying the responsibility and commitment of employees of Chinese enterprises rooted overseas. Let my youth shine and bloom in the vast world of TCDRI.

金鑫的大漠 12 年

金鑫

2003 年加入中国建材

现任中国建材集团埃及 GOE 项目运维项目经理

金鑫是天津水泥院埃及 GOE 包产项目经理。“大漠孤烟直，长河落日圆。”他已经坚守大漠整整 12 年，他所带领的项目团队连续 11 年超额完成生产任务，多次与客户续签包产合同。

埃及 GOE 项目是天津水泥院目前提供运维服务时间最长的项目，金鑫团队共同努力，克服了重重困难，攻克了一道道难关，项目成果赢得了业主的高度褒奖，创造了优异经营效益的同时，有力提升了公司的品牌影响力。

2012 年 2 月 1 日，埃及 GOE 项目正式开始包产运营。项目业主是埃及军方，项目实行军事化管理，在生产技术、文化习俗和思维方式等方面存在诸多差异。项目刚开始时，由于双方沟通不畅，造成了诸多误解。

为此，金鑫每天晚上都要抽出时间主动和水泥厂的经理进行沟通，就工作中存在的问题以及解决的办法提出具体的建议，用自己的专业和诚意消除误解和障碍，增进理解与互信。慢慢地，客户的笑脸多了起来，气氛也逐渐融洽了，工厂的运转效率逐步提高，双方的互信和合作越来越紧密，创造了良好的经济效益和客户价值。

2019 年，埃及水泥市场持续低迷，水泥销售萎靡不振，价格低廉，造成大量熟料外堆。为了满足客户需求、应对市场的冲击，金鑫和项目团队积极开展降本增效活动，在保证水泥质量的前提下，通过提高混合材掺量，降低水泥的生产成本；通过自制备件、修旧利废及技术创新，节约费用超过 600 万元。为满足客户拓展海外市场的要求，他和技术人员积极探索、多次试验，通过不断调整配比、优化操作，终于摸索出一套商品熟料的配料方案，应用后市场反馈良好，为帮助客户开拓海外熟料市场奠定了基础，同时也加快了公司品牌效应的拓展和延伸。

2020 年初，新冠肺炎疫情暴发，身处埃及的金鑫和项目团队面临着“防疫 + 复产”的双重压力。由于文化和理念的差异，很多埃方工人防疫意识不够强，行动上不积极，都不愿

意戴口罩，甚至还在封闭区内随意走动、聚集。金鑫认为，只有转变客户和当地员工的防疫理念、提高防疫意识、开展联防联控，项目的包产服务、人员安全才能得到最大的保证。

为此，他和团队人员不厌其烦地向埃方的将军、生产部长、化验室主任等管理人员介绍中国的抗疫经验，一遍一遍地向埃方员工讲述不戴口罩等不当行为的严重危害。他们的不懈努力终于有了成效，慢慢地，埃方人员也养成了佩戴口罩的习惯，各项防疫措施也处理得当、落实到位。

“一年三百六十日，都是横戈马上行。”驻埃 12 年，金鑫只回国休假过 7 次，仅陪家人度过 1 次春节。他把时间和精力都奉献给了埃及 GOE 项目的包产事业。“无怨无悔，始终如一”是他的真实写照。在每一个日出日落的日子，他都面临着不同的挑战，沉着冷静，善于思考也成了他处理问题的风格。在他的带动下，项目部的每位成员都敬业乐群，精进砥砺，以实际行动践行着对业主的承诺，为公司的国际化业务发展贡献着自己的智慧与力量。

（中材国际所属天津水泥院）

个人体会 我坚信只要扎扎实实、爱岗敬业、甘于吃苦、乐于奉献，干好每一天的工作，一定会在平凡的工作岗位上创造出自己的辉煌。我将勇挑重担，实干笃行，以实际行动践行对业主的承诺，为公司的国际化业务发展贡献智慧与力量！

12-year Work in the Egyptian Desert

Jin Xin

Joined CNBM in 2003

The Egypt GOE O&M Project Manager of TCDRI

Jin Xin is the Project Manager of GOE project contracted by Tianjin Cement Industry Design & Research Institute (TCDRI) in Egypt. The project is located in a vast desert, where solitary smoke seems to rise straight into the clouds and the sun sets perfectly on the endless Nile River. Jin Xin has been working there for twelve years. The project team led by him has completed production tasks exceedingly for eleven years in a row and has renewed the production ensuring contract with the client several times.

The GOE project in Egypt is currently the project for which TCDRI has provided the longest operation and maintenance service. With the efforts of Jin Xin and his team, the project has overcome numerous difficulties and countless obstacles. Its achievements have won high praise from the owner. While creating excellent business benefits, the project has also effectively enhanced the brand image of TCDRI.

On February 1, 2012, the GOE project in Egypt officially began operation. The project was owned by the Egyptian military, and the project was managed militarily. There were significant differences between Jin Xin's team and the project owner in aspects of production technology, cultural customs, and ways of thinking. At the beginning of the project, poor communication between the two parties led to numerous misunderstandings and difficulties.

Therefore, Jin Xin took some time to actively communicate with the manager of the Egyptian cement plant every night, proposing specific suggestions and methods on how to solve problems arising in the work, and using his professionalism and sincerity to eliminate misunderstandings and obstacles, so as to enhance understanding and mutual trust between both sides. Over time, the client's smiles increased, the working atmosphere between both sides became more harmonious, the operational efficiency of the factory improved, and the mutual trust and cooperation between both parties deepened. All these have created good economic benefits and customer value.

In 2019, the Egyptian cement market continued to be sluggish. Sluggish cement sales and low prices resulted in a large number of clinker piles. In order to respond to customer needs and market shocks, Jin Xin and the project team actively carried out cost reduction and efficiency enhancement activities. While ensuring cement quality, they reduced the production cost of cement by increasing the amount of the auxiliary materials added. Through self-made

spare parts, the renovation and recycling of old equipment as well as technological innovation, they saved over 6 million yuan in costs. In order to meet the client's requirements for expanding overseas markets, Jin Xin and his technical personnel actively explored and conducted multiple experiments and finally found a set of formulas for commodity clinkers by continuously adjusting the ratio and optimizing operations. After the formulas were applied, the market feedback was good. This laid a good foundation for helping the client expand the overseas clinker market while accelerating the expansion and extension of TCDRI's brand effect.

At the beginning of 2020, the COVID-19 pandemic broke out, so Jin Xin and his team members were faced with the dual pressure of "epidemic prevention + production recovery". Due to cultural and philosophical differences, many Egyptian workers lacked awareness of epidemic prevention and were not proactive in preventing the pandemic. They all were unwilling to wear masks and even wandered and gathered in enclosed areas. Jin Xin believed that only by changing the mind of the client and local employees on epidemic prevention, improving their epidemic prevention awareness and carrying out the joint prevention and control of the pandemic could the production ensuring services and personnel safety of the project be ensured maximumly.

To this end, he and his team members tirelessly introduced China's epidemic prevention experience to Egyptian generals, production managers, laboratory directors, and other management personnel, and repeatedly told Egyptian employees about the severe harm of improper behaviors such as not wearing masks. His unremitting efforts have finally borne fruits. Gradually, Egyptian personnel have developed the habit of wearing masks. Various epidemic prevention measures have also been properly handled and implemented.

Jin Xin has worked hard around the year. During his 12-year work in Egypt, he only went back to China for vacation 7 times and only spent one Spring Festival with his family. He devoted all his time and energy to the GOE project in Egypt. "No complaints, no regrets, and consistency" is his true portrayal. Along the way, he faced different challenges. Calm thinking and witty decoupling have become his problem-solving style. Under his leadership, every member of the project team has been dedicated and diligent, practicing their promises to the owner with practical actions, and contributing their wisdom and strength to TCDRI's international business development.

Personal Insights I firmly believe that as long as we are down-to-earth, dedicated, willing to endure hardships, willing to contribute, and do a good job every day, we will definitely create our own brilliance in ordinary jobs. I will bravely shoulder heavy responsibilities, work hard, fulfill the commitment to the owner with practical actions, and contribute wisdom and strength to our company international business development.

马来西亚公司的“麦姐”

麦美云

2010 年加入中国建材

现任中国建材天津水泥院马来西亚公司财务经理

账目及财务管理是每家公司都十分重视的工作，中国建材天津水泥院马来西亚公司也不例外。在这里有一位精通财务知识的外籍员工麦美云，人如其名，她具有美丽的外表和过硬的专业能力，办公室的同事们都很喜欢她，亲切地称呼他为麦女士或麦姐。自马来西亚公司 2010 年年底成立以来，麦美云就在公司工作，至今已有 13 年。在这期间，她从一个新人变成了公司的元老，逐渐成长为一名广受赞誉的传奇人物。

刚入职时麦美云是公司的一个普通的职员，她虽然不张扬，但却是个有心人，总是默默地关注着部门业务的每一个运行环节，也正是因为这份细心和专注，她快速熟悉了工作内容，并从中不断学习、摸索、实践。不久之后，她就形成了一套自己的工作方法，不断优化工作流程，积极为公司管理层出谋划策，寻求公司利益最大化。

随着时间的推移，麦美云逐渐成为财务工作中的灵魂人物，她熟悉财务各个环节的工作内容，从凭证整理到复杂的财务决策，无所不精。她就像一只机动灵活的猎豹，无论困境出现在哪里，她总是能迅速捕捉到问题的本质，并勇敢地提出解决方案。

执行 HUME 一线时，公司在最高峰时期大约有三四千名工作人员，麦姐除了要处理凭证和进账的工作外，还需要到税务局处理工作人员的税务注册，工人离开时还需要办理清税的手续。当时，HUME 一线位于霹雳怡保，但税务局却在吉隆坡，来回路程需要至少四五个小时。可麦姐面对这样的辛劳，却开玩笑地说：“正好欣赏路边的风景呢”。

在马来西亚实行 GST 消费税期间，她面临前所未有的巨大挑战，工作量直接增加了一倍，原因是消费税需要每月都提呈给关税局审核。这个突如其来的冲击犹如风暴一般，将她推向了极限。然而，麦姐并没有被击倒，反而以惊人的毅力和过硬的专业素养走出了困境，出色地完成了任务。

HUME 一线的项目完成后，她又马不停

蹄地赶往了槟城南方钢厂项目，随后又回到了 HUME 二线，无论在哪儿，她都能顺利地把工作完成。

在公司工作的这几年间，驻马来西亚的企业领导和财务已经更换了几位，麦姐仍然坚守在财务岗位，领导和同事认可麦姐的工作，麦姐也舍不得离开大家。她说："与大家的工作配合十分顺畅，沟通十分高效，这样的工作氛围对我有很强的吸引力，我永远也不会离开。"

疫情之后，公司业务量有了明显的提升，承接的项目也一个接一个地开始动工了，这可把闲下来的麦姐高兴坏了，她又能回到以前忙碌的状态。

她说："希望中材国际天津水泥院马来西亚的业务越做越大，承接的项目越来越多，这样我就能在这里开心快乐地工作直至退休了。"（中材国际所属天津水泥院）

在努力的过程中，我经历了无数个艰难的时刻。我的肩膀似乎要承载起整个世界的重担，但这并没有击垮我。终于，当工作完成时，我递交了一份完美的成品，我的汗水和努力凝结的果实宣告了我的胜利。

Mai Meiyun from the Malaysian Company

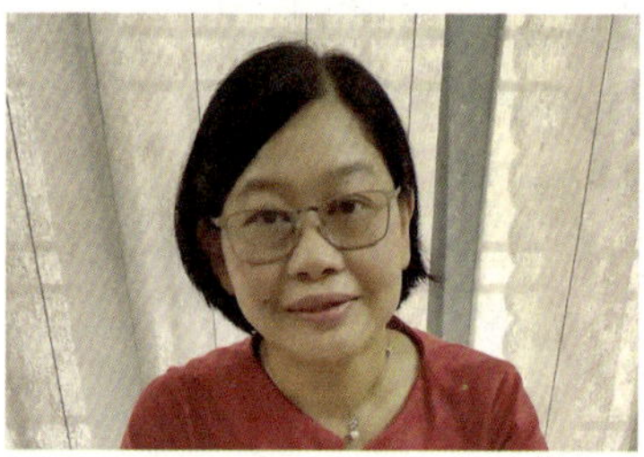

Mai Meiyun

Joined CNBM in 2010

Malaysia Company financial manager of TCDRI

Accounting and financial management are essential departments in every company, including SINOMA Industry Engineering (M) SDN. BHD. I am Mai Meiyun, the finance staff hired by the company in Malaysia. In office, my colleagues usually refer to me as Ms. Mai or Sister Mai. SINOMA Industry Engineering (M) SDN. BHD. was established at the end of 2010 and has been operating in Malaysia for a solid twelve years. I have also transitioned from being a new employee to reaching a senior level within the company.

When Mai Meiyun first joined the company, she was just an ordinary employee. Although she was not outspoken, she was an attentive person who silently paid attention to every operational aspect of the department's business. It was her carefulness and focus that allowed her to quickly familiarize herself with the job and continuously learn, explore, and practice. Before long, she developed her own "working method," constantly optimizing the workflow and actively providing advice and strategies to the company's management team, seeking to maximize the company's interests.

As time went on, Mai Meiyun gradually became the key figure in financial work. She was familiar with every aspect of financial operations, from organizing vouchers to complex financial decision-making. She was like an agile cheetah, able to swiftly identify the essence of problems no matter where they arose and bravely propose solutions.

Just like during my time at HUME, when the company had approximately three to four thousand employees at its peak, I was not only busy with voucher processing and income tracking but also had to handle employee tax registrations at the Income Tax Department. Additionally, when workers left the company, I had to assist in the clearance of their tax procedures. During that time, HUME was located in Ipoh, Perak, while the Income Tax Department was in Kuala, Lumpur, requiring a round trip of at least four to five hours.

In addition to that, during the implementation of Goods and Services Tax (GST) in Malaysia, my workload doubled. This was because the GST returns had to be submitted to the Customs Department for auditing every month. During that period, I never dared to slack off and always worked diligently and responsibly to ensure that all works assigned are able to complete before the deadline.

After completing the project at HUME, I moved on to work at Southern Steel in Penang. Subsequently,

I returned to HUME for another assignment. I feel fortunate that I'm able to successfully complete the tasks in both places.

During these years of work, there have been several changes in the Chinese leadership and finance team stationed in Malaysia. I am grateful and thankful that I have been able to maintain harmonious relationships with each leader and colleague in the corresponding positions, allowing us to collaborate and work well together. In my opinion, a positive work atmosphere is crucial in the office environment.

Although business slowed down during the pandemic, there has been a noticeable improvement in business after the epidemic and projects have started one after another. It is great to see the busy times returning.

Lastly, I hope that SINOMA Industry Engineering (M) SDN. BHD. will continue to undertake more projects in Malaysia so that I can work here until my retirement age.

Personal Insights Throughout the process, I experienced countless challenging moments. It felt like my shoulders were carrying the weight of the world, but it did not break me. Finally, as the final moment of work approached, I submitted a perfect result. The fruits of my sweat and effort declared my victory.

用坚守诠释责任与担当

邓清云

2013 年 10 月加入中国建材

现任成都建材院埃及 Sewedy 水泥厂替代燃料项目项目经理

邓清云是中材国际所属成都建材院埃及 Sewedy 水泥厂替代燃料项目的项目经理，他于 2014 年赴海外工作，长期奋斗在海外项目一线，先后参与完成了沙特 TCC 项目、海德堡格鲁吉亚KASPI项目等多个海外项目建设。

2016 年，邓清云前往海德堡格鲁吉亚 KASPI 项目现场。该项目是一条全欧洲标准建设的熟料生产线。他通过勤奋学习、刻苦钻研，把精力倾注在技术和管理提升上，很快全面系统掌握了各项技术标准，为此后长期在海外工作打下了基础。在海德堡格鲁吉亚 KASPI 项目施工期间，面对人员少、任务重的局面，他主动补位，身兼数职，任劳任怨，加班加点，最终圆满完成工作任务，其中，包括机装管理、材料、技术、现场验收、与业主对接沟通等多个环节。

不讲条件，不辞辛苦，主动自我加压，邓清云用实实在在的工作业绩，展现出建材人敢为人先、艰苦奋斗的良好精神风貌，也给业主留下了不畏艰难、勇往直前的良好印象。

邓清云的精神在国内项目上也彰显得淋漓尽致。2018 年，他来到由中材国际所属成都建材院设计和机电施工总承包的华新昆明崇德项目。该项目的土建施工和设备采购由业主方负责，在土建交付安装和设备到货时间延迟的情况下，业主依然希望在预计时间内实现投产使用，这极大压缩了项目安装时间，给安装工作带来了非常大的挑战。

此时，业务能力过硬，安装经验丰富的邓清云毅然受命，前往华新昆明崇德项目参与安装工作。他在海外连续工作数月，刚从格鲁吉亚回到家里，第二天便马不停蹄，火速赶往项目部开展安装工作。在他的积极参与和同事共同努力下，华新昆明崇德项目高效地完成了紧张的安装任务，按计划顺利点火投产。

2020 年，邓清云担任埃及 Petrojet Φ 110m 原油储罐项目副经理。该项目是埃及国家级项目，也是中材国际成都建材院在做强做优水泥主业的基础上持续深耕埃及市场、首次进军石油化工领域的一项工程项目。全新的行业领域和工艺技

术对他而言都是考验，然而，突如其来的全球新冠疫情给正奋战在项目上的邓清云和他的团队增加了一场大考。

2020 年 3 月中旬至 7 月，项目逐步达到施工高峰期，公司也已在国内精心挑选了 2 支专业化的油罐施工队伍，正准备前往埃及开展施工作业。但由于航班原因，此前所有计划都被迫搁置，为保证项目建设任务顺利推进，项目团队决定采取属地化施工管理模式进行施工。

邓清云协助项目经理迅速组建了埃及项目管理团队和施工作业队伍。在施工高峰期，项目团队只有 5 名中方管理人员，埃及员工和施工作业人员达 600 余人。

属地化施工队伍组建好后，如何让缺乏大型油罐施工经验的埃方人员高质量完成项目建设，成了摆在他面前的另一道难题。

很快，邓清云凭着一股不服输的劲头，开始主动学习、带头钻研，短时间内系统掌握了大型油罐施工步骤、各种焊接材料适用性、制作工装、选配机器等一系列专业知识，并与项目团队一起研究施工细节和焊接工艺，制定了详细可行的施工方案。

目前，该项目已有 4 个原油罐按期、保质建成，并顺利通过业主进行的水压试验。业主方对中材国际的项目建设能力给予了高度认可和充分肯定，并将该施工方案在其他在建原油罐项目中推广。现在，该项目已通过吉尼斯世界纪录认证，成为世界最大的浮顶原油罐。（中材国际所属成都建材院）

多年的海外工作经历开阔了我的国际视野，丰富了我的人生阅历，我也收获了知识和才干，我将继续坚守海外，主动担当，积极作为，为公司国际化、多元化发展作出积极贡献。

A Devoted Man with Strong Sense of Responsibility

Deng Qingyun

Joined CNBM in October 2013

The Project Manager of Alternative Fuel Project for Sewedy Cement Plant undertaken by CDI in Egypt

Deng Qingyun is the Project Manager of Alternative Fuel Project for Sewedy Cement Plant in Egypt undertaken by CDI, a subsidiary of SINOMA International Engineering Co., Ltd. In 2014, he went to work abroad, and he participated in the construction of quite a few overseas projects including Saudi Arabia TCC project and Heidelberg Cement's Georgia KASPI project.

In 2016, Deng Qingyun went to work for Heidelberg Cement's Georgia KASPI project, which was a clinker production line built according to European standard. He studied hard and delved into new knowledge. He channeled all energy into technical and managerial improvement. Not long afterwards, he mastered all technical standards, thus laying a basis for his overseas work for years. During the construction of Georgia KASPI project, there were some tough problems such as understaffing and heavy tasks. He volunteered to undertake several job responsibilities, including management of machinery and equipment installation materials, technology, on-site check and acceptance, and communication and connection with owner.

With no preconditions or complaint, Deng Qingyun chose to assume more responsibilities. In his tangible work performance, the positive image of every pathfinding and hardworking employee in SINOMA International is readily discernible. He impressed owner as an excellent man who feared no adversary and forged ahead with determination.

Deng Qingyun's devotion to work was also noticeable in his work with some domestic projects. In 2018, he joined Huaxin-Kunming Chongde project. The owner was responsible for civil engineering construction and equipment procurement. Because civil engineering handover and arrival of equipment were delayed, the owner still hoped the production line could be put into operation according to original schedule. As a result, the time left of equipment installation became much shorter, so a huge challenge was posed to installation work.

At that time, Deng Qingyun met the challenge resolutely because of his solid business ability and rich installation experience. He participated in the installation work. As a matter of fact, he just came back home from Georgia, where he had worked for several months. But he left home the second day and hurried to the project site to handle installation work. With his participation and all installation technicians' concerted efforts, the installation task was completed on schedule and production line was put into operation as planned.

In 2020, Deng Qingyun was the Deputy Project Manager of Egypt Petrojet Φ110m crude oil tanks. This state-class project represented the first time that Chengdu Building Materials ventured into the petrochemical industry in Egypt after it had developed stronger and better cement business. For him, the new industry and technique was a real test. Yet, the unexpected COVID-19 pandemic became an additional challenge for Deng Qingyun and his team.

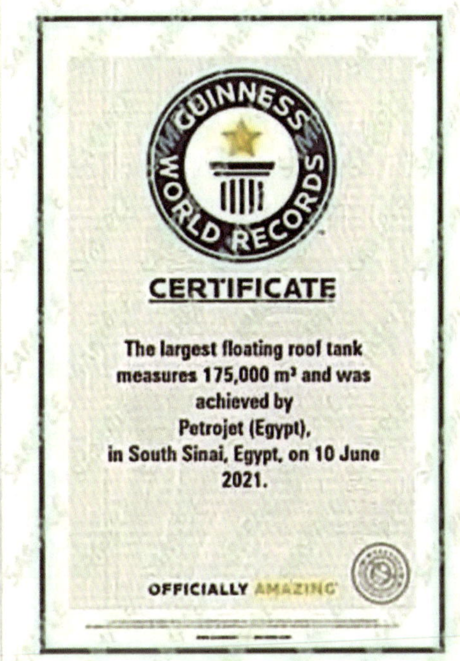

GUINNESS WORLD RECORDS
CERTIFICATE
The largest floating roof tank measures 175,000 m³ and was achieved by Petrojet (Egypt), in South Sinai, Egypt, on 10 June 2021.
OFFICIALLY AMAZING

From mid-March to July, 2020, the project construction gradually reached its peak period. The company had organized two professional construction teams of oil tanks in China, and would arrange the teams to start construction work in Egypt. But the suspended flight crippled all previous plans. To guarantee the sound progress in construction task, the project team decided to handle construction according to the model of localized construction management.

Deng Qingyun assisted Project Manager to build project management team and construction team, which were composed of Egyptian employees. In the construction peak period, there were only five Chinese managerial members, but as many as 600 Egyptian employees and construction workers.

After the local construction team was built, Deng Qingyun had to deal with another thorny problem: how to guarantee those Egyptian construction workers completed the construction task because they lacked any experience in construction of large oil tanks.

Soon afterwards, Deng Qingyun, an unyielding man, began to learn new things and dive into something difficult. He acquired professional knowledge regarding large oil tanks in the shortest time, including construction steps, applicability of all welding materials, making of work clothes and selection of machines and instruments. Together with the project team, he examined the construction details and welding technique and designed a detailed and feasible construction plan.

Now, four crude oil tanks in the project have been completed on schedule and they have passed the owner's water pressure test. The owner spoke highly of SINOMA International's project construction capability and went further to promote this construction plan in other crude oil tanks under construction. The project has been certified by Guinness World Records as the world's largest floating-roof crude oil tanks.

Personal Insights Years of overseas job experiences has widen my international vision, enriched my personnel experiences, and gained myself with knowledge and growth. I will continue to stick to overseas, take initiative to take responsibility, and make positive contributions to the international diversified development of the company.

挑重担排万难的善建者

杨冰峰

2002 年 7 月加入中国建材
现任工程管理二部部长、巴基斯坦日产 7700 吨水泥熟料生产线及配套余热发电和 24MW 煤电站总承包工程项目项目经理

2020 年 9 月 16 日凌晨 1 点 23 分，成都建材院巴基斯坦 PCC 日产 7700 吨熟料水泥生产线项目的（以下简称“PCC 项目”）项目经理杨冰峰发布了动态：“冲转 3000RPM 成功！兄弟们辛苦了，为你们骄傲！”记不得这是第几次工作到深夜，项目建设的每一点进步都在讲述着他数年如一日的坚守与责任。

PCC 项目是成都建材院在巴基斯坦的第一个工程总承包项目，包含配套 12MW 的余热发电和一座 2x12MW 燃煤电站。项目优质高效的履约为公司在当地树立了良好的企业形象。项目建设的每一步都是深深的脚印，每一个脚印都是栉风沐雨、砥砺前行的印记。

2019 年 4 月，项目机械设备安装接近尾声、计划空载试车时，全厂的钢结构综合廊道施工因印巴空战导致人员延期到场而耽误了。钢结构廊道上不仅有通往各个电气室的主电缆，还布置了通往各个车间的水管和压缩空气管道，以及余热发电的蒸汽管道和联通中控与各个电气室的控制光纤。只有廊道贯通全厂调试工作才能开展。为尽快打通这个大动脉，杨冰峰组织队伍开展三班倒的工作模式。本来需要 2—3 个月才能完成安装的架空综合廊道，项目部仅用 20 天就完成组对吊装。

2020 年 1 月 15 日，项目水泥生产线一次性点火成功；21 日，第一吨合格熟料成功产出；27 日，顺利生产出第一吨合格水泥。杨冰峰和他的团队展现出的一流项目管理能力赢得了业主的充分认可。

PCC 项目投产初期，新冠疫情全球大暴发。现场的欧洲设备服务工程师全部撤离。巴基斯坦也关停了所有商业航班，这让正处于考核前生产线调试阶段的项目失去了外部支持，从而变得举步维艰。然而，杨冰峰带领项目部人员一手抓疫情防控，一手抓调试考核，困难和问题被逐个击破。

依靠不轻言放弃的精神，项目部在 3 个月内完成了水泥熟料线及包装车间的所有性能考核。

项目配套电厂的安装调试工作也因厂家服务人员无法到达而面临暂停。电厂的部分安装调试是全新的挑战。

发电厂的心脏——汽轮机，运行精度高、联锁复杂。参数设置错误或联锁设置不合理都有可能造成不可修复的设备损伤。杨冰峰迅速组织项目电气和机械相关专业技术人员成立攻坚小组，研究设备说明书和图纸，查阅相关资料，并与厂家人员视频连线，在线指导解决难题。经过半个多月的努力，顺利完成了汽轮机的参数设置和联锁测试，最终一次性冲转成功。项目位于矿山山脉脚下，2020 年 9 月，项目所在地遭遇百年难遇的暴雨，厂区道路积水达半米。杨冰峰与业主积极商讨，一方面在厂外开挖临时截洪沟引流，及时封堵厂区围墙被冲垮的缺口，避免更多洪水涌入厂区；另一方面在厂区内开挖临时排水沟排除内涝。经过共同努力，尽管暴雨倾盆，厂外洪流滚滚，但项目现场仍机声隆隆，设备正常运转。

闲暇之余，杨冰峰组建项目篮球队、乒乓球队，开辟健身房，组织趣味运动会和卡拉OK 大赛，丰富大家的业余生活，为海外员工营造“家”的氛围。为帮助外聘工程师和当地员工融入团队，他组织双方参加活动，增强了项目部的凝聚力和向心力。

9 月的巴基斯坦秋高气爽，难得的片刻闲暇里，11 个月没回国的杨冰峰脑海中想象着这样一幕：项目全线竣工之后，亲手录上一段项目全景和生产的视频，让默默支持自己工作的妻女看看，让她们和自己一样，感受作为项目建设者的那份骄傲和自豪！（中材国际所属成都建材院）

我将始终秉持“爱岗敬业、无私奉献”的初心，继续加倍努力工作，把平凡的工作做到不平凡，用实际行动践行职责与担当，为公司的持续发展贡献应有的力量。

A Good Builder Who Shoulders Heavy Burdens and Overcomes Various Difficulties

Yang Bingfeng

Joined CNBM in July 2002

The Director of Engineering Management Department No.2 of CDI and the Project Manager of PCC 7700TPD Clinker Cement Production Line and Captive WHR and 24MW Coal Power Plant Project undertaken by CDI in Pakistan

At 1:23 a.m. on September 16 2020, Yang Bingfeng, the project manager of Pakistan PCC cement production line (hereinafter referred to as the "PCC project") with a daily output of 7,700 tons of Chengdu Design Research Institute of Building Materials Industry Co., Ltd., posted a message: "Running at 3,000RPM succeeded! All of you have worked hard and I am proud of you!" He can't remember how many times he worked late into the night. Every progress in the project construction is telling his persistence and responsibility.

The PCC project with a daily output of 7,700 tons of clinker cement production line is the first EPC project of Chengdu Design Research Institute of Building Materials Industry Co., Ltd. in Pakistan, including supporting 12MW waste heat power generation and a 2x12MW coal-fired power station. The high-quality and efficient performance of the project has established a good corporate image in the local area. Every deep footprint of project construction is a mark of the hard work forging ahead.

In April 2019, when the installation of machinery and equipment for the project was drawing to a close and no-load commissioning was scheduled to begin, the construction of the steel comprehensive corridor of the whole plant was delayed due to the postponed arrival of personnel as a consequence of the air war between India and Pakistan. On this steel corridor laid the main cables to each electrical room, water and compressed air pipes to each workshop, steam pipes for waste heat generation and control fibers linking the central control to each electrical room. Only with completion of this corridor could the commissioning of the whole plant be commenced. In order to open this artery in the shortest possible time, Yang Bingfeng organized teams to work 8 hours per shift and 3 shifts per day to have the overhead corridor paired and hoisted within 20 days instead of the usual 2 to 3 months!

The cement production line was successfully started on January 15, 2020. The first ton of qualified clinker was successfully produced on January 21. The first ton of qualified cement was successfully produced on January 27. The first-class project management ability shown by Yang Bingfeng and his team has won the full recognition of the owner.

The PCC project was commissioned at the beginning of the global outbreak of the COVID-19 pandemic. All European equipment service engineers at the site were evacuated. Pakistan completely shut down all commercial flights, which

made it impossible for the project that was in the pre-assessment production line commissioning stage to obtain external support, and the project was stagnant. However, Yang Bingfeng led the project team to focus on pandemic prevention and control together with commissioning, and solved the difficulties and problems one by one.

It is by relying on the spirit of "Never Give up Easily" that the Project Department completed all the performance assessments of the cement clinker line and packaging plant within three months.

The installation and commissioning of the power plant supporting the project were also stopped due to the unavailability of the manufacturer's service personnel. Installation and commissioning of the power plant was a new challenge for the project department.

Steam turbine, as the heart of power plants, required high equipment operation accuracy and complex interlocking. Wrong parameters or unreasonable interlock setting may well cause irreparable damage to the equipment. Yang Bingfeng quickly organized the professional and technical personnel related to the electrical and mechanical discipline of the project to set up an attack team. Everyone studied the equipment instructions and drawings, consulted various relevant materials, and connected with the manufacturer's personnel by video to guide and solve problems online. After more than half month's efforts, parameter setting and interlock testing of the steam turbine has been successfully completed. Finally, the steam turbine was successfully impulse-started. The project was located at the foot of the mine mountain range. In September 2020, the project site experienced a once-in-a-century torrential rainfall, and the road in the plant was waterlogged up to half a meter. Yang Bingfeng actively discussed with the owner to find a solution. On one hand, temporary flood interception ditches were excavated outside the plant to drain the water, and the gaps in the plant wall were blocked in time to avoid more floods entering the plant area. On the other hand, temporary drainage ditches were excavated in the plant to eliminate waterlogging. After our joint efforts, despite the torrential rain and the flooding outside the plant, the project site was still rumbling with the sound of machines and cheerful operation of equipment.

In his spare time, Yang Bingfeng set up the project basketball team and table tennis team, opened a gymnasium, organized fun games and karaoke competitions to enrich everyone's spare time, and created a "home" atmosphere for overseas employees. In order to help external engineers and local employees integrate into the team, he also actively invited them to participate in activities to enhance the cohesion and centripetal force of the department.

September is an autumn month in Pakistan. In a rare moment of leisure, Yang Bingfeng, who has not returned to China for 11 months, imagined this scene in his mind: after the completion of the project, he would personally record a video of the project panorama and production, so that his wife and daughter who have been silently supporting his work could see it and could feel his pride of being abuilder of this project!

Personal Insights I will always stay true to my original intention of “being passionate and dedicating selflessly to work”, keep working harder, try to make the extraordinary out of the ordinary, take on responsibility and commitments by concrete actions, and make my contributions to sustainable development of the company.

带着使命和爱　奔赴世界的各个角落

沈绵鑫

2007 年加入中国建材

现任合肥院工程设计公司工程部副部长

随着国家“一带一路”倡议的实施，沿线国家的基础设施建设大幅增加。如果把建材比作基础设施建设的“粮草”，那么建材人便是“一带一路”出海部队的“排头兵”。在此背景下，中材国际合肥院沈绵鑫带着建材人的使命，踏上了“一带一路”新征程。

2013 年 3 月，新疆项目刚结束，还来不及感受女儿出生的喜悦，沈绵鑫就马不停蹄地投身到了印度尼西亚日产 5000 吨项目。

印度尼西亚地处热带，为千岛之国。岛上荆棘遍布，毒蛇出没，蚊虫肆虐，但这些工作环境上的困难远不及地质问题严峻，复杂的地质才是他需要解决的第一道技术难题。项目临近河流，岩层地质极为复杂多变，有些地方相距几米远，但地质情况决然不同。作为土建负责人的他，深知这一情况事关重大。为此，他与地质勘探队同吃同住，起早贪黑，从勘探记录、钻芯取样到分析实验，每一个步骤都不放过，日晒雨淋，脱了皮也浑然不觉。在取得了准确的地勘报告之后，他立即组织国内专家进

行相关论证，因地制宜地选择地基处理方案，熟料库地沟采用碎石褥垫层加桩基，水泥库采用素混凝土换填桩间土，最大限度地节约工程成本。另一方面，他摆出大量的事实依据，向业主方提出地基处理费用补偿，经过坦诚的交流沟通，业主最终补偿近 150 万美元。

2021 年，他同时担任技术中心项目的现场负责人和卧龙中联商混项目的项目经理，多线作战的他忙得不亦乐乎。

2021 年 3 月底，巴基斯坦 ASKARI 日产 6500 吨熟料水泥生产线及配套项目签约，16

个月工期在国内亦是十分罕见，何况新冠疫情环境下的海外项目，难度可想而知。然而，他丝毫没有犹豫，欣然接受了担任项目经理的挑战。

合同即命令，开工即决战！项目启动后，他首先扑在了设计和采购环节。受新冠疫情影响，很多交流只能在线上进行，效率大打折扣，涉及关键细节，他不厌其烦，耐心沟通。工作上，他一直身先士卒，带领团队日复一日地加班加点，尽可能为现场施工赢得更多的时间。

在项目现场期间，他一直都是睡得最晚、醒得最早、吃住在中控室最多的那个人。在他的带领下，全体成员以“破釜沉舟”的决心，抱着“不服输，我能行”的信念，秉承“逢山开路，遇水架桥”的作风，勇往直前，直至取得最终的胜利。

2022 年 10 月 27 日，项目投料那一刻，业主方的很多人都流下了激动的泪水，不断称赞这是一个“能创造奇迹的项目部”。

尽管与家人聚少离多，也一直无法回答儿女们的“归期之问”，但想到自己投身的事业能够服务“一带一路”项目建设，增进“一带一路”沿线国家的民生福祉，带动中国制造的水泥装备走向国际化，他无怨无悔，无比自豪。（中材国际所属合肥院）

个人体会 作为一名扎根项目的建材人，虽然对家庭有很多亏欠，但想到投身的事业能够服务“一带一路”项目，带动水泥装备走向国际化，我无怨无悔。我愿继续以饱满的热情，带着使命和爱奔赴世界各个角落，用青春和热血去谱写新时代的建材篇章。

Driven by Mission and Passion, Traversing Every Corner of The World

Shen Mianxin

Joined CNBM in July 2007

The deputy director of the engineering department of HCRDI Engineering Design Company

As China's "Belt and Road" Initiative gains momentum, infrastructure development in countries along the route has experienced a remarkable surge. If construction materials are likened to the "nourishment" of infrastructure projects, then those working in the building materials industry are the vanguards of the "Belt and Road"Initiative expeditionary forces. Shen Mianxin of SINOMA International Hefei Cement Research & Design Institute Corporation Ltd. embarks on a new voyage within the framework of the "Belt and Road" Initiative, carrying the noble mission of the building materials industry.

In March 2013, right after completing the Xinjiang project, Shen Mianxin couldn't savor the joy of his daughter's birth. Instead, he immediately immersed himself in the demanding 5,000tpd project in Indonesia, without pausing for a moment.

Situated in the tropical region, Indonesia poses various challenges with its numerous islands, thorny terrain, venomous snakes, and persistent mosquitoes. However, these environmental difficulties are far less serious than geologic problems. His primary concern was tackling the complex geological conditions, which presented the foremost technical obstacle. The project site was in close proximity to a river, and the rock layers exhibited intricate and unpredictable variations even only a few meters apart. Understanding the criticality of selecting an appropriate foundation treatment plan, he dedicated himself to the task. Living and dining with the geological exploration team, he toiled day and night, meticulously examining exploration records, conducting core sampling, and performing analytical experiments. His commitment remained unwavering despite enduring harsh weather conditions and physical exhaustion. After acquiring accurate ground investigation reports, he promptly engaged Chinese experts to assess the findings and devise a suitable foundation treatment plan tailored to the local conditions. For the clinker warehouse, a gravel mattress bedding layer combined with pile foundations was adopted, while the cement warehouse utilized plain concrete to replace the soil between piles, maximizing cost savings for the project. Additionally, he provided substantial factual evidence to support his case for compensation of the foundation treatment costs, engaging in open and transparent communication with the owner. After thorough negotiations, the owner agreed to compensate nearly USD 1.5 million.

In 2021, he assumed the dual roles of Site Manager

for the technology center project and Project Manager for the Wolong Zhonglian Commercial Mix project, effectively managing multiple responsibilities simultaneously.

In late March, the signing of the Pakistan ASKARI 6,500t/d clinker cement production line and its supporting projects presented a unique opportunity. The project's construction period of 16 months, especially in the context of the ongoing new crown epidemic, posed significant challenges. Nevertheless, he embraced the opportunity with unwavering determination and willingly took on the role of project manager, undeterred by the anticipated difficulties.

The contract marked the initiation of the battle, and he wasted no time in delving into the intricacies of design and procurement as soon as the project commenced. Amidst the backdrop of the COVID-19 pandemic, numerous interactions were confined to online platforms, significantly impeding efficiency, particularly in addressing critical details. Nonetheless, he exhibited unwavering patience and perseverance, engaging in continuous communication. Serving as a trailblazer, he led his team by example, consistently working overtime day after day to secure as much time as possible for on-site construction. .

Throughout the project, he demonstrated unwavering dedication, often sacrificing sleep, waking up early, and spending most of his time in the central control room. Under his leadership, the entire team pressed forward with the determination to overcome all obstacles, firmly believing in

their ability to succeed without surrendering, and adopting a proactive approach of forging a path through every mountain and building bridges over every waterway. This unwavering spirit ultimately led them to achieve a resounding victory.

On October 27, as the project was officially commissioned and put into operation, an overwhelming wave of excitement swept through the owner's team, leaving many of them moved to tears and hailing the project department for "creating miracles".

Despite being frequently separated from his family and unable to provide definitive answers to his children's inquiries about his return, he firmly believes that his career is a meaningful contribution to the development of the "Belt and Road" Initiative projects and the betterment of the communities along the route. The thought of serving the construction of "Belt and Road" Initiative, improving the livelihoods of people in the countries involved, and promoting the internationalization of Chinese cement equipment fills him with immense pride and satisfaction.

Personal Insights As a person who rooted in the project of building materials, although I have a lot of guilt to my family, I have no regrets when I associate that the career, I am engaged in can serve the "Belt and Road" project, and drive the internationalization of cement equipment. I would like to continue to go to every corner of the world with full enthusiasm, mission and love, and write a new era of building materials with youth and blood.

感动从来系家国

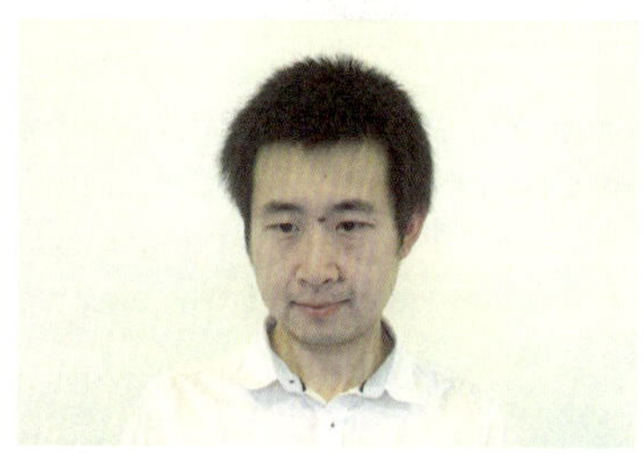

张延龙
2018 年加入中国建材
现任中材海外阿根廷项目部英语翻译

33 岁的张延龙是中材海外阿根廷 L'Amali 二线日产 5800 吨水泥熟料生产线项目现场翻译组副组长。自 2018 年 10 月加入中材海外以来，他执念坚忱，精进恪守，将自己的青春和热血投入到公司在南美这幅画卷的创作中，留下了许多令人感动的事迹。

自加入阿根廷项目以来，张延龙主动放弃回国休假的机会，一直坚守在工作岗位上，成为现场部连续驻外时间最长的员工。2019 年 6 月至 9 月，在现场部开展“大干 100 天”生产建设活动中，他更是放弃了每月一次的休息机会，与其他领导和同事并肩战斗在项目建设的第一线，为公司奉献着智慧和汗水。

日常工作中，张延龙立足本职，倾情敬业，仅 2019 年就参与了 10 余次安装周例会、24 次 Tie-In 例会、7 次 UT 高管会以及多次与业主管理团队之间的重要会议。除了会议口译，他还参与完成会议纪要的书面翻译 40 余份、各类施工方案翻译 10 余份、邮件及信函翻译近百份。作为现场翻译组副组长，他对翻译工作进行全面协调和安排，文件内容涵盖现场安装工作周计划、施工方案及财税政策等，有力配合了现场各项工作的开展。疫情期间，他带领翻译同事对与疫情相关的 100 多份当地政策和法律法规信息进行收集和翻译，为疫情防控以及后续工作提供了有力支持。自加入项目以来，他还对 6000 多封项目函件进行收集整理和分类，极大地方便了项目部与业主的沟通和工作开展。

为满足现场施工需求，张延龙参与了“220t 汽车吊以及生料磨和水泥磨大件吊装所需的 350t 履带吊租赁合同”的签订和执行。尤其是在项目领导的大力支持下，与吊车公司就 350t 履带吊的租赁计算起讫时间进行了艰苦的谈判，最终成功说服对方扣减 3 天时间，为公司节省了至少 15000 美元。在隔离停工期间，他说服吊车公司免除停工期间近两个月的设备闲置费用超过 8 万美元。复工复产后，他对 220t 汽车吊的租赁计算起讫时间与对方展开谈判，再次为公司节约 7000 多美元。

除了本职工作外，为了更好地应对阿根廷当地的疫情，张延龙积极参与现场疫情防控工作，不仅组织同事对疫情相关的政策信息和法律法规进行收集整理和翻译，而且还参与了“一措施五预案”等防疫制度文件的编制、复工复产疫情防控流程的编制和翻译，以及各上级单位对现场疫情防控工作进行巡视的迎检准备工作。2020 年 5 月 19 日，项目所在地奥拉瓦利亚市市长及当地卫生官员一行对项目现场复工复产疫情防控工作进行检查并给予高度评价。

张延龙甘愿放弃自己与家人团聚的机会，以勇于担当、甘于吃苦、乐于奉献的精神，积极投身到公司在南美大陆“桥头堡”项目的建设中，全力支持和参与公司的国际产能合作和全球化战略的实施。这种“黄沙百战穿金甲，不破楼兰终不还”的精神，也是每一个奋斗在一线建材人的写照。（中材国际所属中材海外）

个人体会 非常感谢公司能给我提供一个广阔的舞台施展自己的才能，曾经加入阿根廷项目团队，我感到荣幸，我愿意立足自己的本职岗位，用自己的专业知识和丰富经验，继续为公司的高质量发展贡献自己的光和热。

Work Hard to Serve the Country and People

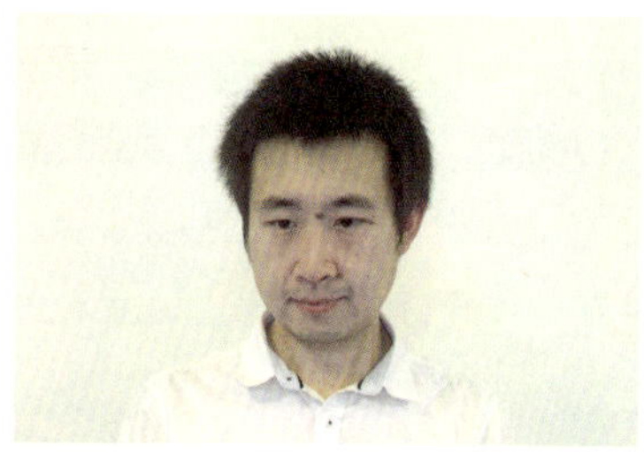

Zhang Yanlong

Joined CNBM in 2018

The English Interpreter of SINOMA Overseas Argentina Project Department

Zhang Yanlong, 33 years old, is Deputy Leader of the On-site Translation Team for the L'Amali No.2 5800t/d Cement Clinker Production Line Project of SINOMA Overseas Engineering Co., Ltd. in Argentina. Since working in SINOMA Overseas Engineering Co., Ltd. in October 2018, he has devoted his youth and enthusiasm to the cause in South America, leaving us countless touching moments.

Since joining the Argentina project, Zhang Yanlong has voluntarily given up the annual leave and stayed in his posts, becoming the longest-staying overseas employee of the Site Department. In the "100 arduous days" production and construction activity launched by the Department from June to September 2019, he has even given up the monthly off days and worked together with other leaders and colleagues at the forefront, contributing wisdom and sweat to the company.

In daily work, Zhang Yanlong is meticulous and dedicated to his job. In 2019 alone, he participated in more than 10 weekly installation meetings, 24 Tie-In regular meetings, 7 UT senior management meetings and several important meetings with the employer management team. In addition to conference interpretation, he participated in the translation of more than 40 minutes of written meeting materials, more than 10 construction schemes and nearly 100 emails and letters. As the Deputy Leader, he coordinated and arranged the translation work in an all-around manner. The documents involved the weekly plan for on-site installation, construction scheme and fiscal & taxation policies. With great efforts, he has played an effective role in the on-site teamwork. During the pandemic, he led his team to complete the collection and translation work, covering more than 100 pieces of documents on local policies, laws and regulations related to the pandemic, providing strong support for the pandemic prevention and control and follow-up work. Since the engagements in the project, he has also sorted out nearly 6,000 project letters, which has greatly facilitated the communication between the Department and the employer.

To cater to the requirements of on-site construction, Zhang Yanlong participated in the signing and implementation of lease contracts for 220t truck cranes required for on-site installation and 350t crawler cranes required for lifting large pieces of raw meal and cement mills. Especially with the powerful support of the project leader, he and his team, with great efforts, negotiated with the crane

company on the starting and ending time for calculating the lease of the 350t crawler crane, and finally persuaded them to deduct 3 days, saving at least USD 15,000 for the company. During the quarantine shutdown, he persuaded the crane company to exempt the equipment idle cost, saving exceeding USD 80,000 for nearly two months. After the resumption of work and production, he negotiated with them on the lease period of the 220t truck crane, saving over USD 7,000 for the company again.

Besides his own work, Zhang Yanlong, aiming to better cope with the local pandemic situation in Argentina, actively participated in on-site pandemic prevention and control. He organized colleagues to collect, sort out and translate policy information, laws and regulations related to the pandemic, formulate the anti-COVID-19 frameworks, such as "one measure and five plans", and prepare and translate relevant procedures for resumption of work and production; also, he completed the preparation for superior departments' patrol inspection of on-site pandemic prevention and control work. The Mayor of Olavarria, where the project is located, and local health officials conducted an inspection on the resumption of work and production on the project site and gave extremely high comments on May 19, 2020.

By sacrificing the opportunity to reunite with his family members, Zhang Yanlong actively participated in the construction of the company's "bridgehead" project in South America with a sense of responsibility and dedication, contributing to the implementation of the company's international capacity cooperation and globalization strategy. As an old Chinese poem says, "We will not leave the desert till we beat the foe, although in war our golden armor is outworn", it interprets the epitome of every builder of SINOMA International struggling at the front-line.

Personal Insights I do feel grateful to the company for giving me such a shiny stage to allow myself to achieve what I can. It is also my great honor to have been working with the Argentina Project Team. In the coming future, I will dedicate myself to my own position and make contribution to the high-quality growth of the company with my own profession and experience.

坚定不移的“青松”

维斯利·昆达

2011 年加入中国建材

现任中材国际赞比亚分公司保税库主管助理

韦斯利是赞比亚本地人，自 2011 年起就加入了中材国际赞比亚分公司，是分公司最早招聘的一批属地化员工。当时他还是个年仅 21 岁的青涩小伙，工作经验欠缺的他从最基础的普工做起，经过十几年，一步步成长为管理人员，目前他的主要职责是管理保税库和监督卡车的装卸货。

2011 年时的赞比亚分公司，承建的 Dangote 水泥厂项目急需用人，韦斯利作为建筑大军中的一员，在施工现场挥洒着汗水与青春，无怨无悔，任劳任怨。虽然工厂离家远，每天往返通勤需数小时，但韦斯利依然坚持按时上班，节假日需要加班也从不推辞。在 Dangote 项目的 7 年时光中，韦斯利打扫过卫生，当过建筑工人，也做过帮厨，他就像一块砖，哪里需要往哪里搬。年复一年，日复一日，他始终坚守在工作岗位上。

Dongote 工厂完工后，韦斯利被调往 Kasumbalesa 仓库，当时仓库人员极为匮乏，也缺少能够信任的员工。韦斯利来到仓库后，在中方员工的带领下，负责招聘并管理 20 多名当地员工，同时记录仓库水泥、煤炭、钢筋等货物的进出。经过之前工地 7 年的锻炼，韦斯利已具备一定的工作管理经验，凭借着谨慎严谨的工作态度，把仓库货物管理得井井有条。在这期间，韦斯利通过处理日常工作中的各种问题，不断优化工作流程，提高工作效率，形成了自己的一套工作方法。

凭借着出色的工作管理水平和认真的工作态度，在工作 4 年后，韦斯利被调往了恩多拉保税库，也就是现在的赞比亚分公司驻地，在这里他继续担任着同样的职务，管理保税库货物的进出与当地员工。虽然如今的仓库场地比之前大数倍有余，员工数量也多于此前，货物量和种类也较之前更多、更繁杂，但韦斯利凭借过去积累的工作经验和工作方法，再管理起来已经能做到得心应手。

在工作之外，韦斯利还非常热爱学习，经常在工作之余与中国员工练习学说中国话，现在他已经能用汉语和中国员工进行日常交流，

在工作中也爱用汉语和人打招呼、开玩笑。他常笑着说：“中国话不简单，中国人更不简单”。韦斯利总是充满热情，他热爱这份工作，也热爱中国文化，不断学习新事物是他保持前进的不竭动力，也是他提升工作能力的基石。

十余年的坚守，韦斯利甚至比不少中国员工来赞比亚的工作时间还要长，在本地员工当中更是元老般的存在。他就如坚定不移的青松一样，扎根在中材的这片土壤之中，茁壮成长，直至枝繁叶茂。

沐风栉雨十余载，苏州中材已在赞比亚闯出了自己的一片天地，而在这片广袤的土地上，应该有更多像韦斯利这样坚韧不拔的青松，为公司的属地化发展巩固土壤，也在公司的呵护下茁壮成长，直至撑起一片更广阔的蓝天。（中材国际所属苏州中材）

我加入中材国际已经十余年了，从最初的普工一路成长为现在的管理人员。我知道，我可以永远相信和依靠公司，对此我非常感激，衷心希望中材国际以及中国能够继续发展壮大。

Wesley: Unswerving Green Pine

Wesley Kunda

Joined CNBM in 2011

The Assistant Supervisor of SINOMA International Engineering Co., Ltd. (Zambia Branch)'s Bonded Warehouse.

Wesley is a native of Zambia and has been employed by the Zambia branch of SINOMA since 2011. He was one of the earliest localized employees recruited by the branch. At that time, he was only a young and inexperienced young man at the age of 21. He started as a basic general worker and gradually grew into a management personnel after more than a decade. Currently, his main responsibilities are managing bonded warehouses and supervising the loading and unloading of trucks.

In 2011, the Zambia branch was still in the initial stage of development, and the Dangote cement plant project under construction was in urgent need of employment. As a member of the construction team, Wesley shed sweat and youth on the construction site, without complaint or regret, working tirelessly. Although the factory is far from home and he had to commute for several hours every day, Wesley still insisted on working on time and never refused to work overtime during holidays. During his 7 years at Dangote, Wesley cleaned the house, worked as a construction worker, and also worked as a kitchen assistant. He was like a brick, moving wherever he needed to go. Year after year, day after day, he persisted in his work.

After the completion of the Dongote factory, Wesley was transferred to the Kasumbalesa warehouse, where there was a severe shortage of personnel and trusted employees. After Wesley arrived at the warehouse, under the leadership of Chinese employees, he was responsible for recruiting and managing more than 20 local employees, while recording the entry and exit of goods such as cement, coal, and steel bars in the warehouse. After 7 years of work at the previous construction site, Wesley had gained some management experience and, with a cautious and rigorous work attitude, managed the warehouse goods in an orderly manner. During this period, Wesley developed his own set of working methods by addressing various issues in his daily work, continuously optimizing workflow, and improving work efficiency.

With excellent management and serious attitude, after 4 years of work, Wesley was transferred to Ndola Bonded Warehouse, which is now the resident of Zambia branch. He continues to hold the same position, managing the entry and exit of goods in the bonded warehouse and the local staff of the warehouse. Although the warehouse space is now several times larger than before, with a much larger number of employees, and a more diverse variety of goods than before, Wesley has been able

to manage it with ease thanks to his work experience and methods accumulated in the past.

Besides work, Wesley also loves learning and often practices Chinese with Chinese employees in his spare time. Now, he can communicate with Chinese employees in Chinese on a daily basis, and he also likes to greet and joke with people in Chinese during work. He often smiles and says, "Chinese is not simple, and Chinese people are even more so." Wesley is always full of enthusiasm. He loves this job and also Chinese culture. Continuously learning new things is his inexhaustible motivation to keep moving forward, and it is also the cornerstone of his ability to improve his work.

After more than 10 years of perseverance, Wesley has even worked longer than many Chinese employees in Zambia, and is a veteran among local employees. He is like an unwavering green pine, rooted in the soil of the company, thriving until the branches and leaves are lush.

After more than 10 years of wind and rain, SINOMA (Suzhou) has broken through its own territory in Zambia. In this vast land, there should be more resilient pine trees like Wesley standing on top of it, consolidating the soil for the company and growing recklessly under care until it can support that blue sky.

Personal Insights I have joined the SINOMA family for more than ten years. Starting as a general worker, deep down, I know I can always count on SINOMA. For that, I will always be grateful and I truly hope that SINOMA as well as China will prosper with each passing day.

与中材国际在一起

卡尔万·卡迈勒·穆罕默德
2015 年加入中国建材
现任中材工贸（伊拉克）有限公司采购专员

2007 年，中材国际所属单位苏州中材第一次走进伊拉克，公司承接了伊拉克苏莱曼尼亚 SCP 日产 5000 水泥熟料生产线总承包项目，正式拉开了在伊拉克的开拓耕耘，也翻开了公司国际市场拓展的新篇章。作为中国建材集团旗下致力于水泥工程板块的骨干企业和央企“走出去”国际化的排头兵，10 多年来，中材国际深耕伊拉克市场，一路高歌猛进，践行了“一带一路”倡议，并成功扎根伊拉克，创造了辉煌的成绩，树立了水泥工程领域的品牌，刷新了中国企业的形象。

然而，成就是来之不易的，与每篇励志故事一样，苏州中材在伊拉克的发展也充满艰难与挑战，当时，在一个刚刚走出战争阴霾的国家里，各项工作开展举步维艰。我们今天故事的主人公——卡尔万，在 2015 年加入苏州中材的团队，作为公司的属地员工，他既是推动公司国际化发展的践行者，也是公司在伊拉克发展历程的见证人。

2015 年 3 月，随着公司 GRD 项目建设高峰期的到来，卡尔万作为司机和翻译第一次来到苏州中材位于苏莱曼尼亚市 Bazian 镇项目建设现场，由于此前多年的英国工作经历，他的英语非常流畅并且拥有丰富的工作经验，所以很快就融入公司的团队，这个渴望以实际行动来建设库尔德美好未来的伊拉克人正式成为苏州中材的一名员工。

2015 年，按照公司长远发展规划，鉴于苏莱曼尼亚位于北部相对安全的库尔德地区，政治也相对稳定，市场前景广阔，经过充分调研，公司决定在这里投资建设钢结构工厂。此时的卡尔万临危受命，被调入钢构厂筹建项目部，他不仅担任司机和翻译，而且还主动承担了筹建前期的各项准备工作及项目所需材料的市场调查和采购工作。

2016 年，钢构厂项目建设完成，看到一个自己亲身参与建设的崭新工厂拔地而起，他感到无比的骄傲与自豪，为自己工作的成绩感到开心的同时，他也放弃了再回英国工作的念头，决定一直留在中材国际。钢构厂建成投产后，由于 ISIS 的影响尚未消除，业务量尚不饱满，卡尔万又积极参与到市场经营工作中，利用他的关系和人脉，为钢构厂开拓市场寻找业务。

2020 年 2 月份以来，突如其来的新冠肺炎疫情席卷全球，伊拉克也没有幸免，当地社会人心惶惶。为了接送公司员工往来轮换，卡尔万经常需要连夜往返机场。因为疫情，项目部要求员工尽量减少外出，很多业务必须要卡尔万出面与外界进行沟通，包括所有员工的食堂食材以及生活用品采购，他都会高效地完成，从来没有怨言，在他心里，以上这些事只需要简单的一句话来解释："这是我的工作"。

十几年来，苏州中材在伊拉克开拓与坚守，耕耘出了自己的一片天地，作为苏州中材的一名员工，卡尔万的生活也随着公司发展变得更加美好，在苏州中材实现了自己的梦想与价值。（中材国际所属苏州中材）

个人体会 我非常喜欢苏州中材，在 SINOMA 工作很愉快，也喜欢跟中国朋友在一起工作。在 9 年的工作时间里，我结交了很多中国朋友，和他们一起共事有很多快乐，我们共同克服工作中的困难，希望中材国际在伊拉克再创佳绩。

Karwan: SINOMA and I, We Are Together

Karwan Kamal Mohamad

Joined CNBM in 2015

The Purchasing Specialist of SINOMA Industry & Trade (Iraq) Co., Ltd.

In 2007, SINOMA (Suzhou) entered Iraq for the first time, with the undertaking of EPC contracting project of SCP 5000T/D cement clinker production line in Sulaymaniyah, Iraq. SINOMA (Suzhou) opened up a new chapter in international market expansion. As a backbone member of China National Building Material Group Co., Ltd(CNBM). dedicated to the cement engineering sector and a pioneer in the internationalization of central enterprises, the company has been deeply involved in the Iraqi market for more than ten years and has made great strides all the way. With brilliant achievements in creativity, the company has established a brand in the field of cement engineering and refreshed the image of Chinese enterprises.

However, achievements are not easily harvested. Just like every inspirational story, SINOMA (Suzhou)'s development in Iraq is also full of difficulties and challenges. What's more, rooting in a country that has just got rid of the shadow of war, it is difficult to carry out various tasks. The hero of today's story is Karwan, who joined SINOMA (Suzhou) in 2015. As a local employee of the company, he is not only a member of this story, but a witness of the company's development in Iraq.

In March 2015, with the peak period of the GRD project construction, Karwan came to this project site in Bazian Town, Sulaymaniyah, working as a driver and translator for the first time. Thanks to the rich work experience in UK, he can speak very fluent English so he quickly integrated into the company's team. This Iraqi, who is eager to build a prosperous future for Kurds with his hands and practical actions, officially became an employee of SINOMA (Suzhou).

In 2015, according to the company's long-term development plan and the goal of taking root in the Iraqi market, since Sulaymaniyah is located in the northern Kurdish region, the site was acknowledged as having the advantages of relatively safe environment, politically stable environment, and broad market prospects. After full research, SINOMA (Suzhou) made the decision to invest in the construction of a steel structure factory. At this time, Karwan was appointed and transferred to the construction project department of the steel structure factory. He not only served as the driver and translator, but also took the initiative to undertake various preparatory work in the early stage of construction and market research as well as procurement of materials required for the project.

In 2016, the construction of the steel structure

factory project was completed, and he felt extremely proud when he saw a new factory that he personally participated in the construction. Giving up the idea of working in the UK, he decided to stay with SINOMA (Suzhou). After the steel structure factory was completed and put into production, the business was not optimistic due to the remaining influence of ISIS. Karwan actively participated in the marketing operation work, using his relationships and contacts to open up the market for the steel structure factory.

Since February 2020, Iraq was impacted by the sudden outbreak of COVID-19 epidemic, and the country was in panic. In order to pick up and drop off company's employees, Karwan often needed to go to and from the airport overnight, and even needed to go deep into the borders of Iran and Turkey. Because of the epidemic, the project department minimized the chances of going out and communicating with the outside world. Many businesses required Karwan to communicate with the outside world, including the purchase of canteen ingredients and daily necessities for all employees. He always completed efficiently and never complained. In his heart, he explained the above tasks only with a simple sentence :This is my job.

For more than a decade, SINOMA (Suzhou) has cultivated its own world in Iraq with the spirits of pioneer and persistence. As an employee of SINOMA (Suzhou), we wish Karwan a better life and realize his dreams and values in SINOMA (Suzhou) .

Personal Insights Karwan said that "I really like SINOMA (Suzhou), and I am very happy to work in SINOMA (Suzhou). I also like to work with Chinese friends. During nine years of work, I have made many Chinese friends and worked with them very happily. We have overcome difficulties in work together. Now, I'm able to deal with foreign affairs, part of material procurement and part of steel structure marketing work independently. I hope SINOMA (Suzhou) continues to achieve good results in Iraq.

运维之花——尼拉

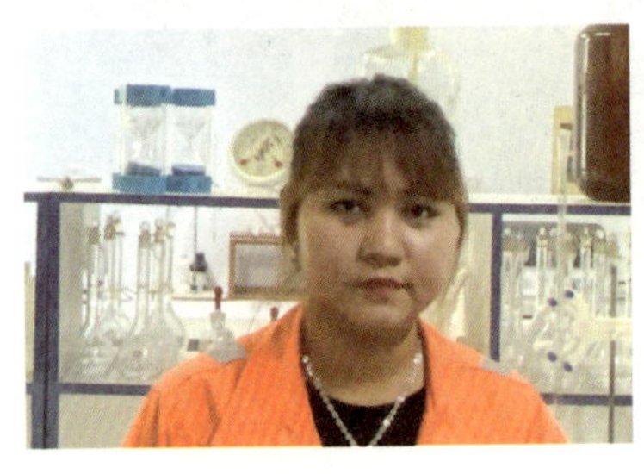

婷·尼拉·邓
2017 年加入中国建材
现任邯郸中材缅甸旦多淼保产项目质检员

有一种经历叫成长，有一种情感叫友谊，有一种情绪叫感恩。邯郸中材缅甸旦多淼保产项目就有这样一位缅籍员工，她就是被称为“运维之花”的尼拉。她以纯朴而务实的工作作风、稳健而敬业的工作态度展现了独有的“风采”，在与中国员工的相识、知识技术的学习中，成为中国建材一名忠实的“铁粉”。

尼拉，毕业于缅甸曼德勒大学，化学专业，化学类研究生，2017 年加入邯郸中材缅甸旦多淼保产项目，从事原材料分析、检测等工作。她深知自己肩上的责任，在日常的工作中，始终严格执行质量控制，对工作认真负责，任劳任怨。在原材料出现结果不一致时，第一时间到现场取样、观察、分析、汇报，做到及时调整物料。无论环境多么恶劣，她从不推诿、不退缩、不计较，雷厉风行，她的精神深深影响到身边同事，也促使大家在工作中更加认真负责，确保进场原材料把控、数据的真实、质量的稳定。

在项目属地化管理中，尼拉以老员工的身份，对新同事耐心辅导，手把手地教。把自己工作中的所学和遇到的各种状态都一一传输给了新同事们，使他们迅速成长。多年来，她为公司培养了不少的优秀人才。

在工作中，当她知道其他员工身体不舒服请假时，总是第一个冲到主管办公室，用“不流利”的中国话说：“我……去……替……

他……工作。”后来主管在一次闲聊中了解到，这份工作对她来说非常重要，她很重视这份工作，对此她的心中充满了感激。

翻看尼拉的工作笔记，在很显眼的位置写着这样一句话：“一个人的思想决定一个人的命运。不敢向高难度的工作挑战，是对自己的画地为牢，只能使自己无限的潜能化为有限的成就。”当问她这句话来源与释义时，她笑了，默默地说了一句：“我喜欢 SINOMA，喜欢中国。这是以前的一个中国姐姐和我说的。”

在国家“一带一路”倡议下，邯郸中材缅甸项目全体人员不忘初心，砥砺前行。结合公司属地化和多元化发展，有力带动了当地员工就业。我们也结识了一批缅甸员工，从相识、相知到无所不谈。从 2017 年到现在，一起走过了 7 年。7 年的青春见证邯郸中材缅甸保产项目的风风雨雨。邯郸中材以“授人以鱼不如授人以渔”的精神，吸引了陪伴公司成长的众多“铁粉”，一起扬帆远航。（中材国际所属邯郸中材）

个人体会

工作岗位是珍贵的，需要我们珍惜，就职岗位既是公司对我们的认可也是对我们的考验，所以来到了岗位上就要时刻坚守，对工作认真负责，为了公司，也为了自己，用辛劳创造价值，用努力回报公司，我喜欢 SINOMA，喜欢中国。

The Flower of Operation and Maintenance - Nila

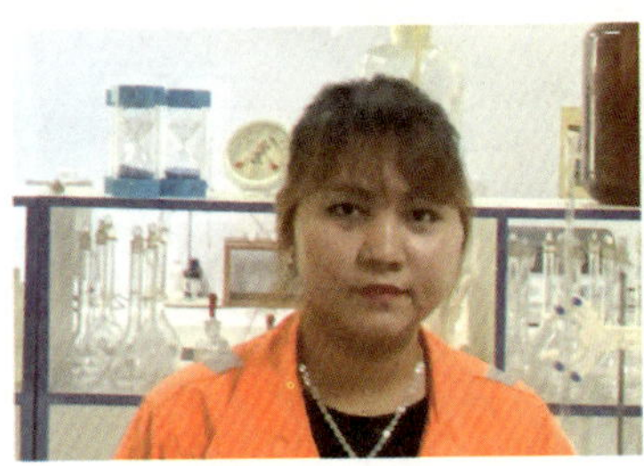

Tin Nilar Thein

Joined CNBM in 2017

The Quality inspector of SINOMA (Handan) Myanmar Than Taw Myat O&M project

There is a kind of accompany called "growth". There is a kind of emotion called "friendship", and there is a kind of mindset called "gratitude". In Handan SINOMA Myanmar Denomiao production protection project, there is such a Burmese employee, known as "operation and maintenance flower" Nila. With her simple and pragmatic work style, steady and dedicated work attitude, she showed the unique "style" of the project, and became a loyal "diehard fan" in the acquaintance with Chinese employees, the influence of corporate culture, and the learning of knowledge and technology.

Nila, graduated from Mandalay University, Myanmar, majored in chemistry, and acquired her master's degree in chemistry. In 2017, she joined Handan SINOMA Myanmar Dendomiao production protection project, engaged in raw material analysis and testing. Controlling raw materials into the market, she knows the responsibility on her shoulders. In the daily work, she always strictly implements quality control, is serious and responsible for the work. When the results of raw materials are inconsistent, she 's always the first to be on site for sampling, observing, analyzing, reporting, so as to adjust the material in time. No matter what the weather is, she never retreats. Vigorous and resolute, she has led the atmosphere for other colleagues as well, ensured the control of incoming raw materials, the authenticity of data, and the stability of quality.

In the "localization" management of the project, Nila, as an old employee, patiently coached and taught hand by hand. The experience learned and encountered in her work were passed down to others, so that they can quickly "grow up". Over the years, many outstanding talents have been cultivated by her for the project.

When she knew that other employees were not feeling well and asked for leave, she was always the first to rush to the supervisor's office, saying in "unfamiliar Chinese" : I... go to ... for ... he...work." She said that, "Without this job, I don't know where to go." Her heart is full of gratitude.

Reading through Nila's work notes, a sentence read: "A person's thoughts determine a person's fate. Dare not to challenge the difficult work, is to make their unlimited potential into limited achievements." When asked about the source and interpretation of this sentence, she smiled and said silently: "I like SINOMA Handan. I like China. "This is what her former Chinese colleague told her.

Under the "Belt and Road" Initiative, all the staff of

Handan SINOMA Myanmar project will not forget the original intention and will forge ahead. Combined with the company's localized management, the company has diversified local development, and promoted the employment of local employees. We get to know a group of Myanmar employees, from mere acquaintance to friends with whom we can talk about everything. Since 2017, we have gone through seven years together. Seven years of youth witnessed the ups and downs of Handan SINOMA Myanmar production protection project. Under the guidance of the company's strategic policy, all the personnel of Handan SINOMA Myanmar Dantomiao production preservation project have attracted many "diehard fans". Let's keep striving together.

Personal Insights Jobs are precious and need to be cherished. The post is not only the company's recognition but also a test for us. Thus we should always stick to the post, and be responsible for the work, for the company, for ourselves. We should work hard to create value to reward the company. I love SINOMA (Handan). I love China.

勇担当　善作为　驻外 10 年献青春

霍建国

2008 年加入中国建材
现任中建材海外经济合作有限公司北京分公司
项目总监兼科特迪瓦项目部经理

习近平总书记在党的二十大报告中指出："青年强，则国家强。当代中国青年生逢其时，施展才干的舞台无比广阔，实现梦想的前景无比光明。"2008 年入职中国建材的霍建国，如今他已驻外工作十余年，分别在利比亚、伊拉克、沙特、科特迪瓦留下工作的足迹。

新时代青年，既要怀抱梦想又要脚踏实地，既要敢想敢为又要善作善成。2009 年，入职刚一年的霍建国怀着"世界很大，想去看看，拓展工作经历"的想法，主动请缨，前往利比亚 FWAM 水泥厂项目，担任控制部经理，负责项目商务计划合约工作。利比亚内战暴乱期间，他仍坚守现场，在最后一批撤侨人员返回国内前，拿到了业主对已竣工项目的确认。利比亚项目结束后，霍建国又先后被派往伊拉克和沙特，负责审计、项目现场经理等工作。十多年来，他一直在"一带一路"上奋力前行，在每个项目上尽心尽责，付出了艰辛的汗水，留下一个个坚实的脚印。

2018 年 10 月，为统筹做好科特迪瓦非洲杯体育设施设计及建设项目，驻外经验丰富的霍建国又被派往科特迪瓦，担任项目部经理，全面负责科特迪瓦体育场项目管理工作，包括安全、进度、质量、成本、合同、信息和协调。原本两年的项目工期，因新冠疫情等原因被迫延后，霍建国在科特迪瓦一待就是 5 年。

科特迪瓦体育场项目位于非洲西部科特迪瓦北部城镇科霍戈，是 2024 年科特迪瓦非洲杯体育场馆之一，项目主要建设内容包括可容纳观众 2 万座的体育场、可容纳 50 个床位的三星级酒店、1 个运动员村及 4 个训练场地。项目于 2019 年 5 月开工，原定合同工期为 24 个月。2020 年突发的新冠疫情打乱了项目工期的正常进度。既要赶项目进度，又要带领项目团队成员克服心理障碍，霍建国通过各种方式突破困境。

疫情期间，他积极落实"稳住人心，稳在当地"的要求，在海外有限的条件下，尽可能在工作之余组织象棋、乒乓球、拔河比赛等各类文体活动，增强员工集体荣誉感和团队协作

精神。针对特殊时期员工家人寻医问药难问题，及时了解情况并汇报公司，调动一切可以调动的资源购买急需药品并送至员工家中，让驻外员工放心安心。

疫情3年，霍建国严格按照公司统一部署，坚持科学组织、周密实施，实现生产防疫齐步走，积极协调处理员工生活、工作及家庭困难，带领项目团队成员克服超期驻外心理焦虑。

蓝图越宏伟，奋斗越艰巨。科特迪瓦体育场项目在执行初期，工程进度、进度款收款工作处于参建企业中下游，每次开会都是被批评的对象，公司也为此承担了比较大的压力。

项目经理，被业界广泛称之为“啦啦队长”，其实还有一种称呼是“救火队长”，霍建国经常将自己称为“救火队长”，哪里有紧急任务，他就出现在哪里。为了扭转局面，霍建国不断改进工作思路，打破以往“等靠要”的思维模式，创造性解决问题。到了项目中后期，项目部逐渐扭转劣势，成为业主方在各种官方场合表扬的对象，赢得科特政府的好评。

历史的大潮汹涌澎湃，时代的洪流滚滚向前。驻外工作十余年的霍建国，从三十而立到如今已过不惑之年，他追求梦想、不负韶华，在推动共建“一带一路”高质量发展的进程中，绽放出火热的青春之花。（中建材海外经济合作有限公司北京分公司）

个人体会 平台很重要，让员工有机会可以通过勤奋、拼搏实现自我价值，树立正确的价值观；祖国的强大很重要，让驻外员工时刻感受到祖国在默默地守护着他们。强烈的民族自豪感让央企员工在海外有足够的勇气面对各种艰难险阻，并战胜困难，取得最终胜利。

10-Years of Youth Devoted to Overseas Work

Huo Jianguo

Joined CNBM in 2008

The Project Director of CNBM Overseas Economic Cooperation Co., Ltd. Beijing Branch, and the Project Manager of Cote d'Ivoire

Chinese President Xi Jinping once said, "The youth is strong, so the country is strong. Contemporary Chinese young people are born at the right time, as the stage for displaying their talents is extremely broad, and the prospect of realizing their dreams is extremely bright." Huo Jianguo, who joined CNBM in 2008, always practiced those words. Now, he has been working abroad for over ten years, leaving traces of work in Libya, Iraq, Saudi Arabia, and Cote d'Ivoire.

Young people in the new era should embrace dreams while being down-to-earth, dare to think and act and be good at doing good things. In 2009, Huo Jianguo, who had just joined the company for one year, volunteered voluntarily to the Libyan FWAM cement plant project as the manager of the Control Department, in charge of project business plan contract work. He sticked to the site during the civil war riots in Libya, and worked hard to get the owner's confirmation of the completed project before returning to the country with the last batch of evacuees. After the completion of the Libya project, Huo Jianguo was sent to Iraq and Saudi Arabia successively, responsible for auditing, project site management, and other work. For more than ten years, he has been working hard on the "Belt and Road", doing his best in each project, and making hard efforts to leave a solid footprint.

In October 2018, to coordinate the design and construction of Cote d'Ivoire's Africa Cup sports facilities, Huo Jianguo, who has rich experience in overseas projects, was sent to Cote d'Ivoire as the project manager and was fully responsible for the project management of the Cote d'Ivoire Stadium project, including safety, schedule, quality, cost, contracts, information, and coordination. The original 2-year project duration was delayed due to reasons such as the COVID-19 epidemic, Huo Jianguo stayed in Côte d'Ivoire for nearly 5 years.

The Cote d'Ivoire Stadium project is in Korhogo, a town in the northern part of Cote d'Ivoire in western Africa. It is one of the stadiums for the 2024 African Cup. The main construction contents of the project include: a 20,000-seat stadium, a 50-bed three-star hotel, an athlete village and four training venues. The project started in May 2019, and the original contract period was 24 months. The sudden outbreak of the pidemic in 2020 disrupted the normal progress of the project schedule. Huo Jianguo used various methods to solve the predicament, not only to catch up with the project schedule, but also to lead the project team members to overcome psychological barriers.

During the epidemic, he actively implemented the requirement of "stabilizing people's hearts and staying put". In the spare time and under limited conditions, he organized various cultural and sports activities such as chess, table tennis, tug of war, to enhance the sense of honor and teamwork spirit of employe. In response to the difficulty of seeking medical advice for family members during the special period, he kept abreast of the situation and reported to the company. With the strong support of the company, he mobilized all resources to purchase urgently needed medicines and deliver them to their homes.

During the three years of the epidemic, Huo Jianguo strictly followed the company's unified deployment, insisted on scientific organization and careful implementation, and realized production and epidemic prevention in parallel. He actively coordinated and handled the difficulties of employees' life, work and family, and led the project team members to overcome the psychological anxiety of overdue overseas stay. The project team has been stationed abroad for more than 15 months, helping the "2024 Africa Cup" at the Cote d'Ivoire Stadium to be held as scheduled.

The bigger the blueprint, the harder the struggle. In the early stage of the implementation of the Cote d'Ivoire Stadium project, the progress of the project and the collection of progress payments were in the middle and lower reaches of the participating companies. The project was the target of criticism at every meeting, and the company took on a lot of pressure for it.

"The project manager is widely called the cheerleader in the industry. In fact, there is another name - firefighting captain." Huo Jianguo often refers to himself as a firefighting captain, and he

appears wherever there are urgent tasks. To reverse the situation, Huo Jianguo tried every means to continuously improve his work ideas, break the previous thinking mode of "waiting and asking", and solve problems creatively. In the middle and late stages of the project, the Project Department gradually reversed its disadvantages and became the object of praise on various official occasions by the owner, winning praise from the Kote government and various ministries and commissions.

The tide of history is surging, and the torrent of the times is rolling forward. Huo Jianguo, who has been working abroad for more than ten years, has been in his forties. He pursues his dreams, and lives up to his youth. In the process of promoting the high-quality development of jointly building the "Belt and Road", he has dedicated his youth.

Personal Insights The platform is very important, so that employees can realize their self-worth and establish correct values through diligence and hard work. The strength of the motherland is very important, so that overseas citizens always feel that the country and the people's soldiers are silently guarding us. Strong national pride makes employees of Chinese enterprises have enough courage to face all kinds of difficulties and obstacles overseas and win the final victory in prevail over.

12 年 与中建投巴新公司“双向奔赴”

亚里士多德·托马斯·莫古纳

2011 年加入中国建材

现任中建投巴新公司首都建材店店长助理

从门店销售员、门店应收账款专员，到门店应收账款主管、总部应收账款主管，再到首都建材店店长助理，亚里士多德·托马斯·莫古纳已经在中建投巴新公司走过了12年光阴。这 12 年里，他一直兢兢业业，勤奋进取，多次被巴新公司评为优秀员工代表，在平凡的岗位上发光发热，和公司共同成长。

亚里士多德是一个勤于学习、善于钻研的员工。最初在莫港肯尼迪店做销售员时，他对计算机软件知之甚少，经常对着电脑手足无措。在中方员工的悉心教授下，他很快学会了相关技术，可以熟练操作销售系统。但是他并不满足于此，在分店担任应收主管期间，他提出了将客户分类为刷卡客户、现金客户、支票客户、电汇客户以及赊销客户的方法，极大地方便了分店日常的应收管理工作。刻苦钻研几年后，亚里士多德逐渐成为总部办公室独当一面的资深主管。在妥善处理自身事务的同时，他也能积极掌握一些公司的外事事务，包括如何准备外国工作许可证申请、外国签证申请以及外国护照申请等。与此同时，他还总结自身工作经验，配合人力资源部门对公司的新员工进行培训，替公司为新员工传道授业解惑。他说：“这种感觉非常好，这让我能清楚自己的不足之处，对知识的渴望也增加了。”如今，亚里士多德又逐步开始学着处理公司的各种保险索赔，包括工伤索赔、公司车辆受损索赔、店面失窃索赔事宜。“通过学习处理这些事情，我对公司层面的各种事情和岗位分工越来越了解，工作也更加得心应手。”亚里士多德自豪地说道。

2021 年是公司发展较为艰难的一年，新冠疫情导致经营发展受阻，员工队伍也因疫情影响青黄不接。关键时刻，亚里士多德临危受命，作为店长助理被派往首都莫港润柏建材店统管分店经营事务，凭借自己 10 多年的工作经验，亚里士多德较为迅速地接手了分店事务，通过管理员工，核查收发货，清点每日营业金，定期向公司汇报经营情况，较好地稳住了店面经营，改善了疫情下公司人手不足的艰难处境，为之后公司经营业务调整打下了坚实基础。

多年以来，亚里士多德始终积极向其他的优秀员工学习，不断提升自己的工作能力，时刻为以后的发展做好准备。优异的表现也获得了总经理的青睐，他们教授亚里士多德项目合同的相关知识，为他提供参与各种商业谈判以及会议的机会，帮助他开阔视野、增长见识。亚里士多德将公司对他的帮助和支持看在眼里、记在心里、体现在行动里。他总是尽最大的努力来完成工作，以此感谢巴新公司和中国同事们对他的耐心指导与帮助，他说：“中国同事们教会我工作技巧和知识，让我的能力得到了很大的提升，他们的热情也时刻感染着我，让我更加热爱这份工作。”

12 年里，也曾有一些公司私下向亚里士多德发出工作邀请，但是都被他拒绝了。“在中建投巴新的团队中，我看到了信任、协作和尊重，学到了乐观、积极和坚持，更为中国企业包容的文化氛围所感染。”他说，“中建投巴新公司给了我一个非常广阔的平台，我愿意在这里继续发掘自己的潜力，发挥自己的能力，继续和公司一起成长。”

中国“一带一路”倡议的实施让巴布亚新几内亚深受其益，亚里士多德实实在在地感受到了国家的发展变化。2018 年，APEC 会议在巴布亚新几内亚召开，亚里士多德更是深受触动，他说：“中国是一个非常友好的国家，‘一带一路’倡议也惠及我的祖国，社会经济得到发展和人民生活得到改善，在巴新的中国企业和中国人也时常向我们伸出援助之手，我特别感谢中国。”（中建投巴新公司首都建材店）

个人体会 我非常荣幸加入中建投巴新这个团队，从销售员到店长助理，我见证了中建投巴新公司的日益壮大，中建投巴新公司也见证了我的成长。我将努力学习中国文化，与巴新文化相融合，为公司发展、为自己的国家建设贡献力量。

Growing up with BNBMPNG for 12 Years

Aristotol Thomas Moguna

Joined CNBM in 2011

The Assistant to Branch Manager of BNBM Pom Hardware branch

From salesperson, cashier, to account supervisor, head account supervisor, and then to assistant manager of Capital Building Materials branch, Aristotol Thomas Moguna has already worked in BNBMPNG for 12 years. In the past 12 years, he has been conscientious, diligent and enterprising, and has been rated as an outstanding employee by the Papua New Guinea Company many times. He shines in ordinary positions and strives to grow together with the company.

Aristotol is an employee who is diligent in learning and good at research. When he first worked as a salesperson at the Kennedy branch in Port Moor, he had little knowledge of computer software and was often at a loss for the computer. Under careful teaching of the Chinese staff, he quickly learned the relevant technology, and he was able to operate the sales system efficiently. But he is not satisfied with this. While serving as the account supervisor, he proposed the method of classifying customers into credit card customers, cash customers, check customers, wire transfer customers and credit customers, which greatly facilitated the daily account management of the branch. After several years of hard work, Aristotol has become a senior executive in charge of the headquarters office. While properly handling his own affairs, he can also actively handle company's foreign affairs, including how to prepare for foreign work permit applications, foreign visa applications, and foreign passport applications. At the same time, by sorting out his own work experience, he cooperated with the Human Resources Department to train new employees. He said: "It makes me clearly understand my shortcomings, and my desire to learn more knowledge has also increased." Aristotol began to learn to how to handle company insurance claims, including workers' compensation claims, claims for damage to company vehicles, and claims for shoplifting. "By learning to deal with these things, I have become more and more familiar with various things at the company level and the responsibilities and work of different positions," said Aristotol proudly.

2021 is a relatively difficult year for the company's development. The COVID-19 epidemic has hindered business development, and the workforce has also been affected by the epidemic. At the critical moment, Aristotol was appointed as the assistant manager. He was sent to the Rainbow branch in the capital to take charge of the branch's business affairs. With more than 10 years of work experience, Aristotol quickly took over the branch's business. By managing employees, checking receipt and

delivery, checking the daily operating funds, he reported the operating conditions to the company on a regular basis. The operation of the branch has been stabilized, the understaffed situation has been alleviated, and a solid foundation has been laid for the subsequent adjustment of the company's business operations.

Over the years, Aristotol has been actively learning from other excellent employees, constantly improving his work efficiency, and always preparing for future development. His excellent performance has also won the favor of the general managers. They taught Aristotol about project contracts, provided him with opportunities to participate in various business negotiations and meetings to help him broaden his horizons and increase his knowledge. Aristotol was moved by the company's help and support. He always tries his best to complete the work in order to thank the company and his Chinese colleagues for their patient teaching and help. He said: "Chinese colleagues taught me work skills and knowledge, and my ability has been improved greatly. Their enthusiasm will always affect me, making me love this job even more."

During the 12 years of working, some companies have privately sent job offers to Aristotol, but they were all rejected by him. "In the company's team, I saw trust, collaboration and respect. I have learned optimism, positivity and persistence. I'm even more affected by the inclusive cultural atmosphere of Chinese companies." He said: "The company has given me a very broad platform, where I am willing to explore my potential, develop my ability, and grow with the company.

Papua New Guinea has also benefited greatly from the implementation of China's "Belt and Road " Initiative. In 2018, the APEC meeting was held in Papua New Guinea, and Aristotol was deeply moved. He said: "China is a very friendly country, and the " Belt and Road " Initiative has also benefited my motherland. The development of society and economy and people's lives has been improved, and Chinese companies and Chinese people in Papua New Guinea often lend a helping hand to us, so I am especially grateful to China."

Personal Insights I am very honored to join the team of BNBMPNG. From the salesperson to the assistant to the branch manager, I have witnessed the growing of BNBMPNG, and the company has also witnessed my growth. I will work hard to learn Chinese culture and integrate it with Papua New Guinea culture. I will contribute to the development of the company and the construction of my own country.

18 年坚守　为公司发展注入“心”动力

科林·罗宾

2005 年加入中国建材

现任中建投巴新公司可可坡店店长助理

“踏实可靠、经验丰富、责任心强”这是同事们对科林的普遍印象。这位 2005 年加入中建投巴新公司的老员工，已经在岗位上辛勤工作了 18 年，从库管员到外场主管、销售人员，再到店长助理，他克服各种压力和挑战，一步一个脚印，和公司心贴心、同奋进、共成长。

作为店长助理，科林主要协助店长进行展厅管理、外场管理和货物的收发管理等，日常工作紧张繁杂，需要各个部门密切合作，科林总能以他出色的沟通和协调能力，确保工作流程顺畅、高效和融洽。他与销售团队密切合作，了解市场情况和客户需求，及时总结反馈，使得分店能及时调整产品线和适应市场需求。

疫情期间，科林带头严格遵守各项疫情防控制度，落实各项疫情防控工作，不惧危险，坚守岗位。并在分店员工出现短缺的情况下，主动承担额外的工作，他出色的管理技巧和解决问题的能力为分店运营创造了稳定和谐的工作环境。

科林以服务客户为宗旨，对待客户始终保持积极的态度。他能够及时处理客户反映的问题，保证客户的满意度。特别是在面对外岛批发客户时，他总以极高的主动性带领团队加班加点，确保装货数量无误，保障货物及时发送，避免了公司的潜在损失。他的出色表现赢得了客户的一致好评，也进一步树立了公司专业高效的良好形象。

科林在担任店长助理期间还展现出卓越的团队合作精神。他积极参与新员工的团队培训，协助店长定期组织召开团队会议，确保团队成员对公司的目标和使命有清晰的了解。科林常说：“新员工是公司发展的新生力量，作为一个在公司 18 年的‘前辈’，我非常乐意把我的经验传授给他们，帮助他们快速成长，一起为公司发展作贡献。”他是这样说的，也是这样做的。在日常工作中他注重帮助新员工提升工作技能，激励和关心老员工，使得大家能对工作充满热情，所在分店员工的流失率也因此较低。他还善于团结同事，能够有效地调和员工之间的矛盾，为分店的团队培养和人员稳定

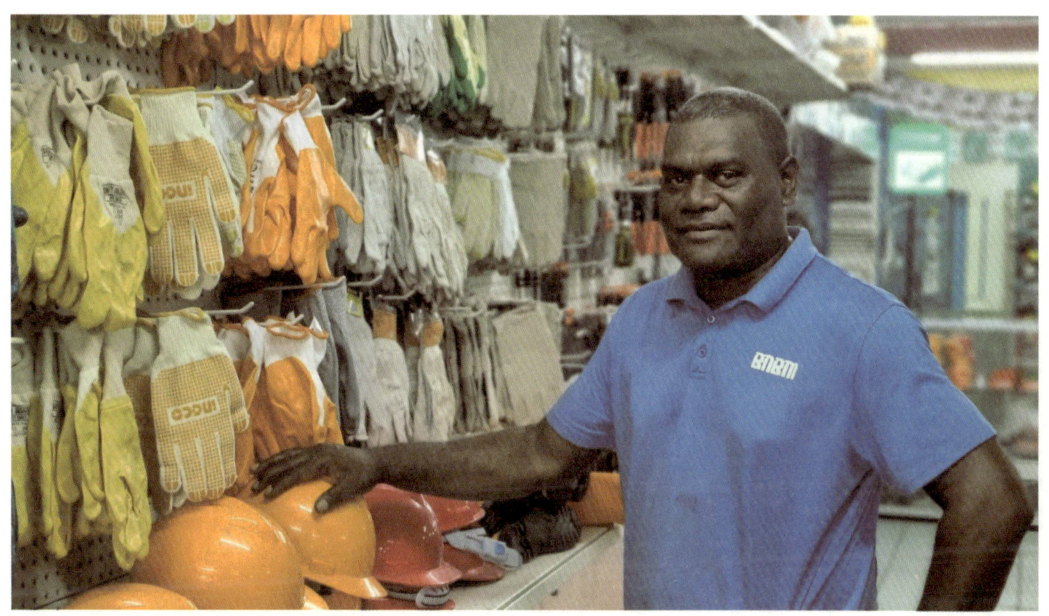

作出了突出贡献。

勤俭节约，树立榜样。除了对员工的关心，科林还展现出极强的勤俭节约的品德。他坚持在每天营业结束后巡视店面，确保水电使用等无异常情况，还主动配合协助中方经理对店面费用进行精细化管理，关注办公耗材的领取使用，检查安保人员的出勤，营运车辆的使用、维修保养和证件更新等，确保分店的费用支出合理有度，避免潜在的损失，确保公司的资源得到合理利用。

去年，由于疫情影响，科林没能来到中国现场参加优秀员工的颁奖，到中国也成了他未完成的一个心愿。他说："我能有如今的工作、生活，全都得益于公司为我提供的平台，让我不断成长和进步，希望以后可以有前往中国交流学习的机会，我也会更加努力工作，为公司发展贡献力量。"

（中建投巴新公司可可坡店）

个人体会 非常开心能加入巴新公司这个大家庭，这里为我提供了很多机会，让我能够发挥自己的潜力、不断成长和进步。我由衷地感谢同事们的支持和鼓励，也祝愿巴新公司未来发展得更好，我将继续和公司共同成长。

18-year Wholehearted Work for the Company's Development

Collin Robin

Joined CNBM in 2005

The Assistant to Branch Manager of BNBM Kokopo branch

"Dependable, experienced, and highly responsible" - these are the common impressions colleagues have of Collin. As a long-standing employee who joined BNBM in 2005, Collin has diligently worked in various positions for 18 years. Starting as a warehouse clerk, he advanced to become a field supervisor, salesperson, and later a store assistant manager. Collin has overcome numerous pressures and challenges, steadily progressing and growing together with the company. Collin works collaboratively as an assistant to the store manager, assisting with showroom management, field operations, and inventory management. His daily work is demanding and requires close cooperation among various departments. However, Collin excels in communication and coordination, ensuring smooth, efficient, and harmonious workflow. He works closely with the sales team, staying informed about market conditions and customer needs, providing timely feedback that enables the branch to adjust its product line and meet market demands.

During the pandemic, Collin took the lead in strictly adhering to all epidemic prevention and control measures, implementing various protocols, and fearlessly holding his post. In situations where the branch faced staff shortages, he voluntarily took on additional responsibilities. His exceptional management skills and problem-solving abilities created a stable and harmonious working environment for the branch's operations.

Collin is driven by a commitment to serving customers, and he maintains a positive attitude when addressing their concerns. He is adept at promptly resolving customer issues and ensuring their satisfaction. Particularly when dealing with wholesale customers from remote islands, Collin demonstrates exceptional productivity. He leads his team in working extra hours, ensuring accurate loading quantities and timely shipment of goods to prevent potential losses for the company. His outstanding performance has garnered unanimous praise from customers and further solidified the company's reputation for professionalism and efficiency.

During his tenure as Assistant Store Manager, Collin demonstrated outstanding teamwork and collaboration. He actively participated in the training of new team members and assisted the Store Manager in organizing regular team meetings, ensuring that team members had a clear understanding of the company's goals and mission. Collin often said, "New employees are the driving force behind the company's growth. As a 'senior'

with 18 years of experience in the company, I am more than happy to share my knowledge with them and help them grow quickly, contributing to the company's development together." He not only spoke these words but also put them into action. In his daily work, he focused on helping new employees improve their skills, motivating and caring for veteran employees, fostering enthusiasm for work, and maintaining a lower employee turnover rate in the branch. He was also skilled at uniting colleagues and effectively resolving conflicts and emotional issues among staff members, making remarkable contributions to team development and personnel stability in the branch.

In addition to his care for employees, Collin also demonstrates a strong sense of diligence and thrift. After the store's daily operations, Collin consistently inspects the premises to ensure that there are no abnormalities in water and electricity usage. He actively cooperates with the Chinese manager to manage store expenses meticulously, paying attention to the procurement and usage of office supplies, monitoring the attendance of security personnel, overseeing the use, maintenance, and documentation of operational vehicles. This attention to detail ensures that the branch's expenses are reasonable and controlled, mitigating potential losses and ensuring the company's resources are utilized efficiently. Collin's efforts have played a significant role in reducing operational costs for the branch. His dedication to thrift and meticulous management contributes to maintaining the financial well-being of the store.

Last year, due to the impact of the pandemic, Collin Robin was unable to attend the on-site award ceremony for outstanding employees in China, and visiting China also became an unfulfilled wish for him. He said, "I owe my current job and life to the platform provided by the company, which has allowed me to continuously grow and progress. I hope to have the opportunity to exchange and learn in China in the future. I will also work harder and contribute to the development of the company.

Personal Insights I am delighted to be part of the BNBM family. It has provided me with numerous opportunities to showcase my abilities, grow, and progress. I am sincerely grateful for the support and encouragement from my colleagues. I also extend my best wishes for the future development and prosperity of BNBM. I am committed to continuing my growth journey alongside the company.

扎根一线拓市场 团结协作创佳绩

王兰菊

2005 年加入中国建材

现任中建材国际贸易有限公司总经理助理兼钢材事业部总经理

王兰菊于 2005 年加入中建材国际贸易有限公司，近 20 年来，她投身钢材外贸行业的初心不变，助力公司开拓海外版图的脚步也从未停下。2023 年她被评选为“中国建材集团有限公司劳动模范”，这既是对她多年拼搏付出的肯定，也是对她和团队矢志深耕国际市场的鼓励。

2006 年，她受命开发新产品。面对庞大的钢材行业，制作产品手册、寻找可靠供应商、专业质检等工作都是从零起步。组建好团队后，他们顶着炎炎烈日，到河北、山东和江浙等地考察工厂，学习产品知识和行业信息，快速建立起供应商体系；为保证产品质量，她和两名同事驻守工厂，在炙热的退火炉车间，轮流亲自做质量检测；为确保订单保质保量按时交货，她几乎每个周末都要到工厂跟进监督；为快速拓展海外市场，她每天都加班到深夜，回到家继续联系客户。曾有一位俄罗斯的大客户在凌晨收到她及时回复的邮件时惊讶地问：“你不睡觉吗？”她深知只有比别人更努力，不舍昼夜地奔跑，才能更快地接近目标。她事务繁杂还要培养新人，却甘于奉献，从未抱怨。

苦心人，天不负。仅用两年时间，她带领团队完成钢材出口销售额 2000 万美元，实现净利润 765 万元人民币。开发新产品的成功，也为后期业务发展奠定了坚实的基础。

从业十多年，她始终以敬畏的心态面对风险，对各环节严格把关，精细管理，保障业务稳健发展。2022 年 2 月起，钢材产品价格因俄乌冲突而飙升，到 9 月份时，又暴跌 30%，叠加人民币贬值约 15%，导致出口报价比最高点时下降 45%；此外，上海的港口不能正常通航，天津出现严重压港现象，不能如期履约，国外客户违约潮汹涌而来。她果断决策，冷静应对，通过转卖、谈判等方式及时止损。

在她的带领下，团队积极调整销售策略，2021—2022 年，钢材事业部分别实现现金净利润 3210 万元人民币和 4149 万元人民币，连续两年被公司授予“优秀团队”称号。

她对团队成员严而有度，爱而有方。在工作中，她是苛刻的领导，坚持高标准和严要求，使钢材事业部的销售数据一直在公司排名前三；在生活上，她是知心的姐姐，关注员工情绪变化并细心安抚，定期为员工举办生日会，及时向遇到生活困难的员工伸出援手，将整个事业部全体员工变成亲密的一家人。她以身作则、勤勉努力、默默奉献，并以“谦恭、敬畏、感恩、得体”的准则指导团队。新员工成长可圈可点，新客户开发势如破竹，新订单喜报频频传来。钢材事业部新员工培养取得优异成绩，以入职两年的新员工为例，人均订单年利润超过 200 万元，单人订单年利润最高突破 500 万元。她打造的团队自信乐观、敢于拼搏、善于开拓，有着超强的战斗力和执行力，坚定不移地为开发海外市场、传播 CNBM 品牌当好先锋队，为落实集团国际化战略贡献他们的“钢铁”力量！

为了更好地推动集团国际化业务发展，王兰菊同志积极推动菲律宾、泰国和沙特 3 个“一带一路”国家的属地化经营落地工作，她积极高效地安排海外市场调研工作、落实属地化人员到位、确定属地化经营目标。我们相信，在王兰菊的带领下，3 个海外市场属地化经营一定会取得优异成绩并为“一带一路”建设贡献力量。（中建材国际贸易有限公司）

习近平总书记提出的共建“一带一路”倡议，在这 10 年间已经不断由理念化为行动，由愿景变为现实。我们要脚踏实地贯彻集团国际化战略，为促进贸易畅通和国际产能对接贡献力量，使我们的国家同“一带一路”沿线的国家共享和平发展的硕果，共筑和谐美好的未来。

Combining Frontline Experience with Team Leadership to Expand International Markets

Wang Lanju

Joined CNBM in 2005

General Manager Assistant of CNBM International Corporation, Manager of the Steel Division of CNBM International Corporation

Since she joined CNBM International Corporation in 2005, Wang Lanju has remained committed to her original aspiration in the steel foreign trade industry, and has never stopped exploring new opportunities overseas for nearly two decades. In 2023, she was honored as a "Model Worker of CNBM," in recognition of her years of hard work and dedication, and her team's steadfast focus on international market development.

In 2006, Wang was appointed to lead the development of a new product. Faced with the immense steel industry, she had to start from scratch, creating product manuals, finding reliable suppliers, and conducting professional quality inspections. Together with her new team, they braved the blazing sun and visited factories in Hebei, Shandong, Jiangsu, Zhejiang, and other places to learn about the product and the industry, and rapidly established a supplier network. To ensure the product quality, she and two colleagues stationed themselves in the factory, taking turns conducting quality inspections in the sweltering annealing furnace workshop. To ensure that orders were delivered with high quality and correct quantity on time, she would almost go to the factory every weekend for supervision. To quickly expand the overseas market, she burned the midnight oil and continued to contact clients after she returned home. Once, an important Russian client received her timely reply email in the early morning and asked surprisingly, "Don't you sleep?" She knew that only by working harder day and night could she achieve her goals faster. Despite a heavy workload and her obligation to train new team members, she has remained devoted and never complained.

The reward for hard work never fails. Within just two years, Wang led her team to achieve sales of $20 million USD in steel exports and a net profit of 7.65 million yuan. The success of developing new products also laid a solid foundation for future business development.

Having dedicated over a decade to the industry, Wang has approached business risks with reverence. She strictly monitors and manages every step, ensuring precise and meticulous management that guarantees stable and robust business development. Since February 2022, the market price of steel products has skyrocketed due to the Russia-Ukraine conflict, only to plummet by 30% in September, compounded by a 15% depreciation of the RMB, leading to a 45% drop in export prices compared to their highest point. Furthermore, the port operations in Shanghai were disrupted, and severe port congestion in Tianjin resulted in significant delays, ultimately leading

to a surge in defaults by overseas clients. Under such circumstances, she made resolute and calculated decisions, deftly managing the situation by reselling and negotiating to protect orders from incurring losses. Exporting steel products is like walking on the blade of a knife, exposed to numerous risks ranging from fluctuations in market prices, shipping costs, and exchange rates to the unpredictability of export tax rebates. For example, in 2007, the government made four policy adjustments to steel product export tax rebates, while in 2021, it twice canceled the export tax rebate for certain steel products. Over 100,000 tons of orders were impacted by these changes, involving a rebate of over 100 million yuan. The policy change allowed only two days notice for compliance, yet Wang and her team worked tirelessly day and night, collaborated effectively with clear work division, and conducted "emergency rescue" that successfully minimized the losses to the lowest possible level.

Under her leadership, the team actively adjusted their sales strategy, and the steel division achieved cash profits of 32.1 million yuan and 41.49 million yuan respectively in 2021 and 2022, earning the "Outstanding Team" award from the company for two consecutive years.

Wang has demonstrated a firm yet caring leadership towards her team members. In the workplace, she maintains exacting standards and strict demands, resulting in impressive sales figures for the steel division that consistently rank among the top three in the company. Outside work, she is a compassionate and empathetic friend to her employees, paying attention to their negative emotions and offering support when needed, regularly organizing birthday celebrations to foster camaraderie, and extending timely assistance to colleagues facing challenges in life. These actions foster a deep sense of camaraderie and unity among the entire department, making it a close-knit family. She sets an example of diligence, dedication, and commitment to work, and embodies the principles of humility, respect, gratitude, and propriety in her leadership. New employees' development has been noteworthy, as new client acquisition is growing rapidly like mushrooms after the rain and news of successful new orders is commonplace. The new employee training program has achieved exceptional results in the steel division, with average annual profits per person exceeding two million yuan and individual annual profits for single orders reaching as high as five million yuan after only two years of employment. She has fostered a team that embodies confidence, optimism, and a willingness to take risks. They excel in opening up new opportunities and demonstrate outstanding combat effectiveness and execution skills. The team remains steadfast pioneers in promoting CNBM's brand and developing overseas market, contributing their "steel" strength to realizing CNBM's internationalization strategy!

To facilitate CNBM's international business, Wang Lanju has been actively promoting the localization of operations in three Belt and Road countries: the Philippines, Thailand, and Saudi Arabia. She has efficiently arranged overseas market research, implemented personnel localization, and determined localization business goals. We believe that, under her leadership, the localization operations in these three overseas markets will surely achieve excellent results and contribute to the Belt and Road Initiative.

Personal Insights Over the past decade, the Belt and Road Initiative proposed by President Xi Jinping has been translated from an envisioned concept into real action and progress on the ground. We must strive to implement CNBM's internationalization strategy, promote unimpeded trade and international capacity cooperation, and contribute to the shared and peaceful development between China and the countries along the Belt and Road. Together, we can build a harmonious and prosperous future for all.

于文化交融中碰撞不一样的火花

延斯·海因里希

2016 年加入中国建材

现任中国建材工程子公司 CTF Solar 技术发展部长

1990 年，延斯 · 海因里希开始在德国凯姆尼茨技术大学学习化学。在获得化学硕士学位后，他又获得了物理化学博士学位，研究重点是化学气相沉积。他的职业生涯始于半导体行业的制造和工艺工程师，后来他在超微半导体公司 / 格芯和英特尔等公司担任过工艺集成和技术转化工程师的角色，在不同国家获得了技术和文化经验。

2016 年初，海因里希博士决定进入不同的技术领域，目的是学习新技术并为新公司提供支持。他作为工艺转化经理加入了 CTF Solar，旨在将自己的经验和技能应用于不同的行业。他将加入 CTF Solar 描述为令人非常兴奋的事情。当时，海因里希博士与他的领导（工艺工程部门部长）一起组建了一个新团队，并从零开始设计基于 CTF 碲化镉技术的大规模光伏组件工厂。他们与中国建材工程的同事在中国四川省成都市启动了首个大尺寸碲化镉发电玻璃生产线工厂项目。他第一次的中国之行与以往的经历完全不同，他受到热烈欢迎和盛情款待，与大家就实现项目共同目标的最佳方式进行公开讨论，这些给他留下了深刻的印象。当然，这个过程并不容易，团队很快意识到德国和中国之间的文化差异可能会带来问题和误解，但每个人都持开放态度，愿意学习和包容。在很短的时间内，目标就确定了下来，大家试图结合两种文化优势来实现项目的成功。开工后不久，第一个项目里程碑（设备设计审查、初始验收测试）实现，且第一部分生产线于 2016 年底已搬入厂房，建设工作仍在进行中 。与大多数 CTF Solar 工程师、科学家和经理一起，海因里希博士多次前往成都，监督设备的安装和调试，现场解决问题，并确保不同供应商的支持和合作。最终，在 2017 年 8 月，在完成项目设计审查不到 1 年后，CTF Solar 与设备供应商共同开发的沉积设备顺利完成试运行，并于 2017 年 8 月 24 日生产出第一个功能组件。这是中国建材集团的第一块碲化镉薄膜发电玻璃，也是全球第一块大尺寸薄膜发电玻璃。在成功展示了

碲化镉技术在制造规模上的能力之后，中国建材工程和 CTF Solar 启动了更多的碲化镉工厂项目。

2018 年，海因里希博士晋升为工艺工程副部长。他的重点和工作任务更多地转移到建立和发展 CTF Solar 工程团队，实施技术变革，以及加强、改进当前和未来的工厂项目。这些新的挑战需要与中国建材工程的同事和工厂运营团队进行更深入的合作。在这里，来自 CTF Solar 中国同事的支持，尤其是来自中国建材工程管理层、项目团队和工程团队的支持，对他的成功起到了重要作用。

2020 年之后的几年对 CTF Solar 团队的每个成员以及海因里希博士本人来说都充满了挑战。新冠疫情对人们的生活产生了影响，特别是 CTF Solar 工厂项目业务受到了冲击。大多数项目都因疫情而延迟，CTF Solar 不得不适应新情况。在这个过程中，跨国团队的好处显而易见。

作为两名不会说中文的 CTF 员工之一，他在新冠疫情期间两次到访中国驻厂。现在，工厂的技术发展得到了不断改进和提升，项目团队和大多数工程正在逐渐回到正轨。CTF Solar 已经在中国建立了一支工程师团队，并提高了发电玻璃的光电转换效率，把工艺和设备引入邯郸工厂。通过邯郸中建材、中国建材工程和 CTF Solar 团队的努力，生产出光电转换效率超过 330W 的“冠军”组件相较中建材之前“冠军”组件的功率纪录提高了 10%，比目前的产品平均水平提高了 15%。这一重大成就让 CTF Solar 的同事们为自己是中国建材团队的一员而感到自豪。

在 2023 年初，海因里希博士成为 CTF Solar 管理委员会的成员，使他能够对 CTF Solar 的进一步发展和业务产生重大影响，并为中国建材工程和中国建材集团的成功做出贡献。他现在期待着未来的挑战，对团队继续创新充满信心，并继续为快速增长的建筑集成光伏 (BIPV) 市场做贡献。（中国建材工程子公司 CTF Solar）

个人体会

感谢中国建材集团在过去的 7 年里让我有机会学习和成长，使我胜任目前的职位。我喜欢为这样一家公司工作，我可以运用经验，发展和应用新的技能，融入团队。从我的角度来看，我们共同努力将碲化镉光伏技术应用于更大的领域，这在过去和现在都是巨大的成功。

Generating Creative Ideas in Cultural Fusion

Dr. Jens Heinrich

Joined CNBM in 2016

Director od Technology Development of CTF Solar

In 1990, Jens Heinrich started studies in chemistry at Chemnitz University of Technology in Germany. After getting a master's degree in chemistry, he continued to get a PhD in physical chemistry, focusing on the studies of chemical vapor deposition. Starting his career in the semiconductor industry as a manufacturing and process engineer, he then assumed several other roles including a process integration engineer and a technology transfer engineer in companies like AMD/ Global Foundries and Intel, gaining technical and cultural experiences in different countries.

In early 2016, Dr. Heinrich decided to move into a different technology area with the aim of learning new technologies and providing support to the new company. He joined CTF Solar as a process transfer manager with the aim of applying his experience and skillsets to a different industry. He described the start at CTF Solar as really exciting, developing a new team together with head of the process engineering department – and designing a factory for large scale PV modules based on CTF's CdTe technology – almost from scratch. Together with the colleagues from CTIEC, they started the project of the 1st CdTe factory for large size modules (> $1m^2$ – almost $2m^2$) in Chengdu, southwest China's Sichuan Province. His 1st trip to China for CTF Solar was totally different from his previous experiences. He was impressed by a very warm welcome and great hospitality he received, as well as open discussions about the best way to achieve the shared goals of the project. Of course, it was not all easy and very soon the team realized that the cultural differences between Germany and China could cause problems and misunderstandings, but everyone was open minded and willing to learn and adapt. In a very short time, the goals were set to try to combine the strengths of both cultures for the success of the project. Soon after the start of the construction, the 1st project milestone (equipment design reviews, initial acceptance tests) was passed and by the end of the year 2016, the 1st part of the production line had been moved into the factory building, while construction work still in progress. Together with most of the CTF Solar's engineers, scientists and managers, Dr. Heinrich travelled to Chengdu multiple times, supervising the equipment's installation and commissioning, solving problems onsite, ensuring the support and collaboration from the different suppliers. Finally, in August 2017, less than one year after completing the design review, the main deposition equipment (CSS – a co-development between CTF Solar and equipment supplier) successfully completed trial operation and produced the first functional midule on Agust 24, 2017. It was the 1st CdTe module for CNBM group and the 1st large size thin film module worldwide. After the successful demonstration of the CdTe technologies capabilities on manufacturing scale, more CdTe factory projects for CTIEC and CTF Solar have been launched.

In 2018, Dr. Heinrich got promoted to deputy head of process engineering. His focus and work tasks shifted more to building and developing the CTF Solar's engineering team, implementing technology changes as well as ramping up and improving current and future factory projects. These new challenges required an even deeper collaboration with the colleagues and partners from CTIEC and with the CNBM factory operations teams. Here, support from Chinese colleagues within CTF Solar, especially from the CTIEC management, project team and the engineering team played an important role in his success.

2020 and the following years were packed with challenges for each team member of CTF Solar and for Dr Heinrich himself. Despite the impact of COVID-19 to the personal life, especially the CTF factory project business was affected. Most of the projects got delayed due to this pandemic situation and CTF Solar had to adapt to the new situation where they could not go to the sites. In this process, the benefits of a multinational team became obvious.

Despite the impact of the COVID-19 pandemic, Dr. Heinrich and his team persevered and adapted to new circumstances, receiving significant support from CTIEC and CNBM colleagues. As one of the two non-Chinese speaking CTF employees, he visited the factory in China twice during COVID-19 outbreak. This crisis highlighted the strength of their multinational team. Now technical development of

factory sites has been continuously improved and enhanced, and the team and most of the projects are back on track. With the support from Mr. Yin, CTF Solar started to build a team of engineers within China and introduced new process and equipment to the Handan factory, which will dramatically improve the performance of the PV modules with respect to efficiency and stability.

Through the efforts of the HDOM, CTIEC and CTF teams, the heromodule with photoelectric conversion efficiency of more than 330W were produced, which is 10% more efficient than the previous record, and 15% more effienct than the current product average. This major achievement makes all the CTF Solar colleagues proud of being a member of this CNBM team.

In early 2023, Dr. Heinrich became a member of the CTF Solar Management board, allowing him to have a substantial say on CTF's further development and business, and contribute to CTIEC's and CNBM's success. He now looks forward to future challenges and is confident in the team's ability to continue innovating and contributing to the rapidly growing market of Building Integrated Photovoltaic (BIPV).

Personal Insights I'd like to thank CNBM group for giving me the incredible opportunity to learn and grow in the past seven years, and ultimately landing me in my current position. It has been a true pleasure working for a company where I can contribute my experiences, continually expand my knowledge and apply new abilities.From my perspective, our joint journey and fight for using CdTe PV technology on a larger scale was and is a big success.

丝绸之路上的坚守

杜荣鹏

2007 年加入中国建材

现任中国建材国际工程集团有限公司高级工程师

2007 年，杜荣鹏入职中国建材国际工程集团有限公司，先后参与沙特 AL-JOUF 水泥项目、阿塞拜疆 QIZILDDAS 水泥项目、哈萨克希姆肯特水泥项目、哈萨克奥尔达玻璃项目，担任项目建设主要负责人。他参与的项目曾获得中国勘察设计协会的工程总承包银钥匙奖，多次获得中国建材工程建设协会的建材行业优秀工程总承包一等奖等荣誉。

时间回到 2017 年，奥尔达玻璃项目启动伊始，杜荣鹏便作为项目部先锋队员之一来到项目驻地。项目建设的浮法玻璃生产线位于锡尔河畔的克孜勒奥尔达市，这里是典型的大陆性气候，大戈壁一望无际，夏热冬寒，昼夜温差极大。随着项目团队的进驻，一座现代化的浮法玻璃生产线即将拔地而起，而杜荣鹏也正式开启了他的坚守之路。

他扎根一线，与业主、分包单位、监理等各方保持密切的联络，推进工程建设属地化的落实。参与项目建设的分包单位多达数十家，有来自中国的公司，也有哈萨克斯坦本地企业。由于语言和文化的差异，想要管理好各家分包单位并非易事。在这种情况下，他奔走于现场各处、联络各方，在不断的磨合中增进施工单位间的协同与配合。工地日常需要处理的问题繁杂，有关于设计落地的，有关于施工组织的，也有关于合同执行的。对于项目建设过程中出现的问题，不论大小繁易，他均能够做到及时应对、灵活处理，不断推进项目建设。

2020 年，全球新冠肺炎疫情的暴发令人始料未及。随着口岸关闭、签证暂停、航班取消等政策实施，中哈之间人员和货物流通受阻，这对正在进行的工程建设可谓致命打击。当时，杜荣鹏恰好在国内，客观的阻碍使得他无法按照原计划返回项目现场。但是，作为项目部核心管理人员，他依然心怀工程进度，克服时差所带来的不便，密切保持与项目现场驻守人员的沟通，对现场遇到的困难积极出谋划策，尽己所能支援项目部团队。后续在赴哈条件具备后，他第一时间启程赴哈。可以说，他的及时到场极大地缓解了当时项目部管理人员不足的

状况，也在项目部中起到了表率作用。

2021—2022 年，他见证了项目追赶工期的关键节点。2021 年 10 月 2 日，熔窑大碹顺利合拢；2022 年 9 月 9 日，生产线点火并启动烘窑；2022 年 10 月 9 日，生产线成功引板并正式投产。由于时间紧、任务重，杜荣鹏积极谋划现场施工工作，优化施工方案。来自中国的安装团队无法及时到达，他便积极寻找哈萨克斯坦本地的安装施工队伍。技术衔接上存在困难，他便第一时间组织相关工程师与施工方沟通解决。接近两年的时间里，他坚守在本职岗位上始终如一，没有片刻的放松，也没有丝毫的懈怠。

杜荣鹏连续多年坚守在海外现场一线，为公司赢得了效益和荣誉，但常年驻外，他牺牲了与家人的团聚时光。回首过去，他依然坚守自己的这份热忱与执着，并表示："我作为一名中国企业员工，为了公司的发展、国家战略目标的不断推进，我会无怨无悔地走出国门，继续努力奋搏。"（中国建材国际工程集团有限公司）

个人体会 通过项目的运作实施，我深深体会到海外项目运作的艰辛，更体会到国家"一带一路"倡议的任重道远。我作为一名中国企业员工，为了公司的发展、国家战略目标的不断推进，我会无怨无悔地走出国门，继续努力奋搏。

The Man Who Dedicated Himself to "Belt and Road" Overseas Project

Du Rongpeng

Joined CNBM in 2007

Senior Engineer of CTIEC

In 2007, Du Rongpeng joined China Building Materials International Engineering Group Co., Ltd. and successively participated in the AL-JOUF cement project in Saudi Arabia, the QIZILDAS cement project in Azerbaijan, the Shymkent cement project in Kazakhstan, and the Orda glass project in Kazakhstan, and served as the main person in charge of the project construction. The project has won many honors such as the Silver Key Award for Engineering General Contracting by China Survey and Design Association and the First Prize of Excellent Project General Contracting Award for Building Materials Industry by China Building Materials Engineering Construction Association.

Back to 2017, at the launch of the construction of Orda glass project, Du Rongpeng came to the project site as one of the pioneers of the project department. The float glass production line to be built by the project is located in the city of Kyzylorda by the Syr Darya River. The city has a typical continental climate, with endless views of the Great gobi, hot summers and cold winters, and extremely large temperature differences between day and night. With the arrival of the project team, the construction of a modern float glass production line was efficiently implemented, and Du Rongpeng's ardous journey began.

He took root in the front line and maintained close contact with the owners, subcontractors, supervisers and other parties to promote the implementation of the localization of project construction. Dozens of subcontractors participated in the construction of the project, including companies from China and local enterprises in Kazakhstan. The language barrier and cultural differences added extra difficulty to managing subcontractors. Under such circumstances, he went all over the site, liaising with all parties, and improving the coordination and cooperation between the construction units. Many problems needed to be dealt with on a daily basis on the construction site, some of which were related to design implementation, some about construction organization, and some about contract execution. For the problems that arose during the project construction, big or small, he responded in a timely manner, dealt with them flexibly, and continuously pushed forward the project construction.

In 2020, the outbreak of the COVID-19 epidemic hugely disrupted the global communication. With the implementation of policies such as port closures, visa suspensions, and flight cancellations, the flow of people and goods between China and Kazakhstan was hindered, dealing a fatal blow to the then ongoing project construction. At that time,

Du Rongpeng happened to be in China, and the unexpected obstacles prevented him from returning to the project site as planned. However, as the core management personnel of the project department, he kept a close eye on the progress of the project, overcame the inconvenience caused by time differences, closely maintained communication with the stationed on-site personnel, actively provided suggestions for difficulties encountered on site, and did his best to support the project team. When the situation allowed him to fly back to Kazakhstan, he departed for Kazakhstan without delay. His timely return greatly alleviated the huge pressure of insufficient management personnel in the project department at that time, and also set a leading example in the project department.

The year 2021-2022 witnessed a critical period in catching up with the project schedule. On October 2, 2021, the furnace arch was successfully completed; on September 9, 2022, the kiln was ignited and launched; on October 9, 2022, the production line was successfully introduced and officially put into operation. Du Rongpeng actively planned on-site construction work and optimized the construction plan. When installation team from China was unable to arrive in time, he actively contacted local installation and construction teams. When difficulties arose in technical connection, he immediately organized relevant engineers to communicate with the construction party. For around two years, he remained committed in his position, without any relaxation and showed no slackness.

Du Rongpeng has been worked at the front line of overseas sites for many years, contributing to the efficiency and winning honors for the company, but he has also sacrificed his time with his family. Looking back, he remains firm in his enthusiasm and perseverance, and says, "As an employee of a Chinese enterprise, for the development of the company and the continuous advancement of national strategic goals, I will continue to work abroad and devote myself to such endeavours if needed."

Personal Insights Through the implementation of the project, I deeply experienced the hardship of overseas project operations, and also realized the heavy tasks and the long way ahead in contributing to the construction of the "Belt and Road". As an employee of a Chinese enterprise, for the development of the company and the continuous advancement of national strategic goals, I will continue to work abroad and devote myself to such endeavours if needed.

“一带一路”上盛开的“蓝莲花”

黎氏香莲

2004 年加入中国建材

现任中国建材国际工程集团有限公司驻越南代表处员工

黎氏香莲，1982 年 1 月出生于越南首都河内，2004 年 8 月在东方大学毕业后加入中国建材国际工程集团有限公司驻越南代表处，从事翻译和管理工作。至今她已在越南代表处工作近 19 年，是公司工作年限最久的海外员工，公司员工按照越南当地的习惯都亲切地称她“阿莲”。

加入公司越南代表处伊始，恰逢越南宜山太平洋水泥项目开始执行，阿莲为了更好地锻炼中文，积极主动要求到现场长期驻厂，承担起项目现场日常的文件资料翻译、会议翻译、施工现场翻译及生活后勤保障工作，帮助工程师及时沟通处理现场问题。工程项目翻译专业性强，阿莲严格要求自己，为了提高翻译准确性，她不怕辛苦和劳累，经常深入施工一线，反复向工程师请教学习，直到把专业技术术语理解透彻并翻译准确，出色高效地完成了项目上的各项翻译任务。工程项目建设条件比较艰苦并且几乎没有个人休息时间，但阿莲工作积极主动，从不抱怨。白天她在工地翻译，晚上还会加班翻译文件资料，合理安排时间，从不耽误现场工作，受到了公司和业主的一致好评。阿莲的中文翻译水平在此阶段也得到了极大地提高。

与此同时，阿莲一直积极参与代表处的日常经营工作，尤其是项目招投标文件翻译、标书制作、合同洽谈等重要工作，同时承担起和越南当地重要客户的沟通交流工作，维系与合作伙伴的关系。阿莲通过几年的学习和努力，成长为一名合格的翻译。她还积极帮助当地其他员工快速融入公司，快速成长。

在中国建材集团的战略引领下，公司在越南先后签署了数十个建材项目，在越南当地员工之中，阿莲的贡献尤为突出。

2016—2017 年，由凯盛科技集团有限公司和越南当地合作伙伴共同出资建设的越南富美超白浮法玻璃项目落地，该项目是国家“一带一路”重点项目，并被列入了 2018 年 4 月 25 日在北京召开的“第二届‘一带一路’国际合作高峰论坛”的见签项目。阿莲负责该项

目的前期沟通联络、技术交流、投资审查、各项手续办理等事宜，付出了很大的心血和努力，她本人也通过各种历练，成长为一名优秀的管理者。

2018—2020 年，越南富美项目执行期间，现场翻译工作量较大，阿莲克服远离家人的困难，主动提出前往现场工作，帮助代表处的年轻员工共同完成现场翻译工作。工地生活和工作虽然辛苦，但每当阿莲与女儿视频通话时，她就会忘记工作的疲惫，工作时她会继续热情地为大家服务。

2021—2022 年，受疫情影响，代表处的中方管理人员入境困难，她作为代表处工作资历最久的当地员工，在代表处上级的指导下，带领当地其他员工积极开展代表处的各项日常经营和管理工作，维护公司与当地客户之间的关系，确保和长期合作伙伴的顺畅沟通，保障了疫情期间代表处正常运作。

加入越南代表处以来，阿莲一直兢兢业业，勤勤恳恳，从一名青涩的大学毕业生成长为一名优秀的翻译和管理人员，她见证了公司在越南近 20 年的业务发展，也见证了“一带一路”倡议在越南从蓝图变为实景。

阿莲常说，加入公司越南代表处是她人生中最重要的决定，未来她希望能够继续为公司贡献自己的力量。（中国建材国际工程集团有限公司驻越南代表处）

个人体会 “一带一路”倡议提出 10 年来，我作为亲历者，见证了中越“一带一路”重点合作项目从蓝图构想到成功落地，再到产生经济效益，这是极不平凡的 10 年，这也是我个人不断蜕变和成长的 10 年，真心祝愿集团未来更加美好。

The "Blue Lotus" Blooming along the "Belt and Road"

Le Thi Hoang Sen

Joined CNBM in 2004

Employee of CTIEC Representative Office in Vietnam

Born in January 1982 in Hanoi, Vietnam, Le Thi Huong Sen joined the CTIEC Representative Office in Vietnam in August 2004 after graduating from Eastern University, working as a translator and management. She has been working in CTIEC Vietnam for nearly 19 years, and is the longest-serving overseas employee in CTIEC. She is affactionately called A-Lian by the colleagues.

When A-Lian joined the CTIEC Vietnam Representative Office, the Nghi Son Pacific cement project was under construction. In order to better practice Chinese, A-Lian, proactively requested to be stationed in the project for a long period, undertaking translation of documents and meetings, and doing translation at the construction site. She also provided living logistics support, facilitating timely communication and resolution of on-site issues for engineers. The translations for engineering projects required high professionalism, and A-Lian maintained strict standards. To enhance translation accuracy, she worked hard and endured fatigue. A-Lian frequently visited the construction site to consult with engineers, ensuring a thorough understanding of technical terms and delivering excellent and efficient translations for various project tasks. Despite the harsh conditions at the construction site and the heavy workload encroaching on her spare time, A-Lian remained committed and never complained. She translated on the construction site during the day and worked overtime to translate documents at night, effectively managing her time without causing delays to on-site work. The company and owners alike highly praised her efforts. A-Lian's Chinese translation skills significantly improved during the process.

Simultaneously, A-Lian actively participated in the daily operations of the Vietnam Representative Office. She played a key role in translating project bidding documents, preparing tenders, negotiating contracts, and engaging in other crucial tasks. Additionally, she liaised with important local customers and maintained strong relationships with partners. A-Lian also proactively supported the integration and rapid growth of other local employees within the company.

Under the strategic guidance of CNBM Group, CTIEC successfully signed approximately ten building materials projects in Vietnam, with A-Lian making outstanding contributions.

One notable project was the Vietnam Phu My Ultra Clear Float Glass, jointly funded by Triumph

Technology Group and local partners. The project achieved tremendous success, positioning it as a national "Belt and Road" key project. It was also featured in the Second Belt and Road Forum for International Cooperation held in Beijing on April 25-27, 2019. A-Lian played a crucial role in the project's initial communication and liaison, technical exchanges, investment reviews, as well as managing various formalities. Through these experiences, she developed into an excellent manager.

During the execution of the Phu My project in Vietnam from 2018 to 2020, A-Lian carried a heavy workload in on-site translation. Despite being far away from her family, she overcame the challenges and volunteered to work on-site, supporting young staff from the representative office in completing the translation work together. Although the work and living conditions were tough, A-Lian's enthusiasm never waned, and when she had video calls with her daughter, the fatigue of work seemed to fade away. She continued to serve everyone with unparalleled dedication.

From 2021 to 2022, the severe COVID-19 epidemic in China posed significant challenges for the Chinese management staff of the representative office in Vietnam. With difficulties in traveling, the most senior local staff in the representative office took charge, leading their fellow local staff members under the guidance of their superiors. They actively undertook the day-to-day operations and management of the representative office, maintaining strong relationships with local customers, ensuring smooth communication with long-term partners, and guaranteeing uninterrupted operation of the representative office throughout the epidemic period. Their efforts were instrumental in sustaining the representative office's functionality despite the crisis.

Since joining the Vietnam Representative Office, A-Lian has consistently demonstrated dedication and hard work, progressing from a young graduate to an exceptional translator and manager. For nearly 20 years, she has been a witness to the company's thriving business development in Vietnam, as well as the successful implementation of the Belt and Road Initiative in the country. A-Lian always says that joining the company's Vietnam office was a profoundly impactful decision in her life. She remains committed to making valuable contributions to the company's future success.

Personal Insights It has been ten years since the Belt and Road Initiative proposed. As a witness of its implementation, I have seen the major collaborative projects between China and Vietnam under this initiative go from being mere blueprints to successfully being realized, ultimately resulting in significant economic benefits. These ten years have been truly extraordinary, not only for these projects, but also in terms of my own continuous personal growth and development. I genuinely hope for an even brighter future for the company.

“一带一路”的坚实“践行者”

苗玉民

2008 年加入中国建材

现任中材节能（菲律宾）余热发电有限公司电站经理

2021 年 3 月，48 岁的苗玉民再次踏上赴菲的征途，这也是他作为中材节能（菲律宾）余热发电有限公司“主帅”的第八个年头。

2020 年由于突发的新冠疫情，菲律宾实施航空管制和闭关政策，正在国内短暂休假的苗玉民被通知不能返回菲律宾。得知消息后，苗玉民心急如焚。为了保证电站安全运营，苗玉民一边与现场菲籍员工视频通话，反复叮嘱他们电站操作细节，指导生产运营，一边远程安排电站员工做好疫情防控工作，确保生产、防疫两不误，同时积极与当地中介机构联系办理返回菲律宾的外交批文。他始终保持 24 小时待机，生怕错过任何一条有效信息。此时对他来说，前往每天确诊病例高达 2 万人的菲律宾并不可怕，不能立刻回到现场安排工作才最让他忐忑不安。终于，在一年的积极努力下，2021 年 3 月，所有赴菲的批文、背书等材料准备齐全。苗玉民迫不及待地拎着他早已准备好的行李箱，带领 5 人团队重新起航，返回菲律宾子公司现场。

刚到菲律宾不久，余热锅炉就出现了一次大的故障。苗玉民带领员工冒着 50℃的高温在锅炉内进行封堵漏管、清除堵灰，进行抢修。菲律宾的天气本就湿热，再加上 50℃的炉内高温，长时间工作让苗玉民全身近乎湿透，而这种高强度的工作对他来说却是常事。2021 年 10 月份，水泥厂停窑检修，余热电站进行连续 6 天的抢修，苗玉民在 3 天的时间里只休息了 2 个小时，连续工作长达 26 个小时，即使腰椎间盘突出的老毛病复发，钻心的疼痛让他直不起腰，他也坚持亲自给员工示范如何进行锅炉封管、如何修复断裂的窑头烟风阀门、如何改造窑尾给水旁通阀。此时的他不是一个站在高台上指挥作战的领导者，而是一个与战友并肩作战的“老兵”，累了就在办公室眯一会，饿了就随便啃几块压缩饼干充饥。

好在这些努力没有白费，余热电站高效运行，逐步建立了一套标准化、程序化、自动化运作的管理体系，并取得了德国 TUV 认证集团 ISO9001-2015 认证。制度转化为效能，

截至目前，余热电站累计供电 2.16 亿千瓦时，同时实现二氧化碳减排 21 万吨，对当地环保事业的发展起到引领示范作用。电站自投运以来，累计向当地纳税约 750 万元人民币，他也成为"一带一路"倡议的优秀践行者。

除了电站日常的生产经营，苗玉民在管理团队上也有一番建树。电站的菲籍员工大都是年轻人，工作闲暇之余，苗玉民就带着大家搞团建。虽然他常开玩笑说，自己是快 50 岁的大叔，但跟员工打起篮球来他就像年轻小伙子一样。转身过人、破防拼抢、勾手远投，一场球赛下来，他跟员工们的距离又拉近了不少。他在融入当地文化的同时，也将中国文化传播给了菲籍朋友。过春节时大家都跟着苗玉民热热闹闹地学包饺子、写福字，还给国内送来了新年祝福。

身在菲律宾，苗玉民将中材节能的企业文化深深扎根在了这里。他走访当地贫困的村庄，进行社会捐赠，积极参与社会公益事业建设，疫情期间代表公司向当地捐赠大米、罐头等生活物资；连续 6 年为当地捐赠树苗数千棵、为社区捐赠警棍、救险队专用雨鞋和雨衣、血压计、医用喷雾器等物资；为学校捐赠桌椅等学习用具，并且为当地成绩优异的贫困大学生募集助学金达人民币 30 万元；为当地解决直接就业 17 人，并带动间接就业、接纳培训 300 多人次，推动了当地经济发展。中材节能这个响亮的名号受到当地民众和政府的一致好评，展现了中国建材集团良好的企业形象和社会担当。

没有哪个冬天不可逾越，没有哪个春天不会到来。苗玉民和他的战友们逆风前行，不惧险阻，乘风破浪，终将在这片金黄的大地上，收获满满。

〔中材节能（菲律宾）余热发电有限公司〕

个人体会 作为电站经理，我始终不忘初心、牢记使命；在工作中积极努力，团结、照顾同事；积极传播中国文化，并融入当地文化；努力为当地创造就业，造福当地人民；积极践行人类命运共同体理念；为节能减排事业作出自己的贡献，为中菲友谊作出自己的贡献！

Dedicated Practitioner of the "Belt and Road" Initiative

Miao Yumin

Joined CNBM in 2008

Power Station Manager of SINOMA Energy Conservation (Philippines) Waste Heat Recovery Co., Inc.

In March 2021, 48-year-old Miao Yumin travelled to the Philippines again, embarking on his eighth year as the "commander" of SINOMA Energy Conservation (Philippines) Waste Heat Recovery Co., Inc.

Due to the outbreak of COVID-19 in 2020, the Philippines implemented aviation control and closed its borders. Miao Yumin was on a brief vacation back in China when he was informed that he could not return to the Philippines. Learning the news, Miao Yumin was anxious and even self-blaming, thinking that it would be great if he hadn't come back home for vacation. Miao communicated with the Philippine staff on site via video link, repeatedly reminding them of the operation details of the plant and guiding them on production operations. At the same time, he remotely guided the employees to carry out epidemic prevention and control work, ensuring that production and epidemic prevention were both guaranteed. He also actively contacted local intermediary agencies to obtain diplomatic approval to return to the Philippines. He stayed on standby 24 hours a day, afraid of missing any information. To him, going to the Philippines, where the daily confirmed cases were as high as 20,000, was not the scariest thing. It was the fact that he could not return to the site immediately that made him uneasy. Finally, after a year of hard work, all the documents, including the approval and endorsement for his return, were ready in March 2021. Miao Yumin eagerly took his already-prepared luggage and led a team of five back to the site of the subsidiary company in the Philippines.

Not long after their arrival in the Philippines, a major failure occurred in the waste heat boiler. Miao Yumin led the staff into the boiler at the high temperature of 50°C to plug the leaking pipe and remove the ash for repairing. The hot and humid weather in the Philippines, coupled with the high temperature inside the boiler, made Miao Yumin almost completely soaked in sweat for a long time.However, this kind of high-intensity work was common for him. In October, during the six-day repair period when the cement plant was shut down for maintenance, Miao Yumin only rested for two hours in three days. He worked continuously for 26 hours. Even when his herniated disc relapsed and the terrible pain made him unable to stand up straight, he insisted on demonstrating to the employees how to plug the boiler and repair the broken kiln head flue valve and how to modify the water inlet valve next to the kiln tail. At this moment, he was not a leader who stood on a high platform to direct the battle, but a "veteran" who fought side by side with his comrades. When he was tired, he took a nap in the office. When he was hungry, he ate a few pieces of compressed biscuits to relieve his hunger.

Fortunately, all these efforts were not in vain. The waste heat power plant operated efficiently, gradually building a standardized, procedural, and automated management system and obtaining TUV certification for ISO9001-2015 from Germany. These institutional improvements were transformed into effectiveness. As of now, the waste heat power station has cumulatively supplied 216 million kWh of electricity, while reducing carbon dioxide emissions by 210,000 tons, playing a leading and exemplary role in local environmental protection. Since the operation of the power plant, it has cumulatively paid RMB 7.5 million in taxes to local authority, becoming an excellent practitioner of the "Belt and Road" Initiative.

In addition to the daily production and management of the power plant, Miao Yumin also has a unique set of management styles for the team. Most of the Philippine employees in the power plant are young, so Miao Yumin leads them in team building activities during their leisure time. Although he often jokes that he is a nearly 50-year-old man, he plays basketball with his employees like a young man, turning around and passing, breaking through the defense and tackling, hooking up for long shots. After a basketball game, the distance between him and his employees was narrowed. While integrating into the local culture, he has also introduced Chinese culture to his Philippine friends. During the Chinese New Year, he taught others how to make dumplings and wrote characters of " 福 " (meaning blessing) and send blessings back to China.

Miao Yumin has deeply rooted the corporate culture of SINOMA Energy Conservation in the Philippines. He visited local poor villages for social donations, actively participated in social public welfare construction, and represented the company to donate rice, canned food, and other daily necessities to the local community during the epidemic period. For six consecutive years, he has donated thousands of tree seedlings to the local area and donated police batons, rescue team-specific rain boots and raincoats, blood pressure monitors, medical atomizers, etc. to the community. He has also donated desks, chairs, and other study materials to schools and raised RMB 300,000 in scholarship funds for outstanding and poor college students in the local area. He has created 17 jobs for locals, and employed and trained more than 300 people, promoting local economic development. The brand name of SINOMA Energy Conservation Limited has received unanimous praise from the local people and government, demonstrating SINOMA's good corporate strength and social responsibility.

Winter will always be over, and spring will come. Miao Yumin and his comrades move against the headwind, overcome obstacles, and will finally reap a fruitful harvest in this golden land.

Personal Insights As a power plant manager, I always keep my original aspirations and missions in my mind. I work hard, unite and take care of colleagues, actively spread Chinese culture and integrate into the local culture. Besides, I strive to create jobs for locals and benefit the local people, and actively implement President Xi's vision of building a community with a shared future for mankind to make my contribution to the cause of energy conservation and emission reduction, as well as the friendship between China and the Philippines!